BIGFOOT

God Bless!

Matt Johnson

"Dr. J."

BIGFOOT

A Fifty-Year Journey Come Full Circle

By Matthew A. Johnson, Psy.D., MSW

Foreword by Bob Gimlin

PUBLICATION
CONSULTANTS
PUBLISHING THE WORKS OF AUTHORS WORLDWIDE

PO Box 221974 Anchorage, Alaska 99522-1974
books@publicationconsultants.com—www.publicationconsultants.com

ISBN Number: 978-1-59433-704-8
eBook ISBN Number: 978-1-59433-705-5

Library of Congress Catalog Card Number: 2017935275

Manufactured in the United States of America

"If you want to find the secrets of the universe, think in terms of energy, frequency and vibration."

Nikola Tesla
Serbian born inventor, electrical engineer,
mechanical engineer, physicist, and futurist
(July 10, 1856 – January 7, 1943)

For in Christ, all things were created, things in Heaven and on Earth,
visible and invisible, whether thrones or dominions or rulers or authorities.
All things were created through Him and for Him. He is before all things,
and in Him all things hold together.

The Apostle Paul
(Colossians 1:16 – 17)

ENDORSEMENTS

In November of 1968, while elk hunting with my father in the Wenaha wilderness in the Blue Mountains of south eastern Washington, I had the opportunity to observe what I have come to believe was a Bigfoot, or more specifically, a Sasquatch. For forty-five minutes, I watched through my riflescope as this creature moved slowly along the hillside grazing on the native vegetation. To say the least, I was fascinated by what transpired during that short time, the memories playing over and over in my mind, as an interest developed that has been with me all these years. To describe the incident completely would fill the space I have been given to write this endorsement, and therefore I will let the incident hang here.

Since that time, I have read everything I could find on the subject of Sasquatch, collecting books and articles which followed me through college, and across the globe during twenty-eight years of military service. By 2002, when I hung up my military uniforms, the 1968 incident seemed almost a dream. But in 2004 I Goggled Sasquatch and was introduced to the BFRO. And an entirely new chapter began in my life.

I attended three BFRO expeditions that year, two on the Olympic Peninsula in Washington State, and the third near Dulce, New Mexico. It was near Dulce, one-month shy of thirty-six years since my first sighting, that I had my second. What I followed into the brush that day and up the ridge for three-hundred-fifty yards, seeing twice in the process, physically matched what I remembered seeing on that Washington hillside so many years ago. This time, it was much closer, around seventy feet. Everything I had read on the subject over the years, and that which I had experienced on those two occasions led me to believe that I was dealing with nothing more than a flesh and blood animal, like any other in the forest. But again, I must let the details hang and get on with the purpose of this endorsement.

I joined the BFRO early the following year. After plotting every report in the Washington section of the BFRO database, I opened a research area on 15 April 2005 near a cluster of sightings northwest of Yakima, Washington. What I experienced on that first night contradicted everything I had come to believe over the past thirty-six years about Sasquatch being merely flesh and blood. Reporting what I had experienced, I received a mixture of guarded support, and condemnation. Since that time, my experiences have continued to become more bizarre and openly discussing them has resulted in a great deal of criticism, and the loss of more than a few friends.

It is here that Dr. Matt Johnson entered my equation. Dr. J, as I have come to call him, had his life changing encounter on 1 July 2000. His encounter landed him firmly in the flesh and blood community of researchers and believers, with no desire to put up with reports about paranormal, shape shifting, inter-dimensional spirit beings with psychic abilities. Granted, I wasn't claiming that I had experienced all of these activities or professed a belief in them, but I openly reported and discussed what I experienced, much of which did not conform to a belief in a simple flesh and blood animal.

In those early years, Dr. J. was quite critical of claims like those I was making. I often felt like I was the target of some of his comments. For several years, I wished, hoped, and even prayed that people like Dr. Matt Johnson would experience some of the strange things that have happened to me and many in my group in the mountains west of Yakima.

I'm happy to say, Dr. J has changed his tune. I've attended two of his conferences in Bremerton, Washington where he presented his experiences at his research areas in southern Oregon. I have to admit, his conferences have been very enlightening, and his presentations have been the most enjoyable I have yet endured. I thought I was "Woo-Woo" but Dr. J has redefined the term, and I don't mean this in a bad way. Dr. J. brought the pride back to the "Woo-Woo" community. I find it refreshing to see someone change so completely in his or her beliefs.

I felt honored when Dr. J ask me to facilitate a meeting with Bob Gimlin in Yakima, where he shared with Bob and I over lunch, his most recent encounters. The information he presented could be the answer to what I have experienced, but failed to fully understand. I find him open and honest in his presentations, and quite emotional about the material he has discovered. But more to the point, I find him morally courageous for putting this information in print for all to share.

I look forward to attending his next conference, and I am honored to pen this endorsement for his book.

By LTC Kevin B. Jones,
U. S. Army Retired

The Study of the Sasquatch is inherently a fantastical endeavor. With the vast majority of evidence relying on the subjective experiences of a few; how does one know whom to trust? How does someone separate the wheat from the chaff? Compounding the issue, claims regarding Sasquatch are, at a minimum, extraordinary, and therefore the bar to believability is high.

Well, there are some best practices that can guide us. When evaluating information, consider two major factors, the veracity of the source and the information itself. On these issues Dr. Matthew Johnson does quite well.

Let's first speak to the veracity of Dr. Johnson as a source of information. First off, we have the incredible dedication of traveling 16 hours, once a month, for five years. Stop to think about that, the monetary expense, the time cost. And in all that time he didn't try and monetize the endeavor. Yes, there were TS-USA buttons/shirts, and maybe a half-hearted GoFundMe for some equipment. However, he has turned down film producers and other big money opportunities. Have you ever seen him on a silly Bigfoot TV show? With his notoriety, the offers were there. People with lesser motivations would have cashed in years ago.

On a personal level, I had known Dr. Johnson for less than a year when he asked me to go to his research area he called the Southern Oregon Habituation Area (SOHA). At the time, calling us friends would have been a stretch. Our interactions had been restricted to the monthly meetings he was hosting. Acquaintances would be more accurate. He knew of my background in Philosophy, namely Epistemology, and my past history as a Counter-Intelligence Agent. I am probably the worst candidate to invite to a research area if shenanigans are afoot. His willingness to bring someone like me up to his research area is a strong indicator he had nothing to hide. Quite the opposite, he was inviting credible people to challenge his findings and observe his research.

As hard as it is to be doubted, Dr. Johnson understands that just taking a person's "word for it" is a tall order, even for those who want to believe. So, he has always been willing to take people with him to corroborate his stories. Another example of this was his invitation to Adam Davies, and John Carlson. These two were not sycophants willing to accept what he told them. In the end, although their interpretations were different, everyone agreed that extraordinary things were happening at SOHA.

Scheduling difficulties prevented me from going to SOHA, but I did go to the interim Southern Oregon Interaction Area (SOIA). I was traveling home from Arizona, and the visit was very Ad Hoc. It was a short camp out. The first night Dr. Johnson showed me the area and explained his methodology. The no light policy, the open air cots, the pacing of the perimeter while playing music. It was an uneventful night, but the first night of his outings usually are.

The second day, the weather looked like rain, Dr. Johnson decided not to go back up; but suggested that if I was willing to brave the weather I should do a solo outing. I ask you, does that sound like someone trying to hide something? To let someone go poking around your research area by him or herself; and poke around I did. I found some large and small prints. There were clear glyph type markings, oddly positioned one the way back into camp, not out. And I could have sworn I heard juvenile voices upstream in the middle of the night. Not as spectacular as many of his guests, but it does demonstrate one key element; his willingness to seek third party verification.

As to his information itself, let's look at two aspects, can it be corroborated and can it be repeated. Much of what Dr. Johnson describes matches the large body of information written about the Sasquatch people, so he isn't far enough away from the body of evidence to raise alarms. But of course, given the nature of the subject, this could be considered self-feeding information. But it is consistent, which is a measure to check.

No, where Dr. Johnson shines is in the repeatability of his methods. It should be intuitive that simply going to the same locations is not enough to repeat his findings. If someone is going to try and replicate, they need to use the same methodologies. There are no short cuts. Over the last few years I've known a number of researchers who have adopted Dr. Johnson's means. Most people, including myself, have had some level of success. Those willing to put in the time, sometimes several years, have made progress. So, in the end, if you doubt what Dr. Johnson says about the Sasquatch, I would challenge you to replicate his methodologies, and see for yourself. Besides, isn't that what most people want? An experience of their own.

It's said that if you cannot learn from the mistakes of the past you are destined to repeat them. Dr. Johnson has spent over a decade trying out various techniques. He has traveled from the unexpected eyewitness, to the "I'll get proof" paparazzi, to the habituator, to the habituatee. Learn from his experiences, and then utilize them to have your own experiences.

Patrick Epistemon
(www.thebigfootportal.com)

Dr. Matthew A. Johnson and I have known each other for well over a decade. Our first meeting was at a convention in 2001 where we were both invited to speak. We have a mutual respect for one another in our efforts to explore the truth. I consider him a very honest and sincere individual, but have occasionally raised an eyebrow when listening to his experiences…who wouldn't, after all, they are quite unique. However, his accounts fall directly into the quantum field of science, which after much research, I've come to realize are the laws of the universe that govern all things and are the basis of our spirituality.

I think it's safe to say that we share the beliefs that these beings [Bigfoot Forest People] display attributes that are enigmatic. However, in the past, we have disagreed as to how they came to have those attributes. Are they good or are they bad, could they have different genomes, etc.? Originally, I think we shared the view that they were a very stealthy, intuitive, and massive, ape-type creature hiding in the woods. As for me, once I wrapped my head around the totality of my experiences, a much-expanded view came into focus. I think we both understand them to be very different now.

That said, my wife, Keri, and I spent the night at the Southern Oregon Interaction Area (SOIA) and listened to him explain what's been happening there. Eyebrows rose again, but I saw in Dr. Johnson's eyes, a very honest countenance. We slept on three separate cots out in the open. That night was very restless for me, most of the time I was in the beta state of sleep. During that night, on three different occasions, something was messing with the bottom of my sleeping bag and moving my feet. However, when I looked up, there was nothing there. Unusual? Yes, but not too surprising.

That night, and again at dawn, Matt and Keri heard several [24 total] loud 'pops' that seemed to come from within the trees. After years of flying and playing music, my hearing is less than stellar and I had put my bionic ears in the truck. I understand that there is a lot more going on at SOIA and I look forward to visiting there again someday.

My advice to anyone who wants to learn more about these beings is to have an open-mind. Don't discredit anyone and, as incredible as it may seem, listen to their story. It may be a good opportunity to learn more. No one knows for sure exactly what these beings represent. That is why we research.

Ron Morehead
Author, Adventurer, and Renowned Bigfoot Researcher
"Voices in the Wilderness/Sierra Sounds"

Dr. Johnson's Southern Oregon Interaction Area (SOIA) is located within a magnetic anomaly and composed of unique geology, minerology and underground water. These things are conductive and respond to the magnetosphere each new day as telluric and magnetic energies run across the landscape to create energetic crossing points—whirling vortices which may someday show to be the ingredients of subtle energy portal manifestation. It's no secret 100 percent of all sacred sites are built upon these natural hot spots. It's here our indigenous ancestors reported communication with compassionate 'other-worldly' Beings.

Since I feel our ancestors genuinely knew what they were talking about—it's no stretch to believe Dr. Johnson's testimony of 'Bigfoot Forest People' who seem to toggle in and out of ordinary reality. The multiverse is stranger than fiction. We'd be fools to think we knew even a whisper of the secrets it still occults from us. Please enjoy reading his book.

Alyssa Runswithwolves Alexandria
Author of *"Influenced: Earth's Power Spots and Their Influence on the Paranormal"* (Published 2017)

TABLE OF CONTENTS

Foreword   19

Acknowledgements   21

Eliminating The Impossible   23

Introduction   25

Part 1 From Myth and Legend into Reality   **29**

 1 Going for a Ride   31

 2 Scared to Death   37

 3 Facing our Fears   49

 4 The Elephant Man   59

 5 The Feeding Frenzy   69

Part 2 The Old School/Paparazzi Money Shot Approach   **71**

 6 The Expedition to Mt. Elijah   73

 7 Come One – Come All   81

 8 My Broken Heart   97

 9 Hotel California   105

10 Persistence   113

11 Joining the Light Side of the Forest   125

Part 3 The Habituation Research Method   133

12 The Southern Oregon Habituation Area (SOHA)   135

13 Taking a Stoll Down Memory Lane   145

14 Clarifying My Intentions   151

15 Come Out and Play in the Dark   157

16 Circumstantial Evidence   165

17 Multiple Eyewitness Testimonies   175

18 Throwing in the Towel   181

19 Dead Man Walking   205

20 The Bigfoot Professor   213

21 The TROLLS invade SOHA   221

Part 4 The Interaction Research Method   225

22 The Southern Oregon Interaction Area (SOIA)   227

23 The Bigfoot Agenda Revealed   233

24 Arguing with Onx   247

25 The Exodus   253

26 A Fifty-Year Journey Come Full Circle   273

27 The Rest of the Story   281

Part 5 Multiple Witness Testimonies   285

Randy Ray   287

Thomas Finley   293

Barb Shupe   295

Judy M. Morton   297

Timothy Collins   301

Samantha Ritchie   303

Ernie Hart   309

Carol Davison and Nola Lightheart   313

Andrea Billups   317

Shelley Mower   331

Steve Bachmann   335

Mike Kincaid   341

Anita Hlebichuk   349

Howie Gordon   353

Tammy Kennedy   359

Scott Taylor   365

Susan Taylor   369

Jacqui Davis, MS, LPC, NCC   373

Kevin Ian Beegle   377

Samara Terpening   389

Grady Johnson   409

Cynthia Kreitzberg   411

Part 6 An Open Letter to my Progeny   **433**

Dear Biological Descendants   435

Part 7 How To Get A Hold Of Dr. Johnson   **441**

Contact Information   443

Foreword

By Bob Gimlin

In October of 1967, Roger Patterson and I ventured to northern California in the hope of finding fresh footprints reportedly left by a Bigfoot Forest Person, and collecting film footage of the area to add to the footage Roger had already collected for a documentary he was planning on putting together. Our greatest hope was to come back with casts of the reported prints, or even better, finding tracks of our own to cast. We both knew that we were facing a task which was next to impossible. However, the reports of recent activity in the area was motivation enough to warrant the trip.

To our surprise, we actually filmed a Bigfoot in the Bluff Creek area walking away from us. The rest is history. Although the film has undergone quite a bit of scrutiny over the decades, I can assure you that it's legitimate. It's the real deal. My life has never been the same.

For over thirty years, the people around Yakima made my life a living hell. Crank phone calls and visits to my house at all times of the day and night, inviting me out to hunt for Bigfoot. They even went so far to harass my wife at her work place, making comments about crazy ol' Bob. It all made me wish it never happened

It wasn't until 2003 at the Bluff Creek Conference, when things really began to change for the better. Surrounded by the likes of John Green, Dmitri Bayanov, Igor Bourtsev, John Bindernagel, Jimmy Chilcutt and a host of other academics and authors, not to mention an audience made up of witnesses, believers and well wishers, I began to appreciate the experience again. And since that conference, the interest has continued to grow and I've met literally thousands of wonderful people who believe in the Bigfoot Forest People, and what Roger and I accomplished that day at Bluff Creek.

As a result of our filming "Patty" in October of 1967, over the past fifty years, many people have gone into the forest trying to find the Bigfoot Forest People. I've traveled all over the United States and I've had the privilege of meeting many of these wonderful researchers. There are too many to name here, but one of many who stands out to me is Dr. Matthew Johnson. Some people call him Dr. J. All kidding aside, he's hard to miss because he stands 6'9" tall. My gosh, he could be a Bigfoot Forest Person.

I've had the pleasure of hearing him present on three separate occasions at Bigfoot conferences. He is passionate, animated, and has demonstrated a true and accurate understanding of who the Bigfoot Forest People truly are.

On July 7, 2016, I enjoyed eating breakfast with Dr. Johnson and Lt. Col. Kevin Jones. During our time together, Dr. J. shared with me what happened up on the mountain in SOIA during the previous month. What a monumental event it was and I wish I had been there to experience it. I'll say this much, what Dr. Johnson shared with me made absolute sense and seemed to tie together many of the loose ends regarding the Bigfoot phenomena. It most definitely fits my understanding of the Bigfoot Forest People.

I'm proud to know that our filming of "Patty" in 1967 started the journey for so many people. I'm also pleased to have learned from Dr. Johnson that our film had a purpose. That the Bigfoot Forest People had an agenda and many of us have helped to fulfill it.

I want to encourage you to read Dr. Johnson's book with an open heart and an open mind. Put away your preconceived notions and ideas and simply enjoy the journey. We all have a journey and can learn from one another. In his book, Dr. Johnson openly, honestly, and courageously shares his journey with you. I know you will enjoy the ride. I know that I have.

Acknowledgments

When my family encountered a Bigfoot on the mountainside above the Oregon Caves National Monument Park on July 1, 2000, I had no idea how my world would be turned upside down. Although my older three children participated in some of the subsequent media shoots and expeditions, their mother chose to shelter them from allowing our family encounter to turn their world upside down too. It's only been recently that my third born child, Micah, has chosen to involve himself with my research again. It's been amazing to watch his desire and excitement to participate grow so quickly. I thank him for his involvement and for our father and son time together up in the mountains. He's hooked. I'm grateful.

On the other hand, my fourth child from my second marriage, Grady, has been out in the research field with me since the age of two. His mother has been very supportive and encouraging of his involvement in my life and in my research of the Bigfoot phenomena. To be quite honest, he's become a better tracker than most adults I bring into the research field with me. This young man knows no fear and he loves the Bigfoot Forest People. He's hooked too. I'm grateful for him as well.

Also, the participation of my third and final wife, Cynthia, has been a godsend (i.e., Third time is a charm). If it wasn't for her, I would have thrown in the towel regarding my Bigfoot research on several occasions. She has been there for me in so many ways. I would have to write another book just to share with you all of the ways she has supported me. Her children have participated as well and have been very supportive. I love all my family members. I respect their choices to participate or to not participate in my Bigfoot research. I'm grateful for their support, encouragement, and interaction with me in life and for hanging out with me up in the beautiful Siskiyou mountains.

In addition, I would never have guessed how many wonderful people I would meet, get to know, and interact with online and in the Bigfoot research field as the result of my family's encounter on that fateful day. I have met Bigfoot researchers and armchair enthusiasts from all walks of life. Interest in the Bigfoot phenomena cuts across all lines, including geographical location, age, gender, socio-economic status, education, political affiliation, religion, ethnicity, professional status, and sexual preference. In short, almost everyone is interested in the Bigfoot phenomena. Most of them are wonderful human beings. Some of them are trolls, haters, and mean spirited people. Ultimately, all of these individuals have impacted my Bigfoot research and my personal life in a positive manner. I am thankful to all of them. Yes, even the trolls, haters, and mean spirited people too.

Finally, I'm grateful to the Bigfoot Forest People who stepped into my life unexpectedly, grabbed me by the scruff of the neck, dragged me into the Siskiyou forest, showed me who they are, and invited me to join their families and clan. My mind has been blown, my body has been healed, and my heart is filled with respect and love for them, my family, friends, and our world.

"Once you eliminate the impossible,
whatever remains, no matter how improbable,
must be the truth."

Sherlock Holmes
(Fictional Character created by the author, Sir Arthur Conan Doyle)

Introduction

Please allow me to begin by stating the obvious regarding my book on the Bigfoot Forest People phenomena: I'm either a lunatic, a liar, or I'm telling the truth.

For those of you who think I'm a lunatic, the trolls and haters have already filed complaints with the psychologist licensing boards in the States of Washington and Oregon alleging psychosis and drug abuse. However, the licensing boards swiftly rejected their complaints as bogus, citing that I've shown no signs of psychosis, drug abuse, nor have I injured any of my patients as a practicing psychologist. They also responded to the complainants by saying that they're not in the habit of regulating the hobbies of psychologists. Finally, I'm still gainfully employed as a Licensed Clinical Psychologist. Just saying.

For those of you who think I'm a liar, although I'm far from perfect, I'm a "born-again" Christian and I value my honesty and integrity. I don't lie and I don't hoax. If I say it happened, guess what? It happened. The cool thing is that I have at least 50+ witnesses who've joined me in my research areas over the past seventeen years and they have all vetted and validated my work. If it was just me, all by myself, reporting what I'm finding, experiencing, and learning, then it would be easy to blow me off as being dishonest. It would be easy to call me a liar.

However, when you include 50+ people confirming my research findings via their YouTube video testimonials, you don't get to call me a liar. You simply have to admit that the issue really lies within you. You're not willing to believe the truth, even if 50+ people are telling you that I speak the truth. The real issue is that you're unwilling to climb out of your little rigid box where you feel safe. You don't want me messing with your current worldview. But, if you proceed reading my book with an open mind and allow me to blow your little rigid box to smithereens, I'll show you a world full of wonder, love, respect, and connection to others and our world.

For those of you who believe I'm telling you the truth in my book, I thank you for your confidence and trust in my honesty and integrity. However, I caution you before you proceed to read my book. Some of you will also have your mind blown by what I'm about to share. Some of you will also learn that there's much more to the Bigfoot Forest People phenomena and to our world than you could ever imagine. In the end, I hope to encourage and assist you in developing a trusting relationship with the Bigfoot Forest People as well as with our mutual Creator.

Finally, for those of you who don't know me, I've always been a passionate educator about the issues and topics that grab my attention. For example, during my junior year in high school, a fellow student died in an alcohol and drug related car accident after attending a party in west Salem, Oregon after we won the Valley League Basketball Championship in 1979. His death hit me so hard that I spent the remainder of my junior year and my entire senior year speaking at all of the local elementary schools and middle schools on the topic of Alcohol and Drug Abuse Prevention. I used my local celebrity status as an All-State and Honorable Mention All-American basketball player to passionately educate the younger members of our community from the ill effects of alcohol and drug abuse.

Also, after we intervened on my mother and her alcoholism, I became passionate about becoming a State and Nationally Certified Alcohol and Drug Abuse Counselor. I also went on to obtain my first Master's degree (MSW) at Rutgers University in New Brunswick, New Jersey. I obtained my second Master's degree and Doctorate degree in Clinical Psychology from George Fox University in Newberg, Oregon (i.e., A Christian liberal arts institution located halfway between Portland OR and the Oregon coast).

Finally, I wrote a book, "Positive Parenting with a Plan (Grades K-12): FAMILY Rules" and spoke in eighty cities per year for over ten years as I passionately educated thousands of professionals and parents regarding how to implement order and structure into their lives as they utilized a successful game plan for parenting in their homes.

Are you seeing a pattern yet? In other words, when something grabs a hold of my attention, it's been my natural response throughout my lifetime to engage in passionate education about the topic. My goal has always been to help others understand and to help improve their lives one way or another.

Regarding the Bigfoot Forest People phenomena, how will learning about them help to improve your life? Well, if you have a better understanding of who they are, where they're from, and why they're here, that information will hopefully cause you to engage in self-reflection and cause you to improve your connection with yourself, others, our planet, and with our Creator. As a Licensed Clinical Psychologist with a professional reputation and licenses to maintain, I have everything to lose and nothing to gain by taking the risk to tell you the truth. I hope you appreciate this fact. On the other hand, you have nothing to lose and everything to gain by taking the time to read my book. In the end, I hope you feel blessed with newly acquired knowledge, understanding, wisdom, respect, and love for yourself, others, the Bigfoot Forest People, and God.

In memory of my father, Arthur H. Johnson, and my mother, JoAnn Johnson. They loved me with everything they had and taught me to stand strong in what I believe, to never give up no matter what, and to always tell the truth.

In memory of Dr. William "Bill" York (Wildlife Biologist). He was my mentor, good friend, and father figure. He taught me the importance of persistence while pursuing eventual contact with the Bigfoot Forest People.

Part I

FROM MYTH AND LEGEND INTO REALITY

CHAPTER ONE

GOING FOR A RIDE

It was 3:00 am on Monday morning, July 10, 2000. The alarm clock jolted me out of my sleep. I had tossed and turned all night long due to anxiety. My mind would not shut off. Although the shower was refreshing, it didn't wake me up. Not even close. Nevertheless, I managed to shave, brush my teeth, comb my hair, get my clothes on, fasten all of the buttons, and get outside to wait for my ride. I wasn't sure if I was shivering due to the temperature or shaking because of my anxieties or both.

At 4:00 am, the dark sky and cold temperatures didn't make it easy for me to climb inside the vehicle that came by to pick me up. Within seconds, after a very polite greeting and welcome, I was off on an adventure. I couldn't believe that I was sitting in the back of a stretch limo, riding north to Portland, Oregon. Ironically, I was listening to "Don't Stop Believing" by Journey over the stereo system in the back of the car. I drank some juice. It was too early to partake of the alcohol. I had to be in the interview chair and ready to go at the Portland NBC affiliate station by 6:00 am sharp.

As the street lights were flashing by the windows and blinding my tired eyes, I was hoping that I didn't overdress for my interview with Jayne Clayson on the "Today Show." Normally, I reserve wearing suits and ties for weddings and funerals. Up until six months prior, I had been a twenty-year resident of Alaska. While living there, I acquired a taste for the low key casual dress code prevalent across America's largest State where some men would wear Carhartt Overalls to church on Sunday mornings. While living there, I developed an allergy to dressing up. However, I've been told that I clean up nicely.

Needless to say, I was scared to death. In less than two hours, several million people were going to be watching me on TV and listening to my unbelievable story. However, I was happy that Bryant Gumbel was home sick that morning and unable to interview me. I just didn't think that he was going to be as kind and polite as I was hoping Jayne Clayson would be when the camera and lights were turned on.

Three days earlier, on Friday, July 7th, I had received a phone call from a producer who wanted to book me for an interview on their TV show. Although several local Oregon TV news shows and radio stations had already contacted me, I was not very media savvy. When she told me that they wanted to book me for a two-minute interview on their show, I told her no. Absolutely not. I told her that I couldn't possibly tell my entire story in two short minutes. I told her that I wasn't willing to do the interview unless they gave me at least four minutes. She responded to me with a very loud frustrated sigh and told me that she would talk with her boss and get back to me in less than an hour. I apologized for the inconvenience I was causing her but I held my ground.

Approximately forty-five minutes later, she called me back and told me that they would guarantee me a four-minute interview. However, she said, "If Good Morning America or any of the other major morning TV shows contact you, we get first dibs for the interview with you." I was very confused and asked, "Who is this?" She said, "We're the Today Show broadcasting live out of New York city. Who did you think we were?" I responded, "I thought you were a local Oregon TV news station." She said, "No sir. You've made it into the big leagues. We're the Today Show in New York city but we are going to interview you at our affiliate NBC station located in Portland, Oregon. The only thing that will bump your interview on Monday morning is if Cuba sends Elian Gonzalez back to the U.S.A."

Once I realized that I was dealing with the "Today Show" out of New York city, I felt both horrible and excited at the same time. I felt horrible because I didn't want her to think that I was some kind of prima donna demanding twice as much time as they were originally willing to give me for the interview. On the other hand, I was excited because they must have really wanted to hear my story and get it out there to the world if they were willing to double their precious interview time from two-minutes to four-minutes. Also, the fact that they wanted me to commit to giving them first dibs, if any of the other major morning TV shows contacted me, demonstrated to me just how much they wanted me on their show. Wow! Was this really happening?

As planned, the stretch limo arrived at the Portland, Oregon NBC affiliate station at approximately 5:30 am. The sun was coming up, I was more awake, and my nerves were jacked up. I was escorted into the building and taken upstairs to the area where the interview chair was positioned in front of a very big camera. A very kind lady sat me in the chair, I received some light touch up with make-up, had an earpiece placed in my ear so I could hear Jayne Clayson's questions, a mic placed on my shirt so she could hear my responses, and I was instructed to wait for the producer to count down over the earpiece for the interview to begin.

In the meantime, my nerves weren't helped by the fact that, in the same room, sitting at their own desks, preparing for their shows, were Lars Larson and Tracy Barry. Both local Oregon news icons. I obviously didn't know it but Lars Larson would eventually become a national conservative commentator icon with his own syndicated radio program. I couldn't believe that I was sitting in the same room with them. I was in awe. The whole experience was surreal.

While waiting to be interviewed by the "Today Show", Lars Larson was talking with Tracy Barry. He was joking, laughing, and telling her about the new recipient of the Darwin Natural Selection Award. Apparently, some lady in her mid-eighties stepped outside of her car while the carwash was in full operation and got herself killed in Hillsboro, Oregon.

I remember him laughing and talking about how stupid it was for anyone to climb out of their vehicle in the middle of their car being washed. I also remember thinking how disappointed I felt when I heard him talking that way about the demise of the elderly woman and laughing.

I thought his humor was inappropriate and I felt sorry for her family. I've never forgotten that moment. Although I like him as a conservative radio commentator and I share his conservative political views, I thought he was being insensitive at that moment in time. However, he did manage to distract me from my overwhelming nerves. Tracy Barry appeared to ignore his humor. In Lars Larson's defense, I have also joked inappropriately in order to cope with the constant exposure to the negative news that has constantly crossed my path as a licensed clinical psychologist over the past two decades.

Suddenly, the producer spoke up through the earpiece and the countdown began. The lights came on, including the light on the very big camera, and I could hear the ending of the previous segment before my interview. Then I could hear that Jane Clayson was introducing me and my interview was beginning. My heart was pounding rather quickly but I was telling myself to remain calm and professional. It was quite odd because I did not have a visual monitor. I could not see Jayne Clayson. The only thing that I could see was the very big camera staring back at me. I felt like I was sitting there talking to the camera.

Near the beginning of the interview, I found myself multitasking in my mind. While I was listening to Jayne Clayson talk, I was worried about Lars Larson and Tracy Berry possibly continuing to talk while I was being interviewed. I thought it was weird that I wasn't placed in a private room without any possible distractions. To my delight, they were both very professional and remained totally quiet while my interview took place. I didn't want America learning about the latest Darwin Natural Selection Award in the background. I'm a perfectionist that way. I always want everything to be spot on.

As Jayne Clayson was interviewing me, I thought things were going well. I thought I was managing my anxiety fairly well while answering her questions intelligently. Then she asked the proverbial question, "Do your friends think that you're crazy?" I could hear that the tone of her voice had changed and that the interview was about to go down a path that I wasn't looking forward to. Fortunately, I had prepared myself ahead of time for the worst case scenario. You know, for the moment when, after helping me to feel comfortable and getting the story out of me, where she sets me up to look crazy to the audience by asking the confrontational question about my sanity.

Because I had rehearsed for this moment several times in my mind in case the situation arose during the interview, I was prepared with a proper response. As my college basketball coach, Harry Larrabee used to say, "Prior proper planning prevents piss poor performance" which came in handy when we played against teams like Georgetown, North Carolina, Kentucky, Louisville, Houston, and other teams. In the spirit of prior proper planning, I chose to dress in my suit and tie rather than my typical hoodie and baseball cap. I thought that the professional look combined with my rehearsed response would shut her up and get her to back away from her attempt to belittle me on national TV. I simply responded to her question in a very calm and professional manner, "No. My friends all know me. They know that I'm a Christian and that I'm a Doctor of Psychology and that I wouldn't lie about something like this." Boom!

During my stretch limo ride back to Salem, Oregon, I was feeling a major sense of relief. I could finally breathe. The interview was over. I couldn't believe how fast it went by. My heart rate was dropping back down to normal. I was extremely pleased when I realized that the interview that I had successfully negotiated to be extended from two minutes to four minutes had actually lasted for a grand total of ten minutes. That's right, five times longer than the initial precious two-minutes that they were originally willing to give me. I chuckled to myself as it became clear to me that I managed to throw off Jayne Clayson, put her in her place, and that she actually eventually became intrigued by my story.

When I returned to my parents' home in Salem, Oregon. I was greeted with fanfare from family and friends. My kids thought daddy was a TV star. We sat down for some breakfast and watched the video tape of my interview. Wow! What a different perspective. It's one thing to be sitting in someone else's office, in front of a very large camera with lights in your face, versus watching the verbal exchange on the TV set.

As I watched the videotape of the interview, two things became very clear to me. First, I was right. She was setting me up for the proverbial question to make me look crazy to her national audience. Second, she was unprepared for my calm and professional response. I could see it on her face and through her body language. I caught her off guard. I could tell that she hadn't been properly prepped regarding my story or my background. The truth of the matter is that Bryant Gumbel was most likely prepped, then he became ill, and stayed home from work. Jayne Clayson filled in at the last minute and conducted the interview instead of him.

When I told her, "No. My friends all know me. They know that I'm a Christian and that I'm a Doctor of Psychology and that I wouldn't lie about something like this," she was blown away. She looked totally shocked. However, she's a professional and recovered very quickly. From that moment on, the entire interview changed and went on for a total of ten-minutes. Grand slam home run! She ended the interview behaving in a very respectful manner and said, "Well there's a story to tell the grandchildren someday." She had no idea.

As things have turned out, it has become a story to tell to the rest of the world – not just a story to tell to my grandchildren. My family's encounter on the mountain above the Oregon Caves National Monument Park, on the right side of the "Big Tree Loop Trail," is not just a story that begins and end on that fateful Saturday on July 1, 2000. Rather, the story also includes everything else that I've experienced and learned during the subsequent seventeen years of research into the Bigfoot phenomena. Buckle up, ladies and gentlemen, you're going for a ride too. An adventure of amazement and wonder.

CHAPTER TWO

SCARED TO DEATH

On Saturday, December 18, 1999, I pulled out of Fairbanks, Alaska in a twenty-six-foot-long U-Haul truck while pulling a twelve-foot-long cargo trailer. Essentially, I was a truck driver in charge of forty plus feet of metal, including the trailer tongue, driving down the Alaska Highway. Although it was my first winter drive, I was not worried because it was also the eighth time that I would be making the two-thousand-five-hundred-mile drive. In my mind, the only difference was that it would be dark most of the day and thirty-five degrees below zero. Actually, close to sixty degrees below zero with the wind chill factored into the equation. No big deal, right? Just another day of driving in the frozen wasteland of the north.

As I began my trip south to the "Lower 48 States", I was reminiscing about my Alaska adventures. The highlights included moving to Anchorage in 1980 on a basketball scholarship to play at the University of Alaska at Anchorage (U.A.A.). I had the opportunity to play college basketball against some of the best teams in the country. I got half my picture in the December 1980 issue of the Sports Illustrated magazine. My silly teammate was in the way of the other half. I was able to play summer basketball in Brazil in 1981 and in Australia in 1983. I started my professional career in the mental health field in Alaska and also volunteered my time with Anchorage Youth For Christ.

Also, while living in Alaska, I was able to see the entire State with the exception of the Aleutian chain. I camped, hiked, fished, and did a small amount of hunting. I pet a Moose and fed it some carrots while she stuck her head inside our home. A buddy and I were chased by a Grizzly bear while on a fishing adventure. I was scared to death. I followed a beautiful jet black Wolf for a couple of miles, on my snowmobile, across a frozen lake above the Arctic Circle. I caught an eighty-five pound Halibut and a thirty-five pound King Salmon. I saw the coast of Russia from the north side of St. Lawrence Island while staying and speaking in Gambell, Alaska. I saw the Northern Lights dance around the top of Denali – "The Great One." I gardened in the daylight at 2:00 am in the morning.

Although I was going to miss Alaska, I was looking forward to raising our children in the State of Oregon where I grew up. The temperatures Were milder in Oregon, there's much less snow, and the Interstate Five corridor makes everything more accessible and closer to travel to without having to buy five airline tickets to get there. Most important of all, my children could play outside without freezing to death or being consumed by a Grizzly Bear in the backyard.

Two-hours outside of Fairbanks, Alaska, the water pump froze in the U-Haul truck and apparently shot the fan through the radiator. I suddenly found myself stranded alongside the highway in the middle of nowhere Alaska. It was pitch dark outside, approximately sixty degrees below zero factoring in the wind chill, and I found myself quickly freezing to death. I had no operational engine and therefore no heat. I turned on my emergency flashers and waited for someone, as stupid as me, who would be out driving on the road in these deadly conditions.

Two hours later, I saw a car in my side-view mirror approaching me from behind. I stepped out of the cab of the U-Haul truck and waved down the car. They came to a stop, rolled down the passenger window two inches, and asked me what the problem was. I explained my situation to them. They asked to see my U-Haul rental agreement. I dug it out of the glove compartment and while I was handing it to them through the two-inch opening, they said, "We have a gun." I responded by partially unzipping my coat and showed them, Buddy, my miniature Sheltie and said, "I have a dog." They didn't appear to be amused.

I begged them to let me inside their car so I could warm up. They said, "Absolutely not. We don't know you. We will contact a towing company when we get into Delta Junction." I said, "But I'll freeze to death before they arrive." They responded, "That's all we're willing to do for you." I found that to be so bizarre and foreign to my experiences while living in Alaska. The rule of the road was to help others because that could be you someday. I found myself climbing back into the cab of my truck, shivering nonstop, with my only source of heat being my little dog, Buddy, inside of my jacket.

Another hour passed and I found myself becoming resigned to the fact that I was most likely going to freeze to death alongside the highway. I was scared to death. I started writing a short note on a piece of paper I found on the floor inside the cab. Suddenly, I saw a pair of headlights approaching my truck from the front. I got out of my truck and started flagging down the approaching vehicle. The gentleman stopped his small pickup truck, rolled down his window, listened to my story, and immediately pulled his truck around to the backside of my truck. He told me to get inside and warm up while he placed flares and reflective triangles on the road behind my truck. He climbed back inside his small pickup truck and told me that he was an off-duty Alaska State Trooper going home from working his shift. I thanked him profusely for saving my life. He had a C.B. radio in his truck and radioed ahead for a tow truck to come take my U-Haul truck to Delta Junction. He also found out that the two women never called the towing company. They left me there to die.

I sat in a cheap hotel for five days before they finally were able to rebuild the engine. I was back on the highway in the freezing cold conditions and drove all the way to Beaver Creek in the Yukon Territory in northern Canada. I woke up the next day and drove towards Haines Junction. The U-Haul truck broke down again about an hour outside of the community. Fortunately, it happened during the daylight hours and a trucker picked me up and took me into town. A gentleman drove me back out to the U-Haul truck and towed it back to his shop in Haines Junction.

It was Christmas Eve and I was supposed to be arriving at my parents' home in Salem, Oregon at this moment in time. Instead, I was still

1,875 miles away from my destination. I asked the mechanic to take a peek at the engine to see if a quick fix was possible so I could get back on the road. He said, "No. My wife and I have a Christmas Eve party to go to." She happened to be in the shop at this time and saw the tears begin to stream down my cheeks. She said, "Come on, honey, it's Christmas Eve. Please look at the man's truck." I smiled at her and gave an appreciative nod. She smiled back. He looked under the hood for about fifteen minutes and said, "You're not going anywhere. This engine is fried. There's a motel across the street and you can stay there until we get this sorted out." I thanked him for taking the time to look at the engine, walked across the street while the snow was coming down, and checked into the motel.

I spent Christmas alone in my motel room with my little dog, Buddy. It took four more days before the U-Haul company decided to drive in a new truck from White Horse, in the Yukon Territory. Only ninety-six miles away. They delivered the new truck and told me that I would have to unload the broken-down truck and reload the new truck by myself. I hired two local high school kids to help me during the Christmas break. Although it had snowed about a foot the night before and was about twenty degrees below zero, we managed to unload the old truck and reload the new truck before 10 pm that night. Those two young men were Canadian angels. I thanked them for their hard work and paid them well.

The next morning, I ate breakfast at the mom and pop restaurant located in the motel. When I was done eating, I got my coat and gloves on. The owners asked me, "Where are you going?" I said, "My new truck is loaded up and I'm driving to Salem, Oregon. I should have arrived there five days ago." They said, "You're not going anywhere. The biggest snow-storm to hit this area in one hundred years is on the way. We're going to get buried in a couple of hours." I stated, "I'm a total of ten days behind schedule and I'm not going to sit around for another couple of days. I'm out of here. Thank you for your kindness and hospitality." I walked out the door, climbed into the U-Haul truck, and started driving.

Two-hours later, the snow storm of the century hit. No problem. I spent twenty years driving in the snow while living in Alaska and this wasn't any different. However, that wasn't quite the truth. In this area, I was driving through steep mountain roads with very tight curves that had five-hundred to one-thousand-foot cliffs alongside the road without any guardrails. At one point, while I was driving around one of those sharp corners on a steep mountain road, my U-Haul truck started sliding across the other lane. Fortunately, no oncoming traffic was in the other lane. However, my U-Haul truck continued to slide toward the cliff. I literally cried out to God and asked for help. The tires on the truck finally gripped the road with about six inches to spare before I went over the side of the mountain. I was scared to death. I slowed down and continued driving down the highway.

The Canadian snow storm of the century encompassed the entire Yukon Territory as well as British Columbia. I plugged away at the miles until I made it to Dawson Creek, the gateway to the Alaska Highway. I checked into a hotel, ordered a pizza and beer, and celebrated the arrival of Y2K with Buddy. It was quite the party. Those miniature Shelties can be major party animals. We woke up the next morning on January 1, 2000. Apparently, the computers did not crash worldwide and civilization did not collapse. Therefore, I was able to pay my hotel bill with my credit card. Miracles never cease.

After I paid my bill, I walked across the street to a 7-11 Store, bought a six-pack of Mountain Dew along with a bottle of Nodoz, consumed way too much caffeine, and drove one-thousand-thirty miles nonstop to my parents' house in Salem, Oregon. The snow storm did not let up until I hit the border separating the province of British Columbia from the State of Washington. After twenty-four hours of nonstop driving, I arrived at my parents' home, got out of the truck, walked like a zombie past everyone waiting for me in the driveway, went to the bathroom, and slept for eighteen hours straight. I'm sure I looked like death warmed over. That was most definitely a "U-Haul trip from Hell." Little did I know what more of a traumatic experience was waiting for me in southern Oregon. A real big hairy deal.

For the next seven months, I busted my butt to build up my psychology private practice in Grants Pass, Oregon. I had to market and network all over town. I joined the Rotary Club. I attended a weekly luncheon meeting for pastors. I worked hard to get myself on provider panels for insurance companies. I advertised, advertised, and advertised some more. Finally, commuted back and forth from Grants Pass to Salem in order to spend the weekend with my family. Only to wake up two mornings later and drive two-hundred miles south again to Grants Pass to do it all over. My wife and children needed to live with my parents until I could generate enough income to provide for our own home in southern Oregon. My hard work paid off and success came quickly. After school was out in June, my wife and children moved south to join me in Grants Pass, Oregon. We finally settled in and boy was I ready for a break. It was time to play with my wife and children.

On July 1, 2000, I found myself enjoying a beautiful Saturday in southern Oregon with my family. My wife and I decided to take our three children on a tour through the Oregon Caves. We drove from Grants Pass, Oregon to the Oregon Caves National Monument Park. What a beautiful drive through Josephine county. The last twenty miles were on a very curvy road that ascended the mountain leading up to the caves. When we arrived, we ate a lunch at a picnic table in the warm sun. The kids were excited to be able to take a tour through the caves. The last time I had taken a tour through the Oregon Caves was eighteen years earlier while on a honeymoon with their mother. The tour was everything the kids had hoped it would be. Except it was a lot colder than they anticipated.

Once we completed the tour of the Oregon Caves, we immediately started hiking the "Big Tree Loop Trail" on the other side of the Visitors Center near the Gift Shop. Although the trail was 3.3 miles long, we didn't think it was a big deal because we had taken our young children hiking in Alaska all of the time. Actually, we were excited because we knew that we no longer needed to worry about running into Grizzly Bears while out in the wilderness. We could finally hike in peace.

The scenery was incredibly gorgeous. We were hiking through tall trees which were surrounded by beautiful plant life on the forest floor. The elevation of the hike is approximately one-thousand-one-hundred feet. The trail also crossed through meadows and ultimately brings the hiker to the widest girthed Douglas Fir tree that one can find in the State of

Oregon. About one mile up the mountain, we came across a horrid smell that was blowing down the mountainside from above our position. All five of us smelled the putrid odor that was as strong as a skunk but it wasn't a skunk. The aroma most definitely grabbed ahold of one's olfactory bulb and ripped it right out of one's head. We all acknowledged the pungent smell and continued hiking. It didn't concern us because we knew it most definitely wasn't a Grizzly bear. Therefore, no worries.

As we continued to ascend the mountain, we started hearing a strange noise paralleling our movement. It was a deep, base, mammal, guttural noise that sounded like "Whoa, whoa, whoa, whoa, whoa." When we would walk, the noise was made. When we stopped, it was silent. When we walked again, the noise was made again. When we stopped, it was silent again. All five of us acknowledged hearing the sound. We were puzzled and could not figure out what was making the noise. We weren't scared because we knew there were no Grizzly Bears in Oregon. Therefore, we had nothing to worry about. After some time, the noise stopped. We weren't smelling anything or hearing anything anymore. The kids, ages 5, 7, and 9, needed to take a brief break. They were doing a great job as always.

I started putting one and one together in my mind and my biological "fight or flight" responses kicked in. I concluded that we were being stalked by something large. I just didn't know what it was yet. I stopped my family on the trail and I told them to stay quiet. The kids used a stick to play with a bug on the trail. I hiked up the hill to our left, through the brush and trees, because I had to go number two as soon as possible. This happens when the biological "fight or flight" response kicks in.

While I was doing my duty, I was scanning the woods down-slope on the mountain on the other side of the trail from where my family was standing. That's when I saw it. I saw it come out from behind one tree to the left and walk in an upright bipedal manner to another tree to the right. Then it looked back and was watching my family where they were standing on the trail. My wife and kids did not know that they were being watched.

I've hiked through the woods in Alaska numerous times and believe me, I know what a Grizzly Bear looks like and I know what a Black Bear looks like. What I saw was not a Grizzly Bear or a Black Bear. What I saw actually walked upright on two legs like a human and it was much taller than a Grizzly Bear or a Black Bear. It had to be at least nine to ten feet tall. What I saw was a Bigfoot, otherwise known as a Sasquatch.

I pulled up my pants immediately. I literally felt the cognitive schema in my head collapse. Everything I knew about the great outdoors came crashing down. I just saw Bigfoot walk off the pages of myth and legend into reality. Then I felt my brain reboot and my protective instincts kicked in. I walked fast down through the brush and trees back to the trail and got my family moving up the mountain immediately. At first, they were in no hurry to move along. I asserted myself and got them to start moving up the trail. They knew that something wasn't right because of the way I was behaving but they didn't know what or why. I decided to move them up the trail, rather than back down the trail, because I sure as heck wasn't going to take my family right back through the area where the Bigfoot was spotted.

At that moment, I chose not to tell my wife or children what I saw because I didn't want them to panic. The adrenaline was rushing through my body and I was very hyper vigilant. I was constantly looking behind us and through the woods. Although the sound had stopped, I wasn't convinced that we were out of danger yet. My heart was pounding fast and I was scared to death.

We hiked a couple hundred yards and around a switchback. When we reached a place where the kids could stop, I sat them down on a fallen log to rest and drink some water, I pulled my wife aside and told her that she wasn't going to believe what I saw. She asked me what I had seen. I told her that I saw Bigfoot and she said, "I believe you." Of course, she believed me, she had smelled the smell and she had heard the repetitive audible cycles of "Whoa, Whoa, Whoa, Whoa, Whoa." She knew that I wasn't crazy. She had also spent decades out in the Alaska wilderness and knew that we weren't dealing with a Grizzly Bear or Black Bear.

My mind was racing as I maintained my hyper vigilance. I quickly came up with a game plan. I told her to keep the kids hiking on the trail and that I would stay back about fifty feet while keeping my eyes on what was behind us. I told her that if anything came up from behind us or through the woods on the left side of us down the slope, that I would run interference to protect them. I told her that if this happened, I wanted her to run the kids along the trail, don't stop, and don't look back. We agreed not to tell the children because we didn't want to panic them.

I was very frightened for my family's safety. Also, I knew that if I had to run interference on my family's behalf, that I would not last very long. What I saw was taller than an NBA player and more buff than an NFL football player. Although I stand six feet nine inches tall and weigh three-hundred-thirty pounds, what I saw could have picked me up, crumbled me up like a wad of paper, and thrown me away. As I previously stated, the Bigfoot I saw had to be nine to ten feet tall. Also, I'm guessing it probably weighed somewhere near one thousand pounds.

Although the situation was tense, fortunately, we never heard the sounds again and I never saw anything after that. We finally made it to the "Big Tree" near the other end of the loop. The kids wanted to stop and check out the Douglas Fir tree that had a forty-foot circumference and was approximately eight-hundred years old. Nevertheless, we had to move them along. We finally made it out of the forest about one and a half hours after our encounter. The longest hour and a half of my life other than when I was freezing to death inside the U-Haul truck alongside the highway in the middle of nowhere Alaska. At least this time I was warm. We sent the kids into the Gift Store to pick out a gift because we had promised to buy them something if they were good hikers and didn't complain. They were super kids.

My wife and I sat on the bench outside the Gift Store and talked about the pros and cons of whether or not we should report what we smelled, heard, and saw. I had just worked hard for six months to build up my private practice. We didn't want to lose business because people would think that I was crazy. Therefore, my wife said it was up to me. I decided that I wasn't going to keep this a secret because it was real and I knew that I was sane. Also, if we had seen a black bear or cougar up on the mountainside, we would have reported it to the Rangers for the safety of other hikers. Why was this sighting any different?

After the decision was made, my wife went into the Gift Shop with the kids. I walked over to the Park Headquarters and reported what I saw to NPS Ranger, Beverly Cherner. I sat in the chair in her office, stunned, and then I began to cry. All of the emotions that I had been stuffing due to the adrenaline began to surface now that my family and I were safe. You don't know how vulnerable I felt being so far out in the woods without the ability to protect my family in that kind of situation. Due to National Park rules, I wasn't allowed to carry my handgun like I normally did while we hiked in Alaska.

I gave Ranger Beverly Cherner my private practice business card which identified myself as a licensed clinical psychologist. I told the her that I was not crazy. I told her that I have two master's degrees and one doctorate degree and that I was an intelligent person. I told her that I know what I smelled, heard, and saw. I told her that I had been a resident of Alaska for twenty years with plenty of outdoor experience. In between the tears and my shaking, I told her that I saw Bigfoot. I expected her to roll her eyes and smirk at me. Instead, she said that she believed me. She said that she didn't think I was crazy. She stated, "Dr. Johnson, we're discovering new species on our planet all of the time. Anyone who thinks that we've discovered everything that is living on our planet is practicing arrogance." I found her words to be very comforting to me. I really needed to hear that.

She took my story, my wife's story, and my oldest son confirmed what the noise sounded like. I was the only one who saw the Bigfoot because I had hiked up off the trail high enough to see it. The Bigfoot stood approximately nine to ten feet tall. It looked half-human and half-ape, walked upright and bipedal like a human, and had very dark hair. A mix of very dark brown and black hair. It had a protruding brow ridge and a cone shaped head. The arms were longer proportionately when compared to the length of human arms. It took a while for the image that I saw to settle in my mind.

We left the Oregon Caves National Monument Park late in the day. While we were driving back to Grants Pass, Oregon, the kids were asking what was going on. My wife said, "Oh nothing. Daddy just saw Bigfoot." The kids went crazy in the back of the car. They responded, "What's a Bigfoot?" They pelted us with one-hundred million questions. Most of their questions were left without answers. I was a newbie to the Bigfoot phenomena. I had no idea how to respond to their questions. We eventually tucked them into bed, said our nighttime prayers, and kissed them good night. Then I drove to my private practice office to type up a report while it was still fresh in my mind.

After I completed typing up my report, I was very curious and started doing some exploring on the internet. I found a Bigfoot website and filed my report online. Within forty-eight hours, the news shot around the world about a clinical psychologist and his family running into a Bigfoot on the mountainside above the Oregon Caves National Monument Park. The Bigfoot was out of the bag. I was worried about my private practice and my future ability to provide for my family. Once again, I was scared to death.

The fun was just beginning.

CHAPTER THREE

FACING OUR FEARS

The following day, Ranger John Roth called me at home to check up on how we were doing. I thought it was a very nice gesture. Then he asked if our family would be willing to return to the Oregon Caves National Monument Park and walk him through where we smelled the smell, where we heard the noises, and where I saw the Bigfoot. I immediately responded by saying, "There's no way that I'm going to bring my family back to the park let alone take them back up on the mountain where that animal is roaming around." He responded, "Dr. Johnson, you know after having lived in Alaska that animals won't approach large groups of people. We will be safe up there on the mountain." I asked if anyone was going to be carrying a gun and he said that it was against the park rules. Once again, he assured me that my family was going to be safe.

He gave me the phone number of John Freitas, a Bigfoot Researcher and retired police officer, from northern California. He told me that John would be coming along with Scott Herriott, another Bigfoot Researcher, and that it might make me feel more comfortable if I talked with him first. I called up John and talked with him for about a half an hour. He reassured me that the Bigfoot would not attack us and that we would be safe. He also told me that he would be packing a handgun but asked me not to tell the park rangers. I talked with my wife and we decided to return to the park on Monday and walk Ranger John Roth through our monstrous adventure on the "Big Tree Loop Trail." We also thought it would be good for all of us to hop back up on the horse and face our fears. We didn't want our children to be afraid to go back into the forest. Heck, who am I kidding? I didn't want me to be afraid to go back into the woods again. I needed to face my fears too.

On Monday morning, July 3rd, we climbed out of our car and walked across the parking lot and into the headquarters at the Oregon Caves National Monument Park. I asked to see Ranger John Roth and he was out in the lobby to greet us in less than thirty seconds. He was a tall gentleman with gray hair and beard who looked very professional in his Ranger uniform and hat. His glasses made him look intelligent. He was soft spoken, kind, gentle in spirit, and worked overtime to assure my wife, children, and myself that we were not in any danger. He expressed much appreciation for our return to the park within forty-eight hours of our encounter. He shared that he was a professional tracker and he wanted to see the area as soon as possible before Mother Nature had an opportunity to cover up any evidence.

As we all stepped outside the headquarters back to the parking lot, John and Scott arrived in their truck. They got out of their vehicle and we all exchanged greetings and salutations with one another. After the introductions, Scott grabbed a couple of trail cams out of the vehicle and we began our walk to the Visitors Center and Gift Store area. I'm going to be very honest and share that my anxiety significantly increased as we neared the trailhead. While we were still in the Visitor Center area, I excused myself in order to use the restroom. I didn't want to find myself having to relieve myself again up on the mountainside. While I was washing my hands, I looked in the mirror and said out loud to myself, "Are you really going to do this? Do you really want to take your family back up there?" I really didn't want to but we were already committed. I walked out of the men's room and we began our ascent up the right side of the "Big Tree Loop Trail."

It was another beautiful warm sunny day as we hiked up the trail. The view at the corner where the cement trail and stairs end was spectacular. I saw the endless sea of mountain tops and thought about all the places that a Bigfoot could possibly hide. As we continued to hike, I got to know everyone better. I learned that Ranger John Roth had authored a book, "American Elves: An Encyclopedia of Little People from the Lore of 380 Ethnic Groups of the Western Hemisphere" which was published in 1997. I learned that John Freitas was a retired police officer who had been investigating Bigfoot encounters for a number of years. Finally, I learned that Scott Herriott had his own encounter with a Bigfoot and allegedly caught it on film. I chuckled to myself as we continued to hike up the mountainside. What an odd bunch we were, but hey, we were having fun and enjoying one another's company. I was also very appreciative of the attention, encouragement, and praise that these three gentlemen were giving to our three young children, ages five, seven, and nine.

When we arrived at the stretch of the trail where we had smelled the putrid stench blowing downwind from the slope above, Ranger John Roth gave the area a very close look over and did not find any Skunk Cabbage. Apparently, unbeknownst to me, some of the park rangers had speculated whether or not we simply smelled some Skunk Cabbage in the area. Nope. Turns out that it wasn't Skunk Cabbage after all. Evidence confirmation box number one was checked off.

When we got to the part of the trail where we were being paralleled by the deep, bass, guttural mammal-like sounds, "Whoa, whoa, whoa, whoa, whoa," everyone saw just how thick the trees and brush were. It would be very easy for something large to stay hidden while following us up the mountainside. Evidence confirmation box number two was checked off.

Finally, we arrived at the area of my family's encounter with the Bigfoot. We showed the gentlemen where the kids were playing with a bug on the path. The stick was still laying there on the path. Then I hiked up through the brush and trees and shouted down to the gentlemen on the trail that this was where I did my business and where I was standing when I saw the Bigfoot watching my wife and children. I asked the three gentlemen to come up to the spot where I was standing so they could confirm my story. They thanked me but said that they didn't think it was necessary.

I asserted myself and strongly insisted that they come up the hill and look at the poop and paper on the ground. I wanted them to confirm that I was telling the truth about everything. I also wanted them to see the vantage point that I had behind the natural blind when I spotted the Bigfoot. They couldn't argue with my logic so they all hiked up the hill. They confirmed that they saw the poop and paper on the ground. Granted, it wasn't a pretty sight, nevertheless, it was necessary in order to confirm the veracity of our story. They also appreciated seeing the vantage point that I had from behind the natural blind. It helped them to see the view and angles I had while looking down the slope of the mountainside. Evidence confirmation box number three was checked off.

We walked back down the slope through the brush and trees and reached the trail where my wife and children were patiently waiting. Then Ranger John Roth asked all of us to stay on the trail while he Walked downslope to the area where I had spotted the Bigfoot. He was a professional tracker and he wanted to give the area a thorough look over without any human interference.

After about thirty minutes, Ranger John Roth called all of us down the slope to where he was standing. He said, "Something very big moved through this area in the past twenty-four to forty-eight hours. I also discovered an animal trail over there that parallels the hiking trail." He started walking us down the animal trail and then he stopped us and pointed to a track on the ground. He squatted down on the ground while we gathered around him being very careful not to step on the track.

While pointing at the track on the ground with his finger, Ranger John Roth stated, "This is not a bear track. It's too long for a bear track." It most certainly was too long for a bear track. I wear a size sixteen shoe which is approximately fourteen and a half inches long. The track we were looking at dwarfed my shoe. Then he stated, "This is a Bigfoot track. However, you need to know that the park has a policy that we will not take a public position with the media regarding the existence of the Bigfoot species within the park boundaries."

I could tell by looking at everyone else that their minds were spinning just like mine was spinning. What did Ranger John Roth just say? The park has a policy that they won't take a public position with the media regarding the existence of the Bigfoot species within the park boundaries? I thought for a moment and said to myself, "In order to have a policy, they would have to have a group of people sitting down around a table in a conference room talking with one another to create such a policy." Then I said to myself, "They wouldn't be sitting down in a room creating a policy unless something had happened in order to cause them to want to create such a policy." Finally, I stated out loud, "This isn't the first time this has happened, is it?" Ranger John Roth simply smiled at me and said nothing. His silence said enough and his smile confirmed my hunch.

Before we hiked back down the right side of the "Big Tree Loop Trail", Scott Herriott asked Ranger John Roth if he could hang up a couple of Trail Cams in the area. Permission was granted and Scott went to work. Afterwards, he asked us not to tell anyone else that he had hung up some Trail Cams because he had a lot of money invested in his equipment. We promised not to tell anyone. Eventually, we returned to the bottom of the trail, said our goodbyes, and drove back home.

Interestingly enough, within thirty days of my family's encounter with the Bigfoot up on the mountain above the Oregon Caves National Monument Park, I received several emails and phone calls from about thirty people with their own Bigfoot encounter stories in the area spanning a twenty-five-year period of time. People shared their stories of encountering a Bigfoot while working at the park, hiking in the park, camping near the park, hunting near the park, and mining near the park. Wow! I had absolutely no idea. However, it was a wonderful confirmation that what I saw was very real and that I wasn't alone. I wasn't crazy after all.

In addition to the Bigfoot stories that were shared with me near the vicinity of the Oregon Caves National Monument Park, several people who had encounters in different parts of the State of Oregon also contacted me. The witnesses came out of the woodwork and were from all walks of life. Pastors, teachers, principals, policemen, businessmen, hairdressers, coaches, biologists, attorneys, judges, realtors, loggers, and hunters.

While sitting in my office, my secretary buzzed me and told me that a Judge was calling me from Portland, Oregon. My mind immediately began brainstorming about which one of my private practice clients could possibly be involved in a legal or civil case two-hundred-fifty miles to the north of Grants Pass. I picked up the phone and received the shock of my life. The Judge told me about his Bigfoot encounter while hunting near the Mt. Hood area a few years earlier.

He said, "I got an early start in the morning while hunting near Mt. Hood. After several hours of no luck, I sat on a stump positioned on a tree line overlooking a clear cut area. While eating my sandwich, I heard some heavy footed bipedal steps coming through the trees approaching the tree line. It was about one-hundred yards upwind from me. All of a sudden, I saw a Bigfoot walk out into the open and he began to walk into the clear cut area around all of the stumps. I could hear a small plane approaching from the south. Apparently, the Bigfoot heard it too and what he did next totally amazed me. He squatted down, bent forward with his arms around his legs, and held his position as if he were one of the several stumps in the clear cut area. After the small plane flew over and was out of sight, the Bigfoot stood back up and completed his walk through the stumps to the other side of the clear cut area. I was blown away, stopped my hunting, and went straight home." Then he stated, "I just had to call you to let you know that I admire your courage for coming out publicly with your story. I also wanted to let you know that you're not crazy. The Bigfoot species are very real."

I was excited and said, "That's an awesome story and thanks so very much for taking the time out of your day to call me and share it with me. When the media contacts me about my story, can I have them give you a call too? It would be great corroboration." He said, "I'm sorry but I won't be able to do that. I want to but I can't. I'm a Judge and coming out publicly with my story would discredit me and cause me to get booted off the bench. I hope you understand." I assured him that I understood and thanked him again for taking the time to call me and share his story with me.

About a week later, another gentleman contacted me at my private practice office. He introduced himself to me as an Oregon State Trooper. He shared a hunting story with me that occurred about two years prior to the phone call. He had been out Elk hunting with his daughter and her husband. He was driving his truck down a logging road up in the mountains outside of Roseburg, Oregon. Then he said, "Suddenly my daughter was screaming from the backseat of the cab, 'Stop the truck! Stop the truck!' So I stopped the truck just in time to see some rocks sliding down the mountainside onto the road in front of us. A few seconds later, an adult female

Sasquatch stepped down the hill, through the trees, and onto the road in front of our pickup truck. It was only about fifty or sixty feet in front of us. She just stood there looking at us."

I said, "Wow! That's an amazing story." He responded, "I'm not done yet, son. Suddenly, an adult male Sasquatch walked up the hill from the left side of the logging road and popped out of the trees onto the road between our truck and the female Sasquatch. He stood there staring at us for about a minute. Then he took three steps in our direction and he looked frustrated with us. My daughter started screaming from the back seat, 'Back up! Back the truck up!' so I did. I backed us up another thirty feet. The male Sasquatch stopped, turned around, and walked back to the adult female. Then they both walked off the logging road into the trees and out of sight. That ended our hunting season for that year. The forest has never been the same since then."

I asked him if I could send the media his way when they contacted me. He replied, "Son, I don't want or need any media attention. I'm a high ranking officer in the Oregon State Trooper organization. I'm two years away from retirement. I'm not willing to take the risk of losing everything that I've worked so hard to gain. But that's why I wanted to call you and share my story with you. I wanted to let you know that your courage to come out publicly with your story is very impressive. Especially because you have a private practice. I also wanted to let you know that you're not alone and that you're not crazy."

I shared with him that my father had been an Oregon State Trooper for twenty-five years. I respected his position, vulnerability, and appreciated his taking the time to contact me to share his story with me. I also took the time to share the Judge's story with him as well as a few other stories that were shared with me. He thanked me for my time and we hung up. Although it was nice to hear about another Bigfoot encounter from a very credible witness, it was frustrating to hear, once again, that he was unwilling to take a public stance. Could you imagine the public response if a Licensed Clinical Psychologist, a Judge, and an Oregon State Trooper all came out publicly with their encounter stories during the same summer?

Finally, a sweet elderly couple who lived in Klamath Falls, Oregon called my favorite story into me. They shared their names with me and told me that they were in their mid-eighties. They told me that they were driving up to the Crater Lake area when they experienced their Bigfoot sighting. The elderly gentleman said, "Dr. Johnson, we saw a Bigfoot walk across the highway in front of our car. It was about fifty yards in front of us. It had to be about eight or nine feet tall. He saw us coming and crossed the road in a hurry. He only took a couple of steps to do it. Anyway, Dr. Johnson, we're just calling to let you know that we saw one too and to let you know that you're not crazy."

My family's encounter with a Bigfoot on the side of the mountain above the Oregon Caves National Monument Park certainly opened my eyes to a species that I never knew really existed. Prior to our encounter, Bigfoot was just myth and legend. A cool campfire story to tell while roasting hotdogs and marshmallows. Suddenly, everyone and his brother and mother were calling me or emailing me and were telling me about their encounters too. It was wonderful corroborative information to receive. Most important of all, it was nice to have it confirmed by so many people from all walks of life that I wasn't crazy. They saw one too.

The phone calls and emails never stopped. I kept meeting so many interesting people, both locally and from abroad. Many of them wanted to hear my story as well as share their story with me too. I lost two private practice clients as a result of coming out publicly with my story. However, I gained one new client too. He said, "I knew that if you were truthful enough to tell the world that you saw a Bigfoot, then you would be truthful and call me on my crap while I'm in therapy with you." That was quite the compliment and affirmed to me that I had made the right decision.

The ultimate affirmation that I made the right decision to report our Bigfoot encounter to the Oregon Caves National Monument Park

Headquarters occurred while I was attending the 2001 Spring Conference of the Oregon Psychological Association (OPA). The conference opened up in a large ballroom at a hotel in Portland, Oregon. A couple hundred Oregon Psychologists were in attendance. The OPA President at the time, Dr. Eric Morel, was addressing his colleagues and was making some opening remarks to kick off the annual conference.

Suddenly, Dr. Morrel asked for Dr. Matthew Johnson to please stand. I was caught totally off guard and was just sitting there. He asked again if Dr. Matthew Johnson would please stand up. His eyes were scanning the large audience in the ballroom. Someone nudged me and I stood up not knowing what to expect. He looked at me and smiled. Then he stated in front of everyone, "Ladies and gentlemen, I would like to introduce to you the psychologist who looked Bigfoot in the eyes and had the courage to speak up and tell the world about it. Thank you Dr. Johnson, for your courage."

I smiled, nodded my head, and gave a quick wave to Dr. Morrel. However, what happened next moved me to the point of silent tears. The entire group of Psychologists stood up on their feet and gave me a standing ovation. I smiled, waved again to everyone, and then sat down and wiped the tears away from my eyes. I received several pats on my back from those who were sitting around me. Everyone sat back down and the conference went on.

Afterwards, several other Oregon Psychologists who had their own Bigfoot encounters approached me or who knew family and friends who had Bigfoot encounters. Many of them wanted to talk with me about my family's encounter, look at pictures, and view my foot casts. Finally, one Psychologist told me that she was now going to have to take her client more seriously about her alleged encounter with a Bigfoot and the subsequent PTSD symptoms that she's been dealing with since her encounter.

I have always been one to stand up for the truth regardless of the consequences. I wasn't about to stop now. I was always taught that a man of integrity does not run from the truth or try to hide the truth. Rather, a man of integrity faces the truth, speaks the truth, and teaches the truth. Besides, I was beginning to make a lot of really cool local friends in Grants Pass, Oregon as well as around the U.S.A.

CHAPTER FOUR

THE ELEPHANT MAN

Within weeks of my family's Bigfoot encounter, when my private practice office phone rang, I never knew if I was going to be talking to a client, a potential new client, someone from the media, someone else who had a Bigfoot encounter, or someone who was simply interested in the Bigfoot phenomena.

On one occasion when I answered the phone at the beginning of my work day, there was an elderly gentleman on the line who spoke very politely and with a British accent. I asked, "Are you calling me all the way from England?" He said, "No sir, I'm actually calling you from next door. I'm renting an office in the same complex where your office is located. My name is Dr. William York and I'm a retired Wildlife Biologist. I now own a mortgage finance company and I fiddle around with lending out small home loans to local residents. I used to be a big game hunter and a wildlife preserve officer in Africa for just over forty years. I was wondering if I could buy you lunch sometime this week and talk with you about your family's recent Bigfoot encounter?"

I immediately responded, "How about this afternoon?" He said, "Well that is delightfully prompt and it would be an honor to buy you lunch today. Can we meet next door at the River Rock Café at twelve noon?" I responded in the affirmative and we met up for lunch about three hours later. I was excited because he sounded like a very fascinating individual with some possible interesting stories of his own to share with me. Also, I enjoyed listening to his British accent. Besides, I never turn down free food.

I ordered my usual Ham Sandwich and small Garden Salad with extra ranch dressing. Dr. William York, who preferred to be called Bill, ordered a bowl of soup. He stated, "I like to eat light because it helps keep the weight off this old man's body." He was only sixty-seven years old at the time. We sat outside at one of the tables with a huge umbrella to keep us out of the hot rays of the sun. He spent some time introducing himself to me and told me about how he went about fulfilling his boyhood dream of moving to Africa and becoming a Big Game Hunter.

Apparently, at the age of seventeen, Bill left his home and moved to Africa to start hunting Elephants for their tusks. After successfully hunting over two-hundred-fifty Elephant, he told me that he felt guilty, put his hunting rifle away, and decided to become a Game Management Officer and studied to become a Wildlife Biologist. Eventually, he informed me, he became a primate specialists and loved studying Gorillas while helping to keep them safe.

Bill shared with me about how he overcame his fear of working with Gorillas in Africa. He developed the habit of going out to the areas where the Gorillas were foraging and he would hang out with them. Occasionally, the alpha male would bluff charge him. Bill told me, "Although I was scared to death, I would raise my rifle and tell myself not to shoot unless the Gorilla passed a certain point. Then I felt comfortable to allow him to come closer before I would raise my rifle. After a while, the alpha male would run all the way up to me and veer off to my left while barely brushing my shoulder but never knocking me over. I started leaving my rifle behind because I realized that he wasn't going to hurt me. All I had to do was treat him and the others with respect and he would allow me to hang around the area with them."

Bill went on to tell me about his Game Management enforcement stories. Over a few decades, he managed to stop a lot of poachers from being successful and saved a lot of wildlife. Also, apparently his reputation led to him leading a Safari for the Queen of England. Finally, he shared with me that he was a consultant to help design and open up the

Animal Kingdom at Walt Disney World in Orlando, Florida as well as the Wildlife Safari in Winston, Oregon. I've actually been to both parks and I was very impressed with the both of them.

Fortunately, both Bill and I had enough time during our business day to block out two hours for our lunch appointment because he took up the first hour with his very interesting stories. It also gave me time to finish my lunch and made me feel more comfortable to open up to him and tell him everything during the second hour. Bill asked me to tell him all about my family's Bigfoot encounter. I shared everything about the encounter with him, including the fear and tears that naturally accompanied my story when I would tell it almost two decades ago. Between the details, my shaking body, and my tears, Bill stated, "That's a very fascinating story and I believe you one-hundred percent." Those words provided me with comfort and encouragement. It was nice to be believed.

Then Bill said something that scared me to death. He said, "We need to get up there as soon as possible." To be honest, I was starting to get a little frustrated with people continually asking me to take them back to the scene of the encounter. Their request involved taking the time to do so, required a lengthy and strenuous hike back up the mountainside again and again, and kept forcing me to face my fears. I had a life to live. I had a family, my children's activities, and a private practice to manage. I couldn't drop everything all of the time just because someone wanted me to take them to the scene of my family's Bigfoot encounter.

I responded to Bill, "You mean take you up to the scene of my family's encounter?" He said, "No, I mean we need to get up there as soon as possible to conduct an expedition. I would think that two nights should do." He could see my automatic uneasiness in my body language. I said, "An expedition? Two nights? You want to go up there and spend two nights with what I saw up there? No offense, Bill, but you've got to be kidding me. That thing was huge! Massive!"

Bill responded by saying, "Matt...... may I call you Matt?" I nodded in the affirmative. He said, "Matt, you know that animals avoid large groups of people. You lived in Alaska and are familiar with this truth. We are not going up the mountain to find Bigfoot. If they're like any other animal that I've ever dealt with in Africa, they will be avoiding us.

Instead, we are simply going up there to find evidence that they're in the area. If they're up there, we will find evidence. Can you get a group of men together for the expedition?"

I said, "I've only lived in Grants Pass for eight months so far. However, recently, several outdoorsman and hunters have contacted me. There's a local pastor and principal of a Christian School who's also expressed an interest in going up to the mountain. His name is Doug Thomas. I'm sure he could help muster up several men to go up on the mountain with us for a Bigfoot expedition. When would you like to go up there?" Bill responded, "How about this coming weekend?" I said, "I'm not sure if we can find enough guys on such short notice but I can sure give it a try. If not this coming weekend, I'm sure we could get enough men together by the following weekend." Bill said, "Well then, why don't you start making some phone calls and get back to me as soon as possible. I'll be free on either weekend."

I promised Bill that I would put together a group of men for a Bigfoot expedition within two weeks or less. In the meantime, I had a private practice to manage, children to parent, and a public and media frenzy to manage. The phone calls and emails were constantly coming in and were starting to overwhelm me.

CHAPTER FIVE

THE MEDIA AND PUBLIC FEEDING FRENZY

I was on the phone with one of the producers for the "Coast to Coast AM" radio show. I said, "Wow! I can't believe that I'm going to be interviewed by Art Bell." She said, "Uhm, no. Art Bell no longer does the show. You'll be interviewed by Mike Siegal instead." I responded, "Who's Mike Segal?" She said, "He took over for Art Bell and he's very good. You're going to like him. Also, he's so excited that you live in southern Oregon, which is where we broadcast out of, so he wants to fly into Medford, Oregon and interview you face to face at the station. Are you okay with that?" I said, "Sure, it sounds like fun."

One week prior to the scheduled interview, my younger brother's friend, Matt Haverly, contacted me and said, "Your brother told me about your story. Wow! What an amazing experience." Then he asked the question, "So, he told me that you're going to make an appearance on the Coast to Coast AM show. What do you have set up to deal with the response?" I said, "I'm just going to give out my phone number and email address." He immediately responded, "No! Are you kidding! There are going to be a million or more people listening to you. Are you going to be able to field that many emails and phone calls?"

About thirty seconds of silence passed. Then I spoke up and said, "Well, I obviously haven't thought that far ahead. No, apparently I don't have a plan. I don't know what to do." Matt responded, "I have an idea. Would you like to hear it?" I responded, "Sure. Please do tell." He suggested the following, "You should put up a website with your story on it. You should also include pictures because people like pictures. This will take care of most people's curiosity. Then you can have your contact information there just in case the media would like to get a hold of you. This way, you only have to give out your website address instead of two sources of information such as your phone number and email address."

"Matt," I responded, "That all sounds really good but there's a couple problems with your idea." He said, "What problems are you talking about?" I said, "The Coast to Coast Am radio interview is going to happen in ten days and I don't have the time, expertise, or money to create and put up a website." He responded to me, "Oh, no problem, I'll do it for you. I know how to make a website and I'll provide my services for free. It would be an honor to help you out. Besides, this is really cool and I want to be involved."

I asked, "Are you sure? You want to do this for free? You think we can get the website done and up in running before the Coast to Coast AM radio interview?" Matt responded, "I can do this. Actually, we can do this. We will need to do this because it's your website. You're going to be the man with the content ideas and the pictures. I'm simply going to be building the website. All I want out of this is to be involved with your research if you decide to go back up there in the mountains." I said, "Deal, I really appreciate you contacting me about your website idea, Matt. I was most definitely inadequately prepared." He said, "My pleasure. I'm looking forward to helping you out on this. It's going to be a cool website."

During the next ten days, Matt Haverly and I were staying up until about 2 am every night, talking on the phone, and passing emails back and forth in order to hammer out the website and get it up and running. The website even included a chat room for interested people to ask me questions and participate in discussions regarding the Bigfoot phenomena. However, my favorite part of the website was the "Banning Option" that Matt created. If we ran into any Trolls or Haters who were creating problems on the website, we could hit the "Ban Button" which placed a cookie on their computer. Thereafter, when they tried to go to our website after we "Banned" them, they were automatically diverted to a "Brittney Spears vs. Mr. T." website. It was hilarious. Eventually, people were figuring it out and simply removed the cookie from their computer. Some website participants were begging us to "Ban" them so they could experience the automatic rerouting adventure. Too funny!

It was time to drive from Grants Pass to Central Point, Oregon to do the "Coast to Coast AM" radio interview with Mike Siegel. Matt Haverly and I had worked hard and completed the website on time. All I had to do was pass out the website address. The drive was only a half-hour long. I was very scared and nervous to be doing a face to face interview, yet also very excited. Mike was also excited to meet me, shook my hand vigorously, and said that he believed me and considered me to be one of the most credible Bigfoot witnesses that he had ever met. We sat down in front of the two microphones and he instructed me as to how to properly place the headphones on my head and how to speak into the microphone. The interview commenced.

Several hours later, I was driving back home and my brain was processing what had just happened. What a whirlwind ride that interview was. Mike Siegel did a wonderful job of interviewing me, slowly but surely bringing out the facts, while also being very sensitive to the emotions that the interview was bringing out in me. There was much laughter as well as tears expressed during the interview. But the thing that was really overwhelming me was trying to anticipate what kind of response the interview was going to generate afterwards.

Well, Matt Haverly was correct. The website received hundreds of thousands of hits. Most people were simply satisfied with checking out what I had to share in print and by looking at some pictures. Others signed up for and started participating in the Chat Group on the website. However, as a result of the "Coast to Coast AM" radio interview with Mike Siegel, I was contacted by many other media agencies.

For an example, I was contacted by the Sci-Fi Channel, the Travel Channel, the ESPN2 Channel, the Animal X program, the In Search Of program, CNN Headline News, the Real Scary Stories program, the BBC, ABC Radio, and over two-hundred radio programs from all over North America. I'll share more later on about some of my media experiences and other interviews. For now, suffice it to say, it was a real fun experience and there was most definitely a learning curve involved regarding the entire process.

What caught me off guard was how some members of the Bigfoot research community responded to my family's encounter and to the attention that the media was choosing to give to me. I had Matt Moneymaker, from the Bigfoot Field Research Organization (BFRO), wanting me to direct all media inquiries to his organization. I told him, "No, Matt, I'm not going to do that. This is my story, not your story. However, I would be more than happy to direct them to you for some supplemental interview information to round out my family's story." Although he wasn't pleased with my response, he agreed to participate in a limited capacity. I must say that I did appreciate the fact that he took me under his wing, initially, and walked me through the Bigfoot experience. My family met with him for breakfast once while we were vacationing in southern California. We also met with him for lunch on another occasion while we were in California. He was very kind to my wife and children.

On the other hand, other experiences with Bigfoot researchers were not so positive. I was invited to participate in Bigfoot email listservs. This was before the advent of Facebook. I was viciously attacked without any moderating from the listserv admins. I was accused of making up the story. I was accused of putting the website together before the encounter until someone went online and learned that the website was created after my family's encounter. I was accused of making up the story as a marketing strategy in order to gain more clients in my private practice. Yeah, right! Like that's a good marketing strategy: "Come see me, I'm the psychologist who saw Bigfoot." Like that was going to generate a lot of new clients for me. Give me a break.

The fun didn't stop there, I was accused by some Bigfoot researchers of manipulating the media to contact and interview me. How silly is that? Like I had some kind of magical powers to make the media contact me and interview me. Others were angry at me and wanted to know why the media was talking with me, a newbie, instead of talking with them. After all, they had a lot more years in the forest than I had. In short, there were a lot of jealous individuals with bruised egos who couldn't understand why they weren't getting the attention.

In retrospect, here's what I think happened. It was the perfect Bigfoot storm. In other words, I think that my family's encounter with Bigfoot drew so much media attention for the following reasons: (1) It happened in a National Park (i.e., The Oregon Caves National Monument Park), (2) The encounter involved an entire family – not just an individual, (3) The witness involved a Licensed Clinical Psychologist (i.e., Me), and (4) The evidence was confirmed by a National Park Forest Ranger (i.e., John Roth). Apparently, all of the above combined together generated a lot of interest from a variety of media agencies at a level never seen before in the Bigfoot research community.

The emails and phone calls continued to come in as time passed. The coolest and shortest exchange of emails that I received was from Dan Aykroyd, one of the stars in the original Ghost Busters movies. He asked me questions about my family's encounter, how we all responded, why I chose to make the decision to continue the loop as opposed to going back down the way we hiked up the mountain, how everyone in my family was doing now, and what were my plans for the future. He graciously thanked me for taking the time to respond to his questions and then I never heard from him again.

One of the classiest Bigfoot Researchers that I had the pleasure of meeting was Derek Randles, the founder of the Olympic Project in the State of Washington. He owns his own landscaping business which affords him the time and money to pursue his passion of Bigfoot research with his many friends. Shortly after my family's Bigfoot encounter, he drove four-hundred miles south from the Olympic peninsula to southern Oregon to interview me. We took a walk along the "Big Tree Loop Trail" above the Oregon Caves National Monument Park and I pointed out to him where we smelled the pungent odor, heard the Bigfoot parallel us along the trail, and where I saw it. Derek was very inquisitive, kind, gentle, supportive, and encouraging. Upon completion of our time together, he rated my encounter and subsequent testimony as a ten on a scale from one to ten. That was quite the confirmation and compliment. Derek Randles is a class act.

On the other hand, my not so favorite exchange of communications occurred between myself and a gentleman named, Erik Beckjord. He was on the fringe of Bigfoot researchers. I was new to the research field and I was learning from others. They identified him as a crazy kook who believed in the "Woo-Woo" abilities of the Bigfoot species. When I asked for clarification, others told me that he was crazy because he believed that the Bigfoot species had paranormal abilities and were able to manipulate quantum physics and mechanics. I was told that people like Erik Beckjord were discrediting serious Bigfoot research and setting the field backwards by decades. Because of people like him, the scientific community would never take us real Bigfoot researchers seriously. I was warned to stay away from the likes of Erik Beckjord.

What I'm about to describe went on and on for over half a year. He would email me several times a day. He would make fun of me on his website because the media was coming to me for information instead of going to him. Finally, he literally called my private practice office about fifty times per day. My secretary quickly learned the tone and pattern of his voice and would hang up on him. However, he was very creative at times and would manage to disguise his voice and trick my secretary into forwarding his call into my office. When I would pick up the phone, he would yell over the phone to me, "Matt, they're in the trees!!! They're in the trees!!!" I would respond, "Erik, you need help and I'm not going to provide it for you. Please stop calling and emailing me. If you don't stop, I will have my attorney file stalking charges against you and I will sue you." Eventually, he stopped and left me alone. Unfortunately for him, he died of cancer a few years ago.

In spite of some of the Trolls and Haters, I was viewed and treated as a hero by most everyone in the Bigfoot community, which I later dubbed as "Bigfootdom" (i.e., The kingdom of Bigfoot members which consists of researchers, armchair enthusiasts, and lurkers). They appreciated the fact that I was willing to put it all on the line in order to come out and share publicly about my family's Bigfoot encounter. The appreciative emails still come almost two decades after the Bigfoot encounter. It's such a privilege and honor to read so many positive and encouraging emails from kind people with good hearts.

However, eventually the Bigfoot encounter started having a negative impact on my family. My ex-wife and children began to grow tired of the endless inquiries from the various media agencies. We would spend all day out in the mountains shooting an episode for their program. I'm talking hours and hours of filming. Then when we would sit down and watch the TV program once it aired, most of the filming hit the editing room floor. I was the main focus of the interviews while they showed very little footage of my wife and children. They began to rebel and asked to opt out of future interviews. It was a very fair request. Although it was frustrating for the media agencies who wanted to include the entire family, the cost/benefit analysis wasn't worth it for the rest of the family.

Part 2

THE OLD SCHOOL PAPARAZZI MONEY SHOT APPROACH

CHAPTER SIX

THE EXPEDITION TO MT. ELIJAH

Dr. William York, otherwise known as Bill, had previously assigned me the task of assembling an expedition team to go up on the mountain within one to two weeks of our lunch meeting. Although I was eight months new to Grants Pass, Oregon, a local gentleman interested in the Bigfoot phenomena had contacted me and offered his assistance if it was ever needed. His name is Doug Thomas.

Doug is a local pastor and principal at the Vineyard Christian School. He's a very kind soul who would give anyone the shirt off of his back. He's an avid outdoorsman and knows the mountains in southern Oregon, including the logging roads, like the back of his hand. He stands about 5 feet 10 inches tall, is handsome, always smiling, and is missing his right arm. When I first met him, he joked about how he lost it to a Sand Shark in the dessert. In case you haven't caught on, he has a great sense of humor too.

I contacted Doug and told him all about Bill and his years of experience in Africa. I told Doug about Bill's request that I assemble a Research Team and asked him if he could help me put it together. Doug enthusiastically responded in the affirmative and we brainstormed about all the guys that we both knew and thought would make good team members. We managed to put together a ragtag bunch of guys who were equally enthusiastic to join us up on Mt. Elijah to help us look for evidence of Bigfoot roaming around in the wilderness near the Oregon Caves National Monument Park.

There was a total of fifteen expedition team members, including Dr. York, Doug, and myself. The remaining twelve individuals consisted of a bunch of local avid outdoorsmen, including the sixteen-year-old neighborhood kid down the street who was dying to go out into the mountains with us. Also, accompanying us were Bill Lee, a national radio broadcaster for ABC Radio at the time, and his cousin, Darrel Stout. Both hailing from the State of Texas. Finally, my father, Art Johnson, accompanied us too.

My father was seventy years old at the time of our first expedition and a retired Oregon State Trooper. He served for twenty-five years and closed out his law enforcement career by helping to run the Fingerprint Bureau. My father was very fascinated by the Bigfoot phenomena because of his own alleged experience that occurred during a deer hunting experience thirty-six years earlier in 1964. To be clear, he never called it a Bigfoot encounter. You'll understand why in just a moment.

Apparently, on a cold Fall morning, my father took my older brother up into the logging roads in the mountains above Seaside, Oregon. My brother was ten years old at the time, which would have made me only three years old. I was too young to remember anything about what was conveyed by the both of them upon their return home. The only reason that I know anything about this story is because, at the age of twelve, I found and read a copy of my father's typed up Oregon State Police Report of the alleged encounter while I was rummaging through some boxes in the upstairs attic. When I asked him about what I had found and read, he only spoke to me about it once and then never again after that.

My father had reached a point on one of the logging roads where he thought it was a good place to park the Chevy station wagon, hike up the hill, and see if he and my older brother could spot any deer in the area. After they made it to the top of the hill, they hunkered down, and waited quietly for about ten minutes. They did not see any deer at all. Matter of fact, the whole area appeared to be void of any animal or bird activity. It was eerily silent. The kind of silence that can scream to your sixth sense while in the woods.

Suddenly, my father reported that there was an extremely loud scream that sounded as loud as a jet engine. He said that it was like someone flipped on a light switch. The scream transitioned into a repetitive, "Whoop! Whoop! Whoop! Whoop! Whoop!" that got louder and louder and louder until it reached a point that they had to cover their ears. Then the light switch flipped off. The sound had stopped as quickly as it had started.

My father reported that both he and my older brother were alarmed and could not tell where the sound was coming from. Still hunkered down, my father decided to make some noises in order to flush out whatever it was that was making the extremely loud noises. Well, my father received a response. It wasn't an audible response. Rather, he reported that something large started running toward them through the brush and trees. My father and brother were high up on the hill and they were looking downwards from an elevation that was about one-hundred feet higher than where the mystery screamer was positioned.

The next thing that my father reported was very unusual and sent goosebumps up and down my body when I read about it in his report. He described that both he and my older brother heard and saw something running through the brush toward them from below the hill. They could see the brush moving and some smaller trees being pushed over. Yet, they could not see whatever it was that was running through the brush or displacing the trees. It was as if the aggressive screamer was invisible. He reported that it stopped charging toward them when he raised his hunting rifle and pointed it in the direction of the breaking brush.

My father immediately guided my older brother down the other side of the hill that they had hiked up in order to reach the Chevy station wagon. He opened up the front right passenger door, directed my older brother to lay on the floor under the dashboard, covered him up with a blanket, and told him not to move or come out from under the blanket until he returned to the car. My father took his hunting rifle and hiked back up to the top of the hill. He started making noises again, including blowing his nose, in order to get the attention of whatever it was that was down the other side of the hill.

According to my father's report, the brush started breaking again and trees were being pushed over. However, he still couldn't see anything. The charging stopped. Then he said that he heard what sounded like a clanking heavy metal door. Then the scream occurred again, followed by the high pitch "Whoop! Whoop! Whoop! Whoop! Whoop!" that got louder and louder and louder like a jet engine. Once again, my father found himself covering his ears with his hands. Then the noise stopped again like a light switch was flipped off. Then he heard the clanking heavy metal door again. Then the charging started coming up the hill again. My father raised his hunting rifle again but this time the aggressive approach did not stop.

My father ran down the other side of the hill toward the station wagon, threw his rifle in the back seat, quickly climbed into the car behind the steering wheel, started the car, put it into drive, and drove like a mad man down the logging road to flee the area. Two minutes later, my father and brother found themselves in a cul-de-sac area at the dead end of a logging road. Needless to say, they were both scared to death.

My father reported that he spun the Chevy station wagon around and high-tailed it back down the logging road where they had just come from. My father allegedly passed the spot, where he had parked the station wagon earlier, while driving fifty miles per hour. He returned my older brother to our home and then went to the Oregon State Trooper Office located in Astoria, Oregon. He typed up his report and submitted it to his commander. The next morning, he went back up to the area with two other Oregon State Troopers. Apparently, they were armed to the teeth with some real heavy duty fire power.

They spent a couple of hours hiking all over the area where the alleged encounter occurred. Other than the broken brush and pushed over trees, they found no other evidence. No footprints, no hair samples, and no visuals. The only other thing that they did manage to find was a tree, located right by the logging road, that had been snapped off about nine feet off the ground and the top of the tree was laying across the road. Apparently, this happened while they were searching the area. The tree was snapped over across the road on the side of their car that was closer to the dead end of the road.

They went back to the State Police Office and reported to the commander what they found. They were all told never to mention the event again. As ordered, my father kept his mouth shut. He filed a copy of his report in a box in the attic and never mentioned it again until I found the report. He was adamant that he didn't know what he and my older brother encountered because they never saw what it was.

My father, Art, was excited and grateful that I invited him to come along with us on our expedition. As previously stated, he was seventy years old. He knew he wasn't going to be able to join us while we hiked up and down the sides of the mountains in the area. However, he could stand guard while we all slept through the night. He had already been retired for fifteen years and had worked some occasional side jobs as a graveyard security guard. Therefore, he was used to staying awake all night long. Although the rest of us younger Bucks were excited to be there together, we were also very happy that my father was willing to pull the graveyard shift and make sure that we were all protected while we slept.

On Saturday, September 9, 2000, we met in the morning in the parking lot where the Hellgate Jet Boat Excursion business is located in Grants Pass, Oregon. Dr. York's and my private practice office were also located in the same building complex. Once all fifteen members of the expedition were assembled, we proceeded to drive toward the Oregon Caves National Monument Park. There are rules about not camping inside the park boundaries. I had previously purchased a map of the local logging roads from the BLM Office and located a spot that would keep us out of trouble with the Rangers. Once we reached the dead end of the spur logging road on the eastside of Mt. Elijah, near the Bigelow Lakes area, we packed up our gear and hiked in on a trail.

Dr. York wanted us to camp up on the ridgeline of Mt. Elijah on the south side of the park boundaries of the Oregon Caves. He chose the ridgeline camping spot based on his years of experience of working with Gorillas in Africa. Although Dr. York knew absolutely nothing about Bigfoot, he assumed that they were more apt to be hanging out on the ridgeline during the summer than they were to be hanging out around the Bigelow Lakes in the valley below on the eastside of the ridgeline.

We stopped several times along the way to give my father some rest. Truth be told, we needed the rest too. We eventually made it up on top of the ridgeline and found a meadow surrounded by trees. We had our camp set up, tents and all, before noon. We consumed some snacks for lunch and then I gathered everyone together. We reviewed the BLM map, divided up into seven teams of two men, Dr. York assigned all seven teams to their areas, and we began to go over every nook and cranny of Mt. Elijah. We covered the west side and east side of the mountain. We covered the south side and the north side of the mountain. We covered the valleys below, including the Bigelow Lakes.

We were ready to deploy our Old School research tactics, otherwise known as the "Paparazzi Money Shot" approach. In a nutshell, this approach philosophically believes that the Bigfoot species are descendants of Gigantopithecus, which is Latin for giant mountain ape. It was believed that these descendants migrated over the Bering Sea Land Bridge along with all of the other animals and humans during the Ice Age.

Since the Bigfoot species were simply giant mountain apes, or wood apes as some researchers referred to them, then we could aggressively pursue them in the forest just like any other animal. Therefore, "Old Schoolers" were in the habit of utilizing high-tech equipment to assist them in their research such as Trail Cams, Seismic Sensors, Night Vision Equipment, Thermal Imaging Equipment, etc.

After hours and hours of relentless searching, all expedition party members returned to our base camp hidden in the meadow surrounded by trees on top of Mt. Elijah. It was late and the sun was starting to go down. We scrambled to get our dinners ready. Some gentlemen simply brought sandwiches or snacks. Others brought camp stoves so they could cook up their dinners. While we were eating, we all shared the evidence that we had found in the area. We found all sorts of very large human-like looking footprints. We found tracks that appeared to belong to a very large adult male, an adult female, and to an adolescent child. We also found one sunning area and three bedding areas that were all freshly used. We also found scat piles.

After we were all fully fed and done sharing about what we all found, I waited for about an hour and then pulled out my ghetto blaster stereo box. I had managed to create a cassette tape of a repetitive loop of a very loud and annoying crying baby. I played the tape over and over again and again for over an hour while I was cooking up some bacon in a frying pan. No man and no animal could resist the alluring aroma of bacon cooking in a frying pan.

By the way, the theory of playing the repetitive loop of a crying baby over and over again and again was that it would either sound like a wounded animal and bring in the Bigfoot or they would simply be curious about the crying baby and want to come in and take a peek. This theory made sense to me. Both Dr. York and I believed that the Bigfoot that my family and I encountered was drawn to us because of our three young blonde haired children. Why not try playing a repetitive looped taped of a crying baby? Also, who could resist the aroma of bacon frying in a pan? Guess what? It worked!

We were all exhausted and started dropping like flies. Dr. York and I were the last ones to hit the hay right around midnight. We were all sound asleep in our pup tents and snoring up a storm. All of us except for my seventy-year-old father who was up guarding the camp. He had slipped himself inside a sleeping bag and then sat still in a camp chair in the middle of our base camp. He was hoping that he looked like a stump.

Three hours later, he was kicking at my feet which were sticking outside my pup tent because I'm almost seven feet tall. He kicked and kicked at my feet until I finally woke up. I stuck my head outside of my tent and whispered loudly, "What?" My father responded, "Look over there!" He then turned on his flashlight and lit up an adult male Bigfoot who was standing on the perimeter of our base camp. As soon as he was lit up, he ran to his right, our left, and you could see the branches and brush moving as he ran away. Later on, after I fell back to sleep, my father saw two more Bigfoot on the perimeter of the base camp. This time, he didn't bother to wake me up and he kept his flashlight off.

The next morning, after we all woke up, my father was like a kid in a candy shop. He shared with all of the men how he had successfully kept us safe from the encroaching Bigfoot by lighting them up with his flashlight. The men were captivated by his story and thanked him for being willing to pull the graveyard shift while guarding camp. My dad was smiling with pride regarding his contribution. He was also elated that he actually had a visual of a Bigfoot.

After we were done eating breakfast, Bill Lee videotaped everyone regarding their experiences up on top of Mt. Elijah. He ended his interview with Dr. York. He proceeded to say that he didn't come up to Mt. Elijah to find Bigfoot. Rather, he came up to the mountain to look for evidence of Bigfoot in the area. He then shared with everyone that he started his journey as a skeptic but he was leaving a believer. He acknowledged all of the evidence that was found by everyone, including the tracks, sunning area, and bedding area that he saw with his own eyes. He concluded in his interview that Bigfoot is very real. Finally, he expressed confidence that if we kept coming out into the forest to look for Bigfoot over and over again and again, we would eventually learn more about their patterns and behaviors and it would eventually become easy to find them and interact with them, just like many animals he had worked with back in Africa.

The expedition to Mt. Elijah on the south side of the Oregon Caves National Monument Park boundaries, was a success. We had confirmed that they were in the area. We had found evidence which was confirmed by visuals. Fifteen men confirmed all of the above. It turns out that I wasn't crazy after all and that Bigfoot really existed. Little did I know; I had officially become hooked. I became addicted to the Bigfoot phenomena and I wanted to learn more. Much more. At that time, I had no idea that my newfound hobby would keep me coming back out into the mountains looking for the big hairy guy for the next two decades. However, it didn't matter because I wanted answers. The truth is out there.

CHAPTER SEVEN

COME ONE, COME ALL

During the remainder of the summer of 2000, we continued with repeated expedition trips to Mt. Elijah and the Bigelow Lakes area. We found additional evidence and had a couple more visuals. I decided that it would be a good idea to report our research results to the nearby Park Rangers. After all, they were very kind to my family and me and I thought they would appreciate it if I kept them up to speed. I dropped by the Oregon Caves National Monument Park and gave Ranger John Roth an update. He pulled out a map and asked me to point out where we were finding our evidence and what road we were using to access the area. I was more than happy to accommodate his request.

The following weekend, a couple of guys accompanied me back up to our research area outside of the boundaries of the Oregon Caves National Monument Park. We turned off one of the main logging roads on to the spur road that took us to our spot. Halfway up the spur road, we came to a sudden stop. We couldn't go any further. It appeared that someone took a rather large backhoe and dug up the spur road to make it impassible. They succeeded. There was absolutely no way that we were going to get my Suburban past the newly created crater in the middle of the road. There was only enough room to pass by if you were riding a horse, 4-wheeler, dirt bike, or were walking on foot.

We were shocked, angered, frustrated, and yet, very curious as to who did it and why they did it. We got back into the Suburban and drove back to the main logging road. We drove up and down a few other spur roads in the nearby area and none of them had been dug up. We drove back to the spur road that led to our research area and stopped once again at the newly dug up crater in the road. I parked the Suburban and we exited the vehicle. We decided to walk the remaining two miles in order to check out our research area.

We finally reached our destination area. We walked off the road and through the trees in order to reach the meadows near the Bigelow Lakes area. From a distance, I could see what appeared to be a puppy pen in the middle of the meadow. I walked through the tall grass and as I got closer to the puppy pen, I saw something inside of it resting on the ground. When I reached the puppy pen, I realized that what I was seeing was a rabbit. We looked at one another with puzzled expressions on our faces. Then one of the guys noticed a video camera on one of the trees which was pointed directly at the puppy pen. Then we noticed another video camera on a different tree which was on the other side of the meadow and was also pointed at the puppy pen.

We managed to put one and one together as we quickly assessed the area, including the newly formed crater in the spur road created by a backhoe. It became very clear to us, rather quickly, that the spur road had been dug up to prevent us from reaching our research area. Also, whoever dug up the road wasn't just interested in preventing us from reaching our research area. They were also very interested in commandeering our research area. Thus, the puppy pen, rabbit, and video cameras. I was no longer a big fan of the Park Rangers at the Oregon Caves National Monument Park. I regretted the day that I told Ranger John Roth anything about the evidence that we were finding in the area near the park boundaries.

I was fuming by now. I reached over the top of the four-foot-high puppy pen fence, grabbed the rabbit by the scruff of the neck, and released him into the wild. Then I walked over to one of the video cameras which was mounted on a tree pointing at the puppy pen, gave the video camera the bird, said a few choice words that would be bleeped out on TV, and walked away. I didn't know what we were going to do now regarding our Bigfoot research efforts but I knew it wasn't going to happen in this area any longer. The Oregon Caves National Monument Park staff made sure of that.

As we were walking the two miles back down the spur road to my parked Suburban, Dr. York saw that I was discouraged and said, "Cheer up, ol' chap. There's plenty of mountains to go about looking for our big hairy friends. This is just a small temporary setback. We'll be back at it before you know it." I responded, "I hope you're right, Bill. I just feel so stupid that I ever said anything to John Roth about where our location was and about the evidence that we were collecting. I never figured that they would commandeer our research area."

Shortly thereafter, fall arrived. As typical in southern Oregon, it was another Indian Summer. The temperatures were still incredibly warm. As the sign says, which is hanging across 6th Avenue in downtown Grants Pass, Oregon, "It's The Climate." Matter of fact, within a five-year period of time, Grants Pass had made the cover of three different magazines as the number one place in America to retire due to the climate, small population, low cost of living, and growing medical services for the elderly retirement population. Grants Pass rivals Mayberry RFD.

Well, it turned out that Dr. York was right. He told me that another opportunity would arise and he was correct. A deer hunter, named John, had given me a call at my private practice office and reported a Bigfoot sighting to me. Dr. York and I met with him for breakfast the following Saturday morning. It turns out that John was retired from the Marines and was working for a logging company in the local area. He shared with us about how he was up in the mountains, about ten miles away from the Oregon Caves National Monument Park, and he had just dropped a deer.

John began to walk toward the carcass to retrieve it when he heard a loud stomp on the ground coming from behind him. He immediately spun around and quickly surveyed his surrounding environment like a well-trained Marine. He couldn't see what had made the loud noise behind him. He continued to survey the logging road and surrounding brush and trees when he heard the loud stomp once again. This time he had acquired a better sense for where the noise was coming from and turned his head to the right to look up the mountainside. That's when he saw a Bigfoot standing up on the hill about a third of the way up the slope. He stomped the ground a third time.

John shared that he wasn't completely caught off guard by what he was looking at because he had grown up in southern Oregon and he had heard several stories about Bigfoot. He had also read about my family's encounter at the Oregon Caves National Monument Park and saw the TV interviews. He told me, "I knew you weren't lying when I saw you on TV and your body was shaking and those tears were coming down your face."

John reported to Dr. York and me that he just stood there on the logging road in amazement and held his ground. I asked him, "Weren't you scared, John?" He said, "Nah. I wasn't going to run off like one them army or air force boys would have. By God, I'm a Marine. We are the first to fight and the last to leave." Then he laughed and said, "Leave no deer behind. I shot the damn thing and I wasn't going to give it up to some Bigfoot no matter how big he was." All three of us laughed.

What John described next stunned both Dr. York and me. Apparently, the Bigfoot stomped the ground a fourth, fifth, and sixth time while he was motioning with his right hand and arm for John to leave the area. John refused to budge, nor was he willing to give up his deer. After the two-minute standoff proved to be fruitless for the Bigfoot, he turned around and started to walk up the mountainside. John immediately took three steps in the direction of the ascending Bigfoot. Not a good idea.

The Bigfoot immediately turned around and took three large steps down the mountainside toward John, stopped, and stomped on the ground several times while whacking the ground with a big branch. Then he growled and screamed at John. He raised his hunting rifle at the Bigfoot and yelled, "I'll shoot you, you son of a bitch, if you take one more step towards me!" The Bigfoot sighed out of frustration, turned around, and started walking up the mountainside again and on into the tree line. John lowered his rifle, walked back toward the carcass, collected his deer, placed it in the back of his truck and drove away.

Even with all of his forty years of big game hunting in Africa, Dr. York couldn't come up with a story that was equivalent to the one we just heard John share with us. We both sat there with our jaws dropped while John continued to munch down his breakfast. We gave each other the look, nodded our heads in agreement, and then Dr. York asked, "John, would you be willing to drive us up to the area where this fantastical story took place?" John said, "Sure. When would you like to go?" Bill and I both said at the same time, "Now!" John responded as he at his last bite of breakfast, "Okay, I have some time to spare this morning. Let's go."

We pushed away from the table, paid our bill, utilized the bathrooms, and departed for the mountains. Although John lived in the Cave Junction area, he was gracious enough to drive into Grants Pass to meet with us for breakfast. However, it also meant that Bill and I were going to have to follow him back out to the Oregon Caves in order to go investigate the area of his alleged encounter.

While we were following John in his Ford pickup truck, I said to Bill, "You know, he could be lying to us, right? I've already had some other people attempt to hoax me so I would turn the media on to them so they would get some TV time." Dr. York responded, "If you'll recall, when you brought up the possibility of turning the media on to him so he could tell his story, he respectfully declined your offer. I don't think he's lying to us. If he is, we still had a wonderful breakfast and an opportunity to spend some time in the mountains." I responded, "All good points, Bill. You're right, it's been a great morning so far and I love being up in the mountains."

After driving several miles up into the mountains, we finally reached the spot where John claimed his encounter took place. We got out of our vehicles and John began to tell us his story all over again. This time with the benefit of seeing the surroundings as his very consistent story unfolded again. We walked over to the location where he had shot the deer and there was plenty of blood on the ground.

As we stood on the logging road, he pointed up the mountainside and told us approximately where the Bigfoot was standing and stomping on the ground. We proceeded to hike up the mountainside to the very spot that he was pointing out from below. Sure enough, there were several very large footprints on the ground. Some were deeper than others, most likely due to the stomping. We could see where the Bigfoot had turned around and started walking back up the mountainside.

When Dr. York and I were done exploring the area, Bill asked John, "Would you mind if we turned this into a research area? We just lost our previous research area and we're looking for another one. However, we don't want to take over your hunting area." John responded, "Oh Hell, that's not a problem. I have several hunting areas and the others don't have a ten-foot-tall Bigfoot trying to intimidate me. I'll just hunt in those areas and you two crazy fools poke around in these woods all you want." All three of us laughed.

Dr. York and I thanked John for his time and for his willingness to share his story with us. We followed him back down the logging road for several miles and off the mountain back down into rural civilization. He turned left and we turned right. While turning in opposite directions, everyone waved to one another and then we never saw John ever again. What a character he was. I'll never forget his forthrightness, bravery, and friendly nature. A true Marine.

Dr. York and I were able to make a couple more trips into the area before the snow hit in early November. We found many fresh tracks as well as two bedding areas which indicated that we were most definitely dealing with a family group that consisted of an adult male, adult female, and an adolescent child. The two bedding areas were exactly the same. The adult male slept on the left side and left an impression that was about nine feet long and four feet wide. The adult female always slept on the right side and left an impression that was about seven and a half feet long and about three feet wide. Finally, the adolescent always slept in the middle and left behind an impression that was about six feet long and almost three feet wide too.

Our last visit to the area in the Fall of 2000 was just after a very light snow fall hit. Bill and I were still able to make it up the logging road and to our research area. We hiked up the mountainside, found some fresh tracks, and followed them up the mountainside and into the tree line. The tracks went over to a place where a very large stump in the ground had been located.

We observed the surrounding area and it became very clear to the both of us what we were seeing. The Bigfoot had wrapped his arms around the rotting stump, ripped it out of the ground, and threw it off to the side. Then he began to dig through the ground to eat the grubs. After he had finished his work in this spot, we could tell by the tracks on the ground that he turned and walked over to where the stump had landed, and started digging at the bottom of the stump for more grubs. After he had finished his meal, based on the tracks in the snow, he had turned and walked away along the ridgeline.

I said to Dr. York, "Can you imagine the strength that it took to uproot that stump and toss it fifteen feet away?" He smiled as he shook his head and responded, "It would take a great deal of strength to do what has obviously been done here. I'm beginning to think that based on the estimated size, visuals by witnesses, and the foot tracks in the ground that these creatures are much stronger than the Gorillas that I was dealing with in Africa. They're an amazing animal."

Bill and I carefully walked back down the snowy mountainside, climbed back into my Suburban, and warmed up as we drove down the logging road, and back to Grants Pass, Oregon. We understood that was going to be our last trip to our research area until the Spring of 2001. However, it wasn't like we weren't going to see each other ever again because our offices were located right next to each other in the business office complex located near the Rogue River in Grants Pass, Oregon.

During the rest of the winter, Bill and I saw each other several times per week. Sometimes we would simply make our way over to one another's office during down time. On other occasions, we would meet up at the Hellgate Café for lunch. We would talk about Bigfoot, our families, Bigfoot, our businesses, Bigfoot, local community affairs, and Bigfoot. We also took the time to develop a game plan to assemble a research team that would help us gather as much evidence as possible for the following Spring, Summer, and Fall of 2001.

When the Spring of 2001 arrived, we implemented our "Come One, Come All" strategy in order to obtain as many boots on the ground as possible. We needed as much help as we could muster up in order to help us collect evidence of the Bigfoot family in the area. I put the word out via friends and the internet. As a result, we had men, women, adolescent, children, and the elderly all participating in our monthly outings. Sometimes, twice a month outings. We even had some people who were gracious enough to cook breakfast, lunch, and dinner for only fifty dollars a person. Their sole contribution to the weekend outings was to make sure that everyone else was well fed Friday evening through Sunday morning. They just wanted to sit around the campfire with everyone else and listen to the stories and see the evidence that we brought back to camp (i.e., Foot casts, scat samples, hair samples, pictures, etc.). We all ate like kings and queens.

The campfire stories were my favorite thing about spending time up in the mountains. Quite often, everyone would look to Dr. York to tell us all about his adventures while being a big game hunter and guide. He talked about the elephants, giraffes, gorillas, and lions. He shared with us about how he led an African Safari for the Queen of England. He talked about the gun battles with African poachers as well as his time fighting in the Korean War. Apparently, he still had a bullet in his body that they could not remove without risking paralyzing him. His stories and his British accent were captivating to everyone.

Other group members also had fascinating and entertaining stories to tell around the campfire at night. Doug Thomas would share with all of us about his adventures up in the surrounding mountains and logging roads with all of his friends. He certainly had more than his fair share of Bigfoot stories that he had heard about from others who lived in southern Oregon. He would tell these stories to everyone and captivate his audience. Some of them were very scary and others were ended with a punch line that got everyone laughing. It was very cool for me to have a fellow Christian involved with the Bigfoot research. The fact that he was a pastor and principal at Vineyard Christian School was icing on the cake.

Some of my favorite stories from this particular research area include the following:

1. We probably had a group of people on one weekend that totaled close to forty souls. Although most were men, we also had some women

and children along. As per my request, most everyone brought along walkie talkies and we tuned all of them to the same channels. Our base camp was located at the intersection of three logging roads. When darkness arrived, we spread out an equal number of people down all three logging roads. They were instructed to pair up in twos, keep their flashlights off, maintain a distance of fifty feet between parties, and quietly radio the base camp if they saw or heard anything.

Approximately two hours later, the two gentlemen who were stationed down one of the logging roads at the farthest point away from base camp, came running back to camp, both screaming and crying. Needless to say, everyone else came running back to the base camp too. Once I was able to calm the two men down, we learned that they had been sitting on the side of the logging road in the pitch dark behind a bush. Suddenly, they saw the silhouette of a tall, upright, bipedal walking creature coming down the logging road in their direction. They were very scared and instead of following protocol, they decided to light up the creature in order to stop it in its tracks before it came any closer to them. Well, they apparently succeeded. The Bigfoot stopped in its tracks, turned around, and ran back down the logging road in the direction it just came from. Then it took a right and ran up the side of the mountain.

Although not everyone was willing to come along with Dr. York and me, I managed to get twenty guys who had enough courage to follow. We ran up the logging road to the area where they had spotted it take a right and run up the mountainside. Sure enough, there were two huge human looking tracks on the side of the hill close to the road, where it had run up from the logging road and into the brush and trees. Someone brought along a pair of headphones and a parabolic microphone dish. We took turns listening to the Bigfoot pacing back and forth up in the trees and the brush while mumbling to himself.

I quickly put together a game plan and gathered the guys around me to tell them what we were going to do next. I told them that I wanted them to spread out along the logging road in both directions with a distance of fifty feet between each individual. That way we could cover a lot of ground and get another sighting if he decided to come down to the logging road again. There was absolute silence for about thirty seconds. Then one of the men spoke up, "Fifty feet apart alone? No way! How about two of us together spaced out fifty feet apart from the next couple of men?" All the other guys were nodding their heads in agreement. I wasn't going to argue with these volunteers about how their game plan just chopped in half the amount of distance that we could cover along the logging road. I could clearly see that they were all terrified. To get them to spread out in groups of two was a significant accomplishment so I took what I could get. After an hour, without any success, we all headed back to the base camp and told the story to everyone else sitting around the campfire.

2. Another favorite story from this research area involved a much smaller group of men. One of our volunteer researchers was an electronics specialist from Eugene, Oregon. His name is Don Moser. He brought along a seismic sensor and we positioned it alongside the logging road a couple hundred yards away from the base camp. The setting was placed in a position that it would take something very heavy to set it off. That would prevent something as small as a squirrel or deer from triggering the device.

Just before dark, we placed one bunch of bananas on the road next to a cantaloupe that we cut in half. In other words, there were three large items that would have to be picked up and taken away. The alarm was turned on inside of Don's vehicle and we sat around the campfire, sipping on hot coffee, and listening to one another's stories. Suddenly, the alarm went off in the car, "Beep, beep, beep, beep. Beep, beep, beep, beep. Beep, beep, beep, beep." I grabbed my million candle flashlight and aimed it down the logging road and turned it on. You need to understand that my million candle flashlight could light up the entire mountainside. I turned it on within a matter of seconds.

When the million candle flashlight was turned on, we saw absolutely nothing. There wasn't anything waiting for us. No bear, deer, elk, cougar, or Bigfoot. Then someone noticed that all of the food was gone too. We walked to the area and couldn't believe our eyes. Whatever it was that was heavy enough to trigger the seismic sensor was also able to grab one bunch of six bananas and two cantaloupe halves, and take them off the road in less than the three seconds it took me to light up the area after the alarm started sounding off in Don's car. Whatever managed to pull that off had to be heavy enough to trigger the device, have hands to scoop up the food, and manage to get off the road before the light came on. No animal that only had its mouth to use could have pulled off such a task. Simply not possible. Hands and speed were needed to grab the food and avoid being tagged by the flashlight. Although we were bewildered, we were also excited.

We walked back to our base camp, grabbed our next round of food for the bait pile, headed back to the seismic sensor, and put everything in its place. Don Moser tinkered around with the seismic sensor to make sure that the setting was correct and that it was still functioning. Then we went back to our base camp and waited for the alarm to go off again. This time, I placed my camp chair away from the campfire so I could turn on my million candle flashlight within one or two seconds of the alarm going off. There were two other guys sitting right next to me. The rest of the guys were staying warm around the fire and enjoying Dr. York's stories.

About an hour later, "Beep, beep, beep, beep! Beep, beep, beep, beep! Beep, beep, beep, beep!" I immediately turned on my flashlight within one to two seconds tops. I was going to light up that Bigfoot whether he wanted to be lit up or not. Dang! There was absolutely nothing there again. No animal to speak of and the food was all gone. How in the world were they able to pull that off two times in a row? We walked down the logging road and examined the area. The summer temperatures were constantly in the 80's and 90's so the road was baked as hard as cement so we couldn't find any foot tracks. All of the food was gone. The device was still working.

We walked back to the base camp totally stumped. We knew that it had to be a Bigfoot that was pulling off the heist of our food in the bait pile. It had to be really heavy to set off the device and it had to have hands to scoop up all three food products and get off the road within one to two seconds. We were befuddled yet amazed. There was so much more to learn about these incredible animals.

One hour later as we were wrapping things up around the campfire and we're talking about climbing into our sleeping bags inside of our tents, we suddenly heard, "Beep, beep, beep, beep! Beep, beep, beep, beep! Beep, beep, beep, beep!" I ran for my flashlight and lit up the road. In the midst of the excitement, Don Moser was yelling, "Guys! Guys! It's not the seismic sensor! I brought it back to camp and the alarm is turned off inside my vehicle."

Then we heard it again, "Beep, beep, beep, beep! Beep, beep, beep, beep! Beep, beep, beep, beep!" The noise sounded exactly like Don Moser's alarm. However, we finally realized that the noise was coming from the brush and trees on the edge of our base camp and not from Don's car. Wow! No freaking way! The Bigfoot was imitating the sound of the electronic alarm and was messing with us just for fun. Well, one of our guys on the research term got a little angry and excited and decided that he was going to walk right into the brush and trees and let the Bigfoot know what he was thinking and feeling. I had to grab him by the shoulder and pull him back. I told him, "You're not going to put yourself in danger under my watch. You're also not going to put me in the position of having to explain to your wife and children what happened to you while you were up here." He stood down and we stood back away from the perimeter of camp.

3. On another occasion, we had just finished up a weekend of Bigfooting in this research area. Once again, several foot casts were collected in the area. I gave all of my foot casts away to the visitors and kids and waved goodbye to them. Then Don Moser and I commenced with "Operation Lollygagging." After everyone left, we started to set up a video camera hidden under a fake rock with a waterproof container nearby which contained the battery and other electronics. We decided to give this a try because, previously, we had noticed that the Bigfoot always seemed to walk around the base

camp area after our departures (i.e., Based on foot tracks found in the area upon our return to camp).

Don Moser was up on the hill overlooking the base camp. I was standing on the logging road in base camp acting as his potential Bigfoot so he could make sure that he was visually covering the entire area. As he was taking care of things and setting up the equipment, we both heard a very loud growl coming from behind him. He stopped doing what he was doing and his eyes got as big as saucers. I'm sure mine did too. However, I immediately told Don that I didn't see anything behind him and that he was okay.

I backed away from him to see if I could get a better view of what it was that was behind him and growling so loudly. Still I could see nothing. Then suddenly, something standing right behind me growled and was breathing down the back of my neck. I seriously thought I was a dead man at that moment in time. I slowly turned around prepared to meet my fate when I saw absolutely nothing. I stuck out my hand and felt a hairy chest right in front of me. I took five steps back very quickly and turned around and walked back over to where Don was. I said, "Don, I just had one over there growl at me too. I think they want us to go now." He said, "I'm done setting everything up so, yes, let's go. This is getting weird." I retorted, "You're telling me?" We left in a hurry.

4.   Finally, my most favorite story from this research area occurred when a writer and photographer for USA Today came with me in the middle of October in 2002. It was just the three of us alone without anyone else. The gentleman's name was Marco R. Della Cava. He was a city boy from the San Francisco Bay area and was not a big fan of camping in the outdoors. Neither was his photographer.

Although it was winter and the sun set early in the evening, we managed to arrive and set up camp before it became dark. We drove about a mile down the logging road and put out some food for the bait pile up on the mountainside where John had shot the deer and was confronted by the adult male Bigfoot. We sat down at the bottom of the mountainside and waited in the dark for something to come and hit the bait pile. Nothing ever did. However, we did hear a lot of heavy footed movement up in the tree line at the top of the mountain. Something up there was not comfortable with us hanging around at the bottom of the hill.

We drove a mile back to base camp, warmed up around the campfire, and then got ready to go to bed. The photographer refused to sleep inside the pup tent. He insisted on sleeping inside the car. I asked him, "So, you don't think that a Bigfoot is capable of smashing through a window if he really wanted to get to you?" He said, "At least I'll see him coming. I can't see him coming if I'm inside the tent." On the other hand, Marco stated, "I don't want to see him coming so I want to sleep in the tent. Let's get in there before I start freaking out."

We climbed into the tent and got inside our sleeping bags. I said, "Goodnight", to Marco and began to close my eyes. He asked me, "What are you doing?" I said, "I'm going to sleep. It's bedtime." He asked, "How are you going to do that?" I said, "Well, I'm going to close my eyes just like this and fall asleep. Watch me." I quickly faded away into dreamland.

The next morning, I woke up, opened up my eyes. Marco was laying on the other side of the tent just looking at me with his eyes wide open. I asked him, "Didn't you get any sleep?" He responded, "No! How could you sleep?" I said, "I was tired. That's what people do when it's night time. Why didn't you sleep?" He said, "I couldn't sleep because something or someone was walking all around the camp last night. He even stood by my side of the tent for an hour just breathing really loud. I tried to wake you up but you were sound asleep." I responded, "Welcome to my world, Marco", and laughed.

We crawled out of the tent and I heated up some water so I could make some coffee for the three of us. I was apologizing up one side and down the other because they hadn't seen a Bigfoot, didn't get any pictures of a Bigfoot, nor saw any tracks left behind by a Bigfoot. Fifteen minutes later as we were sipping on our hot coffee during the cold morning hours, we all heard a noise coming from the area down the logging road where we left the food for the bait pile the night before. Marco summed it up best near the end of his front page USA

Today article which was published on October 31, 2002. He concluded his article by writing the following:

And just as the coffee is brewing, it happens. From up a winding fire road come sounds: The high-pitched chatter of a chimp, suddenly intercut by the low groan of a scream in slow motion. Ears prick up. Breathing becomes optional. For 15 seconds, this unearthly racket floods the camp. Then it vanishes. Other than humans, most animals known to man are incapable of such broad sound ranges. Bigfoot or not, something odd has spoken.

"Hmm, not a bear, not a cougar," says Dr. Johnson. "You ever hear anything like that before?" Dr. Johnson's visitor, suddenly busy taking down the tent, offers to discuss his myriad theories in town. The tall man in search of an even taller thing smiles and pops open the Caddy's trunk. "You have to admit," he says. "This sure beats golfing."

Well, what Marco didn't include in his front page USA Today article was the fact that I responded to the scream by saying, "Let's go." He said, "Yes, let's go. I want to leave immediately." I said, "Nope. You guys came up here to write about a Bigfoot encounter. We're not leaving here until we go check out the bait pile first." Marco replied, "I don't want to go anywhere near the bait pile." I said, "Okay, you guys wait here. However, for the record, I have the gun and the car. If I don't make it back, start walking down the mountain on that road right over there." Marco replied, "We're coming with you."

We climbed inside my car and drove the mile toward the bait pile area. We got out of the car and checked out the bait pile. All of the food was gone, there were Bigfoot tracks in the area, and something heavy footed was moving around inside the tree line at the top of the mountainside. I asked, "Are you convinced now?" Marco said, "Yes! Yes, I'm convinced. Can we please leave now?" We climbed back into my car, left the mountain, and drove to Herb's Restaurant in Grants Pass, Oregon. A nice and toasty restaurant that serves great food and an awesome breakfast. We took some time to process everything and then they left from there.

Apparently, Marco forgot to include the above in his article, including the pictures of the footprints. I think the city slicker was coming to spend time with me in order to mock me for a front page Halloween article and, instead, left the mountain a believer. Good for him. On the other hand, my Bigfoot adventures were about to take a sour and sad turn for the worse.

CHAPTER EIGHT

MY BROKEN HEART

It was in the early Spring of 2002, Dr. LeRoy Fish accompanied Dr. York and me in our research area. He was a Wildlife Biologist and a member of the Bigfoot Field Research Organization (BFRO). Our reports and TV interviews were generating a lot of interest in the community of Bigfootdom. By this point in time, Dr. York and I had been interviewed together by multiple media agencies, including the Travel Channel, In Search Of, Real Scary Stories, the BBC, a French Documentary Film Crew, some children's TV shows, and many news channels too.

As a result of all the media attention that we were receiving, and the evidence that we were producing, Dr. Fish chose to contact me and expressed a strong desire to come to southern Oregon to visit with the both of us. Dr. York and I spent a couple nights with Dr. Fish in our research area. Both he and Dr. York enjoyed one another's company. They quickly became members of the "Mutual Admiration Society" because of the great respect that they had for one another.

We gave Dr. Fish the "Red Carpet Tour", including the spot along the logging road where a creek ran underneath the road through a culvert. We showed him where an alleged dispute took place between two Bigfoot adult males. In this spot, approximately ten Willow trees had been snapped over between eight to nine feet off the ground, right next to the creek. Also, a five-hundred-pound boulder had been placed right next to the strand of snapped-over trees. Five of us very large and strong men could not lift up the rock together.

The rock had not rolled down the hill as some research teams initially speculated. The evidence on the rock was clear. The base of the rock, where it was stuck in the dirt, was very dirty. There was no other dirt to be found on the rock. Also, the top layer of the rock had a light flakey layer of moss spread all over it. The flakey moss was so fragile that you could scrape it off with the slight movement of a single finger. Yet, all of the light flakey moss on the top of the rock was completely intact. If that large rock had rolled down the mountainside, it would have dirt all over it and the light flakey moss would be gone. Dr. Fish looked very closely at the rock, examined the mountainside above the rock, and arrived at the same conclusion we did. The very large and heavy rock had been intentionally placed on the road right next to the snapped over Willow trees for a reason.

He asked how we knew that there was a dispute that led to the snapping of the Willow trees and the placement of the large rock. We proceeded to tell him about our informant, "Crazy Jack." A gentleman that we had met during the early summer of 2001. He occupied the lookout tower on the top of the ridgeline and was trying to communicate with us by flashing a mirror at us. I had a map and figured out how to reach the tower via the logging roads on the other side of the ridgeline. Unfortunately, the last two-hundred yards of the road were steeper than steep and we had to walk up the hill on foot. There was no way that I was going to drive my Suburban up or down that incredibly steep hill.

When we made our way to the top of the hill and stood at the bottom of the lookout tower, "Crazy Jack" came down the tower stairs screaming and cussing all the way at the top of his lungs. He was telling us about how he fought in the Vietnam War and that he had killed a lot of men and he had no problem killing a few more. He also said something about cutting off our heads, crapping down our throats, and mailing our skulls to our next of kin.

We were all kind of looking at one another and smiling, acknowledging to each other that we thought his bark was worse than his bite. He wasn't carrying any weapons so we knew that we were safe. When he finally reached us, I walked up to him, stuck my hand out, and said, "Hello, I'm Dr. Johnson and these are my friends. We are the group of men that you were trying to communicate with this morning by flashing your mirror at us from on top of your tower." He responded, "Well, why didn't you say so. I apologize for being so rude but you never know who you're going to run into up here in the mountains. So what are you guys doing down there every two to four weeks?"

I told him about our new found hairy hobby (i.e., That we were Bigfoot researchers). "Crazy Jack" thought it was cool and stated, "Those animals are very real. I had one down here at the foot of my tower just the other night. My dog was going crazy and barking up a storm. I looked over the edge and I could see him moving around. Then he started up the stairs and I started yelling and screaming at him and I fired a couple of warning shots. He jumped off the stairs and ran away in a hurry. It didn't take him many steps to cover a lot of ground."

We exchanged cell phone numbers and kept in touch with "Crazy Jack" every time we drove up to our research area. He kept an eye on things to let us know whether or not other people were visiting our area. Also, he kept us informed about whether or not he saw or heard any Bigfoot activity in the area. That's how we learned about the alleged dispute between the two Bigfoot males at the bottom of the hill, near where the creek was coming down the mountainside and crossed underneath the road through a culvert.

Thereafter, when we drove up to the area, "Crazy Jack" would give me a call or I would give him all call. He told us about the dispute that took place in the middle of a pitch dark night. We went and investigated and that's when we found the snapped over Willow trees and the large heavy rock that had been placed on the road right by them. He had no knowledge about the snapped over trees or the placement of the large rock. He could not see them from the tower.

The story that "Crazy Jack" told fascinated Dr. LeRoy Fish. He wanted to go up to the tower and meet the storyteller. I made a deal with both Dr. Fish and Dr. York that I would transport them to the base of the steep hill, then they would have to wait while I went and got "Crazy Jack" to come on down the hill and meet with them. They agreed. However, when we reached the base of the hill, both Dr. Fish and Dr. York told me that they thought they could make it up the hill just fine without any difficulties. Please keep in mind that Dr. Fish was 59 and Dr. York was 69. Neither one of them were in very good shape. Matter of fact, it was my assessment that their egos were getting in the way of proper decision making. I kindly stated as much but they both argued with me that if they took their time, they could reach the top without the trip killing them. Well, they made it. We stopped several times along the way and I was scared to death. The journey was much tougher than either one of them anticipated. Nevertheless, they were able to enjoy meeting "Crazy Jack", listening to his stories, and they both enjoyed the view. They were correct, the journey up the mountainside did not kill them. Well, at that moment in time, it didn't kill them.

However, approximately one week later, Dr. LeRoy Fish died in his shop from congestive heart failure. I felt so bad when I heard about his passing. I kicked myself in the butt over and over again regarding the fact that I should have made both he and Dr. York wait at the bottom of the steep hill like they had promised that they would. It broke my heart to know that his hike up the very steep hill may have been the catalyst for his early demise. I told this to Dr. York and he responded to me by saying, "Matt, when it's your time to go, it's your time to go. At least he enjoyed being here with us, learning more about Bigfoot, meeting "Crazy Jack", and he got to enjoy the incredible view. He died doing what he loved doing. There's no better way to go than that."

Well, I didn't tell Dr. York this but I sure as heck wasn't going to allow him to march up anymore steep hills in the future. Matter of fact, Bill had talked about going up the hill to visit with "Crazy Jack" to catch up on any stories and I simply called him on the cell phone and handed it to Dr. York. I watched over him like a baby. We grew to become best friends and he was like a father figure to me.

Around this time, Dr. York and I had turned our research team into a non-profit organization because we wanted to raise funds for better high tech equipment. We figured with all of the media attention that we were receiving, that we could obtain tax-deductible donations to help us out with our goals. We were too dependent on the kindness of

Don Moser and his high-tech equipment. He wasn't always available to come out with us every time we were in the field. It was a long three-hour drive for him to make it every time from Eugene, Oregon. Also, he had a life, a wife, a family, and he enjoyed playing tennis and acting on the side. We simply couldn't expect Don to come down to southern Oregon and play with us every time we were ready to go out into the field.

Therefore, the Southern Oregon Bigfoot Society (SOBS) was formed and established as a non-profit organization. We were not only active in the Bigfoot research field inviting anyone and everyone to come and join us, we also sponsored monthly meetings in Grants Pass, Oregon. We held monthly Bigfoot meetings at the Black Forest Restaurant in their meeting room. We always filled the room to capacity. It was fun to meet with the regulars plus see new people visit with us from time to time. Unfortunately, we had a member in the Southern Oregon Bigfoot Society who took it upon himself to use the non-profit status for his own personal gain. Dr. York and I didn't want anything to do with his unethical behaviors. We certainly didn't want the IRS breathing down our necks because of him.

In November of 2003, we were experiencing a warmer winter than usual in southern Oregon. There was no snow in our research area yet. Dr. York and I had made our way out to the research area for some alone time. We didn't have the large crowds with us, it was just the two of us. We enjoyed our walks through the forest and our time sitting around the campfire at night. I always enjoyed listening to his stories about his time in Africa. One night, while sitting around the campfire, we discussed the individual who was taking advantage of our nonprofit status for his own personal gain. I was the President of the SOBS and Dr. York was the Vice-President. We decided that we were going to have to boot this individual from the organization and turn him into the IRS. It was a difficult decision to make but we knew we had to do it.

The next morning, Dr. York wanted to drive to the other side of the ridgeline and go up the steep hill to visit with "Crazy Jack" and see if he had any stories to share. I pulled out my cell phone and called "Crazy Jack's" number several times but there was no answer. I told Bill that

I thought it was too late in the year and that "Crazy Jack" most likely wasn't up in the tower watching for fires now.

However, at Bill's insistence, I drove him around to the other side of the mountain. When we reached the bottom of the hill, I practically begged Bill to let me go see if "Crazy Jack" was up in the tower. If he was there, I would fetch "Crazy Jack" and bring him back down. Bill expressed an appreciation for my concern but assured me that I didn't have to coddle him. We hiked up the hill slowly but surely. When we reached the top, it was clear that "Crazy Jack" was not up in the tower. As I predicted, it was too late in the year and fire season was over. There was no need for "Crazy Jack" to man the lookout tower. Bill said, "Well, Matt, we still get to enjoy this incredible view." Incredible it was. The views were spectacular. I enjoyed this moment of quiet solitude with my very good friend. I can still see him standing there taking in the view and taking deep breaths of the fresh crisp air on top of the mountain.

About a week later, I was driving back to Grants Pass, Oregon from my parents' home in Salem, Oregon. I received a call from my wife who informed me that Dr. York had passed away the previous night in his sleep. I almost drove off the highway. I felt my heart break in half. I cried, and cried, and cried the rest of the way home. I was sobbing so hard that I couldn't see straight. I felt like I had just lost my best friend and father all wrapped up in one package.

While driving my Suburban, I became angry and started yelling at Bill, "Why wouldn't you listen to me? I told you that you shouldn't have hiked up that damn steep hill. I told you that that hill probably killed Dr. Fish and that it might kill you too but you wouldn't listen to me." I cried and cried some more. The wind was officially out of my sails. I was numb. I was done. I threw in the towel.

The following week, I resigned from the Southern Oregon Bigfoot Society. I no longer had Bill on my side to take care of business and clean house. Therefore, I turned the reins of the organization over and walked away from everything. I stopped going out to the research area and I stopped involving myself in anything Bigfoot related. I was done. Shortly, thereafter, I lost my marriage and had no motivation to keep going out into the field.

I had met my second wife during this time, and started focusing more on our relationship and the transition that my three children were going through. Don't let anyone fool you, divorce sucks for everyone, no matter how hard you try to smooth things out for the kids. I didn't have time to go out and conduct Bigfoot research in the middle of this significant transition that was occurring for my children and myself. I spent time playing with them and coaching their teams.

My second wife enjoyed hearing about my Bigfoot research stories and she strongly suggested that I get back up on the horse and go back out into the mountains. I really wasn't that interested. However, I would occasionally take her, family members, or some friends passing through the area out to the woods. I had to admit, it was nice to get back out there into the forest every once in a while. We created some fond memories sitting around the campfire at night while talking about past Bigfoot adventures. But seriously, I was done. My broken heart took all of the motivation out of me and the wind out of my sails. I was no longer planning to go back into the woods to look for Bigfoot. Little did I know; I may have given up on looking for them but that didn't mean that they were going to give up on looking for me. The saga continued.

CHAPTER NINE

HOTEL CALIFORNIA

One of my favorite songs in my youth was "Hotel California", produced and performed by the Eagles in 1977. Let's face it, the 1960's, 1970's, and 1980's created some of the best music known to mankind. I love the Facebook meme that says, "I may be old but we had all of the best music." Well, it's true. We did.

"Hotel California" was an instant classic that will never be outdone by today's music artists. I loved the lyrics in the song, especially "Last thing I remember, I was running for the door. I had to find the passage back to the place I was before. Relax said the nightman, we are programmed to receive. You can check out anytime you like but you can never leave." Little did I know how true these lyrics would play out in my own life regarding the Bigfoot phenomena.

One night, during the Summer of 2005, I was sitting at home alone in our 5,000 square foot house. The home was situated on two and one half acres on the Rogue River, three miles east of Grants Pass, Oregon. My wife was in Texas visiting her family and friends. I was watching a show on the large flat screen TV in the living room. Both Spencer, an Irish Wolfhound, and Sophie, a Chocolate Labrador, were sleeping on the floor right next to me.

Suddenly, both Spencer and Sophie jumped up on their feet from a sound sleep and began ferociously barking at something standing at the doorway from the living room to the foyer. The only problem was that I couldn't see anything at all. I told them to be quiet and stop barking. They continued to bark ferociously. I had never seen them kick into such a defensive posture before. Normally, they were both very mellow dogs and seldom ever barked at anything. No matter what I tried, they wouldn't stop barking. I threw a pillow at them, I yelled at them, and I even swatted Spencer in the butt. They kept on barking at something standing in the foyer that I couldn't see.

Just as suddenly as they began to bark, they stopped. They looked confused and came over to me right away looking for reassurance and praise. They acted like they had just put their lives on the line to protect me. They wanted to hear that they did a good job and that they were good dogs. I sang their praises, loved on them, and petted them non-stop. While I was thanking the dogs for being so protective, I was puzzled by the fact that they both woke up from a deep sleep, barked ferociously at something that they both could see, and yet, I couldn't see it at all. Very puzzling.

Thanks to the pause button on the DVR, I was able to resume my show and finish it. About a half-hour later, I walked from the living room, through the foyer, and into the kitchen for a snack. Then I sat down at the computer on the other side of the kitchen and began to surf the internet. About an hour later, I heard three loud knocks at the front door. I wondered who it could be because I didn't see any cars drive through the locked gate and onto our fenced property. I went to the front door, turned on the porch light, and was met by absolutely nobody. There was no one there.

I closed the front door and returned to sitting in front of the computer. The funny thing was that I was surfing the internet looking up information about the latest Bigfoot stuff online. Yes, I had missed being out in the field and wanted to see what was going on. About a half-hour later, I heard three loud knocks at the front door. Once again, I was puzzled because I didn't see any cars drive through our locked gate. I opened up the front door and no one was there.

I returned to the computer again, sat down, began to surf online and the three knocks came to the front door for the third time. This time,

I ran to the front door, opened it up anticipating that no one would be there, and ran around the front yard conducting a perimeter sweep of our fenced yard. I was going to find those kids who snuck onto our property and nail their butts for pranking me. The only problem was that the gate was secured and I never found anyone on our property. Neither did our two dogs, Spencer and Sophie. I was very perplexed by the events of the evening but the fun wasn't over yet.

Just after I entered the home with the two dogs, closed the front door, and made it back into the kitchen, we all heard an incredibly loud noise that sounded like something really big was crashing down on the ground and exploding. The dogs began to bark uncontrollably. I grabbed the flashlight again and returned to the front yard. I found absolutely nothing. We extended our sweep to the backyard. We started walking down the hill down toward the Rogue River and that's when we found the very tall tree that fell over away from the river and in the direction of the house.

I walked back inside the house with Spencer and Sophie, sat down in the living room, and called up my wife. I told her that I wasn't crazy and please listen to everything that I had to share before passing judgment. She listened to everything and asked me, "What do you think it is? Something is obviously trying to get your attention. The question is who or what?" After we hung up, I sat there alone in the living room with the two dogs and thought about her questions. Who or what is trying to get my attention?

The next day, I went to work at my private practice office. When I was done seeing my last client, I walked out of the office, locked the front door, and walked around the corner of the building and across the parking lot to my car. While doing so, I swore that I saw a Bigfoot standing by one of the trees next to the building. I saw the same thing the next two nights as I walked to my car. Finally, on the last weeknight, I locked the front door of my office and walked around the other side of the building to get to my car. As I walked by the building, I swore that I saw the same Bigfoot standing by a tree on the side of the building. It was like he knew that I was going to switch sides of the building that I chose to exit in order to reach my car.

I began to question my own sanity. However, the dogs barking ferociously in the living room happened. The knocks at the front door happened. The tree pushed over in the backyard happened. Finally, I was actually seeing a Bigfoot every time I left my office to go to my car in the back parking lot. Therefore, I decided to outwit the Bigfoot and started parking my car in the front of the building. I would walk by Dr. York's old office that he occupied prior to his death. I said out loud as I walked by his office, "Where are you when I need you, Bill. I don't know what's going on but I really wish I could talk with you right now."

About six months later, a friend and I were standing on the front porch of our home late at night. He was about to leave when we heard a very loud, bloodcurdling scream come from the mountain top across the Rogue River Highway. We turned and looked at each other. Kevin said, "That's a Sasquatch. I guarantee you one-hundred percent that's a Sasquatch." I said, "I agree with you. I don't think they're willing to let go of me quite yet. I'm not sure why but I think they want me back out in the woods." Kevin agreed with me.

A couple days later, I was walking on a trail adjacent to the Rogue River Highway. I was simply out getting some exercise and wanted some alone time. As I was walking along the trail in the woods, I felt like I was being watched. My sixth sense was kicking in very strongly. As I continued to walk, I smelled the pungent smell once again. I hadn't smelled that smell since my family's trek up the mountainside above the Oregon Caves National Monument Park. I stopped and started looking up the mountainside through the trees and brush. After about two minutes of searching, that's when I saw the Bigfoot standing between two trees. It was as if he wanted me to see him. I said, "Will you please leave me alone. I'm done with you guys. I threw the towel in a while ago." I turned and walked away toward home.

To be honest, I was still missing Dr. York big-time. Bill's death left a hole in my heart that I felt could not be mended. I missed him so much. He was a good friend and father figure. To go back out into the woods conducting Bigfoot research would only remind me of the pain of missing his presence, wisdom, humor, and the endless stories that he had to share around the campfire at night. I just couldn't go on without him. Besides, I was making the necessary adjustments to go on with my life without pursuing the Bigfoot phenomena.

One day, during the Summer of 2006, I dropped by the "Why Not Market" to purchase my Diet Mt. Dew, maple bar donut, and to shoot the breeze with Jason. His parents owned the store and he and I became friends over time. When I walked into the store, Jason said, "Matt, I have got to talk with you." He sounded desperate and I was preparing to put on my psychologist cap when all of a sudden he started talking about Bigfoot stuff. I thought to myself, "Oh no, here we go again."

Jason shared with me about how he grew up in a home at the base of a mountain in rural Grants Pass, Oregon. As a boy, he spent countless hours and days playing by himself or with his friends up on the mountain. Recently, he went back up on the mountain for old time's sake. He wanted to revisit some of his childhood play areas and hiding spots. Then he told me that when he visited the "Hidden Pond", he found some very large Bigfoot tracks right next to it in the mud. He wanted me to go up the mountainside and check them out.

I said, "Thanks, Jason, but I'm done with Bigfoot research. I don't want to go out there anymore looking for the big hairy guy." Jason responded, "But Matt, you have got to see these foot tracks. They're huge and they're perfect." We argued back and forth in a very friendly manner until Jason managed to break through my wall and secure my compliance to his request.

Two days later, I showed up on his front porch at the base of the mountain. The directions he gave me were good and the scenery was beautiful. I rang the doorbell and he answered it about a minute later. He appeared to be so happy that I followed through on my promise to show up. He started do give me directions about how to go up the mountainside and where to find the "Hidden Pond." I said, "Wait a second, Jason. Aren't you going to take me up the mountain and show me where the pond and tracks are?" He said, "Are you kidding? I don't want to go up there with that thing running around up there." I laughed and said, "Jason, you're kidding me, right?" He responded, "No, Matt, I'm not kidding you. Please go up there, check out the tracks, and let me know what you think."

I drove up the mountainside on a quasi-road that cut through other people's properties. I went up as far as I could before I ran into a road block that prevented me from reaching the logging road. However, I was prepared for the road block because Jason told me it would be there. At least I knew that I was in the right spot. My two younger kids, ages 11 and 13, came along with me for the ride. They hadn't been out in the woods in a long time and wanted to go on an adventure. They also wanted to see the tracks on the side of the "Hidden Pond."

We walked down the logging road about 100 yards, as directed by Jason, until we reached the bend of the road. It was at that point that Jason said we were to cut into the woods on the left side of the road and we would discover a pond about 50 feet or so off of the logging road. Just as Jason predicted, we found the pond. It was beautiful, surrounded by trees, and full of fairly clear water. We walked up to the edge of the pond and my kids pointed out the two very large human-like footprints in the mud. They were approximately 22 inches long. It looked like a Bigfoot had walked up to the edge of the pond, squatted down, and drank some water. All three of us were excited.

However, we were not able to cast the two tracks because they were partially submerged in the water at the edge of the pond. We turned and looked back towards the hill and I saw a set of tracks walking away from the pond. I found a perfect track to start casting. While we were working on filling the large foot impression with the Plaster of Paris that I mixed together, the three of us suddenly heard a very low, loud, mammal-like, guttural growl coming from the other side of the knoll only about fifty-feet away from us.

I put my casting equipment down on the ground and starting walking toward the knoll. My daughter whispered to me rather loudly, "Dad! Dad! What are you doing?!" I said, "There's a Bigfoot on the other side of the knoll and I want to see him." She then whispered even louder, "Yes, we know! Get back here! What if he kills you? What are we supposed to do?" Well, she had a point and I couldn't argue with her so I came back and finished my casting. Then we quickly left the area for the Suburban and drove back down the side of the mountain.

I parked my Suburban in Jason's driveway and walked up to the door and rang the bell. He answered the door and asked, "Did you find anything?" I said, "Please come out to my car." He came outside and I opened up the back door and showed him the very large foot cast. I said, "Jason, I don't mean to offend you by asking you the following question but you aren't messing around with me are you?" He said, "No! Matt, you know me. I would never do that to you. I didn't make those prints. I found those prints and that's why I wanted you to check them out. Am I going crazy or are those real Bigfoot tracks?" I said, "Jason, you're not going crazy. They are real Bigfoot tracks." I asked his permission to revisit the area in a couple days and he granted me access to the area through his property.

A couple days later, I returned to the "Hidden Pond" all by myself. I found the tracks and began to follow them up the mountainside through the brush and trees. I wasn't walking along a paved path. I was climbing over the top of fallen trees, ducking under branches, walking around thorny bushes, and trying my best to stay on the right path following the tracks up the mountainside. Eventually, I reached the top of the mountain and walked out onto a logging road along the ridgeline.

I turned right and walked down the road a couple of miles until I came to a junction. I looked around and memorized all of the geographical features of the area. Then I walked back up the logging road until I reached the area where I stepped off of the road. Rather than going back down the mountainside, I decided to follow the logging road in the opposite direction to see where it led to. A couple of miles later, I reached the dead end of the logging road which ended up in a cul-de-sac. Since the tracks were headed up in this direction, I thought that this might be the perfect place to establish a new base camp. I was hooked once again.

I walked back down the logging road and found the path that I walked on to reach the top of the mountain. I retraced my steps all the way back down to the half-way point up the mountainside. I got into my Suburban and drove it back down to the bottom of the mountain, passed Jason's home, and back to my house. I couldn't believe that I was climbing back up on the saddle again. I was certain that I threw in the towel regarding any further Bigfoot research. If it hadn't been for Jason's relentless insistence, I would never have returned to the research field.

The following weekend, I purchased a map of the area from the Bureau of Land Management (BLM) office. I drove around on logging roads for two days straight until I finally found the junction that I had memorized. I was so excited. I now had a new research area and it was well hidden up in the mountains just outside of Grants Pass, Oregon. The location made it easy to access which meant more frequent trips to the area. I had also learned my lesson about how "come one, come all" wasn't the best approach to Bigfoot research. That approach led to the demise of the last research area because friends told friends who told friends who brought more friends to the area. Eventually, people wanting to see a Bigfoot overran the area. I wasn't going to let that happen again in my new area. The Southern Oregon Research Area, otherwise soon to be known as SORA had been found.

CHAPTER TEN

PERSISTENCE

It was now the Summer of 2006 and I found myself to be totally rejuvenated, excited, and motivated to jump back into the Bigfoot research field. Although I truly missed my mentor, good friend, and father figure, Dr. Bill York, I knew that he would want me to continue with our work. Matter of fact, I felt a nudge coming from him every now and then.

I was constantly reminded of his words regarding persistence that he had talked with me about on several occasions. He also wrote about the necessity of persistence as a Bigfoot researcher prior to his death on November 12, 2003:

"Persistence is the Most Important Attribute to a Bigfoot Researcher"
by William York, Doctor of Science in Wildlife Biology

Those who search for Bigfoot are certain to experience much disappointment and frustration. Starting with high excitement and enthusiasm, most casual searchers soon become frustrated by the lack of actual sight or sound of the creatures. Despite, perhaps, an abundance of evidence, a failure to have more tangible contact causes a reduction in enthusiasm and many people give up after only a few trips into Bigfoot country.

I have just returned from a weekend trip (September 9th and 10th) with Dr. Matthew Johnson, psychologist, who actually saw a Bigfoot while hiking with his family on July 1, 2000. Several of Dr. Johnson's friends were also of the party. We discovered a good deal of evidence indicative of the recent presence of Bigfoot in the area of search (i.e., snapped trees, bedding area, large foot impressions, etc.). We even had a nocturnal visitation by a very large animal on Saturday evening, but no actual confirmed sighting of Bigfoot. Although very sporting in their comments, I did note disappointment and believe that some of the party will not continue to search for Bigfoot in the future.

Being a neophyte in the Bigfoot field, I held low expectations. Matter of fact, I began our research expedition as a skeptic and stated as such at the end of our time together. I was, however, thrilled by the indisputable evidence we gathered over the weekend. The lack of tangible evidence (i.e., not being able to see Bigfoot) reminded me of my early years as a professional hunter in Africa.

There is a very large (up to 850 lbs.) antelope inhabiting the mountain forests of Kenya, called Bongo – Boo cercus Eurycerous. It is very secretive and shy and rarely seen. Being a very prized trophy, it was, in past years, hunted by sportsmen, guided by professionals, on many scores of safaris. There are professionals who have conducted a dozen hunts for Bongo and never even seen one.

My experience could have been the same. I conducted six safaris, each about fourteen days long, without seeing a single Bongo. It was deeply frustrating, not to say humiliating, to hunt a known animal, finding abundant sign of its presence, and yet not catching a sight of it. I almost gave up hunting Bongo.

On my seventh hunt, however, things changed. Probably because of the past failures, I had acquired a good deal of knowledge and understanding of Bongo. Much of it, no doubt, unconsciously. On this seventh hunt, we were successful in obtaining a fine trophy. Subsequent hunts were equally successful; showing that in fact Bongo were quite numerous, showing that earlier failure was due to the lack of knowledge of Bongo.

From similar experiences with other rare animals, I have concluded that persistence is the most important attribute to a Bigfoot researcher. I fully intend to be persistent, in the complete confidence that I shall eventually have repeated encounters with this elusive and very real creature.

How could I not jump back into the Bigfoot research field? How could I not remain committed and persistent in my pursuit of the truth? My friend, Jason, had just handed me a major gift on a silver platter (i.e., Two 22 inch tracks along the side of a pond halfway up the mountainside from his home). Those tracks led me up to the top of a mountain with a logging road on the ridgeline and to a brand new base camp.

Not only was there track evidence that led me there, as I started to explore the surrounding area, I also found several tree structures. For the newbies, tree structures are obvious manipulated trees and branches placed in certain positions that could not occur via natural circumstances such as windstorms, snow snaps, or age and gravity. Instead, these trees have been picked up, moved, placed, and woven with other trees and branches that demonstrate intelligence and design – not a natural occurrence.

I named this new location the Southern Oregon Research Area (SORA) so it would be easier to refer to it when I would generate any reports online. While living in Grants Pass, I spent a lot of time up there in SORA and I never went alone. I always brought one or more people with me because I wanted witnesses to verify what I was observing or experiencing.

If all I ever did was go alone and report on what I was seeing and experiencing, it would be easy for people to blow me off as a liar or hoaxer. However, if I brought along other people who were also seeing, hearing, and experiencing what I was, then it would be a lot harder for the skeptics to dismiss what I was reporting. I now preferred to have these people come from long distances because I had learned that most local guests from southern Oregon couldn't be trusted.

In the past, my "come one, come all" policy turned out to be altruistic and naïve. I believe that my intentions were good and that I meant well. I truly wanted people to come along, experience, and learn more about the Bigfoot phenomena. I've always been passionate about education and I wanted people to have the opportunity to get out and experience something that they would never do on their own. Previously, everyone who came along with Dr. York and me were grateful and expressed their gratitude. Everyone promised that they would never come back to the research area without us. They also agreed to never tell anyone else about the location of our research area.

However, I was obviously naïve, because on a couple of occasions, we caught people on video tape bringing up carloads of their friends to our research area. On another occasion, we caught one of our members bringing his friends up to the area for some target shooting. They didn't even realize that they were setting up targets all around our hidden video camera and came close to hitting it on a few occasions.

By the way, the fact that they almost hit the video camera was the least of my worries. What astonished me was the ignorance of the shooters and the total lack of respect for the Bigfoot in the area. How in the world were we ever going to gain their trust and get them to come closer to us if we were going to turn their home into a target shooting location? It made no sense to me at all.

When Dr. York and I confronted the gentlemen involved, they became defensive and offended. They thought that we were making a big deal out of nothing. They dropped out of the group which was fine with me. The experience also taught me to be more selective about who I invited to come along with me on my Bigfoot research expeditions. With a new research area, I had the opportunity to start all over again with a new approach to screening and selecting guests.

Truth be told, I also had people tag along with me because I was still scared to death to ever go alone. I had yet to achieve the courage and confidence that Dr. York displayed during past expedition trips. When the campfire was dying at night and people were starting to climb into their tents, Dr. York would walk away from the base camp, in the dark, to his tent several hundred yards away from everyone else. He wanted to be alone and sleep alone at night.

On one occasion, I tried to convince him to take my 44 magnum handgun with him but he adamantly refused to do so. I asked why and he responded, "Matt, earlier in my life, I shot and killed way too many animals. I've carried a lot of guilt with me throughout my life as a result. I put my guns up for a reason and I have no intention of borrowing yours."

I asked, "But Bill, what if you're walking to your tent tonight and a cougar or black bear decides to make you a meal?" He retorted, "How many people do you know or have you heard about in southern Oregon being killed and eaten by a cougar or black bear?" I responded, "None." He quickly stated, "Precisely. I'm perfectly safe walking the logging road at night as well as sleeping alone at night. Besides, Bigfoot isn't going to visit anyone in this base camp full of so many people and tents. If he comes to say "hello" to anyone, it will be me who's sleeping all by myself far away from everyone." Well, Bill had a point. I wasn't going to argue with his logic. I just never had the courage to follow suit. At least, not yet.

In SORA, our experiences were equivalent to my two previous research areas. We experienced occasional heavy footed bipedal steps around the perimeter of the base camp. They were very stealthy and would walk very quietly for such a large animal. Occasionally, we would hear the large snap of a stick or branch that they would step on. Oops! We would also see some occasional silhouettes, eye glow, and hear a growl or two.

On one occasion, I had a couple from England contact me via the internet and they informed me that they would be traveling through the Pacific Northwest while on a summer vacation. They asked if they could join me in SORA for two nights. Well, they most certainly met my screening criteria for living far away from southern Oregon. I didn't have to worry about them coming back to SORA without me. I also trusted that they wouldn't give up the location of SORA to anyone else so I brought them with me.

Not much activity happened on the first night. We heard what we thought were some heavy footed bipedal steps at a distance accompanied by one wood knock. However, on the second night, we hiked up the trail to the other logging road and conducted a night sit up there. About an hour into it, we had movement around the perimeter. Then, about one-hundred-feet down the logging road, we all heard a very deep, bass, mammal-like, guttural growl that lasted for about thirty seconds. Then there was a thirty-second pause. Then the growl happened a second time. Another pause. Finally, the growl occurred a third time.

The British couple was sitting in their chairs with their eyes wide open as saucers. They were obviously terrified. The gentleman said in a panicked voice, "That's a Bigfoot, isn't it? That's a Bigfoot! What are we going to do?" I responded, "Relax. We're going to be just fine."

Then I stood up in the pitch dark of night, looked down the road in the direction that the growl was coming from and said rather loudly, "Is that it? Is that all you got? Step up on the road so we can see you! Quit being afraid of us and hiding behind the bush." The Bigfoot responded to me by verbalizing a very big, deep sigh, turned around, and started walking back down the mountainside.

The British couple was astonished by my bravery and the lady asked, "How did you know that you weren't going to anger it and cause it to come over and kill all of us?" I replied, "I had a very good friend who taught me to let the facts rule my judgment and decisions out here in the wilderness rather than my fears. I've been out here for six years now and the Bigfoot have never been aggressive towards me nor have they ever killed me. He was bluffing us and trying to intimidate us to get us to leave. I simply called him on his bluff and he just realized that I figured it out. As I said, we're going to be just fine."

The next morning, the British gentleman walked over to the spot where the Bigfoot was standing behind the brush and growling at us. He found some very large human-like footprints. He also found some tracks leading down the mountainside where he walked after I had called him on his bluff. They left SORA happy campers and enjoyed their Bigfoot experience.

During the following four years, I persistently returned to SORA one to two weekends per month. I would stay for two to four nights at a time. As previously stated, I would always have one or more people with me because I wanted witnesses and I was too afraid to be up there by myself. However, in my defense, I would make daytrips to SORA on my own. I would always carry my 44 magnum handgun with me for backup. When I walked around SORA in the daylight, I could sense that I was being followed and watched. My sixth-sense or Spidey senses developed over time.

On one occasion, during a daytrip to SORA, I was by myself. I was walking around and looking for evidence such as tracks or new tree structures. At one point, I really had to go to the bathroom. I pulled my pants down to my ankles, grabbed a hold of a branch with one hand, and leaned back as if I were sitting on an invisible toilet. This would allow me to conduct my business without soiling the backside of my legs, socks, shoes, etc.

While I was doing my thing, I felt like I was being watched from behind. I turned my head and looked over my left shoulder. Sure enough, there was a juvenile Bigfoot looking over the top of a very large fallen tree at me. He was only about thirty feet away from me. He had a dark cone shaped head and black eyes.

I said, "Hello", turned my head and continued with my business. I looked back in his direction about ten seconds later and he had ducked down behind the fallen tree. Just before I finished my business, I looked back at him one more time and he was looking at me again from behind the log. Suddenly, he cocked his head to the side and gave me a puzzled look as if to say, "That's how you guys do it?" I started laughing, cleaned up, pulled my pants back up, and walked away. That was my first introduction to Ceska. I didn't realize it then but I would literally watch him grow up and come to know him much better over the years.

I persistently continued to utilize the Old School Paparazzi Money Shot approach in SORA. I would hang up Trail Cams and take advantage of others who offered to bring their Night Vision or Thermal Imaging equipment. However, we ran into the same problems that we ran into in my previous research location. It appeared that the Bigfoot could see the infrared light and would avoid it at all cost. In both research locations, there was clear and consistent evidence of the Bigfoot approaching an area where a Trail Cam was hanging on a tree, then we could see that they altered their course in order to avoid the Trail Cam. However, when the Trail Cam was turned off, the Bigfoot would walk right in front of the device without any worries.

Also, unlike in my previous research area, the Bigfoot in SORA would not take the food that I was leaving for them. Every night, I would put out fresh fruit, fresh vegetables, fresh meat, bread, and candy. Every night, they left my food alone. They wouldn't touch it.

I'm talking for four straight years. For the record, nothing touched the food for four straight years. That includes little critters and birds too. I was totally befuddled.

In the previous research area that Dr. York and I worked on together, the Bigfoot would take the food that we left for them as long as we turned off the Trail Cams. If we left the Trail Cams on, they wouldn't touch the food either. However, if we turned off the Trail Cams, they would take the food. I should note that the Bigfoot not only took our food, they would peel the Bananas and leave the peelings in a neat pile. They would husk the corn, eat it, and then place the husk in one neat pile and the corn cobs in a different neat pile. It was amazing.

Yet, the Bigfoot in SORA wouldn't touch the food at all no matter what we tried. In the spirit of Dr. York's wisdom, I remained persistent and continued to leave them food even though I was flushing a lot of money down the toilet every month. On one occasion, my buddy, Howie Gordon joined me in SORA. I first met Howie Gordon when he wrote me asking if he could join me in my research area. He had been on the Big Brother reality TV show in seasons six and seven. He shared with me that he had been interested in the Bigfoot phenomena since he was a young boy. What he didn't know is that I was a Big Brother fan and a major fan of his during those two seasons. When Howie and I first met, we both were members of the Mutual Admiration Society (MAS) for about twenty-four hours. Then we calmed down and started to get to know one another better while we were up in the mountains engaged in Bigfoot research.

As usual, Howie and I placed the food in a bait pile outside of the base camp. The next morning, as usual, all the food was right where we left it. They didn't take any of the food at all. However, something new and different did happen. For the first time in four years, they finally responded to my leaving them food. Although they didn't take any food, they acknowledged my gift and left a very large branch on the ground right by the pile of food. Kind of like a calling card or a thank you.

Howie Gordon and I thoroughly examined the trees in the surrounding area and determined that the large branch absolutely did not fall from above. Matter of fact, the large branch that was placed by the pile of food was aged, gray, and did not come from any tree in the local area. Therefore, it was not only not fresh, it was obviously carried in from another area and placed by the pile of food. We were both excited that they finally did something to respond back to my leaving them food after four years of persistence. Progress was slowly but surely being made. Emphasis on slowly.

Matter of fact, to be honest, after spending four enthusiastic persistent years in SORA, I was starting to hit the proverbial brick wall again. However, this time, it wasn't because I was grieving the loss of my friend, Dr. Bill York. I had worked through my grief and loss issues and that was no longer affecting me like it once did. Rather, I was hitting a ten-year proverbial brick wall regarding the fact that no matter what I did or tried to do, the Bigfoot simply weren't coming in any closer. They always kept their distance from me. My sense was that they were merely tolerating my presence in their home but they certainly weren't interested in interacting with me.

I started thinking about some of the leaders in the field that most Bigfoot researchers and armchair enthusiasts looked up to and I began to recognize a pattern that I actually found to be very discouraging. For example, the four horsemen of Bigfootdom, although respected by all researchers and armchair enthusiasts in the field, did not fan the flames of enthusiasm for me because of their own lack of success. What do I mean by making such a blasphemous statement? Well, first things first, I absolutely intend no disrespect at all. Truly. Rather, I'm simply stating the facts and pointing out the truth.

Although John Green, a Canadian Journalist, did a wonderful job of collecting a plethora of stories over several decades, he never saw or interacted with a Bigfoot. Although Grover Krantz, a Professor of Anthropology at Washington State University, helped to bring the subject of Bigfoot into academia, he never saw or interacted with a Bigfoot. Peter Byrne, an acclaimed Monster Hunter, spent almost fifty years of his life looking for Bigfoot but never saw one. Finally, Rene Dahinden, a famous Bigfoot researcher also never laid his eyes on a Bigfoot, let alone interacted with one. Yet, these are the Four Horsemen in Bigfootdom? These are our role models for Bigfoot research?

What's my point? Well, my point is a simple one. In 2010, I came to the realization that I had just spent ten years of my life engaged in Bigfoot research. Yet, I was not doing much better than the leaders I had just mentioned. What did I have to show for after ten years of Bigfoot research? Several foot casts, a couple of visuals, some growls, screams, and a few tree knocks. So what! I felt like I was about to spend the next ten, twenty, thirty, or forty years of my life doing the same thing and not getting any further than the Four Horsemen of Bigfootdom. The only thing that was separating me from them was that I actually had some sightings.

Was this it? Was this all I could expect from my efforts? Is this all anyone could expect from their efforts? No! I wanted more than this. I wanted to be able to interact with them on a consistent basis. I wanted to experience Dr. York's "Bongo Moment" that he wrote about after his seventh hunt. Ultimately, I wanted to be able to show up to my research area, sit down with the Bigfoot, share some food with them, and hold one of the toddlers on my lap. Foot casts, growls, screams, and tree knocks were no longer working for me. I wanted more. Much more. But how was I going to get there?

Well, first, I had to come to the realization and understanding that replicating the approach of the Four Horsemen was not the way to do it. I'm a Psychologist and a problem solver. I helped other people solve their problems and I knew if I thought this one through, I could come up with a new and more productive game plan. I thought about it and thought about it and my problem-solving skills led me to the doorstep of the fringe Bigfoot researchers. The crazy kooks. The "Woo-Woo" gang.

However, there was just one tiny, itty-bitty problem. These were the people that I had been treating like crap online for the past ten years. Before the advent of Facebook, I participated in Bigfoot email listservs like most all other Bigfoot researchers. Whenever the crazy kooks would raise their silly heads, speak up, and talk about interacting with Bigfoot on a regular basis, I would slice them and dice them. Like many other Bigfoot researchers, I would tell them to go crawl back into the hole that they came from and to stop discrediting us serious researchers. Now I found myself seriously considering changing things up and trying their approach to Bigfoot research.

Well, why not? My persistence in utilizing the Old School Paparazzi Money Shot approach wasn't paying very many dividends. I just gave the approach ten years of my life. Why not give a different approach a try for the next ten years? So, I threw in the towel and joined the other side. I left my high tech equipment at home and adopted the Dr. Jane Goodall approach. I adopted and adapted some of her Habituation Research Methods and started implementing them with the Bigfoot in SORA. As a result, SORA ended up being renamed to the Southern Oregon Habituation Area (SOHA). The only problem was that I was completely clueless about the Rabbit Hole that I was about to fall into. Alice in Wonderland ain't got nothing on me.

CHAPTER ELEVEN

JOINING THE LIGHT SIDE OF THE FOREST

In August of 2010, I attended my thirtieth high school reunion. I couldn't believe that thirty years of my life had just flashed by like that. It seemed like it was only yesterday that I graduated from South Salem High School in Salem, Oregon.

I was staying at the Grand Hotel in the downtown Salem area. It was Saturday morning and I had just slept in because I was up late the night before. I had attended a Reunion Social that was hosted at a home in West Salem the night before. I found myself rushing to get downstairs in order to partake of the free breakfast buffet offered by the hotel for its guests.

I exited the elevator and began to walk towards the breakfast area when I ran into Cynthia Kreitzberg. Apparently, she had just finished eating breakfast and was headed back up to her room. I was about to walk past her when she actually spoke up and said, "Hello" to me. My jaw just about hit the floor. I thought to myself, "Wow! Cynthia Kreitzberg just said hello to me. She's way out of my league." Please keep in mind that we had five-hundred-twenty-five graduating seniors in our class. Although I knew who Cynthia was in high school, I never really knew her. Our paths never crossed because we ran in different social circles during high school. As a high school kid, I perceived myself as unworthy to hang out with someone like her.

On the other hand, little did I know, she thought the same thing about me when we were in high school. I was an All-State and Honorable Mention All-American high school basketball player. All the major universities recruited me during my junior and senior years. She thought that I was way out of her league. Fortunately for me, she was brave enough to ask me the following question: "Would you like some company?" I was shocked, dumbfounded, and happy that Cynthia Kreitzberg would ask me if I wanted her to join me for breakfast. I responded, "Yes, please. I would be honored."

We caught each other up to speed regarding our current life circumstances. We found ourselves in the same exact boat. We were both leaving our second failed marriages. We both had three children the exact same age who were very successful in school and life. The only difference was that I also had a younger child, Grady, who is a fine, young, smart boy with a good heart. We both were enjoying some time off from the stress of a 40 hour per week work life, although I was still busy speaking in 80 cities per year teaching my "Positive Parenting with a Plan" seminars. Finally, we both were mutually attracted to one another but we obviously didn't want to say anything about it at that point in time.

After breakfast was over, I had to check out of my hotel room. I was going to give a friend of mine, David Long and his wife, a tour of Salem. Apparently, Cynthia had some other commitment to fulfill as well. She offered to allow me to store my suitcase in her room for my convenience. I was no dummy. I knew that her gesture was a way of saying that she wanted to see me again so I enthusiastically agreed to her offer. However, when David called me and canceled the tour, I contacted Cynthia right away and informed her that I was free the rest of the day.

We walked all over the downtown Salem area. We talked and talked and talked while we were window shopping. Eventually, we stopped at the Food Court at the Salem Mall to sit down and eat some lunch. By this time, I knew that there was a possibility of dating Cynthia but I knew that I had to break the news to her. I'd rather tell her and lose her now rather than wait until later and hurt all the more because of being more deeply involved. So, I took the risk and opened up and told her about my Big Hairy Hobby.

I told her about my family's Bigfoot encounter at the Oregon Caves National Monument Park on July 1, 2000. I shared with her about my subsequent research expeditions in southern Oregon. I informed her that I had no intention of giving up my hobby and that it was my goal to learn who they were, where they came from, and why they are here. I expected her to roll her eyes or to kindly and graciously thank me for lunch, walk away, and never hear from her or see her again.

Instead, she believed me. She was all in. I didn't know then she was originally a Montana girl who moved to Salem with her parents. She loved the outdoors and had lots of experience in the woods. She was even kissed by a Black Bear while sleeping at her grandmother's cabin in Montana. The clouds opened up, the sun shone down, and the angels were singing.

We spent the rest of the afternoon and early evening just talking, talking, and talking some more. We finally went to our thirtieth high school reunion that night. Although it was great to see and visit with my classmates from South Salem High School, all I could think about was Cynthia. We would occasionally cross paths during the evening but we both agreed that we wanted to spend that time catching up with everyone else since we just spent the entire day together. When our thirtieth high school reunion had come to an end, we eventually said our goodbyes, I gave her a kiss, and I drove away knowing that Cynthia Kreitzberg was going to eventually be my wife. The third time is a charm.

Fast forward about nine months to June of 2011. By this time, I had moved north to Puyallup, Washington to live near Cynthia. We were spending all of our free time together. We walked, hiked, swam, and biked together. We talked about anything and everything under the sun, including the Bigfoot phenomena. I had just been invited by Toby Johnson to speak at his Sasquatch Symposium just outside of Eugene, Oregon. Cynthia and I were excited to attend the conference together. It would be the beginning of our shared Bigfoot journey.

As Cynthia and I were driving south from Puyallup, Washington to the Eugene, Oregon area, I began to catch her up to speed regarding the different theoretical camps in Bigfootdom. I told her about the traditional researchers, which was the group I had been a member of for the past ten years. Then I told her about the fringe group of Bigfooters who believed in the "Woo-Woo" (i.e., The alleged paranormal abilities of the Bigfoot species). I told her that they had a reputation of making it difficult for those of us who were conducting serious scientific research. I also shared that after ten years of research, I was becoming more open minded to explore their point of view. I encouraged her to be friendly to them, nod her head, smile, and take anything they had to share with a grain of salt. Although there could be some truth to what they were sharing, they were still the "crazy kooky" people. I had not yet learned how to communicate with them, respect them, or speak their language.

After I completed my presentation on "Bigfoot and Post Traumatic Stress Disorder (PTSD)," I sat down in the front row and had the opportunity to listen to Thom Powell present before lunch time. I whispered to Cynthia, "This is one of those crazy kooky people that I was talking with you about. At least he's funny and keeps the attention of his audience."

During Thom's presentation, he discussed conducting a double blind study regarding the long distance telepathic communication of the Bigfoot Forest People. If I remember correctly, he referred to the Aborigines in Australia and the ability of their Shamans to communicate telepathically via long distances. I believe Thom referred to this ability as the "Coconut Express." As he spelled out the details of his experiment, I leaned forward to listen more closely. He had captured my attention. As a psychologist with two Masters degrees and one Doctorate degree, I understood the utilization of the scientific method as well as double blind studies. If this guy was a "Crazy Kook", he was a very intelligent "Crazy Kook."

After Thom Powell completed his presentation, it was time to eat lunch. Cynthia and I enjoyed our meal as well as our discussions with the couple sitting across the table from us. When the couple finished eating their lunch, they dismissed themselves. Just when Cynthia and I were about to get up and leave the dining hall, Thom Powell sat down across the table from us. He looked into my eyes, and into my soul, and asked, "So, what really happened up on the mountain that day?"

I couldn't figure out how he knew that I had never told the entire story to anyone during the past ten years, including my ex-wife and children.

I responded to Thom Powell by saying, "You know what, Thom? I'm going to tell you what really happened up on the mountain that day. However, before I tell you, I'm going to take Cynthia outside and tell her first. I've never told a soul what happened and she's going to be the first one to hear it. When I'm done, you can come outside and I'll tell you too." He politely agreed to my terms and patiently waited to hear my story.

I took Cynthia outside of the dining hall and on to the very large deck and told her what I had never told another soul. I shared with her that when I was up on the mountain above the Oregon Caves National Monument Park, behind a natural blind answering my call to Mother Nature, that I didn't see the Bigfoot walk out from behind one tree and see it walk to another tree. Rather, I saw the Bigfoot appear out of nowhere and then walk to another tree. I saw a Bigfoot do what only the kooks describe, I saw it uncloak.

As my body was shaking, and I was in tears while reliving the experience, I shared with her that I literally felt my cognitive schema of the world and the great outdoors come crashing down inside my head. After my brain rebooted, I felt my protective instincts kick in. Then I shared with her that while I was coming back down the hill through the brush and trees to reach the trail, I actually didn't avoid eye contact with the Bigfoot as I had always reported. Rather, I maintained my visual focus on the Bigfoot as I descended the hill. When he saw me coming down the hill, he immediately cloaked again.

As I was approaching my family to get them out of the area, I was absolutely, totally, and completely one hundred percent terrified by what I had just seen. I didn't want to freak out my family by telling them that I saw a Bigfoot. I especially didn't want to freak them out by telling them that I saw a Bigfoot uncloak and then cloak again. Instead, as best I could, I calmly moved them up the trail. As we journeyed up the trail, I was totally scared and overwhelmed by the impossibility of protecting my family from something that was so much bigger than me and who had the ability to appear out of nowhere and just as quickly disappear again. At that moment in time, I seriously doubted my ability to get my family off the mountain alive.

As I stood there shaking and crying, Cynthia reached out to comfort me and reassure me that she didn't think I was crazy. I felt a great sense of relief. Her support and encouragement was just what the doctor ordered. With perfect timing, Thom Powell emerged from the Dining Hall with his ears perked up and ready to listen to my story. I shared it with him just as I had just done so with Cynthia. I waited quietly for his response. He looked at me and said, "Now I believe you. I knew by your expressed emotions during your media interviews that something more had to have happened up on the mountains besides you just seeing a Bigfoot."

Thom Powell asked me why I didn't share the entire story ten years earlier with my family, friends, and the media. I responded in a defensive manner and said, "Are you kidding me? I'm a psychologist with a private practice. I was taking a big enough risk sharing with the world that I simply saw a Bigfoot. There was no way on God's green Earth that I was also going to share with the world that I saw that Bigfoot uncloak and cloak again. Everyone would have thought that I was crazy and I would have lost everything." He nodded his head in agreement and responded, "Good decision. I agree. Are you going to start telling people now?" I said, "I'll start telling people when I'm good and ready. Right now, I'm not good and ready. I'm still wrestling with my own denial of what I saw up on the mountainside that day. However, someday, I'm sure I'll be ready to tell the world."

As Cynthia and I were driving back to Puyallup, Washington, I realized that I was no longer a full-fledged member of the traditional researchers group. I was now transitioning from the "Old Schoolers" research group to the "Woo-Woo" group. Although Thom Powell had just enthusiastically welcomed me to the club, my membership came without any instructions or guidance. Fortunately, I now had a partner who was eager to learn along with me.

Upon our return home, Cynthia and I were exhausted. We went to bed early that night. It was summertime so we slept with our second story master bedroom window wide open. As we laid there engaging in "pillow talk", our jaws hit the floor when we both heard a nine-hundred-pound owl sound off in the greenbelt behind our home (i.e., A Sasquatch with very large and loud lungs attempting to imitate an owl). We had never heard anything like it before in the greenbelt. All of a sudden, right after the "Woo-Woo" conference and my subsequent confession, there they were sounding off. We couldn't believe what we were hearing. Needless to say, we were motivated to get out there into the greenbelt area and start trying to reach out to the Bigfoot Forest People.

In September of 2011, Howie Gordon was visiting with us. He is a Bigfoot junkie and travels out west at least once per year to spend time with me out in the woods. One night, Howie, Cynthia, and I carried our camping chairs out into the greenbelt. It was pitch dark but the ambient light from the Moon allowed us to make our way through the forest to our "Night Sit" area.

We set up our camping chairs in the dark right next to each other. Yes, we were afraid to be out there in the dark. Within thirty-minutes or so, we appeared to be surrounded by several Bigfoot Forest People. We knew that we were surrounded because we could hear them moving around, some of them whispering to one another, and a couple of them were tossing small pebbles and pine cones at our feet. They weren't trying to hit us and hurt us. Rather, they were simply saying "hello" to us and getting our attention.

Suddenly, to the east of our location, a very large Bigfoot Forest Person left us and ran down the hillside to the Orting Valley about nine-hundred feet below. He ran down the hill through the trees and brush in the pitch dark of night. Very impressive. When he reached the bottom of the hill, the three of us heard several dogs sound off in the neighborhood below.

While we were sitting there, both Cynthia and I asked Howie to turn off his cell phone. We reminded him that we had a 'no light' policy while conducting 'Night Sits" in the forest. He said, "I left my cell phone at your house. What are you talking about?" Cynthia and I both pointed at his right elbow and I said, "Right there by your right elbow." Howie said, "Crap, Doc! What the hell is that?" I told him not to move.

The three of us watch this small ball of faint light move from his right elbow up to his right hand. Then it moved back down to his right elbow again. Finally, it moved up to his right shoulder. Howie did a great job sitting still while the orb was scanning his right arm. Afterwards, we saw the faint white orb fly from Howie's right shoulder up into the sky about thirty feet above the ground. It hovered there for about thirty seconds and then it zipped away to the east. Talk about a mind blowing experience.

We continued to sit in the dark for another thirty-minutes or so and then I stood up in the dark and started to talk to them. I said, "Hello, my name is Matt. This is Cynthia and this is Howie." Both Cynthia and Howie said "hello" to them too. Then I said in my very calm and soothing psychologist voice, "We're here to be your friends. We don't want to hurt you and we believe that you don't want to hurt us. It would be really nice if at least one of you would step forward and say 'hello' to us."

No sooner than I said that, we had an eight-foot-tall Bigfoot Forest Person start to walk toward us from the 12:00 o'clock position on the perimeter of our 'Night Sit' area. The ambient light from the moon above clearly illuminated the upright, bipedal, silhouette that was walking straight toward us. It was about fifty feet away and closing. I stood up while Cynthia and Howie remained seated in their camp chairs.

Suddenly, along its way toward our location, the eight-foot-tall Bigfoot Forest Person cloaked. However, he continued to walk straight toward us. We could see the branches, ferns, and leaves moving as he came closer. We could hear his upright bipedal steps progressing in our direction. Howie started shouting, "Doc! Doc! It's coming right toward you, Doc!"

As the Bigfoot Forest Person passed me on my left side, I felt him bump my left shoulder. He spun me around like I was a little kid. However, I'm 6'9" tall and I weigh over three-hundred-pounds. I'm not a little kid. I would like to point out the fact that if he wanted to hurt me or knock me flat on my butt, he most certainly would have. However, he exercised restraint as he bumped my left shoulder while passing me. As he passed me, I literally watched the bipedal footsteps walk through the ferns and leaves on the ground. Then I saw the branches move as high as eight feet off the ground as he stepped back into the trees and brush. Afterwards, all three of us talked about how we all felt our central nervous systems light up with some kind of energy. Quite frankly, the three of us were so jacked up by what happened during the 'Night Sit' that we didn't go to bed until 5:00 am the next morning. The paranormal abilities of the Bigfoot Forest People had just been confirmed by the three of us and could no longer be denied or ignored.

Part 3

THE HABITUATION RESEARCH METHOD

CHAPTER TWELVE

THE SOUTHERN OREGON HABITUATION AREA (SOHA)

During the summer of 2011, I took Cynthia and her two youngest children, Claire and Morgan to the Southern Oregon Habituation Area. By this time, I was in transition from the 'Old School' approach to the Habituation Research Method. I left all of the high tech equipment at home. I started putting the food out in large stainless steel dog food bowls which I referred to as gifting bowls. I was no longer baiting a big dumb giant mountain ape. I was now trying to establish a trusting relationship with a sentient being with paranormal abilities. By the way, another way of saying paranormal abilities is to simply say beings who have the ability to manipulate quantum mechanics.

The four of us set up camp and then we went for a hike. We were off road and off trail, deep in the woods. As we were walking, Claire pointed out an interesting indentation in the ground which had been covered up by leaves that fell from the trees above. I carefully removed the leaves from the impression and found a large adult male Bigfoot track. It was twenty-two inches long, nine inches across at the toes, and six inches across at the heel. It dwarfed my size sixteen shoes which are fourteen and one-half inches long. The impression had obviously been made several months earlier when the ground was very moist. By this time, the summer sun had baked the ground hard.

I was talking about what it would take to cast the track when Morgan pointed out another track which was only about eight feet away from the impression that Claire discovered. Once again, I carefully removed the leaves from the impression in the ground. It turned out that we discovered an adult female track that was about seventeen inches long.

The cool thing about Morgan's discovery is that, after closer examination, there was a juvenile track inside the mother's track. It reminded me of when I was a kid and our family would occasionally visit the beach in Seaside, Oregon. As a young child, I would have fun following my mother and trying to step from one of her tracks in the sand to the next track in the sand. It was clear to me that the juvenile Bigfoot was having fun doing likewise with his or her mom.

I left Cynthia and her kids behind to explore the area while I drove off the mountain to purchase some Plaster of Paris. I also bought some food coloring so I could dye the plaster with two separate colors when I casted the combined mother and juvenile track. I returned to SOHA and casted the tracks while teaching both Claire and Morgan how to do so. It was a very nice day and I enjoyed spending time with all of them.

That night, we conducted a 'Night Sit' far away from the SOHA base camp. To be honest, I wanted to conduct the 'Night Sit' there because I didn't feel comfortable having them up close and personal at the SOHA base camp which was a much smaller area. Claire and Morgan had a fun time playing some kind of pretend Ninja fighting game. I'm sure that the younger Bigfoot Forest People enjoyed watching them play with one another. Then we sang and Cynthia played her flute for a while.

After the sun went down, we noticed some silhouettes and eye glow around the perimeter. There wasn't much activity around us and it was getting late. We turned on our flashlights and walked back through the woods in order to return to the SOHA base camp. We climbed into our tent and started to go to sleep. As I lay there, I was pleased that we had such an awesome experience for their first Bigfooting trip.

Around 4:00 am, I was woken up by some noise outside the tent. I remained still and quiet. I could clearly hear two sets of bipedal steps tiptoeing around camp. I nudged Cynthia a couple of times until she woke up. Then I whispered in her ear, "They're here. They're tiptoeing around the base camp and checking out our stuff." Cynthia acknowledged that she could hear them too. My heart was pounding because I was so excited.

Cynthia fell back to sleep and I nudged her a couple of times again. I whispered to her, "They're still here. Stay awake so you can listen to them." She said that she would and then immediately fell back to sleep. She was exhausted from all of the driving that she had done in the days before coming to SOHA. I decided to let her sleep and I lay quietly on my back inside the tent and continued to listen.

I could hear them pick things up off the table, obviously checking out the objects, and then put them back down on the table. I could hear them take items out of the garbage bag, check things out, and then stuff them back inside the garbage bag. Finally, I heard them unzip the zipper on a duffle bag, check things out, finally zipping the bag back up again. Then I heard them walk out of camp. After that, I fell asleep.

Around 7:30 am, I woke up again. I could hear the younger Bigfoot Forest People at the 2:00 o'clock position on the perimeter. They were moving around and whispering to one another. Cynthia woke up right around this time and I whispered to her, "There right on the other side of the bushes on that side of the tent. They're only about eight feet away from us." Suddenly, one of them picked up a very large piece of wood and threw it into the brush right near our tent which was followed by a very loud thud. Then they ran away from us near the 3:00 o'clock position on the perimeter. Both Cynthia and I chuckled because they were behaving like two young pranksters having fun together.

When we got out of the tent, we took our time checking out all of the items in our camp. Although we could tell that some items had been looked at and moved ever so subtly, absolutely nothing was missing. The only thing that was out of place was Morgan's duffle bag that had been removed from the camp chair and placed on the ground. Everything else that they had looked at had been put back into the same place they found it.

It was our first family trip up in the mountains Bigfooting together. It was also going to be our last Bigfooting trip together as a family. Both Claire and Morgan weren't thrilled about getting back out there. I was more excited about the two tracks that they found than they were. I told them that they were the best tracks I've ever seen pulled out of the ground in all my years of Bigfooting. They gave me the tracks. Love those kids.

In May of 2012, I went to SOHA with my buddy, Karl Haeckler, and my son, Grady. Karl was a former Bigfoot Field Research Organization (BFRO) Investigator. He was also a Medford Swat Cop who had served overseas in Afghanistan and Iraq. We conducted our 'Night Sit' inside the SOHA base camp rather than hiking so far away. It proved to be a great decision. We had lots of activity on the perimeter. We observed silhouettes, heard several heavy bipedal steps, as well as some tree knocks up close and personal.

Although I had made the decision to leave all of the high tech equipment at home, I decided to try something new. I purchased a Bionic Ear parabolic microphone dish so I could start recording what was going on around the SOHA base camp at night while we were sleeping. I didn't think that it would be a problem because it was passive technology which was anchored down in the base camp. There was absolutely nothing aggressive or invasive about the device at all. I started recording all night long for anywhere from eight hours to twelve hours.

That night, Karl, Grady, and I went to bed inside the tent after I set up the parabolic microphone dish and digital Sony recorder. I explained to Grady the necessity of remaining quiet while I'm recording. I told him that it was okay for him to whisper to me but that he should not be overly rambunctious. He is a good kid, well behaved, and did a wonderful job of following the protocol that I was slowly but surely establishing in SOHA. I will eventually describe the protocol that I established so you can attempt to replicate it in your own research area.

The next morning, Grady woke me up from my sleep and whispered in my ear, "Dad, I have to go to the bathroom." I directed him to go ahead and leave the tent and use the porta-potty. He unzipped the flap of the tent, went outside to use the toilet, and then came back into the tent and whispered, "Dad, the water jug is too heavy for me to pick up and flush the toilet." I apologized to him and told him to go ahead and use the toilet and that I would be right outside. I was half asleep and should have realized that before I sent him outside on his own.

After we returned home from SOHA, I had to start listening to my audio recordings. I listened to every second and never skipped around. I was afraid that I would miss something if I didn't exercise the discipline and take the time to listen to every sound. It was like going to SOHA twice in one trip. I was amazed at how much activity was going on at night while we were asleep inside the tent.

Well, I eventually reached the moment when Grady left the tent for the first time to use the porta-potty. He came back inside the tent and then went back outside again. While listening to the audio recordings, I heard something that blew my mind. It was a game changer for me. When Grady exited the tent the first time, the parabolic microphone dish and Sony digital recorder captured the Adolescent Bigfoot Forest Person on the perimeter whispering, "Aye-ga-y-ate." The second time Grady exited the tent, the Adolescent male uttered the same word once again, "Aye-ga-y-ate." No way! They have a spoken language. This didn't sound anything like the Samurai Chatter that Ron Morehead recorded up in the Sierra mountains during the 1970's. Instead, what I recorded sounded like a North American Indian language with staccato syllables.

Later on, I played the recording for an Indian friend who is a member of the Klamath Indian Tribe in southern Oregon. She said that the word was very similar to one of the words in their vocabulary that means "urination." I was blown away.

However, the fun was just beginning in SOHA. As I continued to record all night long, every night I was there, I was coming up with more and more spoken language. I was recording them singing and humming. I recorded a crying baby Bigfoot shortly after its birth. The mother could be heard comforting the baby all night long as it cried and fussed. I recorded one of them tapping out a drum solo on the camp stove table after I had played the eleven-minute drum solo from Iron Butterfly's song, "Inagodadavida." A 1960's classic.

As time progressed in SOHA, I found it necessary to establish a strict protocol that would guide the behaviors and attitudes of all the guests that I was bringing up on the mountain with me. The protocol was also established for my own behaviors and attitudes. I also created a strict protocol in order to remain consistent and predictable to the Bigfoot Forest People. I concluded that if I behaved in a consistent and predictable manner, it would eventually make it easier for them to trust me.

Here's the protocol that I established over time in SOHA, instructed my guests to follow in a strict manner, and followed religiously with great results. I'm sharing my protocol with you in order to help you improve your results in your research area. Others who have listened, learned, and implemented my protocol in their areas have reported back to me with great success too:

1. Upon arrival, I would park my vehicle in the SOHA base camp in the same exact spot every time. I tried to discourage others from driving their vehicles to SOHA. Instead, I encouraged them to park their cars lower on the mountain, throw their gear in my truck, and ride up the hill with me. There simply wasn't enough room for multiple vehicles to park in SOHA. Also, the road to SOHA is rutty, overgrown with vegetation that has scratched the heck out of my vehicles and torn the mirrors off my Suburban, and quite frankly, the road is becoming dangerous and will eventually become impassable.

2. Immediately upon exiting my vehicle, I would grab the large cow bell and ring it at the 2:00 o'clock position on the perimeter of the base camp, nonstop, for one minute. I would pause for thirty seconds and then do it again. If my guests were interested in ringing the cow bell, I would allow them to take turns.

3. Before we did anything else, we would set up the base camp in the same exact manner every time. The campfire was always in the same spot. Eventually, we stopped using campfires or any source of light at all. My reasoning was because if they thought we were going to try and light them up if we heard or saw anything on the perimeter, they would keep their distance. Also, keeping the camp dark with a 'no lights' policy was a demonstration of trust towards our Bigfoot Forest People friends. I'll talk more about this later in the book.

4. We positioned our camp chairs in the same exact spot every time.
5. We put the camp table and garbage bag in the same spot every time. Yes, you read that correctly. We placed the garbage bag inside the base camp for the exact reason that you're not supposed to leave the garbage bag inside of camp. I wanted to see what wild animals were in the area. I wanted them to come into camp. None ever did. Yes, you read that correctly, no animals ever came into base camp while we were there during a ten-year period of time. That's significant data.
6. We placed our storage bins in the same exact spot every time.
7. Like clockwork, at sunset every night, we would place the gifting bowls outside of the SOHA base camp approximately one-hundred-fifty feet away. The bowls were always washed squeaky clean while wearing surgical gloves. We never served the food in dirty bowls. We also removed any and all fingerprints from the bowls so if we found any fingerprints on the bowls in the morning, we knew that they didn't belong to us. As we carried the bowls from the base camp to their position, we would sing two repetitions of "Row, Row, Row Your Boat" and then whistle the tune once. A couple of years later, I recorded the adult female Bigfoot humming the tune. We would place the gifting bowls on the ground in the same exact spot every time. Then we would take a before picture and then head back to the base camp. Once we reached the base camp, we would never breach the perimeter of the base camp until the sunrise the following morning. They needed to know that we weren't going to try to light them up and we weren't going to try and chase them through the woods either.
8. Also, we always placed a dozen eggs out every night next to the gifting bowls. The eggs functioned as a control variable to rule out the possibility of little critters hitting the gifting bowls. By the way, when opportunistic little critters hit any source of food left out for them, they always make a mess. The next morning, it always looks like nuclear devastation. Also, opportunistic little critters will always take the eggs. They would never leave eggs behind. On the other hand, the Bigfoot Forest People are very neat, clean, and never

overindulge. They're only interested in taking what they want. More often than not, they wouldn't touch the eggs. Although on one occasion, they cracked two eggs in half, swallowed the yoke, and then placed one half shell inside the other half shell and then placed both back inside the egg carton. A little critter would never do that.

9. Once we placed the gifting bowls outside of camp and we returned to camp, we would always introduce ourselves by saying our first names only while tapping our own chest. Eventually, I recorded them over fifteen times, saying my name, "Matt." Then we would play instruments, sing songs, whistle tunes, and I would play music on my MP3 player while attached to my portable Bose speaker. The Bigfoot Forest People love, love, love music. They especially love music when your heart is into what you're singing or playing. We never played heavy metal or rap music. No loud, angry, negative, aggressive music allowed. We played instrumental music, Native American Music, melancholy pop music, classical music, female vocals, children singing, and music with a beat. Once again, we eventually learned that the most important thing is that your heart is into the music that you play, sing, or whistle to them. That's how they connect with you. If your heart isn't into the music that you're playing, you will not draw them in.

10. Regarding bathroom options, we established a place inside the base camp where the women felt comfortable using the porta-potty. They were not allowed to pee and poop outside of the base camp. The guys also had to use the porta-potty to poop. They also weren't allowed to poop outside of camp. The guys had two designated spots on the perimeter of the base camp where they could pee. However, they had to say, "I'm just going potty. Just going potty. Just going potty." This way, the Bigfoot Forest People knew why the men were approaching the perimeter and it wasn't because we were going to try and chase them. Finally, I didn't think it was appropriate to pee and poop outside of the base camp where the Bigfoot Forest People were walking around the perimeter. We didn't want them stepping on our biological messes and getting upset at us.

11. Like clockwork, at sunrise every morning, we would retrieve the gifting bowls while wearing surgical gloves. Before touching the bowls, we would take an after picture. This gave us a means of comparison with the before picture from the previous night. By collecting the bowls while wearing surgical gloves, we wouldn't put any fingerprints on the bowls while we were checking the bowls out for fingerprints. Sometimes we had to lightly breathe on the bowls to illuminate any fingerprints that were left behind. However, more often than not, the fingerprints stood out like a sore thumb. Pun intended.

12. We would eat breakfast in camp, go off the mountain during the day in order to give the Bigfoot Forest People some space, and then return in the late afternoon and start the protocol all over again. While off the mountain, I would take my guests sightseeing to the local various tourist sites in southern Oregon such as Crater Lake, the Oregon Caves, the Redwood Forest, the California coast, and the Hellgate Jet Boat Excursion ride on the Rogue River, including an awesome buffet dinner in a rustic lodge setting. Regardless of where we ate our one large meal at a restaurant while off the mountain, we would always use their toilet before returning to SOHA. Ahhhh!!! Then we would go to the grocery store, buy snacks and beverages for the evening, and fresh food for breakfast the next morning.

Now, to be honest, you can create your own protocol for your own area. The important thing is that you must be persistent and consistent. All of the above helped to make myself and my guests predictable. Predictability made us dependable. Dependability made us trustworthy. Trustworthiness eventually brought the Bigfoot Forest People closer, and closer, and closer for improved and desired personal interactions. My goal has always been to have the Bigfoot Forest People feel comfortable enough to come into camp, hangout, and hold one of their young ones on my lap. It's going to happen someday soon. I'm one-hundred percent confident.

CHAPTER THIRTEEN

TAKING A STROLL DOWN MEMORY LANE

The activity level in the Southern Oregon Habituation Area (SOHA) was slowly but surely beginning to increase. We were beginning to experience more and more visuals, vocals, and tree knocks on the perimeter of the base camp. We were hearing bipedal steps and seeing eye glow on the very edge of camp, only ten to fifteen feet away from us. We were beginning to occasionally see evidence that the younger children were watching us on the perimeter too and also visiting the gifting bowls as evidenced by their tiny fingerprints combined with the much larger fingerprints. Those little fingerprints were so cute.

One night in SOHA, Grady and I entered our tent, climbed into our sleeping bags, and went to sleep. More often than not, I sleep so much better up in the mountains than I do in my own bed at home. Being in the mountains is therapy for this psychologist. However, around 2:00 am, I woke up because I heard some heavy footed bipedal steps approaching the backside of our tent where are heads were positioned.

All of a sudden, I felt myself being zapped. What does being zapped mean? Well, the 'Old Schoolers' will try to convince you that the Bigfoot Forest People are using infrasound to paralyze their prey. The only problem with their theory is that we aren't prey to the Bigfoot Forest People nor are they using infrasound. The effects of infrasound do not match what is actually being experienced while one is being zapped. The effects of infrasound include fear, sorrow, depression, anxiety, nausea, chest pressure and hallucination. Instead of experiencing the listed symptoms associated with infrasound, I was experiencing a feeling of relaxation, comfort, and peace.

When the Bigfoot Forest Person was zapping me, it was like my body was being immobilized while I was still very consciously alert. I liken it to going into surgery and the anesthesiologist places a mask over your nose and mouth. Then they tell you to count backwards from ten. When you get to five, you're totally passed out. When you're being zapped, it's like you're at 7.5. You can think but you can't move. You're not wide awake and mobile like you were at a 10 before you started breathing from the mask. At the same time, you're not at a 5 and totally passed out and unconscious either. Once again, I felt relaxed, comfortable, and peaceful.

As I laid there in the tent with my body immobilized, yet wide awake, I felt a hand about the size of my own slide between my head and my pillow. Keep in mind that I stand 6'9" tall and I have the hands to match. I can palm a basketball without any difficulty at all. Now, I know what you're thinking right now. How did the Bigfoot Forest Person stick his hand between your head and pillow? Was there a hole in the back of the tent? Nope. There was no hole in the back of the tent. Now you're asking, well then how did he do it? My answer is that I'll get to how he did it later in the book. For now, stay with me as I finish addressing the more important aspects of this story.

As I laid there in my sleeping bag, inside the tent, with a large hand between my head and pillow, I could see what appeared to be a very fast slide show going on in my mind. The slide show with pictures quickly flashing by began from my infancy. Before I knew it, fifteen minutes later, pictures of being in first grade at the John Jacob Astor Elementary School in Astoria, Oregon were flashing through my head. Although I was enjoying taking a stroll down memory lane, I wasn't enjoying the fact that our connection appeared to be coming across to me as being very one-sided.

Although my body was immobilized, I began to wrestle in my mind with the Adolescent Bigfoot Forest Person in order to sever our connection.

How was I attempting to do so? Well, all I can explain to you that in my mind, I was pushing, pulling, yanking, leveraging, twisting, and turning in order to stop the memory reading process. By the time we reached my middle school years at Leslie Junior High School in Salem, Oregon, I managed to stop the process. I won. He had to stop and listen to me.

I said in my mind, "This isn't fair. This isn't right." The adolescent Bigfoot Forest Person mind spoke back to me, "What isn't fair? What isn't right?" I said, "You get to read through all of my memories and get to know everything about me but I don't get to know anything about you. If you want to continue reading through my memories, then I need to be able to ask you some questions too." He immediately responded, "I have to speak with the elders first." I said, "Okay." He disconnected from me, I shot back up to a 10, and he walked away from the SOHA base camp through the woods.

As I lay there in my sleeping bag inside of my tent, I couldn't believe I experienced what had just happened. I turned my head and looked at the tent wall and there was no hole in the side of the tent. I couldn't, for the life of me, figure out how he managed to put his hand between my head and my pillow without leaving a hole in the side of the tent. Then I just lay on my back, in the dark of the night, and waited for his return.

About an hour later, as I lay there in the dark, I heard two sets of heavy footed bipedal steps returning to the backside of our tent in the SOHA base camp. I have to say that I was excited, not scared, and my heart was beating faster as the adrenaline was flowing. Suddenly, I felt myself being zapped again. I dropped from a 10 back down to a 7.5 again. My body was immobilized but I was very conscious and aware of what was going on. Next, I felt a much larger hand slide between my head and the pillow. This very large hand pretty much covered most of my head. The palm of the adult male Bigfoot Forest Person was down by the base of my skull while his fingertips were wrapped over the top of my head and resting on my forehead. In short, the very large hand dwarfed my hand and I don't have little hands.

The adult male Bigfoot Forest Person mind spoke to me, "My son said that you wanted to ask me some questions." I responded, "Yes, why is he reading through my memories?" The elder answered, "That's our way of knowing what is going on with the human race." Well, that made sense to me. It's not like they have CNN or FOX News to watch every day at home.

The elder then asked me, "Do you have any other questions?" I responded, "Yes, who are you?" He immediately answered nonchalantly, "We are guardians of the forest and we protect all who dwell within. Do you have any other questions?" I responded, "No. I'm fine." Then he asked me, "May my son continue to read through your memories?" I replied, "Yes, he may." The elder said, "Thank you" and removed his hand from between my head and the pillow.

I felt the smaller hand of the adolescent male slide between my head and the pillow again. I remember thinking right there and then about the amazing difference in the size of hands. I couldn't believe that the father's hand pretty much wrapped around most of my head. That was a freaking huge hand. Then the adolescent male began reading through my memories again. I was amazed that he was able to pick up where he left off. He didn't have to start all over again from my infancy.

It was actually kind of fun as I lay there in the tent enjoying a slide-show review of the life that I had lived. The weird thing was that I wasn't just seeing all of my memories flash before my eyes, I was also feeling all of the feelings associated with the memories in fast forward speed. I was feeling happy, sad, afraid, and mad in a quick repetitive cycle, over and over and over again. Naturally, I preferred the happy memories.

When the adolescent male had completed reading through my memories, he said, "Thank you" to me. I responded, "You're welcome" back to him. Then he disconnected, slid his hand out from between my head and pillow. I shot back up to a 10. The adolescent male walked away from the SOHA base camp with his father. It was really cool laying there and listening to the heavy bipedal footsteps walking away through the woods.

Next, as I continued to lay in my sleeping bag inside the tent, I began to question everything. Did this really just happen? Was I dreaming? Was I hallucinating? Did I have a psychotic break? Nope. This really happened. I was wide awake the entire time and nothing about it smacked of dreaming, hallucinating, or psychosis. Then I suddenly thought to myself, "Oh no! What about Grady?" I turned my body and head to my left to check on him. Grady lifted his head up off of his pillow, looked me straight in the eyes, and said, "They spoke with me too, daddy." Then he laid his head back down on his pillow and fell quickly back to sleep.

I just laid there stunned. Crap! This really did happen. I wasn't dreaming, hallucinating, or experiencing a psychotic break. Grady just told me that they spoke with him too. Wait! Grady said "they" and not he. Grady referred to them in the 'plural" form rather than using the 'singular' form. In other words, "they" referred to both the adolescent male and the father (i.e., "They spoke with me too, daddy"). Wow! I laid there wondering what they spoke to Grady about. I decided that I would let him sleep and not make a big deal of it with him. After all, he was only five years old at the time. I thought I would just wait and hear from Grady about his experience if and when he wanted to share it with me.

I reached for my cell phone, turned it on, and began to blow up Cynthia's cell phone with a million text messages. I typed everything that I could remember. I'm sure she was thinking, "Uh oh! He's lost his marbles." It didn't matter. I had to tell another adult. Cynthia is my soul mate so she's going to have to put up with my craziness no matter what. Well, she responded back in a very excited and inquisitive manner. She too was blown away by Grady's response to me: "They spoke with me too, daddy." She also was wondering what they talked about. To this day, I have no idea. Grady can only remember the event but he doesn't remember the specifics of what they talked about. It doesn't matter to me. What does matter is that he was there with me, at the age of five, experiencing things that most other kids on planet Earth never have the opportunity to experience. Those are memories with his father that he will never forget. Grady has stories to tell to his children and grandchildren.

Since that time, as I review the event over and over again in my mind, I'm struck by the cultural differences between the human race and the Bigfoot Forest People. They seem to do whatever they want to do whenever they want to do it (i.e., Zapping, reading through memories, healing, etc.). In other words, they don't ask for permission, they just do it. When they're doing it, they're kind, gentle, and respectful. I was never harmed nor did I feel afraid. On the other hand, when humans attempt to get close and personal with another human, we ask for permission first. If we don't ask for consensual participation, then we are violating human customs and possibly breaking some laws too.

The other thing that comes to my mind when I'm reviewing this experience is the fact that the mind speak communications with the adolescent male and his father were all very respectful. The adolescent wasn't going to answer any of my questions without speaking to the elders first. I can think of a whole lot of human adolescents who couldn't give a crap what their elders thought and often proceed with doing what they want to do on their own free will. I was also impressed with how kind and gentle the adult male Bigfoot Forest Person treated me. Quite frankly, his hand was so huge that he could have simply popped my head open like it was an egg. Instead, he was kind and gentle, asked me questions, allowed me to ask him questions, and then thanked me for my willingness to participate in the memory reading process. In short, there was a whole lot of respect that occurred during the mind speak exchange in spite of our cultural differences. However, I soon realized that I was only beginning to scratch the surface. There was a whole lot more for me to learn about the Bigfoot Forest People.

CHAPTER FOURTEEN

CLARIFYING MY INTENTIONS

It took me thirteen years before I was willing to camp and sleep out in the woods all by myself without another human being with me. I never counted bringing Grady along with me as being by myself. Yes, he's a young boy but he was still there with me. Grady was another person to interact with and distract myself from my ongoing fears of what I didn't know about the Bigfoot Forest People. For some silly reason, I believed in my mind that the Bigfoot Forest People would never attack me if I had my son along with me. Also, I thought that they would never attack me if I had Maggie with me.

Who's Maggie, you ask? Maggie is my nickname for my 44 magnum handgun that I've always carried into the woods with me. I always brought Maggie along with me just in case I ran into bear, cougar, wolves, or stupid human beings. I mainly feared running into stupid human beings. I didn't ever want to get caught up in some kind of "Deliverance" movie scenario with one or more crazy men in the woods. I figured that I would simply cap their asses if anyone ever threatened my family, friends, or myself. Fortunately, I've run into none of the above. I've was never threatened by any animal or human in SOHA.

Finally, there I was in the SOHA base camp, setting up the area for my first solo trip. Dr. William York, who always hiked far away from the established base camp to sleep alone at night, would have been proud of me. I was all alone except for my seven-pound Toy Fox Terrier, Atlas. He was my eyes and ears for anything trying to sneak up on me when I had my back turned or was simply being distracted by other activities. After I had rung the large cow bell, set up the tent, chair, bins, table, and other items, Atlas and I took a hike in the woods. I wanted to see if the Bigfoot Forest People had created any other large and noticeable tree structures. Nope, didn't find anything. However, Atlas and I most certainly enjoyed the refreshing walk through the beautiful woods.

Later that night, I started a campfire and was kicking back in my chair. I had strategically placed my chair with my back against the Suburban so nothing could sneak up from behind me. As usual, Atlas was sitting on my lap. Around 10 pm at night, the local Bigfoot Forest People family started to arrive at the SOHA base camp area and position themselves around the perimeter. They all seemed to have their favorite spots that they would occupy more often than not when they were visiting. Eventually, I could hear them make their way from the edge of the perimeter and head over to the gifting bowls that were located about one-hundred-fifty feet away from camp.

Occasionally, I could hear them out by the bowls talking to one another. I would imagine them passing the gifting bowls around while they were snacking and talking. Although I couldn't understand their language, every once in a while, I could tell it was the adult male or adult female or one of the kids talking. Around midnight, I was contemplating peeing in the designated area on the perimeter, one last time, and then crawling into my tent to go to bed. Well, right at that moment, I suddenly heard very heavy and loud bipedal steps come running from the gifting bowl area toward the base camp.

My heart began to beat very fast, my adrenaline kicked in full force, and I was scared to death. The running sounded very aggressive. I thought I was going to see one of the Bigfoot Forest People run straight into the SOHA base camp. I seriously thought I was going to die up there on the mountain. However, at the last moment, the adolescent male veered off to my right, his left, and stood behind the bushes at the trailhead. He just stood there watching me as I continued to sit there in my chair with my back against the Suburban. I eventually calmed down, and said "hello" to him. After a few more minutes, he turned and walked back to the gifting bowl area.

The fact that my adrenaline just got jacked up to full throttle made me not so tired at the moment. I stayed awake for another hour and played some music on my MP3 player which I had hooked up to my portable Bose speaker. I knew that they loved the music and, quite frankly, I needed to listen to it as well so I could calm down. Afterwards, I returned to my chair and started talking with the family members who had now returned to the perimeter of the base camp. I explained to them that I was there because I wanted to be their friend. I told them that I was grateful to them for allowing me to be there with them.

Atlas, who was sleeping on my lap, lifted his head up and looked over toward the 3:00 o'clock position. He cocked his head and looked as if someone was talking to him. I heard absolutely nothing. He stood up on my lap and his little tail started wagging a million miles per hour. Suddenly, he jumped off of my lap and ran straight over to the 3:00 o'clock position with his tail still wagging. He ran into the brush and trees and into the dark.

I was desperately calling out his name, "Atlas! Atlas! Get back here, Atlas! Come here, boy! Come on! Atlas! Come here now!" Well, normally he would come back to me if I called him like that but he didn't. I began to fear that I was going to hear him scream and see his little legs being tossed back into the base camp. A couple minutes later, Atlas came back into camp with his tail still wagging one million miles per hour. He was as happy as he'd ever been and he looked like he just spent several minutes with his best friend. I thought to myself, "What the heck, they can mind speak with dogs too? Wow!" They obviously were calling him out of the base camp to come visit with them. After that, I didn't worry any longer when he would act like someone was calling him and he would run out into the brush and trees and the dark.

The following day, I went off the mountain and spent the day with my son, Grady. He lives with his mother in Grants Pass, Oregon. After a fun day of playing with Grady, I returned to the SOHA base camp. Along the way, I had stopped at the Albertson's grocery store to purchase some peanut butter, wheat bread, raspberry jam, and other goodies for the Bigfoot Forest People as well as some goodies for me too. Upon my arrival to base camp, I quickly made the peanut butter and jelly sandwiches, put them in the cleaned out gifting bowls, and delivered them to the gifting spot just before the sun set. Yes, I sang "Row, Row, Row Your Boat" to them twice and then whistled the tune as I delivered the goodies. I took the before picture and then returned to the base camp.

Once in the SOHA base camp, I relaxed in my chair with my back against the Suburban. I snacked on some of my goodies and gave Atlas some dog treats too. Eventually, I got up and walked around the campfire in the center of the base camp while I played my music to the local family. I would sit down and rest, snack again, and talk to them from my position of safety. Then I would stand up again, throw a couple logs on the fire, and play some more music.

At bedtime, I would routinely pull up the same song on my MP3 player and play it before I would go to sleep. Guess what the song was? Yep, you're right, "Row, Row, Row Your Boat." I would play the song and then sing it to them. I would thank them for allowing me to be in their home and remind them that I wanted to be their friend. As the fire was dying down, both Atlas and I crawled into the tent and fell fast asleep.

Around 3:00 am, I woke up from a sound sleep. I could see that the fire had burned itself out and it was pitch dark outside. Surprisingly, I heard some heavy footed bipedal steps approach the right side of my tent. I slowly reached for my gun which was on the floor to my right side. I had my hand on the gun and my finger on the trigger. Then I clearly heard mind speak inside my head, "Take your hand off the gun." I removed my hand. The steps came closer to my tent. I slowly reached for my gun again. Then I heard again, "Take your hand off the gun." I complied and put my right hand back inside my sleeping bag.

The adolescent male Bigfoot Forest Person began the process of zapping me. I felt my body relax and become immobilized. My mind was clear and alert. Although I was comfortable, Atlas was not so comfortable. He was inside my sleeping bag digging a hole through the left side of my chest and I couldn't do anything about it. After a short period of time, he stopped and lay down beside me in my sleeping bag.

The adolescent male accessed my memories from earlier in the day while I was shopping at the Albertson's store. He showed me grabbing the peanut butter, the raspberry jam, and the wheat bread off of the store shelves and paying for it. Then he showed me washing the gifting bowls while wearing the surgical gloves, making the sandwiches, putting the goodies inside the bowls, and then placing the gifting bowls outside of camp in their designated spot right off the trail. Then he asked me a question via mind speak, "What are your intentions?"

Well, that came out of left field. I didn't see that one coming. Matter of fact, as I laid there thinking through his question, I became frustrated. Seriously? I've been out here for several years doing the same thing over and over and over again. I've constantly told you guys my name and that I wanted to be your friend. I've consistently been leaving food for you and playing music for all of you and you're asking me what my intentions are? Well, I didn't answer him. I thought my actions clearly spoke about what my intentions were.

I guess I frustrated him too like he was frustrating me. He decided to run me through the same exact memories for a second time. He showed me grabbing the peanut butter, the raspberry jam, and the wheat bread off of the store shelves and paying for it. Then he showed me washing the gifting bowls while wearing the surgical gloves, making the sandwiches, putting the goodies inside the bowls, and then placing the gifting bowls outside of camp in their designated spot right off the trail. Then he asked me the same exact question again via mind speak, "What are your intentions?"

Well, I could be just as stubborn as him. I laid there saying nothing. Once again, I thought that my consistent behaviors spoke clearly as to what my intentions have been over the years. I've clearly told them what my intentions were while standing up in the base camp and addressing them while they stood behind the bushes and trees. Why on God's green Earth was he asking me such a silly question?

Well, the adolescent male Bigfoot Forest Person proved to be more stubborn than me. Guess what? Yup! He ran me through the same dang memories for a third time. He showed me grabbing the peanut butter, the raspberry jam, and the wheat bread off of the store shelves and paying for it. Then he showed me washing the gifting bowls while wearing the surgical gloves, making the sandwiches, putting the goodies inside the bowls, and then placing the gifting bowls outside of camp in their designated spot right off the trail. Then he asked me the same exact question for a third time via mind speak, "What are your intentions?"

I felt and heard myself let out a frustrated sigh in my mind and I finally answered his question: "To earn your trust and friendship." He immediately responded, "Thank you!"

Now, I'm going to try and do my best to help you comprehend what happened at that exact moment in time. You see, I didn't just hear him respond, "Thank you!" I actually felt his emotions behind his expression of "Thank you!" That's right, I felt his emotions. They were not my emotions. They were most definitely his emotions. He was very happy. Really happy. I even felt him let his guard down and felt him bond emotionally to me. Suddenly we were connected. We had a male bonding moment. We became close friends.

He stopped the zapping process and I shot back up to a 10 while he walked away from the SOHA base camp. I laid there in the pitch dark totally elated. I was so happy to have heard and felt his "Thank you!" I liken that experience to watching an episode of Star Trek and seeing Spock engage in a Vulcan mind meld. The viewers watched Spock connect telepathically with his subject and read their mind and go through their memories. However, he could also feel their emotions. That's exactly what I experienced with the adolescent male. We were telepathically connected and I heard his thoughts and felt his emotions. I also felt his affection toward me. I knew that I no longer ever had to reach for my gun. My fear was gone. In the end, I was grateful that he was more stubborn than I was.

Starting from that day forward, things started getting wildly crazy at SOHA. I'm talking exponentially off the charts. They started coming to the edge of the base camp and would show themselves much more often. Occasionally, they would breach the perimeter, step inside the base camp area, stand there for a minute or two, and then walk back out of camp. I was looking forward to seeing where all of this was going to go. The rabbit hole just got way deeper.

CHAPTER FIFTEEN

COME OUT AND PLAY
IN THE DARK

After my male bonding experience with the adolescent Bigfoot Forest Person in the Southern Oregon Habituation Area (SOHA), I simply had no more fear. I was no longer worried about the possibility that one of them was going to, sooner or later, hurt my family, friends, or me. After all, there's so much misinformation on the internet in various Bigfoot Facebook Groups regarding how the Bigfoot species are malevolent and waiting for the right time to cannibalize all of humanity. Well, I had firsthand experience that I was absolutely in no danger at all. Whew! It was nice to kiss my fear goodbye. But was it really gone for good or did I have more room for growth regarding my learning how to trust the Bigfoot Forest People?

As I continued to make multiple trips to SOHA, with friends or by myself, I started to hear the same mind speak message over and over again: "No lights!" At first, I wasn't sure what was meant by that message. Then during one trip, Cynthia and I were camping out in SOHA and we had the lantern on top of the hood of the Suburban. It wasn't quite dark yet and we both happened to be looking in the direction of the vehicle at the same time when we saw the lantern fly off the hood and land on the ground about ten feet away. No, gravity didn't cause it to slide on the curved hood and slide off the front of the car. The lantern did exactly what I said it did. It flew off the hood of the Suburban in a horizontal direction and landed on the ground ten feet in front of the Suburban. Then, you guess it, "No lights!"

We began to carefully warn and instruct our guests to SOHA that we had implemented a "No lights" policy. When asked why, we would simply explain to them that the Bigfoot Forest People did not want us to have any lights on at night. They preferred to interact with us in the dark. Therefore, no more lanterns, campfires, headlamps, or flashlights. Well, we would allow the use of flashlights if someone had to dig through a duffle bag to find something in the dark. However, no one could use their flashlights to point toward the bushes and trees. Matter of fact, we went out of our way to make sure that we had everything staged before it got dark so we didn't have to dig through our bags or the vehicle to find something later in the dark.

Well, it worked. The Bigfoot Forest People started coming in closer and closer to the base camp. They had no fear of us trying to light them up with a flashlight or with the flash of a camera. They appreciated us respecting their request as well as our demonstration of trust in them because we no longer feared being around them in the dark. In a nutshell, we were submitting to their requests and giving them the upper hand. Well, they've always had the upper hand. Nevertheless, spending time in the base camp without any light, all night long, definitely felt like being placed in a submissive and vulnerable position.

You wouldn't believe the number of men who came out to SOHA with me who had a problem with the "No lights" policy. Some of them were very honest with me and admitted that they were afraid of the dark. They would go out of their way to tell me that they didn't fear any animals in the forest, including the Bigfoot Forest People, but they could never get over their personal fear of the dark. One gentleman said to me, "Matt, I've been afraid of the dark ever since I was a kid. To this day, I have to sleep with a nightlight on in my bedroom." I assured him that he was going to be fine. The first night was always the scariest night for most of the attendees in SOHA. However, when they woke up alive the following morning, they weren't as scared on the second and third nights.

During one solo trip to SOHA, I was snuggled inside my sleeping bag in the tent. Atlas was resting on top of the sleeping bag down by my feet. As I was starting to drift off, I was startled by a noise over by the Suburban about thirty feet away from me. The adolescent male had lifted up the camp stove on the table and then set it back down. Then I heard him drag the garbage bag, slowly but surely, across the ground from the table all the way over to in front of my tent. Please keep in mind that the garbage bag wasn't so heavy that he had to drag it all the way. He could have carried it over to the tent. Instead, I believe that he playfully wanted to get my attention. Well, he most definitely had my attention.

He then swiped the front of my tent at the ground level with the garbage bag. I felt it brush against my feet at the front of the tent. Atlas jumped up, ran up the sleeping bag to my head, and then dove inside the sleeping bag. The adolescent male picked up the garbage bag and swiped the front of my tent for a second time at the ground level. Finally, he did it a third time. I was laying there wondering what the heck he was trying to do. Then he dragged the garbage bag across the dead end cul-de-sac at the end of the dead end logging road and walked away.

I laid flat on my back inside my sleeping bag totally perplexed as to why he just did what he did. Eventually, I fell asleep. When the sun came up later that morning, I got out of my tent and made my way across the cul-de-sac and found the garbage bag tied to the trees. Yes, that's right, tied to the tree with the plastic ties from the garbage bag itself. Wow! Why did he do this? Well, I eventually concluded that he did it because he wanted me to come out of my tent and sleep outside.

Well, that wasn't going to happen. Instead, it freaked me out so I started sleeping in the back of my Suburban. I know, I know. My fear was all gone, right? Well, apparently not. I obviously still had some fear within me and I believe that the adolescent male was carefully and gently confronting my fears. One night, while sleeping in the back of the Suburban with Grady, I woke up because I thought I heard a knock on the window but I fell quickly back to sleep. I was very exhausted and I don't think that anything or anyone could have kept me awake at that moment in time.

When I returned home from my trip to SOHA with Grady, as usual, I started to listen to hours and hours of audio recordings. Sure enough, during that moment in time, I clearly heard the adolescent male walk into the base camp, mess with a couple of items on the table, and then walk over to the Suburban and knock on the window a couple of times. Then he walked away.

After the tent incident and the window knocking, I couldn't conclude anything other than the fact that the adolescent male Bigfoot Forest Person wanted me to start sleeping outside in the open under the stars. Once again, he was giving me an opportunity to show him that I trusted him rather than feared him. I was learning that I still had lots of fear to overcome. I was learning that fear was a barrier to relationship building with the Bigfoot Forest People. They don't like it when we fear them.

I thought it through and concluded that the wall of a nylon tent or the glass window of a Suburban wasn't going to stop a Bigfoot Forest Person from getting a hold of me and killing me if they really wanted to do so, right? Isn't it silly that so many people feel safer within their tent at night than they do sleeping out in the open under the stars? Too funny. We're like little kids, hiding under blankets in bed, because if the Boogie Man can't see you, then it can't get you. News flash! A Bigfoot can get you through your tent wall, your camper wall, or through the glass window of your vehicle. Also, if they were as dangerous as some Bigfoot researchers would like everyone to believe, then why did I keep waking up alive every morning after morning after morning, month after month, year after year? Simple applied logic leads to only one conclusion: The Bigfoot Forest People aren't dangerous and they want us to be outside with them in the dark. They want us to trust them. They don't want us to fear them.

Once I amended the protocol in SOHA to include the mandatory sleeping outside on cots, the activity level started increasing again. I began to see a pattern develop, the less fear we displayed and the more trust we demonstrated to them, the more they reached out to us. Also, I learned that some people simply weren't willing to overcome their fears. When I told some potential guests that they weren't going to be able to sleep inside a tent or their vehicle, they opted out of coming to SOHA.

Although they wanted to see and possibly interact with the Bigfoot Forest People, the thought that they could wake up in the middle of the night with one of them standing right next to their cot and checking them out was just too scary for them to overcome.

As time passed, we were viewing more and more silhouettes with eye glow on the edge of the perimeter of the SOHA base camp. We were also beginning to experience them coming into our main camp area cloaked. They would playfully poke our back or arm or pull on our clothing. Occasionally, someone sitting in a camp chair was lucky enough to resolve a shoulder and neck rub. We were also starting to see more orbs zipping around the base camp too. SOHA was starting to become a very magical place. The happiest place on Earth.

In November of 2013, I was out in SOHA with Michael Beers and Gunnar Monson. They were sitting in their chairs with their backs to the Suburban while I was walking around the edge of the perimeter playing my music. The light on my device was lighting up the attendees while I was playing my music to them. I walked from the 9:00 o'clock position on the perimeter to the 12:00 o'clock position and then over to the 3:00 o'clock position. During my musical sweep of the perimeter, I managed to count the presence of eight juvenile belly crawlers, three toddlers, and three adolescents. It was obvious to me that we had way more attendees than just the local family.

I walked over to the Suburban and told the guys what I had seen and counted. Michael said that while I was at the 12:00 o'clock position, he saw a juvenile walk out of the brush behind me. When I started to turn back in the young one's direction, he darted back into the brush. They both suggested that I sweep the perimeter again and count while I played some more music to them. I did as both Gunnar and Michael requested and I counted fourteen of them again: Eight juvenile belly crawlers, three toddlers, and three adolescents.

While I was standing at the 9:00 o'clock position on the perimeter and playing my music, I had three belly crawlers right in front of me on the other side of the berm. They didn't seem to care that I could see them. They were more interested in watching the music video on my cell phone while the music was playing. Suddenly, off in the distance about sixty feet back from the edge of the road, I saw two Beings of Light appear. They were about eight feet tall and they were translucent. I could see right through them. I could see the outline of their head, neck, shoulders, arms, trunk, and legs.

If that wasn't shocking enough, I began to see a fog of light emanate from their feet. It was flowing across the ground like fog on a Broadway stage created by using dry ice and water. The fog of light was illuminating the entire area. While I stood there looking at these two Beings of Light, I began to feel a strong sense of unconditional love. Overwhelming, unconditional love. I was moved to tears as I stood there. In the meantime, the three belly crawling juveniles were still watching the music video on my cell phone and didn't seem to be bothered by the event. I seriously contemplated walking up the berm, past the juveniles, and straight to the Beings of Light. However, I didn't want to upset the parents of the little ones.

As quickly as the Beings of Light appeared, they disappeared, and the illuminating light was gone. It was dark again. I walked over to Michael and Gunnar and sat down. They could tell that I was emotionally moved by something. They could see the tears rolling down my cheeks. They asked what happened and I told them. They told me that they saw the area light up but they weren't sitting in a position to be able to see the two Beings of Light off in the distance. Those two gentlemen were very kind and supportive. They never once disrespected me or questioned the veracity of my experience.

The next morning, we awoke at sunrise and went out to check the gifting bowls. We knew that more had shown up to join us on the edge of the perimeter of the SOHA base camp so I had placed eight peanut butter and raspberry jelly sandwich halves into each gifting bowl. There was a total of sixteen sandwich halves. When we arrived at the gifting bowl area, we were amazed by what we found. There were only two sandwich halves left in the bowls. In other words, the fourteen younger Bigfoot Forest People that I counted on the perimeter the night before each took one sandwich half (i.e., Sixteen minus fourteen equals two). All three of us were blown away. Not to mention that we found fingerprints on the bowls too.

It turned out that sleeping out in the open and implementing our "No lights" policy helped to enhance our experience at SOHA. The more that we demonstrated that we trusted them and had no fear, the more they would notch up the interaction level. By the way, at the time of the event, I had absolutely no idea who the Beings of Light were. All I knew was that if we hadn't implemented the "No lights" policy, I would have never seen the light. There's more to come.

CHAPTER SIXTEEN

CIRCUMSTANTIAL EVIDENCE

People are funny. No matter how much Bigfoot evidence I share with them, they always want me to show them more. I'm convinced that ninety-five percent of Bigfoot Researchers must live in the State of Missouri – "The Show Me State." There's also the possibility that ninety-five percent of Bigfoot Researchers are direct descendants of 'Doubting Thomas.' He refused to believe in the resurrection of Jesus Christ unless he saw him with his own eyes, touched the wound on his side, and the wounds on his hands. He wasn't going to believe the witness testimony of the other disciples who did see him after Jesus' resurrection. Talk about a hard sell.

Some people demand that you do things their way in order to satisfy them even though their way is producing little if any evidence at all. In actuality, they should be doing things my way because my way is producing results. Nope. Not good enough for them. Some individuals are extremely narcissistic and think that the world revolves around them and their demands. They want what they want and they want it now. Give me! Give me! Give me!

Over the years, I've been sarcastically asked where all of my Trail Cam pictures or videos are. I remind them that when I was actually using the high-tech equipment in the past, we never captured a Bigfoot Forest Person on film or video. We did catch a Black Bear, once, licking the lens of the video camera and obtained a nice shot down its throat. Other than that, we got absolutely nothing significant. Then I reverse their question on them, and ask them, where are all their pictures and videos of the Bigfoot Forest People. Naturally, they don't have the very thing that they're demanding me to produce for them.

I've learned over the years that Trail Cams and Video Cameras function as repellent to the Bigfoott Forest People. They get frustrated with me and say something like, "Well, if you have them so close to you every night, then you should be able to produce a picture or video." The silly knuckleheads never let it sink in through their thick heads that the reason why we have them up close and personal every night is because we aren't trying to take their pictures. We're simply interested in building a trusting relationship with them. I encourage them to put their high-tech equipment away and do likewise. Some have honestly confessed to me that they're too afraid to do what I'm doing out in the field. They prefer to keep the Bigfoot Forest People at a distance. We're talking about big names in Bigfootdom who fear the dark, fear being vulnerable, and fear that the Bigfoot Forest People are going to hurt them, kidnap them, or kill them. They're not willing to allow logic to override their irrational fears (i.e., If the Bigfoot Forest People wanted them dead, they would be dead one-hundred times over already by now).

Let's face it most Bigfoot evidence is circumstantial at best. Without a body, we will never have direct evidence that the Bigfoot Forest People exists. Please DO NOT misinterpret this factual statement as some kind of 'Pro-Kill' endorsement. I'm NOT 'Pro-Kill' and we can't kill them anyway. By the way, anyone who claims that they have killed a Bigfoot Forest Person is a liar. I'll explain why later in the book. Anyway, my point is that all any Bigfoot researcher has is circumstantial evidence. Now, between you and me, I believe that Bigfoot researchers over the decades have collected enough circumstantial evidence, combined with witness testimony, to prove that the Bigfoot Forest People exists. A jury of their peers would agree.

In other words, we don't actually need a body to prove that they exist. Nevertheless, there's enough Missourians and 'Doubting Thomas' out there in society that they will never accept the existence of the Bigfoot Forest People based on circumstantial evidence and eye-witness testimony. It's a hopeless cause. Well, just so I'm clear, I'm NOT writing my book for them because it doesn't matter what I or anyone else says or what evidence we provide, they're simply not going to believe it unless they see Bigfoot with their own eyes. Doubters are going to doubt and haters are going to hate. It's in their DNA. Hopefully, they'll have their own life-changing encounter someday.

Instead, I'm writing this book for kind people with good hearts and open minds. Those individuals who don't need to see direct evidence to believe that they actually exist. Instead, they're open to being influenced by convincing circumstantial evidence and witness testimony. Therefore, to help you understand what I mean is that circumstantial evidence in a trial, which is not directly from an eyewitness or participant, requires some reasoning to prove a fact. There is a public perception that such evidence is weak ("all they have is circumstantial evidence"), but the probable conclusion from the circumstances may be so strong that there can be little doubt as to a vital fact ("beyond a reasonable doubt" in a criminal case, and "a preponderance of the evidence" in a civil case).

Particularly in criminal cases, 'eyewitness' ("I saw Frankie shoot Johnny") type evidence is often lacking and may be unreliable, so circumstantial evidence becomes essential. Prior threats to the victim, fingerprints found at the scene of the crime, ownership of the murder weapon, and the accused being seen in the neighborhood, certainly point to the suspect as being the killer, but each bit of evidence is circumstantial (Law.Com).

During my years of Bigfoot research, I've collected a lot of convincing circumstantial evidence from my various research areas. We've collected Bigfoot Forest People foot casts of all sizes on a variety of mountainsides. We've collected toddler tracks, juvenile tracks, adolescent tracks, and adult tracks. The longest set of tracks actually came from Zorth in the Southern Oregon Interaction Area (SOIA). They were twenty-six-inches long, eleven inches across at the toes, and seven inches across at the heel.

If you pay close attention, finding and collecting the Bigfoot tracks out in the wilderness can provide more information than just who left the tracks behind. For example, in one research area, Dr. William York and I found a set of tracks that were obviously made by a young juvenile and adult female. They were walking up a hill onto a logging road. Once they reached the logging road, you could clearly see that the young juvenile was playfully walking across the dead end cul-de-sac. The young one was digging his heel in the ground and then sliding his right foot forward. Then digging the other heel in the ground and sliding the left foot forward. We could picture the scenario in our minds and enjoyed a laugh together. We had fun trying to mimic the young one.

On another occasion, during my 'Old School' researcher days, we found an eighteen-inch track across a gulley where a Bigfoot Forest Person was watching our camp during the previous night. We had a media crew out there with us that night and the producer was extremely angry with the cameraman for not bringing enough juice to power up their night vision camera for more than thirty minutes. The really cool thing was that six months later, approximately six miles away from our campsite, we actually found the same track on another mountainside. It was a perfect match, including a tiny outgrowth on the side of the foot in the same exact spot.

Finally, regarding cool Bigfoot track stories, I had a guest, Andrea Billups, with me at the Southern Oregon Habituation Area (SOHA). Although she is a Bigfoot Forest People enthusiast, she was not a camper. She is a girlie girl. Pink is the color of her national flag. Yet, to her credit, she didn't let her lack of camping experience or fear of sleeping out in the open on cots deter her from coming along with me. However, she did have conditions. She wanted me to place her cot parallel to my F-150 pickup truck and about three feet away from it. I had to place the table at the foot of her cot. I had to be sleeping close by on the other side of her cot and we had to place the head of our cots near the brush. In short, Andrea wanted to be surrounded on all sides so there would be no room for the Bigfoot Forest People to come up to her at night, while she slept, and check her out.

Guess what? The next morning, Miss Andrea was shocked to find juvenile tracks around her cot. Based on the fingerprints that we found on the floorboard of my F-150 pickup truck, a juvenile managed to shimmy across the ground on his back underneath my truck. Then he used his hands to grab the floor board and pull himself out from underneath the truck. Needless to say, Miss Andrea was blown away that, in spite of the fortress built around her, they were still able to get to her anyway.

Speaking of fingerprints, we managed to collect a hand cast out of the ground in my early 'Old School' days. We had set up a 'bait pile' for the 'dumb giant mountain apes' and raked out the ground around the tempting food. Well, they weren't so dumb. One of them got on his knees and leaned on one hand while grabbing the food with his other hand. In other words, the indentations in the ground clearly told a story that the Bigfoot Forest Person noticed that the ground was raked and did everything possible to avoid the raked area. By the way, this wasn't the first time that we saw circumstantial evidence showing them avoiding our other raked areas.

During my time in the Southern Oregon Habituation Area (SOHA), while utilizing the stainless steel dog food bowls otherwise known as gifting bowls, we were able to collect numerous fingerprints and hand-prints. Please remember that I would wear surgical gloves, clean the bowls out, place the food in them, and then carry the bowls out about one-hundred-fifty feet from the SOHA base camp. Then I would retrieve the bowls in the morning, with witnesses present, while wearing surgical gloves again. In short, any fingerprints found on the gifting bowls did not come from me or any members of my research party.

Every morning at sunrise, when we would go out to retrieve the gifting bowls before the forest woke up, it was like Christmas morning. I loved taking my guests out there and watching them respond to what we would find waiting for us. What food did they take? What food did they leave behind? Was there any evidence of little critters or birds hitting the gifting bowls? Never, I might add. There was never any evidence that little critters or birds were hitting the gifting bowls. Anyway, then the best of all possible circumstantial evidence, were there any finger-prints or handprints on the gifting bowls? When my guests saw all of the circumstantial evidence in the gifting bowls and around the gifting bowls (i.e., Footprints on the ground), combined with the fingerprints and handprints, they were sold. They were amazed. Santa delivered the goodies in the SOHA stockings. My guests learned that I don't lie and I don't hoax. If I say it happened, guess what? It happened. All of my guests left SOHA as believers.

We also found very large nonhuman handprints on the windows of our Suburban and Subaru. With the help of Jaime Alvarez, we were able to lift the handprint from the window and secure them to a large piece of paper. Cynthia works for a law enforcement agency as a Justice Systems Support Supervisor. She makes sure that the data is available to a variety of law enforcement agencies to help catch the bad guys. She took the prints to their fingerprint specialist of twenty years. He concluded that they weren't human. He also concluded that they didn't come from any known primate that he ever studied at the zoo in Seattle, Washington. Now that's pretty cool.

Speaking of eating food out of the gifting bowls, when you put gifting bowls out between three to nine times per month for a total of five years in SOHA, you begin to recognize patterns. For example, the Bigfoot Forest People seldom, if ever took the food on the first night. Although we could hear and see them hanging around the perimeter, it was like there was some social custom that prevented them from taking the food on the first night it was offered. Occasionally, when I would arrive at SOHA, I wouldn't put out any food on the first night. Then I would put it out for the first time on the second night. Guess what? They wouldn't take the food on the first night it was offered even though it was offered during the second night we were there. Very fascinating.

The only violation of this social custom occurred when the toddler was allowed to start visiting the perimeter of the SOHA base camp with his adolescent brother and juvenile sister. It was really cute; the toddler was just as impulsive as any young human child. Also, just like a human child, the toddler would pull the sandwich halves apart, lick out the peanut butter from the one half and then lick out the raspberry jam from the other slice of bread and then put them back together and place them back inside the gifting bowl. The toddler did the same thing with the Oreo Cookie. As time passed, the toddler learned to comply with the social custom of not taking the food on the first night it was offered.

On a side note, just a brief rabbit trail moment, when the toddler was introduced to the perimeter of the SOHA base camp, the daddy walked up the hillside and walked completely around the entire perimeter as loud and heavy footed as possible – two nights in a row. He was clearly sending us a message, "That's my baby and you better not mess with him." Trust me, we never tried to mess with any of them. We just talked, laughed, sang, played instruments, whistled tunes, and played recorded music.

Back to the gifting bowls. After about three years of placing the gifting bowls about one-hundred-fifty feet from the perimeter of the base camp, I decided to change things up. I decided to place the gifting bowls only twenty-five feet away from the perimeter. Although the bowls were still hidden behind trees and brush from our viewing them from the base camp, daddy was not pleased with the change. As we sat there in the dark in the middle of camp, we could hear them at the gifting bowls. When one of the kids reached for the food in the gifting bowls, daddy let out a very loud, gruffy, grunty whoop. It was so loud; we almost fell over backwards in our chairs. How did we know that daddy responded to one of his kids reaching for the food? Well, the next morning we checked out the bowls and found only one chocolate covered peanut missing. Even though we moved the gifting bowls back to their original positions, daddy wouldn't allow his children to take any food from the gifting bowls during the remainder of that trip to SOHA. He apparently put us in timeout. The following trip, he allowed them to take food again.

During one trip, when I placed the sandwich halves inside the gifting bowls along the edge, I placed ten pieces of Candy Corn in a circle in the center of the bowl with the white tips facing toward the center. The next morning, when we went out to retrieve the gifting bowls, the ten pieces of Candy Corn were found to be repositioned inside the bowl into two straight lines of five. After the second night, the circle of ten Candy Corn were repositioned inside the bowl into a Triangle shape. Please tell me what little critter or bird is going to rearrange geometric figures into different geometric figures inside a gifting bowl filled with other food? That's right! None! No little critters or birds can engage in such behaviors. Not possible.

On another occasion, Johnny Manson and I went to check on the gifting bowls during December of 2013. Although there was some food missing, the major circumstantial evidence that we found was several Peanut M&Ms in the bowl that had been obviously sucked on and then spit out back inside the bowl. They were sitting there waiting for us in a pool of saliva. We cleaned out a Tupperware container with rubbing alcohol and then placed the M&Ms and saliva inside and sealed the container with duct tape. It's been sitting in our freezer for the past three years waiting to be analyzed by a trustworthy DNA expert.

Why haven't we had them analyzed yet? Well, because it cost thousands and thousands of dollars. Also, the analyst has to be trustworthy. In other words, some of the go-to experts that most people have relied upon in the past appear to be self-serving rather than sincerely seeking the truth. When the right opportunity comes along, we will have them analyzed.

Once we placed a basket out in the gifting area and put food inside of it. In order to get the food out, the individual had to hold it open. When we came back a week later to check on the basket, the lid had been torn off of it. We found fingerprints on the bottom of the basket. We also found long strands of black hair caught by the woven basket. I sent the hair samples off to an analyst in Australia who confirmed that they were not human hairs, black bear hairs, or any known primate hairs. That was nice confirmation. No, he doesn't analyze saliva.

Some other circumstantial evidence that we discovered in SOHA was the massive tree structures on the ridgeline. They picked up large trees and would move them around, lean them on one another, and weave them between each other to create designs and structures. On other occasions, they would take a tree and snap it about nine feet off the ground and then lay it over the top of another tree that they bent over in order to hold it down after they wove that bent tree in and out of other trees in front of it. There was no way that structures like this were the result of snow snaps or wind storms. They were intentionally manipulated by very large upright beings.

On another occasion, Cynthia and I left the SOHA base camp to go for a hike. When we came back awhile later, we found about twenty pinecones laid in a row on the trail leading back to camp. At the end of the straight line of pine cones, was a geometrical design made of sticks, pinecones, and rocks. None of that was on the trail when we left the camp for our hike. However, it was amazing to find it waiting for us upon our return to camp.

On another occasion, while I was in SOHA on a solo trip, Atlas and I hiked away from camp for about two hours. When we returned to the base camp, I found one of his old hollow chew sticks with a feather stuck inside of it waiting for me on my cot. That was an awesome gift from them to me. Oh, I neglected to mention that within a minute of our initial arrival at SOHA, Atlas and I were greeted with a rock that was tossed into camp by my feet. One minute later, a large pinecone was tossed into camp by my feet. That was their way of saying "hello" to me.

Is that enough circumstantial evidence for you? Are you convinced yet that I've been habituating with a family of Bigfoot Forest People? Just in case I still need to push you over the edge into belief, I would like to remind you that I had been using a Bionic Ear parabolic microphone dish and a Sony digital recorder to capture the Bigfoot Forest People talking, singing, humming, whistling, whooping, hooting, barking, and tree knocking. Would you like to listen to them? Lean closer to the book. Shhhhhhhhhhhhhhh!!! Do you hear them? No? Well then, you'll have to go online to SoundCloud.Com and type in "Team Squatchin USA" and listen to a plethora of recordings.

By the way, I'm not talking about listening to hours of record-ings. I'm actually talking about you needing to take days and days to listen to all of my recordings. If you're smart, you'll scroll down to the bottom of the page and begin with the oldest recordings and then move forward to the newer recordings. Oh, please don't forget to listen to them with your HEADPHONES. Not your cell phone speaker. Not your earbuds. Not your crappy computer speakers. Please listen to them with your HEADPHONES.

Well, there you have it. There's my circumstantial evidence. If you would like to look at pictures or read more about my evidence, please go to my website: TeamSquatchinUSA.Com. There are lots of pictures there along with blogs and other interesting information to learn from. I would also like to invite you to join my Facebook Group by going to the search window and typing: Team Squatchin USA. We have over 8,000 members who have lots of good information to share with you. Many of them are still learning about the Bigfoot Forest People phenomena just like you.

CHAPTER SEVENTEEN

MULTIPLE EYEWITNESS TESTIMONIES

Eyewitness testimony is a legal term. It refers to an account given by people of an event they have witnessed. For example, they may be required to give a description at a trial of a robbery or a road accident someone has seen. This includes identification of perpetrators, details of the crime scene, etc. (SimplyPsychology.com).

When it comes to the Bigfoot Forest People phenomena, eyewitness testimonies are greatly relied upon as important data to support or back up the circumstantial evidence. Just look at various Bigfoot investigation websites on the internet. They will list numerous eyewitness sightings, classify them, and then supplement the reports with a Bigfoot investigator who has gone into the area afterwards to confirm the reported sighting through the collection of circumstantial evidence (i.e., Footprints, handprints, hair samples, etc.). In short, a solid and credible eyewitness combined with circumstantial evidence is a hard case to refute. Over the past five decades, the kingdom of Bigfootdom has been built, brick by brick, upon this simple truth: Eyewitness testimonies plus circumstantial evidence.

Just a reminder, this is exactly why my family's encounter on July 1, 2000, stood out like a sore thumb. An entire family experienced an encounter, a psychologist saw the Bigfoot Forest Person, and a National

Park Ranger found circumstantial evidence two days later. The credibility of my family, my credentials as a psychologist, and the confirmation of Ranger John Roth was very hard to dispute. That's why the media was all over my family's encounter like a cat on catnip.

Now, I'm smart enough to realize that the testimonies from multiple witnesses far surpasses the testimonies of the few or the one. Therefore, when I began to conduct my research in the Southern Oregon Research Area (SORA), which eventually changed to the Southern Oregon Habituation Area (SOHA), I knew that my individual testimony of the results that I was starting to glean from my research approach was not going to be enough to appease the skeptics. In other words, anyone can go out into the forest and make all kinds of claims, but if they're the only one experiencing those events, then it's easy for the masses to write them off as crazy or a hoaxer. Therefore, over a ten-year period of time, I managed to bring over forty witnesses with me to SOHA. Either we're all crazy or we're all liars or we're all telling the truth.

Likewise, if you want to establish credibility as a Bigfoot Forest People researcher, it's not enough to go out there by yourself, experience them, and then come back and report your data. Once again, you can be written off as crazy or a hoaxer. However, when you go to the great lengths to document your research as I have done, and I still do, utilizing multiple eyewitness testimonies, then it's harder for others to blow off your results.

I brought people out with me who are teachers, principals, attorneys, janitors, hairstylists, policemen, businessmen, avid hunters, military personnel, engineers, grocers, artists, investigators, computer technicians, pastors, mental health clinicians, music DJ's, financial planners, TV personalities, etc. Most have testified publicly about their experiences with me up in the mountains via my YouTube.com channel. Just go to YouTube.com, type in "Team Squatchin USA", and you'll come across over one-hundred-fifty videos to watch and learn from. Many of those videos include eyewitness testimonies from SOHA and SOIA.

I would like to share with you how I went about screening individuals to join me in my research area. It's very important that you don't just bring anyone along with you. First things first, do not bring anyone along with you who reeks of negativity. If they're dark on the inside, constantly treat others rudely and disrespectfully, and all they care about is themselves, I guarantee you that the Bigfoot Forest People will spot them a mile away and have nothing to do with them. They don't like 'A-Holes.'

In a couple of cases over the years, I've had people ask me to provide them with some consultation in order to assist them in improving the possibility of success in their research area. I always have them openly and honestly tell me about their research team members. Then if necessary, I'll hone in on an individual team member who is coming across to me as a potential 'A-Hole.' If my suspicions are confirmed, I'll tell them to cut the 'A-Hole' off of their team. Those who listen to me and have followed through with my advice started to see improvement in interactions almost immediately. Those who ignored my advice continued to experience very little, if anything at all, in their research areas.

In one case in the Midwest, a gentleman who ignored my advice at first because the guy that I identified as the proverbial 'A-Hole' on his team was his best friend, eventually cut his best friend off of his research team. As a result, he noticed an increase in visuals and interactions almost immediately. I don't care if the 'A-Hole' on your research team is your best friend or spouse, either they change their ways or you cut them from the team if you want to experience results. Serious Bigfooting is not about going out into the woods to have a fun time with your friends. Rather, it's about doing anything and everything to increase the likelihood of experiencing increased sightings and interactions. If you have to cut someone from the team, then cut them from the team. You can spend fun times with them doing other things besides Bigfooting with them.

Next, I screen for people to accompany me to my research area who are (1) kind, with (2) good hearts, and (3) open minds. They also have to be teachable and willing to submit to my protocol. If you have established a successful protocol in your research area and are experiencing the Bigfoot Forest People multiple times, why would you risk bringing someone out with you who thinks they know it all and who's un-teachable? They will set your research success backwards.

A couple of years ago, I had to withdraw my offer to bring a well-known figure in Bigfootdom with me to SOHA. I had been pestered for years to bring this gentleman to SOHA with me. However, when it came time for me to vet him like I do everyone else who comes to SOHA with me, this person became offended. They thought that they should be able to come to SOHA simply because of who they were and their status in the kingdom of Bigfootdom. I was left with no other choice but to inform this person that they weren't going to be able to come along. He most definitely did not have a teachable spirit about him.

The next thing that I would do when it came to inviting potential eyewitnesses to SOHA, I would have them sign a nondisclosure agreement (NDA). Contrary to the rumors that the TROLLS in Bigfootdom were spreading, the NDA did not prevent anyone from talking about their experiences in SOHA. Why on God's green Earth would I invite multiple witnesses to SOHA and then prohibit them from talking about their experiences while being there with me? That doesn't make any sense at all. Instead, the NDA encouraged them to talk about their experiences at SOHA. The only thing that the NDA prohibited anyone from doing was (1) not to tell anyone else where SOHA was located, and (2) never go back to SOHA unless they were coming back as my guest. Oh yes, plus I got their first-born child. Muhahahahahaha!

I always explained my protocol to my potential guests and told them that they would follow it to the letter of the law or I would escort them off the mountain and that they would never be welcomed back. This included no alcohol or drugs, peeing and pooping only in the identified areas, smoking in the designated spaces, no fires or lights, and absolutely no freaking out allowed. I always had to chuckle when individuals would respond to me with, "Freak out about what?" I would tell them about all of the potential things that they could see or experience while in SOHA, including waking up in the middle of the night to a Bigfoot Forest Person right next to their cot.

As I just said, they were told that they could not freak out. I would tell them that they were to act like they were a Navy Seal and that they were as strong as steel. Almost everyone who comes with me is totally scared to death on their first night to my research area. It's kind of cute. When they wake up the next morning, I'll look at them and ask them if they're alive? Naturally, they respond to me with a "Yes" and ask me why. I just remind them that the Bigfoot Forest People surrounded us last night and that it's important data to note that absolutely no one woke up dead in the morning. They get my point and manage to relax much more during their second and third nights to my research area.

Finally, I require my attendees to speak out about their experiences when they come to my research area. Multiple witness testimonies, that all see, experience, and say the same things over and over again, provide some serious credibility to my research methods and results. Their eyewitness testimony is especially compelling when combined with circumstantial evidence. Most of my multiple eyewitnesses have been willing to give their testimonies via my YouTube videos (please watch them in order from the oldest video first to the newest video last). Afterwards, they have talked with their family and friends about what they experienced in SOHA as well as participated in group discussions via my "Team Squatchin USA" Facebook Group page. Finally, several of them have provided written testimonies which you can read at the end of the book.

However, every once in a while, I'll run into individuals who hesitate to testify publicly, out of fear of retaliation from others. In other words, the kingdom of Bigfootdom can be very political and there are people out there who, don't want to hear the truth, nor do they want others validating the truth that I am sharing with the world. For example, initially, Ron Morehead and his fiancé, Keri Campbell, didn't want to testify publicly about coming to my research area nor share what they experienced in SOIA. Ron is well known and connected in Bigfootdom and he feared that some individuals might shun him or get on his case for hanging out with me and verifying my research results. Eventually, he spoke up and even submitted a write up for my book. Thank you very much, Ron and Keri.

Another example would be my third child, Micah. He came to my research area with me twice during the 2016 research season and was totally blown away. He told me that it turned out that his dad wasn't crazy after all. I needed to hear my son say that. Nevertheless, he wanted me to delay any public mentioning of his coming to my research area because he needed some time to process everything before he was willing to go public with his experiences. Micah plans to return to SOIA in the future.

Finally, I brought a world renowned Cryptozoologist to SOHA with me and he was so overwhelmed by what he experienced that he didn't want to tell anyone anything for fear of public ridicule. I'll discuss our 'out of this world' experience in the next chapter.

In conclusion, there's absolutely nothing wrong with you going out into your own area and keeping your experiences private. In that case, you're not trying to share your data with others nor are you trying to educate the world. Keep on Squatchin in privacy. On the other hand, if your goal is to share your data with others and you want to help educate the world about the Bigfoot Forest People phenomena, you're going to need to collect circumstantial evidence and you're going to need to supplement it with a whole lot of credible eyewitness testimonies. There's truth to be found in a multitude of eyewitnesses, especially when combined with a whole lot of circumstantial evidence. The skeptics can doubt or disbelieve you but they're much less likely to successfully deny information provided by a whole bunch of credible eyewitnesses.

CHAPTER EIGHTEEN

THROWING IN THE TOWEL

In June of 2014, I almost threw in the towel and walked away from my Bigfoot research adventures. I really believed that I was on the cusp of blowing the lid off of the Bigfoot Forest People phenomena. I thought I had most of it figured out. Then we experienced some events in the Southern Oregon Habituation Area (SOHA) that greatly overwhelmed and frustrated me. These events humbled me and showed me exactly how much I didn't know. I wasn't sure if I wanted to take the next step in my research. Was it going to take me another fifteen years to arrive at the next level of insight and knowledge? If it wasn't for many nights of pillow talk with Cynthia, I would have thrown in the towel and walked away from it all. I would have taken up something more mundane and boring like golfing or deep sea fishing. Please allow me to backup and explain to you exactly what happened during those four eventful nights in SOHA.

In early May of 2014, I was contacted by Adam Davies. He asked to spend four nights with me in SOHA. He's a British gentleman and an author, world-renowned cryptozoologist, adventurer, and tracker. He has participated in numerous documentaries for Monster Quest, National Geographic, and has been on the Finding Bigfoot TV show. I was excited to have someone with such a well-known reputation to accompany me in my research area. Talk about incredible validation of my research methods and results by someone whose reputation for telling the truth is impeccable. My response, "Heck yes, Adam, you can come to SOHA with me!"

Once Adam received the 'green light' from me that he could come to SOHA, he then asked if he could bring a friend of his along. My heart sank because if his friend was an 'A-Hole', I would have to say no. His name is John Carlson and he lives in New Jersey. Adam told me that he has known John for a long time and that they're good friends. He also shared that he's a paranormalist and very interested in the Bigfoot Forest People phenomena. I called John, vetted him, and approved him to come along with Adam. John is a true gentleman, courteous, friendly, and has a wonderful sense of humor. As time passed, I grew more and more excited about hosting Adam and John in SOHA.

Just before Adam flew over from England to the west coast of the United States, we had a Skype session and he informed me that he was going to be spending time at a well-known Bigfoot research center on the Olympic Peninsula, west of Seattle, Washington. Then he was going to spend four nights with me at SOHA. Finally, he was going to spend a few more nights at a well-known research area in northern California and then return home to England.

With bold confidence, during our Skype session, I told Adam, "Let me tell you exactly how your trip to the west coast is going to play out." He looked a little caught off guard by my statement but appeared curious to hear what I had to say. He said, "Okay", so I proceeded to share my bold and confident prediction with him.

I said, "Well, Adam, you're going to arrive to the location on the Olympic Peninsula and be blown away by the beauty of the area. You're going to meet and brush elbows with the 'who's who' in Bigfooting, enjoy good food and drinks, and spend time swapping Bigfoot stories with really nice people. Then you're going to hike up a mountain with way too many people, in an area infested with trail cams everywhere which act as Squatch repellant, and in the end, you will experience very little if any Bigfoot activity at all because that's not how you're supposed to go about Bigfooting. However, the good news is that you're going to enjoy the scenery, the food, the drinks, and the people because it's a very nice

Bigfoot social club. I know what I'm talking about, Adam, because I've been there before. You're going to have lots of fun but you're not going to experience anything significant regarding the Bigfoot phenomena."

I continued to share my bold and confident prediction with Adam by saying, "Then you're going to come to SOHA with me, spend four nights, and have your freaking mind blown to smithereens. Afterwards, you're going to travel to northern California, and enjoy the scenery, the food, the drinks, and the friendly people. However, just like on the Olympic Peninsula, you're not going to experience anything significant regarding the Bigfoot phenomena because, likewise, they're going about their research in the wrong manner. Nevertheless, you're going to have a fun time with them. Oh, and you're also going to be spending your time in northern California processing what you experienced with me in SOHA."

After I was done sharing my bold and confident prediction with Adam, silence filled the air for a moment followed by Adam's nervous laughter. I'm sure he was thinking, "What am I getting myself into with this Dr. Johnson guy?" He then spoke up in his British accent and gentlemanly manner and said, "Well, I look forward to experiencing everything that the west coast has to offer regarding the Bigfoot phenomena." That was a very polite and neutral response. However, at this point in time, I must say that after Adam returned home after his west coast Bigfoot tour to the United States, he said to me, "Matt, you called my Bigfoot trip to the west coast one-hundred percent spot on. The trip played out exactly the way you predicted it would. I will never forget my time in SOHA for the rest of my life."

So, would you like to know what happened up on the mountain in SOHA in June of 2014? Okay, before I begin, I'm going to warn you that it's going to sound very 'out of this world' and bizarre. It may cause you to question the sanity of the author of this book (i.e., me). However, I would like to remind you that three adult men who were not drinking or using any drugs witnessed the events that took place in SOHA. The events were also witnessed by my son, Grady, who was seven years old at the time. He still remembers this unique trip to SOHA to this very day. Finally, the events in SOHA were witnessed by Atlas, "The Official

Mascot of Team Squatchin USA" but he's dead now so he can't talk about it. I know, I know. Sick humor. Hey, I loved that little dog and miss him very much. My point is that even Atlas saw what the four of us humans saw and he was responding to the events too in his little seven-pound Toy Fox Terrier way. He cocked his head, perked up his ears, growled and looked in the same direction that we were looking at when the events were playing out. Canine confirmation. Additionally, we talked to Cynthia on the phone each night, and Adam, John and I shared our experiences with her as the weekend unfolded.

Adam and John had completed their visit to the well-known Bigfoot research center on the Olympic Peninsula and drove their rental car over to our home in Puyallup, Washington. I had cooked up some Rib-eye Steaks for dinner and invited Adam's wife at that moment in time, Lori Simmons, to join us. As predicted, Adam and John enjoyed the scenery, the food, the drink, and exchanging Bigfoot stories with the very nice people. However, nothing significant happened regarding the Bigfoot phenomena. Adam stated, "I made a grunt sound and I heard a grunt back." Cynthia and I looked at each other, smiled. We silently acknowledged to one another, "Wait until he goes to SOHA." Too funny.

The next morning, we took the honorary pictures outside in the driveway. The three adult men, acting like little boys, posed for our pre-expedition pictures. We had a fun time and laughed a lot. With the photography obligations out of the way, I proceeded to drive eight hours south to southern Oregon. Keeping with tradition, we began our time in Grants Pass, Oregon with a late lunch at the Black Bear Diner on 6th Street. Then we drove to the Albertson's grocery store on the other side of the Rogue River in south Grants Pass in order to purchase our supplies. We drove through the Dutch Brothers coffee stand to get our caffeine fix, and then on up to the mountain top and the SOHA base camp.

The drive to SOHA is a very precarious experience. The road is over-grown with vegetation, guaranteed to thoroughly scratch up the outside of one's vehicle. On occasion, the vegetation grabbed a hold of my side mirrors and ripped them off of my Suburban. Also, the road is full of very deep ruts that make the road impassible for most vehicles except for those with four-wheel drive and high clearance. Finally, the decaying road is on the side of a very steep mountain and will undoubtedly collapse under the weight of a heavy vehicle sometime in the near future. In short, the trip to SOHA is on a road less traveled.

When we arrived at the SOHA base camp, we unpacked and set up. Once again, as I always do with all of my guests, I reminded them of the strict protocol that we were all to follow in SOHA. Once again, as usual, my new guests respectfully rolled their eyes and agreed to comply with my established protocol. I gave them a tour of the surrounding area and then allowed them to explore on their own. I reminded them that they were being watched. Not by me. The local Bigfoot Forest People family was watching them. I'm sure that Adam and John thought I was off my rocker. I didn't care because I knew that I would be proven right. All I had to do was give it time.

I mean, think about it for a moment, please. Do you actually think that I would bring forty plus eyewitnesses to SOHA over a ten-year period of time so they could all tell the world that I was a liar and a hoaxer? Do you really think I would bring someone of Adam Davies' caliber up to SOHA to bust me as a hoaxer? No, just the opposite was true. I brought everyone up to SOHA over the years because I was confident regarding my habit-uation research methods and subsequent results. I brought everyone up knowing that they would have no other choice but to tell the truth that what I said that I had going on in SOHA was actually really happening in SOHA. To think otherwise about me and my motives for bringing others is totally ludicrous.

On our first of four nights in SOHA, we placed the gifting bowls outside of the base camp in the established gifting area about one-hundred-fifty feet away. The sun set and we were sitting in the pitch dark of night in the middle of the SOHA base camp facing the 12:00 o'clock position on the perimeter. Facing this direction also allowed us to see the 9:00 o'clock posi-tion to our left as well as the 3:00 o'clock position to our right. We hadn't been sitting in the dark any longer than an hour when a very loud grunt came from the 11:00 o'clock position on the perimeter. Adam nearly fell over backwards in his chair. He couldn't believe what he had just heard. , John was also very impressed by the Bigfoot Forest People vocal.

Please keep in mind that at this point in my research, I was recording every night for eight to twelve hours with my Bionic Ear parabolic microphone dish and Sony Digital recorder. I have posted a plethora of audio clips from our four nights in SOHA on my "Team Squatchin USA" channel at SoundCloud.com. I've also posted our testimonial videos from this trip on my "Team Squatchin USA" channel at YouTube.com. In other words, you can hear Adam's response to the grunt on the perimeter. You can also hear what happened during the remaining nights at SOHA. In short, despite how crazy the rest of what I'm about to write in this chapter sounds to you, it all really happened. It truly did. I don't lie and I don't hoax. Four credible humans experienced the events. The events were documented with audio recordings (i.e., Circumstantial evidence). None of it was hoaxed.

Also, the reader needs to keep in mind that there's a theoretical difference between myself and Adam as to how the Bigfoot Forest People are perceived. Adam is still stuck in the 'old school' approach and thinks of them as a descendant of Gigantopithecus. To be fair to Adam, I also thought this way during the first ten years of my research. It's the traditional theoretical model that's crammed down the throats of all who are new to Bigfooting.

By this time, three years earlier in 2011, I had made the official leap from the 'old school' theoretical approach to the orientation that the North American Indians have been right all along. The Bigfoot species are a people. Hence, I refer to them as the Bigfoot Forest People. We were dealing with a sentient being – NOT a dumb giant mountain ape only capable of grunting. They talk, sing, hum, make geometric designs, live in family groups that belong to clans, etc. That's why Adam was mainly interested in hearing grunts because dumb giant mountain apes grunt. He was not buying into the fact that the Bigfoot species were a people of the forest. He was politely humoring me because of his mindset.

Anyway, back to the story. The rest of the first night was filled with occasional vocals, bipedal walking, silhouettes, and eye glow. As usual, I played my music on the perimeter and also sang some songs. I introduced myself to the local Bigfoot family by saying, "My name is Matt. Matt. My name is Matt." I would tap my own chest when I would say my name. Then Adam and John took turns introducing themselves, while tapping their own chests while saying their names. The cool thing is that I have one of the Bigfoot Forest People saying, "Adam", after he said his name. For the record, I have them recorded over fifteen times saying my name, "Matt." Go to SoundCloud.com, type in "Team Squatchin USA", and listen to days and days' worth of audio recordings. Please start with the oldest recording first and move forward from there.

The next morning, we checked out the gifting bowls at sunrise. You can see the results on YouTube.com. Afterwards, as I normally do, I drove my guests off the mountain for the day and we did some sightseeing. I took them to the Redwood Forest in northern California. I took them to the "Stout Grove" to be specific. All of my guests enjoy going there and viewing the majesty of some of the oldest, tallest, and biggest trees on the planet Earth. Besides, the area is very 'Squatchy' and gets the Bigfooting juices flowing. As usual, we ate one big meal off the mountain, shopped for our evening snacks and fresh breakfast supplies, and then returned to the SOHA base camp for a second night. It is very important to note that while I drove the two hours to our destination as well as the two hours back from our destination, both Adam and John were napping in the Suburban. Obviously, I was not allowed to nap while I was driving.

During our second night at the SOHA base camp, we placed the gifting bowls in the gifting area just before the sun set. Then, once again, we sat in our camping chairs in the middle of the base camp in the pitch dark of night. As always, we had lots of Bigfoot activity on the perimeter of the SOHA base camp. I played my music, sang songs, whistled tunes, and we introduced ourselves by name while tapping our own chest. Surprisingly, Adam stood up and sang some songs too. That was very cool to see. On a personal side note, it was nice to see both Adam and John relax a little more during their second night at SOHA. I believe that they were caught off guard by the level of Bigfoot Forest People activity in SOHA and were somewhat nervous as a result. I believe that they were expecting more of the same regarding what they experienced on the Olympic Peninsula (i.e., Not much at all).

As we went to bed on our cots, sleeping out in the open underneath the stars, John asked me if I had just turned on a flashlight. You can hear this audio clip at SoundCloud.com. I responded, "No." He went on to describe that a light flashed off the top of the trees in front of us and he was wondering if I had turned on a flashlight. Well, I hadn't turned on a flashlight. However, after having been up in SOHA for eight years at that point in time, I had noticed the light flashing on the tops of the trees at the 12:00 o'clock position in SOHA on numerous occasions. At first, I thought it was the headlights of a vehicle driving up to camp on the road at the 6:00 o'clock position. But there was never a vehicle driving into camp. Eventually, I simply grew to accept that the flashing white light on the top of trees at SOHA was just an anomaly that would go unsolved. After all, as I was experiencing and learning in SOHA over the years, Bigfoot Research began to involve anything and everything but the expected. Please buckle up. The ride is about to get a little bumpy from this point on.

After the second active night in SOHA, we retrieved the gifting bowls at sunrise. You can see the results on YouTube.com. We snacked on our fresh breakfast supplies and then we went off the mountain for another day of tourist sightseeing. Let all attendees to SOHA utter these words, "Matt is the best doggone host that anyone could ever have while visiting southern Oregon." Although I've seen these tourist sightseeing spots a hundred times, I always enjoy seeing my guests' faces light up when they visit the spots for the first time and witness their mystery, majesty, and beauty. It never gets old for me to bring pleasure to my guests and friends.

By the way, if you're getting frustrated with me because I'm continually referring you to my "Team Squatchin USA" YouTube channel or my SoundCloud.com channel rather than writing about all the details in this chapter, I'm doing it for two reasons: (1) This book is probably going to be four-hundred or more pages long. If I wrote about all of the details, it would probably be closer to eight hundred pages long. You and I both know that it's going to be a challenge for you to finish a four-hundred plus page book let alone a five-hundred-page book; and (2) Believe it or not, it will make everything more 'believable' for you if you actually watch it with your own eyes and listen to it with your own ears. In short, the videos and audio recordings back up and support what I'm writing about in this book. If you're interested in pursuing the truth and confirming the truth, then you'll take the time to watch the videos and listen to the audio recordings in order to supplement what you're reading in my book.

As weird as things are about to get in this chapter, the events that occurred in SOHA during June of 2014 are nothing compared to the other events I'm going to write about later on in this book. If I can help you to believe what I'm saying is true now by suggesting that you supplement your reading my book with YouTube.com videos and SoundCloud. com audio files, then you're more likely to believe me later when the story becomes even crazier than it's about to get.

In other words, if I'm telling the truth now why would I turn around and lie about things later? What's the point in lying? Exactly my point! I have no reason to lie. I have consistently and steadfastly told the truth from the day my family encountered a Bigfoot on the mountainside above the Oregon Caves National Monument Park on July 1, 2000. I have absolutely no other motivation than to continue to tell the truth. Once again, that's why I supplement everything I do with multiple witness testimonies and circumstantial evidence.

During the second day off the mountain, I took Adam and John to the Oregon House of Mystery, otherwise known as the Oregon Vortex. It's a place worthy of your time to visit if you're ever passing through southern Oregon. At this location, there is a magnetic vortex that swirls around nonstop. We took their one-hour tour and enjoyed all of the various points of interest and education inside the Oregon Vortex. On a personal side note, I would encourage you to visit the Montana Vortex in Columbia Falls, Montana. My friend and fellow Bigfoot Forest People researcher, Joe Hauser, own it. Cynthia and I visited the Montana Vortex during the summer of 2016 and visited with Joe and Tammy. They're a sweet couple. Also, we obtained a cool picture of a Bigfoot Forest Person after hearing a whoop. We also obtained some cool pictures of some orbs too. But I digress. Back to the Oregon House of Mystery.

In a nutshell, the location where the Oregon House of Mystery stands today was discovered over one-hundred fifty years ago by the local Indians when they realized that animals were avoiding the area. Especially, large mammals such as horses, elk, bear, and deer. Eventually, the white man came along and homesteaded on the property and eventually built an assayers office there. Why did they put an assayer's office smack dab in the middle of the electromagnetic vortex? Well, they realized that both people and gold weighed less inside the vortex than it did outside the vortex. Therefore, they were able to rip off the miners by paying them less money inside the vortex. Then they would take the gold outside the vortex and sell it and make a better profit. God bless America! Anyway, the point is that the magnetic vortex is real and they have lots of educational stations set up on the property to demonstrate the various effects caused by the magnetic field. It's an amazing place to visit.

After we were done visiting the Oregon House of Mystery, I drove Adam and John to visit the Crater Lake National Park. Once again, they were able to nap while I was driving the Suburban. It was a beautiful day and the water inside the Crater was bluer than blue. Mt. Mazama blew its top around 5,700 BC with a force, supposedly, forty-two times greater than that of Mt. St. Helens in May of 1980. Mt. Mazama lost a mile of its elevation after the explosion and rocks landed as far away as California, Nevada, Arizona, Utah, and New Mexico. Although the destruction in the area was beyond horrific at the time, it is dead drop gorgeous there today. We sat on the back porch of the Crater Lake Lodge, put our feet up, and sipped on a beer while taking in the view of the lake. Crater Lake is a must see tourist spot if you ever visit southern Oregon.

After we were done with our visit to Crater Lake, I drove Adam and John from there to Miguel's Guadalajara Restaurant on the Rogue River in Shady Cove, Oregon. Guess what they were doing while I was driving the Suburban? Yes, you got it! They were napping while I was driving. Why do I keep pointing that out? Well, you'll eventually understand as you continue to read. We enjoyed a nice Mexican dinner while sitting out on the deck overlooking the Rogue River. When we finished eating, I drove us back to the Albertson's grocery store in Grants Pass, Oregon. Yes, they were napping while I was driving.

After we purchased our goodies from the Albertson's grocery store for our third night up on the mountain, we drove through the Dutch Brothers coffee stand, obtained our drug of choice, and got high on caffeine as we drove back up to the mountaintop and the SOHA base camp. Needless to say, everyone was tuckered out because we spent over six hours on the road going to and from our various destinations earlier that day. The caffeine in my Annihilator coffee drink at least was able to keep me awake until around 1:00 am later on that night. Given all the driving that I did during the three days, most people wouldn't have been able to stay up until 9:00 pm. The truth is all of the driving I had been doing during the three-day period was catching up with me. I almost resorted to using toothpicks to keep my eyelids open. I was seriously dead tired.

After we returned to the SOHA base camp on the third night, I had to rush to prepare the gifting bowls for delivery before the sun went down. We got them out in time, just before dark, and returned to the base camp for another night of experiencing the Bigfoot Forest People in the pitch dark of night. However, I noticed a difference on this third night regarding Adam's and John's behaviors. Instead of spending most of their time in their chairs in the middle of the base camp, they appeared to be spending more and more time on the other side of the parked Suburban around the 5:00 o'clock and 6:00 o'clock positions on the perimeter.

While I was continuing to implement my habituation research methods with the Bigfoot Forest People, playing music and interacting along the perimeter from the 9:00 o'clock position to the 12:00 o'clock position and on over to the 3:00 o'clock position, I noticed that Adam and John were nowhere to be found anywhere near me. Instead, they were spending an inordinate amount of time away from all of the activity on the perimeter. To be honest, they were coming across to me as being overwhelmed by all of the Bigfoot Forest People activity and that they wanted a break from it all. They spent their time on the other side of the Suburban, laughing, talking, and smoking Backwoods Cigars. Occasionally, I went back their way and invited them to return to where all of the activity was but they preferred to stay put right where they were. I thought it was a bit odd but I wasn't going to be rude and insist on them returning to the center of the base camp. If they needed a break from all of the activity, well then, they needed a break.

Around 11:00 pm on that third night, Adam and John were yelling at me to come join them on the other side of the Suburban. Well, to be honest, I was frustrated that they weren't spending time with me on my side of the Suburban. I had major Bigfoot Forest People activity going on and I wanted them to experience it. Again, they yelled at me to join them. I told them to come join me. Finally, they demanded that I come over to where they were immediately so I walked around the back end of the Suburban and my jaw dropped and hit the ground.

At the 6:00 o'clock position on the perimeter, on the road that we have to drive up on in order to reach the SOHA base camp, was a portal that was wide open over a very large mud puddle. I couldn't believe what I was seeing. It looked similar to the portals that they showed in the Sci-Fi TV series, "Stargate." It was about ten to twelve feet in diameter. What I saw was a completely different world than ours. It was a world with a red sky and dark scraggly vegetation. Adam asked, "What the hell is that?" I said, "I have no idea. I've never seen that up here before. What did you guys do?"

Adam and John explained to me that they were having a fun time, talking and joking, and had inadvertently made their way down toward the muddle puddle when a sparkly light began to appear. Then eventually, it looked like a blind opened up and the next thing they noticed was the portal. At that time, we all described what we were looking at to confirm that we were all seeing the same exact thing (i.e., A world with red sky and dark scraggly vegetation).

Suddenly, John said, "What are those things?" Adam and I looked a little closer and then we saw them too. There were what appeared to be two, three-foot-tall dark beings with glowing red eyes. We later referred to them as guardians of the portal. They seemed to be just standing there near the portal and didn't appear to me to be malevolent or up to no good as Adam and John would later describe them to be. We shined a flashlight on the portal and it shut it down. Everything was gone.

I walked back over to the regularly occupied area of the SOHA base camp to spend more time with the Bigfoot Forest People. After all, that's exactly why we were there, right? I invited Adam and John to return with me but they opted to stay back at the 6:00 o'clock area. I played some more music and enjoyed see the silhouettes, eye glow, and hearing the vocals. After a short while, Adam and John were summoning my presence back to the 6:00 o'clock position on the perimeter. I walked around the back of the Suburban and the portal was open again. I asked, "How did you open it up?" They told me that they didn't know how they opened it up, all they did was walk down in the direction of the portal again and it opened all by itself.

We shined a flashlight on it and shut it down again. This time, I stayed there with them as we stood closer to the portal area. Then I finally saw what they had been talking about. There were sparkling lights which opened up like a shade into the portal. We saw the two guardians again who appeared to me to be minding their own business. We shined the flashlight on the portal again and it all disappeared again.

I walked back to spend more time with the Bigfoot Forest People on the perimeter while Adam and John remained down by the portal area. Eventually, they made their way back to me in a panic letting me know that the guardians had rushed them. I asked if the guardians had actually touched them and they told me no. They informed me that they had shined the flashlight on the portal and shut it down again.

By this time, I was majorly frustrated and pissed. I wasn't scared, instead, I was pissed. This portal thingamajig and the guardians were raining on my parade. I had brought Adam and John to SOHA in order to experience the Bigfoot Forest People. We were enjoying a lot of activity on the perimeter and all of a sudden, this portal is distracting my guests from the reason we were all there. I understand that some of you think that the portal is a more significant discovery than interacting with the Bigfoot Forest People, however, that's not the way I was viewing it at the time. I brought Adam and John up to SOHA to vet and verify my research – not to discover an inter-dimensional portal.

Having been up in SOHA for eight years already, I was not worried about the portal or the guardians. I figured that the portal and guardians had been up there the whole time I had been there. I also realized at that point in time why the white light had been flashing on the top of the trees at the 12:00 o'clock position for all of those years. It wasn't headlights from a vehicle driving up the road. Rather, the white light flashing off the trees at the 12:00 o'clock position had to have been coming from the portal opening and closing. In conclusion, I knew that for eight straight years, I never woke up dead in SOHA. I knew that we were safe but I had to do something to calm both Adam and John down.

Therefore, I grabbed my 44 magnum handgun and walked past Adam and John and down to the portal area. They asked where I was going and I told them that I was taking care of business. I walked right up to the mud puddle where the portal was opening up. I was also carrying a flashlight with me too. In the name of Jesus and 'Maggie' (the nickname for my handgun), I commanded the guardians to go away and leave us alone. I told them that if I saw them again, that I was going to stick my gun down their throats and blow their heads off. I walked back up to Adam and John, passed them, and returned to the main area of the base camp. They followed me there. I told them how to shoot the gun, left it for them, and then told them that I had to go to bed. As previously stated, I was seriously dead tired and needed my sleep. I encouraged Adam and John to go to sleep too but they were worried that the guardians would attack us in our sleep.

At this point, I would like to address all of you who are already familiar with my story, and the rest of you who are reading about my story for the first time and wondering the same thing: "How could you go to sleep at a time like that?" Well, as I already wrote on the previous pages, I had been driving my guests around for three straight days. On the first day, I drove eight hours from Puyallup, Washington down to Grants Pass, Oregon while my guests napped in the Suburban. On the second day, I drove a total of five hours while my guests slept in the Suburban. On the third day, I drove a total of six hours while my guests napped in the Suburban. Guess what? I was going to have to drive my guests around on our fourth day too while they most likely napped. Finally, I was going to have to drive for eight hours all the way back from Grants Pass, Oregon to Puyallup, Washington.

So, I'm not sure what some of you don't understand about the fact that I didn't get to catch up on sleep after multiple late nights while I was driving for three straight days, but I was exhausted and I needed to sleep. Also, as previously stated, up to that point in time, I had been up in SOHA for eight straight years and managed to wake up alive every morning. Based on the flashing light off the top of the trees at the 12:00 o'clock position on the perimeter, I concluded that the portal had been there the whole time. If the portal and the guardians were dangerous, I would be dead one-hundred-times over already. Therefore, we were absolutely in no danger at all. Once again, please go to SoundCloud.com and listen to the audio recordings.

On the fourth morning, we retrieved the gifting bowls at sunrise. Once again, we had some awesome results as the Bigfoot Forest People took some food items. Please watch the YouTube videos. More importantly, Adam and John were dead tired because they stayed awake for the whole night until the sun started to rise. Although they were amazed that I was able to sleep through the rest of the night, I was equally amazed that they chose to stay up rather than go to bed. However, to be fair to Adam and John, they didn't have eight years of research experience in SOHA to draw upon to form a rational conclusion that we were not in danger. Instead, they chose to interpret a bluff charge from the guardians as a nefarious attempt to take their lives. Adam seriously thought he was going to die that night. In my mind, he was over-killing the situation. Yes, pun intended.

On the fourth day, we eventually went off the mountain after Adam and John were able to catch up on some of their lost sleep. We picked up Grady and went on the Hellgate Jet Boat Excursion trip down the Rogue River. We chose the 'Dinner Cruise' and enjoyed a great meal and drink at the rustic lodge down the river. It was a beautiful day off the mountain, an awesome and fun boat ride, and appeared to help distract both Adam and John from what they had experienced the previous night.

When we were done with our boat ride, we headed back up to the top of the mountain and to the SOHA base camp. While driving up to the top, Adam and John asked me if I thought the portal and the guardians were going to be present again. I told them that I had no idea. I reminded them that the portal and guardians were just as new to me as they were to them. Finally, I encouraged them to join me in the center of the base camp and focus on our Bigfoot Forest People friends.

Upon our arrival, I had to hurry and put the gifting bowls together. At Adam's insistence, I put double sided white tape on the outside of the gifting bowls. He was hoping to collect some hair samples. I complied with his request and we placed the gifting bowls out in the gifting area. Upon our return to camp, Adam and John decided to take their chairs and set them up near the portal area at the 6:00 o'clock position. After a while, they called to me and informed Grady and I that the portal had opened up again. Grady was impressed. He said, "Dad, that's so cool."

Grady and I observed Adam and John for a while opening the portal and then closing it with a flashlight. Opening the portal and then closing it with a flashlight. Grady whispered to me, "Dad, they're acting like two scared little girls." I responded to Grady, "Son, you need to keep in mind that you've been coming to SOHA with me since you were two-years-old. Based on your experiences, you know that we have nothing to fear up here. On the other hand, this is Adam's and John's first trip to SOHA. This is only their fourth night up here. You need to cut them some slack because they don't know any better." Grady agreed.

Eventually, Grady and I went back to the center of the base camp and spent the rest of our time with our Bigfoot Forest People friends. Around 11:00 pm, I informed Adam and John that Grady and I were going to bed. Once again, they couldn't believe that I was going to sleep. I encouraged them to go to bed too but they responded in the same manner as they did the previous night. They were afraid to go to bed because they feared for their lives and thought that the guardians had a nefarious plan and that they would attack us in our sleep.

While I was sleeping, Ceska visited me in a dream. He informed me that the portal had been there the whole time and that the guardians weren't going to hurt anyone. He said that they were there to make sure that none of us tried to go through the portal. He said that the guardians were simply doing their job. Finally, he shared that bright white light shuts down the portal because it's a safety mechanism built into the portal to keep humans out at night. He reminded me that most humans travel through the forest with bright white lights on at night (i.e., Flashlights, headlamps, headlights on cars, motorcycles, and quads). He said that the guardians were frustrated by my friends because they kept on opening and closing the portal like two young kids playing around with a garage door opener.

The next morning, as the sun rose, we collected the gifting bowls one final time. Adam found fingerprints on the white double sided tape.

He also found what he thought was a possible Bigfoot Forest Person hair sample but it turned out to be one of Atlas' hairs. We packed up camp and dropped Grady off at his mother's home. Then Adam, John, and I drove to Herb's Diner in Grants Pass, Oregon. We enjoyed our breakfast and then shot an awesome testimonial video outside in the parking lot. Yes, this is where I encourage you to go watch my YouTube videos again. After all, they did an awesome job with their testimonials. Finally, for obvious reasons, they chose not to discuss their experience with the portal and the guardians while we were shooting their testimonial video. But if you're sharp, you'll pick up on the fact that they both look dead tired. Well, now you know why. It's because they stayed up for two nights straight.

At the beginning of our eight-hour drive from Grants Pass, Oregon back to Puyallup, Washington, Adam said, "I can't believe that I shushed a Bigfoot at the 8:00 o'clock position on the perimeter so I could do battle with the guardians of an inter-dimensional portal. I didn't sign up for this sci-fi adventure." Also, before he fell asleep, Adam said to me, "From now on, Matt, if you tell me that you've discovered a pink Unicorn at SOHA, I will believe you." We all laughed because it turned out to be a very crazy adventure. Much more than anyone had bargained for. Afterwards, like I had mentioned at the beginning of this chapter, Adam told me that I called his west coast experience one-hundred percent spot on. Nothing happened up north on the Olympic Peninsula and nothing happened in northern California. All the action took place in SOHA and his mind was blown as I had boldly and confidently predicted. I hadn't realized my mind would also be blown yet again during this weekend.

Afterwards, I continued to go back to SOHA for one to two weekends per month. Every time I was there, I would always go down to the portal area to see if I could open it up. Nothing would happen. Three months later in September of 2014, I actually saw a Bigfoot Forest Person walk out of the portal and immediately step off the road and into the woods. The portal opened and closed rather quickly. In spite of the fact that I had a visual confirmation that the portal was still there, I was unable to open it up.

During the time shortly after the portal experience with Adam and John, I almost threw in the towel. I was frustrated by the fact that the whole equation of the portal was thrown into the mix. What the heck was I supposed to do with that? How in the world was I going to crack the mystery of the Bigfoot Forest People phenomena with this crazy portal addition to the proverbial puzzle? Fortunately, Cynthia kept me anchored to the ground as well as motivated to figure out what was going on.

In April of 2015, we were about to host our first ever Team Squatchin USA Bigfoot Forest People conference. Although it was ten months after the portal incident, Adam had yet to speak up publicly about it. His silence bothered me for two reasons: (1) A true man of science does not withhold important data from others based on fear of ridicule. Rather, like Galileo, a true man of science is willing to speak up and tell the truth regardless of who it may upset. The withholding of the portal information as it was related to the Bigfoot Forest People phenomena was not helping everyone else to solve the mystery. Also, (2) I was concerned about his emotional well-being. I knew that the portal and guardian experience had traumatized him and that it wasn't good for him to stuff it all inside. Rather, the best way to deal with such experiences is to talk about it and normalize it. I went through a similar experience with my encounter above the Oregon Caves when I saw the Bigfoot uncloak and then cloak again. I didn't talk with anyone about it for ten years and I didn't start feeling better until I finally told Cynthia and Thom Powell. As a licensed clinical psychologist, I know that talking about traumatic encounters is the key to becoming free from the emotionally paralyzing effects of traumatic encounters.

Therefore, at my conference near the end of April in 2015, I released information about the portal and guardians in SOHA. Boy did the poop hit the fan in Bigfootdom. That revelation shot around Bigfootdom like a bolt of lightning. The responses from the Bigfoot community varied from "that's awesome" to "you're freaking crazy." Immediately, the TROLLS and haters wanted proof. They were saying that I was making it all up. Although John Carlson spoke up immediately in our "Team Squatchin USA" Facebook group and confirmed that the story was true, the TROLLS and haters were waiting to see some proof.

After a while, I released my audio recordings. Once again, more people jumped on board the train of belief and acceptance while the TROLLS and haters now shifted their focus to "we want to hear from Adam." Well, after some time, Adam finally spoke up and confirmed that it had all happened. He confirmed that the portal and guardians was a true story and that it was an experience that he wasn't expecting. He shared that he feared for his life during his last two nights in SOHA. Once again, more people were convinced and several people who were mocking me ended up apologizing to me. Just a public service reminder, I don't lie and I don't hoax. If I said something happened, guess what? It happened. Don't ever doubt my veracity.

Now, although both Adam and John came out publicly during an interview and confirmed that I most definitely had Bigfoot Forest People activity going on at SOHA and that the portal incident accompanied by the guardians truly did happen, that's where we parted our ways. You see, they chose to interpret the portal and guardians differently than I did. In a nutshell, because John had an experience in his youth with what he believes to be some demonic beings, they chose to interpret the guardians as being demonic beings also (i.e., I strongly believe that John's past experience skewed his perception of his present experience). Adam, who had no paranormal background at all, chose to jump on John's bandwagon. Together, they concluded that the guardians were demonic beings guarding the gateway to hell. They chose to interpret their experience in SOHA as two separate events simultaneously occurring: (1) Bigfoot Forest People activity, and (2) Demons guarding the gateway to hell.

At this point in time, I have to ask you, "How lucky am I?" I mean think about it. How lucky am I to have two very different events going on in the same area at the same time? Heck, I should go buy some lottery tickets, don't you think? You see, in the minds of Adam and John, they chose to dichotomize their experience. They chose to separate the two events. That's not uncommon when someone is majorly stressed out by a traumatic situation. In short, it's our psyche's way of helping us to handle a traumatic event in a way that we can process it and live with it.

The only problem with Adam's and John's conclusion is that they're completely ignoring three very important pieces of data: (1) Ceska visited me in a dream and told me who the guardians were and that we were safe, (2) I saw a Bigfoot Forest Person walk out of the portal three months later in September of 2014, and (3) One year later in June of 2015, I finally figured out how to reopen the portal and Satan didn't take all of us to hell. You're responding, "What? You figured out how to reopen the portal?" My answer is a solid and unequivocal "yes."

You need to remember that I'm a licensed clinical psychologist. It's my job to engage in problem-solving. That's what I do for a living. I collect various pieces of information, put the puzzle together, and help my clients to understand the problems that they're facing and how to overcome them. I simply applied my same problem-solving skills to the portal issue. What I eventually figured out was that before the portal opened up on the third evening in June of 2014, I took both Adam and John to the Oregon House of Mystery. We spent an hour inside the electromagnetic vortex. I concluded that we must have brought some residual electromagnetic 'juju' back with us on our bodies that functioned as a key to unlock the portal.

Therefore, based on this hypothesis, I conducted an experiment with a small group of people who I brought to SOHA in June of 2015. With their permission, and without telling them what I was up to, I took my friends to the Oregon House of Mystery. Likewise, we spent an hour inside the electromagnetic vortex. When we came back to SOHA, and the sun had set and darkness filled the night, I asked my friends to accompany me down to the portal area. Guess what? The portal opened up. However, this time, it did not open up to a world with red sky and dark scraggly vegetation. Instead, the portal opened up to a dimension of energy and light.

As we stood there, we were all seeing the same sparkling lights along with the fog of light that was emanating from the portal area. The fog of light was similar to the fog of light that I saw emanating from the feet of the two Beings of Light in November of 2013 while Michael Beers and Gunnar Monson were up in SOHA with me. But this time, the fog of light was up in the air as high as twelve feet and extended up the road on both sides of us. Also, this fog of light was faint and dim rather than bright. For the record, there was no real fog in the area that night. Matter of fact, the wind was blowing yet the fog of light was not moving. Why? Because the wind can't blow light around. The wind can move misty fog but the wind can't move light that appears to be fog. There's a major difference.

During June, July, August, and September of 2015, I was able to reopen the portal with a total of ten witnesses viewing the event. Once again, if I did it all by myself and reported the results to the world, it would be very easy and wise to blow me off. However, when I am able to replicate reopening the portal with multiple witnesses present, it's not so easy to blow off my results.

We also conducted two additional experiments related to the portal: (1) Some of us went to the Oregon House of Mystery and spent an hour inside the electromagnetic vortex. A fourth individual, Shelley Mower, did not go to the Oregon House of Mystery. That night, we sent Shelley to go stand down by the portal area. She bravely did so, all by herself, for about thirty minutes and nothing happened. Then we called her back up to the base camp while the three of us went down to the portal and managed to open it up. While Shelley was standing alone by herself in the base camp, she was experiencing Bigfoot Forest People activity around the perimeter.

Eventually, we called Shelley back down to the portal area again. We wanted to see if (A) Shelley could see what we could see. If yes, then the electromagnetic energy simply functioned as a key to unlock the portal. On the other hand, if Shelley couldn't see what we were seeing, then (B) the electromagnetic energy functioned as a key to unlock our perceptions and create the ability to see the portal. Well, it turned out that Shelley could see what we could see, therefore, the electromagnetic energy at the Oregon House of Mystery functioned as a key to unlock the portal.

The second experiment that we conducted with the portal was (2) After going to the Oregon House of Mystery and spending an hour in the electromagnetic vortex, we were able to reopen the portal in SOHA. Then the next day, we went swimming in the Illinois River. Later during our second night, after swimming in the river, we were unable to reopen the portal. In short, swimming in the river apparently washed off the residual electromagnetic 'juju' from our bodies. We were able to repeat both experiments successfully.

When it comes to Adam and John's interpretation of who the guardians are and what the portal was, we will have to agree to disagree. I will say this much, I spent a total of ten years in SOHA and I think that I might have a much better idea regarding what is going on up there than they do. I have much more experience and data to draw upon in order to put the pieces of the puzzle together accurately and successfully. They only had two nights up there to draw upon to help them arrive at their conclusions. Although Adam is a world-renowned cryptozoologist, he's not an expert of SOHA. He was a guest in my research area and lacked the data to formulate an accurate conclusion.

I recently found out from some mutual friends that Adam had gone back up to SOHA with some other individuals. He spoke about his trip at a recent conference in the state of Washington. Allegedly, they had two individuals who were utilizing night vision equipment. Both of them saw a ball of orange light move through the forest while wearing their night vision equipment. The significant thing about that is that all you can see is a variety of green hues while utilizing night vision equipment. You're not supposed to see any other colors besides a variety of green hues. Yet, these two individuals saw an orange ball of light moving through the forest in their separate night vision viewers at the same exact time. Apparently, some other activity happened up in SOHA including bipedal steps, silhouettes, and Samurai chatter (i.e., Spoken language that sounds like Japanese Samurais talking). However, they didn't reopen the portal and no guardians dragged their research party off through the gates of hell. Just saying.

In closing this chapter, I would like to say two very important things: (1) If anyone is going to go to SOHA in an attempt to determine whether or not I'm telling the truth, they're going to have to replicate everything that I did up there to the letter of the law regarding the implementation of my protocol. If they don't implement my protocol exactly the way I did, then they're comparing apples and oranges. They can neither confirm, nor deny any of my research results. Also, (2) as previously stated, what happened in SOHA is nothing compared to what you're about to read in the remainder of my book. In short, SOHA was both a classroom for me as well as a classroom for the younger Bigfoot Forest

People. Today, based on present data, SOHA has become outdated and irrelevant. Bigger and better events have occurred since June of 2014.

As you read the rest of my book, I'll be taking you down the same Rabbit Hole that the Bigfoot Forest People took me down. I'm going to remind you of the fact that anything short of producing a body (i.e., Direct evidence) means that no one can prove that the Bigfoot Forest People actually exists. Once again, I'm NOT endorsing the "Pro-Kill" philosophy. Matter of fact, as previously stated in my book, humans can't kill the Bigfoot Forest People. Anyone who claims to have killed a Bigfoot Forest Person is a liar. You'll find out later why. I'm not suggesting that we attempt to kill one (which can't be done). I'm merely reminding you that we will never have direct evidence to provide to the world to prove their existence. Therefore, we only have both circumstantial evidence and eyewitness testimonies to draw upon to arrive at our conclusions about the Bigfoot Forest People. For the record, many court cases over the years have been settled based solely on circumstantial evidence and eyewitness testimony without any direct evidence being provided. Likewise, that's the only way that the Bigfoot Forest People phenomena is ever going to be settled.

With all of the above stated, I've provided you with both circum-stantial evidence and eyewitness testimonies that verify that I'm telling you the truth. Why would I change my ways now? Why would I lie to you now? In other words, while we continue to slide down the Rabbit Hole together, please buckle up, and hang on. Together, we will end up in the land of truth. By the time you're done reading my book, as I promised Adam Davies before he visited SOHA, your mind is going to be blown. However, when the dust settles, you're going to have your answers regarding (1) Who are the Bigfoot, (2) Where are they from, and (3) Why are they here.

CHAPTER NINETEEN

DEAD MAN WALKING

I need to hit the rewind button and take you back to February 14, 2012. Although it was Valentine's Day, Cynthia was very gracious and agreed to share a romantic date with me on the following night so I could play in a city-league basketball game. We were playing against a younger and faster basketball team. Most of their team members were in their twenties and thirties, while most of our team members were in our forties and fifties. In spite of the age difference, it was a very close game.

I stand six feet nine inches tall and weigh over three-hundred-pounds. Because of my size, the young bucks thought that they could pound on me inside the key near the basket. Also, because of my size, most referees allow the pounding to take place without calling any fouls on them. Well, this old fart wasn't about to allow that to happen. I started throwing young bodies all over the court. The young bucks were very competitive and becoming upset because I wasn't rolling over and dying. Although I was grossly out of shape, I wasn't going to allow these puppies to win. I was sucking air and felt like a dead man walking. Nevertheless, I kept taking the ball to the hole and scoring at will. They couldn't stop me from scoring no matter how much they beat on me.

During the second half of the game, I dove for a loose ball and was very proud of myself for out hustling the younger guys to get my hands on the ball and secure it for my team. However, during my act of competitive hustling, the guard from the other team stepped on the back of my left leg. In all my forty years of playing competitive basketball, I never felt so much pain in my life. I managed to get myself off of the floor so the game could resume without me. I hopped over to the corner of the gym on my right leg and leaned against the wall. I lifted up my left leg and tried to move my left foot. Nothing! My foot was just dangling there. That was a confirmation for me that I most definitely severed my Achilles tendon. I thought to myself, "Crap! Sometimes I hate growing older."

Two days later, I went in for surgery to reattach my severed Achilles tendon. During the surgery, I almost died on the operating table. Apparently, I was allergic to the medication that they used to help my throat relax so they could slide a breathing tube down my throat. I stopped breathing and they had to get me breathing again. Although I was obviously knocked out and had no idea what had happened, I was happy to see that they got me breathing again. I'm a big fan of breathing. I like breathing. Nevertheless, it appears for a minute or two, I may have been a dead man sleeping.

Three days later, Cynthia and I were on a plane flying from Seattle, Washington to New Orleans, Louisiana because I had a speaking engagement regarding my "Positive Parenting with a Plan" book. At this point in my life, I was still speaking in eighty cities per year all over the United States, training thousands of professionals and parents to use my parenting program in their agencies, private practices, and in their homes. While I was pushing myself around on a knee scooter, Cynthia was running behind me carrying my bags. I hate to admit it but it was a blast zooming through the airport. I had to stop several times so Cynthia could catch up with me. After I was done speaking in New Orleans, Cynthia and I enjoyed some time staying in the French Quarter and the fun on Bourbon Street. I'm now a big fan of beads.

Cynthia and I flew from New Orleans, Louisiana to Las Vegas, Nevada. Another way of saying it is we flew from Sodom to Gomorrah. I spoke in Las Vegas, once again, training professionals and parents. Afterwards, Cynthia and I took in a Cirque Du Soleil show called "O" and it was awesome. Once again, I had fun zooming around on my knee scooter and had to exercise self-discipline so Cynthia could keep up with me. To be quite honest, if I didn't have Cynthia along with me, there was no way that I could have fulfilled all of my speaking obligations.

The next day, Cynthia drove the rental car from Las Vegas, Nevada to Los Angeles, California. Over the next couple of days, I spoke in different communities in the vast concrete jungle of humanity. By the end of my speaking tour, both Cynthia and I were exhausted. We were looking forward to returning home. We flew from Los Angeles, California back to Seattle, Washington, drove back to the home in Puyallup, Washington, and face planted in bed. Home sweet home! Not bad for someone who just went through surgery and almost died, right?

After my speaking tour through Louisiana, Nevada, and California, my left leg ballooned like an elephant leg. No matter what I tried to do, it remained as an elephant leg. My leg was totally numb from my calf down to my toes. I could feel absolutely nothing. I put up with it for three years until I finally convinced my family physician to give me a referral to a specialist.

On March 3, 2015, Cynthia and I were sitting in a vascular surgeon's office in Puyallup, Washington. The physician had his gal lube up my left leg with some gel and she started doing an ultrasound on my upper thigh. Suddenly, she stopped and said, "Oh, my God!" Cynthia and I looked at each other with surprised looks on our faces.

I said, "What? What's wrong?" She just shook her head.

As she continued to conduct the ultrasound on my upper left thigh she said, Oh my God!"

Again, I said, "What? What's wrong with my leg?"

She responded "Oh, I'm sorry. I'm not supposed to say anything. The doctor will talk to you about it.

She started lubing up my upper thigh on my right leg and said, "Let's take a look over here. Okay, everything looks good. Now let me take another look over here on your left leg. Oh my God. I'm so sorry. I'll go talk with the doctor and let him talk with you." She walked out of the room and Cynthia and I just sat there in the room, alone, staring at each other. We could hear the young gal talking with the vascular surgeon out in the hallway, on the other side of the door, but we couldn't tell what they were talking about. I was worried that I was going to have to go into emergency surgery.

The vascular surgeon finally entered the room, quietly and calmly walked over to a chair near me, sat down, looked at me and said, "Let me begin by telling you just how lucky you are. You should be dead. You had what I would diagnose as a 'big ass DVT' in your left leg that went from your groin to your knee. A deep vein thrombosis. A very large blood clot. If you walked in here with that large DVT in your leg, I would tell you to get your affairs in order because you're going to die. If I attempted to operate to remove the DVT, you would die. If I gave you medication to dissolve the DVT, you would die. If it broke up naturally on its own, you would die. You should be dead."

Needless to say, Cynthia and I were completely stunned. I asked, "Well, is the DVT still there?" He responded, "No. That's just it. You should be dead. It's gone. The DVT is gone. I don't understand it. I've been a vascular surgeon for over twenty years and I've never seen anyone survive DVT like the one you had. You should be dead. It's a miracle that you're not dead. You should be dead."

I asked, "Well, if the DVT isn't there, then how do you know that I even had a 'big ass DVT' in the first place?" The vascular surgeon responded, "Because of the vascular damage the DVT left behind. It blew out the valves in your veins. We can see where the clot was. You should be dead. This is amazing. It's a miracle. You should be dead."

Then I asked, "Well, do I need to go in for surgery?" He responded, "No. The DVT is gone. All you need to do is wear a compression sock and take an aspirin every day." I said, "That's it? A sock and an aspirin are going to get rid of my elephant leg?" He said, "The compression sock will help to get rid of your elephant leg. The daily aspirin will help to reduce the likelihood of you developing another "big ass DVT" in the future. By the way, you should never fly on a plane so quickly after surgery." I responded, "Well, no one told me not to do so. I had no idea." He said, "Now you know. I still can't believe this. I'm looking at a miracle here. You should be dead."

After forty-five minutes of hearing "you should be dead" about a thousand times, Cynthia and I had to dismiss the vascular surgeon from our appointment with him. We had other errands that we had to run, including purchasing some compression socks and a bottle of aspirin. Besides, there's only so many times that we could sit there and hear that I should be dead. I got the point, I'm a dead man walking. Although I should be dead, I wasn't dead. It's a miracle. But wait a second, who performed the miracle?

Fast forward to July of 2015, Cynthia and I went to the Southern Oregon Habituation Area (SOHA) to enjoy three nights with the Bigfoot Forest People family. There was no one else with us. We were enjoying some alone time. Yes, we were able to reopen the portal again. Later on that night, Cynthia and I finally went to bed after entertaining our friends with music and singing. It had been a very hot day. Therefore, we slept in our sleeping bags but left the upper flap open. We didn't want to cook inside our bags. Cynthia had brought some sheets to cover us with so we could be protected from mosquitoes and other bugs. We both slept great.

In the middle of the night, I woke up from a deep sleep and realized that I had been zapped. Although I was wide awake, my body was immobilized. I felt a large hand on top of the sheet sliding back and forth over my left leg, from my groin to my knee and back to my groin again. There was some kind of energy emanating from the hand into my leg. After about five minutes, I heard the Bigfoot Forest Person engage in mind speak to another one, "His leg is still okay." Immediately, I thought to myself, "My leg is still okay? Still okay? Wait a second, you guys healed my leg?"

Then the hand slid over to my crotch area and, once again, I could feel the energy emanating from his hand. No, nothing sexual happened. Get your mind out of the gutter. After a couple of minutes assessing the area, I heard some more mind speak, "His prostate is still okay." I thought to myself, "What? You guys are the reason why my prostate levels returned back to normal?" You, the reader, need to know that I had been struggling with prostatitis for twenty-years. I almost ended up in the hospital twice. At one point, a few years earlier, I was told that my levels were nearing the possible cancerous stage and that they might have to obtain a biopsy.

Finally, the hand slid up to my abdomen and rubbed over my stomach in a circular manner for approximately thirty minutes. I felt the energy penetrating my body and I could feel something happen on the inside. You need to know that during the previous month, I had to go to the Emergency Room twice because of overwhelming pain in my abdomen. They gave me a CAT scan and discovered a golf ball-sized growth in my intestinal tract. They scheduled a colonoscopy for me so they could go inside and get a better look and obtain a biopsy.

After thirty minutes of circular rubbing of my abdomen, I heard the Bigfoot Forest Person say to the other one present, "His stomach is okay now." I immediately, engaged in mind speak and said to him, "My mouth. My mouth. Please heal my mouth." He immediately said to the other one, "I'm not touching his mouth." I had some unresolved dental issues at that time and thought I would give it a shot. Why not? They healed my leg, prostate, and apparently my stomach.

A couple days later, Cynthia and I were back in Puyallup, Washington. I was breathing in a mask that was covering my nose and mouth while counting backwards from ten. I passed out by the time I reached five. When I woke up after the colonoscopy, the physician sat there amazed and said, "I couldn't find anything. I went up there twice and gave your intestinal tract a thorough look and the growth is not there. It's gone. It's most certainly there in the CAT scan but it's no longer there in your stomach. It's gone. I'm not sure how or why it isn't there. It's a miracle."

Well, this dead man walking is happy to be alive. I'm grateful to God and to my Bigfoot Forest People friends for taking great care of me, above and beyond the call of duty. When I think about it, in theory, I should have died sometime in February of 2012. Yet, five years later, I'm still alive. I've experienced five extra years that I wasn't supposed to live. Yet, by the will of God and by the healing hands of the Bigfoot Forest People, I'm still alive today. I have no idea how much borrowed time I have left. Nevertheless, I do know that I'm grateful for every day that I wake up alive.

Regarding the healings that I've experienced over the years, when most people are seriously sick, they pray to God for a healing. They also ask their friends to pray to God on their behalf for a healing. In many cases, they ask God to provide the right medication, the financial support, and to guide the hands of the healing physician through surgery. In other words, although the surgeon does the work, the appreciation for success is often given to the surgeon but ultimately to God (i.e., God worked through the healing hands of the physician). When it comes to the healing hands of the Bigfoot Forest People, I don't see any difference. I'm grateful for their healing hands but ultimately, I give the credit and glory to God. No physician or Bigfoot Forest Person can heal anyone outside of the will of God.

The cool thing about the healing hands of the Bigfoot Forest People is that there are no appointments needed, no releases need to be signed, no co-pays are required, and the insurance companies are never billed. Oh, and no HIPAA either. Matter of fact, in the case of my leg and prostate, they obviously spotted my medical problem and chose to do something about it without even asking me if they could do something about it. I was their friend and they simply chose to help a friend out. In other words, they have a different cultural custom than we do. Today, our society is so litigious that we fear helping anyone out without having waivers and contracts signed by all parties involved first. Granted, there are still some humans who will see a need and jump in to help, whether or not they're asked to do so. Litigation be damned. Our culture is not their culture. Our customs are not their customs. They simply have a loving heart and want to help if they see that their friend has a need.

On another occasion, Kevin Beegle, a good friend of mine, had his foot healed and his leg was lengthened to match his other leg. They worked on him intensely for two nights in a row while in the Southern Oregon Interaction Area (SOIA) with me. Although he ended up in the hospital due to the intense work, he came out of the hospital doing well. His healing is medically documented with before and after X-Rays.

I'm aware of another gentleman who accompanied me to SOIA on a few occasions who was healed. At this point in time, he wishes to remain anonymous. He's one-hundred percent convinced that the Bigfoot Forest People healed him of cancer. They began their intense work on him while up on the mountain top. They followed him home and continued to work on him for several weeks afterwards. By the time they were done, he went in for a physical and was pronounced healthy. Matter of fact, the physician reviewed all of the tests that he gave to him and said that he had the test results of a twenty-five-year-old. The Bigfoot Forest People that followed him home also provided healing for one of his children and one of his parents. His family members saw that he was healed by the Bigfoot Forest People and asked him to send his friends over their way for a healing too. They quickly did so. Once again, amazing!

At this point in time, I wish to address the issue of whether or not the Bigfoot Forest People are demonic or not. The quick answer is no. They're not demonic. How can I be so certain that they're not demonic? Well, I have asked them whether or not they believe in God and that Jesus Christ is his only begotten son. I recorded them saying, "Yes, (pause) we do believe." I've also recorded them saying "Yahweh" (Hebrew for 'God') in the middle of the night while I was sleeping. Many people across North America who've been able to develop close and personal relationships with the Bigfoot Forest People, like I have, all discuss how they feel an overwhelming sense of unconditional love when they're in their presence. Finally, they're able to heal those who are sick, and in my case, prevent me from dying. I'm sorry, but demons don't do any of the above and I'm sure that they would prefer to take human life, not save human life. I strongly believe that no living being can heal anyone else apart from the will and power of God. I have much more to say about the Bigfoot Forest People and their relationship with God but it will have to wait until a later chapter.

CHAPTER TWENTY

THE BIGFOOT TEACHER

For years in the Southern Oregon Habituation Area (SOHA), I continually asked my Bigfoot Forest People friends if they would please provide me with a teacher. During every trip, I would ask, "May I have a teacher? Provide me with a teacher? Can one of the elders be my teacher? I sure would like to learn more from you. May I have a teacher?" I would ask over and over again and again. I'm sure that I sounded like a broken record to them or fingernails on a chalkboard.

In October of 2015, I took Miss Andrea Billups to the Southern Oregon Habituation Area (SOHA). Although Miss Andrea grew up in West Virginia, she most definitely isn't a mountain girl. As I pointed out in a previous chapter, she is a girlie girl and pink is the color of her national flag. She did go camping once at age eleven and then didn't repeat the act until she came out with me several decades later. By profession, she's a journalist and has written for several major publications. She has participated in presidential campaign pools following the candidate around the country as they were running for president. She teaches journalism at the University of Florida.

Upon her arrival to Oregon, keeping with tradition, we ate our first meal at the Black Bear Diner on 6th street in Grants Pass, Oregon. I carefully instructed Miss Andrea that she was to follow the established protocol in SOHA to the letter of the law. Also, she was to behave like a Navy Seal and be as strong as steel. Well, she managed to do all of the above. Matter of fact, she acted like she had been camping her whole life. I was impressed.

While we were in SOHA, Miss Andrea had the opportunity to sort through her own curiosities and fears related to the Bigfoot Forest People. She had the opportunity to hear heavy footed bipedal steps move around the perimeter of the base camp. She was able to see silhouettes accompanied by eye glow. She was able to hear some very awesome vocals. One night, when we had several Bigfoot Forest People all around our base camp area, both close and distant, we heard them taking turns trying to imitate an owl and eventually turned the noise into whooping and barking. It was both awesome and eerie. We were laying on our cots in the pitch dark of night when it took place. Although she was scared, she handled herself with great composure. Please go to SoundCloud. com and listen to the compilation of noises from her trip to SOHA in October of 2015.

On another occasion, we were standing at the 12:00 o'clock position on the perimeter of the SOHA base camp in the pitch dark of night. Standing at the 11:00 o'clock position was an eight-foot-tall Bigfoot Forest Person. Also, standing at the 1:00 o'clock position was a nine-foot-tall Bigfoot Forest Person. They were less than ten feet away from us. Talk about awesome and intimidating at the same time. I'm almost seven feet tall and it's not that often that I'm made to feel small. On this occasion, I felt very small.

Miss Andrea said, "Matt, remember that Navy Seal thing? Well, on the outside, I'm a Navy Seal and I'm as strong as steel. However, on the inside, I'm freaking out." She chose to stare at the ground in order to avoid looking at the very tall and large beings standing right in front of us. I told her that I thought she was doing a wonderful job managing her fear. I also reassured her that if the Bigfoot Forest People were menacing and dangerous, then we would be dead already. I'm not sure if she found those words to be very comforting. Nevertheless, she did a great job.

My favorite interaction with the Bigfoot Forest People in SOHA, during my trip with Miss Andrea, was when we had our sleeping cots together one night. We had a very large tarp covering the lower half of our sleeping bags. I strategically positioned the very large tarp so it would be easy to grab and pull up over the rest of our sleeping bags and our heads just in case in started to rain.

In the middle of the night, I woke up and was laying there on my back. I had my hoodie up over my head to keep my noggin warm. I also slept with a t-shirt over my eyes. No matter where I sleep, I always have to place a t-shirt over my eyes. It's a quirky little habit that I developed while in high school. Anyway, as I lay there on my back, it started to rain. All of a sudden, I felt a tug on the tarp and it was pulled from my waist up to my shoulders. Then I felt a second tug on the tarp and it was pulled from my shoulders to over the top of my head. Then I felt a third tug on the tarp and it was pulled from just over the top of my head all the way over to the ground so no moisture could reach me. I thought that was very nice of Miss Andrea to take care of me like that and to keep us dry.

I asked, "Andrea, did you just pull the tarp over the top of us?" She didn't answer me. Silence. Once again, I asked a little louder, "Andrea, did you just pull the tarp over the top of us?" Still no answer. I reached my hand over to her sleeping cot and I couldn't feel her there. I immediately pulled the tarp from over the top of me and took the t-shirt off of my eyes. I turned my head to see if she was sitting on the porta-potty positioned near the head of our cots just in case she needed to use it at night. She wasn't there. The next thing I envisioned was myself sitting on the other side of a table at the Josephine County Sheriff's Office trying to convince them that I didn't bury her body anywhere.

Now I desperately shouted her name, "Andrea!" She responded, "Yes, Matt." I asked, "Where are you?" She replied, "Down here at the bottom of my sleeping bag." Well, did I ever feel the most awesome sense of relief. I was happy to learn that she was okay and that I wasn't going to jail. You see, Miss Andrea is a tiny gal and managed to curl up in a ball near the bottom of her sleeping bag. I asked her again, "Did you pull the tarp over the top of us?" She said, "No. You just woke me up."

Suddenly, I realized who had pulled the tarp over the top of us. It was one of our Bigfoot Forest People friends. He saw that it was beginning to rain and decided to pull the tarp over both Miss Andrea and me to keep us dry. How cool is that? Talk about personalized service while Bigfooting up in the mountains. However, I do have to say that I'm just a tad bit disappointed that he neglected to turn down our beds earlier in the evening nor did I find a mint on my pillow. He's going to have to step up his game.

After I took Miss Andrea to her hotel near the Medford Airport, so she could fly back to Florida the following morning, I drove myself back up to SOHA for a solo night. I had the time to spare and wanted some alone time with my Bigfoot Forest People friends. The usual stuff took place while I was up there alone. I heard heavy footed bipedal walking, saw silhouettes and eye glow, saw the mom standing at the 3:00 o'clock position with her toddler on her shoulder, and heard vocals. Once again, this broken record asked for a teacher. I told them that I loved them and considered them to be a part of my family. I hoped that they considered me to be a part of their family. I was practically begging them to provide me with a teacher. No response.

Eventually, I went to bed and slept like a baby that night. There's absolutely nothing like being up on a mountain top all by yourself, in the pitch dark of night, totally surrounded by several Bigfoot Forest People, and knowing that you're one-hundred-percent totally safe because they've got your back while you're sleeping. They will even pull the tarp over you if it starts raining. I was very pleased with the progression of our developing relationship.

The next morning, I packed up camp into the back of my F-150 pickup truck. After I had everything loaded, I heard a mind speak asking me to read from my Bible to them. Over time, I've learned that they love to listen to the four gospels as well as the epistles of Paul. After I was done reading to them, I closed my Bible and started walking toward my truck. Suddenly, I was stopped in my tracks by a very strong and loud mind speak: "You're our teacher. That's why we bring our children to you." I responded in my own mind, "Excuse me?" The Bigfoot Forest Person repeated himself even more strongly, "You're our teacher. That's why we bring our children to you. We trust you to teach them. We have given you a guardian to protect you and keep you safe because you are our teacher."

Suddenly, the tarp being pulled over Miss Andrea and me on the previous night finally made sense. He must have been the guardian that was assigned to me because they gave me the designated role of a teacher to their children. I asked, "Who is my guardian and may I know his name?" I was told that my guardian was the adolescent male in SOHA and that his name is Ceska. I was so happy to hear the news because I literally watched Ceska grow up during my ten years in SOHA. I saw him grow from approximately five feet tall, the first time I saw him, to around seven and a half feet tall by this point in time. I used to look down at him but now I look up at him. Needless to say, I drove off the mountain one very happy camper.

During the following month, Mike Kincaid came up from the San Francisco Bay Area to spend a couple of nights with me in SOHA. We didn't allow the cold November nights to discourage us from being there. I first came across Mike, a few years earlier, when he contacted me to let me know that he found SOHA online. I had no idea who he was and responded, "Uh huh. Sure you did." He responded back, "No, seriously, I did." Then he sent me a Google Earth pic of the SOHA base camp and my heart sank. I thought to myself, "Crap! A troll finally found SOHA." However, with Mike, that wasn't the case. He was genuinely and sincerely concerned about the security of the location of SOHA. He advised me what I needed to do in order to make the area more secure. His integrity and sweet spirit won him a trip to SOHA. Over the past few years, we've become great friends. I love him like a brother.

The Bigfoot Forest People at SOHA love Mike too. They playfully interact with him every time he comes to visit. On one occasion, they saw him playing with a rather large and thick stick that had obviously been snapped in two. We were a couple hundred yards away from camp when he found it. It was about a foot and a half long. Mike was playing with it like it was a puzzle. He kept putting it together and pulling it apart. Eventually, he laid it back on the ground and we walked all the way back to camp.

The following morning, we got up to go retrieve the gifting bowls at sunrise. As we began our short trek on the trail to reach the bowls, I stopped Mike and said, "Come back here please." He walked back to the trailhead at the base camp. I asked, "Isn't that the same stick you were playing with yesterday at the other end of the trail?" He replied, "Yes." Then I asked him, "You didn't carry it back to camp did you? I thought I saw you put it back down on the ground where you found it, right?" He responded, "Yes." I said, "Mike, I think they saw you playing with it and they brought it to the base camp to leave it as a gift for you."

Mike picked up the long and thick stick and noticed that one of the pieces had been snapped in half again. Now, he had three pieces to play with as he put the puzzle together, took it apart, and then put it back together. I asked Mike to give me one of the pieces. I tried with everything I had to snap that piece in half and I couldn't even come close to doing so. I said, "Mike, they obviously like you. You're going to take that home with you because they gifted it to you." Mike insisted that I take it home with me since SOHA was my research area. I said, "No, Mike. That's their gift to you. I don't want to take your gift home with me. Besides, you can show it off to your family." Mike smiled and said, "That would be cool."

Back to our November of 2015 trip, Mike and I were enjoying our time together in SOHA. While we were walking around, I noticed that Mike was limping. Apparently, his leg was sore from playing so much basketball. Well, I wasn't the only one who saw him limping. The next morning, the blanket and tarp had been pulled off of Mike's sleeping cot and placed neatly on the ground at the foot of his bed. We both thought it was very peculiar. When he finally got up out of bed and started walking around, he noticed that his pain was gone. He wasn't limping anymore. He said, "I think they healed me in my sleep." I told him that I agreed with his assessment. However, being a friend who loves him like a brother, I also said to him, "Unfortunately, I don't think they healed your face. It's still hurting me." We both laughed. We have both my son, Grady, and Howie Gordon to thank for their endless face jokes.

During our last night at SOHA, I was sleeping like a baby again. My cot was placed in a parallel position about three feet away from my truck. I had my Bionic Ear parabolic microphone dish and Sony digital recorder running all night long. I woke up shortly after 4:00 am. I was sleeping on my left side facing the truck. As always, I had my hoodie over the top of my head to keep my noggin warm. I also had a t-shirt draped over my eyes. As I laid there on my cot, I asked in my mind, "Are you still there?" My guardian, Ceska, walked between me and the truck, bent over and said in my ear, "Yes (pause), right here beside you." I immediately took the t-shirt off of my eyes and I couldn't see him because he was cloaked. Nevertheless, I heard him walk back to his position at the head of my cot and stand there. I looked at my watch and saw that it was 4:05 am.

When I returned home, I did the math. I knew that I started recording at 8:00 pm sharp on the previous night. I knew that he said, "Yes (pause), right here beside you" at 4:05 am. Therefore, all I had to do was fast forward eight hours and five minutes into the recording in order to find the vocal. Well, I did exactly that. Guess what I found? That's right, "Yes (pause), right here beside you."

Now, please think about this for a moment. Ceska is not dumb. He knew that I was recording all night long. He could have responded back to my question via mind speak. Instead, he intentionally chose to walk between me and the Bionic Ear parabolic microphone dish and vocalize, "Yes (pause), right here beside you." Don't believe me? Think I'm full of crap? Well, guess what I'm going to tell you to do? That's right, please go to SoundCloud.com and type in "Team Squatchin USA." Go listen to the vocal for yourself. Please keep in mind that he said it in his Squatchy tone of voice rather than in a human dialect. It's an amazing recording!

All of the above was a major confirmation that, indeed, I had been assigned the role of teacher for the youth of the Bigfoot Forest People family and their clan. That, indeed, I had been given a guardian because of my designation as the teacher. He not only stood by the head of my cot all night long in SOHA, every night, but he also followed me home and spends more nights than not standing in my bedroom watching over me. How do I know? I've heard him shifting his weight on the wood floor. I've heard him talk in his Squatchy tone of voice. The first few nights he was in my room, he let out the Squatchy smell full force. I almost gagged on the smell. No, it wasn't me farting underneath the bed covers. My farts don't smell anything like the unique Squatchy smell. After a few times, I asked him to tone it down several notches so he did. Finally, after the very first night he showed up in my bedroom, without having said anything to anyone, Grady told me that he saw Ceska walking down the hill in the backyard toward the Rogue River. Grady described him perfectly.

I know all of the above sounds crazy to you. However, just a public service reminder, I don't lie and I don't hoax. If I said it happened, guess what? It happened. My track record is perfect. Multiple witnesses and circumstantial evidence back up my research. Go watch the YouTube videos, listen to the SoundCloud.com audio recordings, and read the individual testimonies in the back of the book. Besides, you haven't seen crazy yet. There's still more to share with you as we slide down the Rabbit Hole together.

CHAPTER TWENTY-ONE

THE TROLLS INVADE SOHA

On December 25, 2015, Cynthia and I spent Christmas night in the Southern Oregon Habituation Area (SOHA). Little did we know; it would be our last night there. It was chilly and snow partially covered the ground. Because the sun was going down fast, we put some bread products in the gifting bowls and set them out in the gifting area away from the base camp.

Shortly after our return to the base camp, our SOHA Bigfoot Forest People family immediately surrounded us. I explained to them what Christmas was about and Cynthia and I proceeded to sing various Christmas Carols to them. Although we could clearly hear them walking around the perimeter of the base camp that night, we were perplexed the next morning when we couldn't find one single track in the snow. As we drove off the mountain, we were clueless about the plans that were already in progress for the TROLLS to invade SOHA a couple days later.

No matter where you go on planet Earth, you will always find kind people with good hearts and open minds. You will always find people who are willing to help others out at the drop of a hat. They're willing to give others their time, money, and emotional support. These kind people are an inspiration to all of us and motivate many to 'pay it forward' to help others. Finally, these kind people help to bring light into the darkness and love to the unlovable. The Bigfoot Forest People are drawn to these kinds of humans.

However, to everything, there is an opposite. We have Yin and Yang. The light side and the dark side of the force. God and the devil. Jesus and the demons. Good and evil. Why do you think the Star Wars movies are so successful? Simply put, it's because the storylines are all centered on this simple truth: Good vs Evil. Everyone enjoys the Star Wars movies because they want to see Good triumph over Evil. In the end, no matter how bad it gets, everyone wants to see faith, hope, and love prevail. The greatest of these is love.

Well, almost everyone. Then again, we do have the TROLLS among us. The TROLLS are a small group of individuals who have found one another in the dark cesspools in cyberspace. Birds of a feather flock together. They're also known as HATERS. They're the group of people who plot against others and love to rain on their parade. No matter what evil acts they engage in, they will find a way to justify their behaviors in a way that makes sense to them. In the meantime, everyone else's jaws drop in disbelief that any human being would intentionally behave that way toward someone else.

In a nutshell, TROLLS hate others because they hate themselves. They project out their own self-loathing perceptions on to others in order to avoid their own interpersonal pain. Misery loves company. They have no understanding of 'love your neighbor as yourself' because they have no love for self. As a result, they feel best when others are in pain. They rejoice when others are in tears. They celebrate their nefarious triumphs while others grieve the loss of their accomplishments. In short, they shun the light and love of God while dancing in the dark with the devil. They are blinded by their own self-hatred and mock all that is truthful and good. The life of a TROLL is a very sad life indeed.

Two days later, the TROLLS arrived at the SOHA base camp, spent about thirty minutes there, shot a video, declared that I was hoaxing, and posted the coordinates online for the rest of the world to see. By the way, I will not mention them by name because they're not worthy of penning their names in ink on the pages of my book. They're not worthy of the time or attention. The funny thing is that they thought they were going to receive positive responses online from the Bigfoot researchers' community after they posted their video. Instead, they were hammered by everyone for violating the unwritten and unspoken researchers' ethic: "Thou shalt not invade another's research area."

How did they find the location of SOHA? Well, because one of the forty plus people that I brought up there threw me under the bus and revealed the location to the TROLLS. I know exactly who did it too. Although my natural response is to want to respond in kind, I refuse to lower myself down to their level of pond scum.

By the way, this wasn't the first time that the TROLLS attacked me in a very personal way. On a previous occasion, they filed a false complaint with the psychologist licensing board, alleging drug use and psychosis. They actually attempted to go after my livelihood. Fortunately, the board saw through their disingenuous motives, dismissed their complaint, and gave me their contact information because the complaint was so inappropriate. The psychologist licensing board made it clear to those filing the false and bogus complaints that I've not harmed any of my clients and that they're not in the habit of monitoring the hobbies of psychologists. Case closed.

When Cynthia and I learned that the TROLLS had invaded SOHA and watched the video online, we both cried. We both felt like we were kicked in the stomach. We grieved the loss of ten years of work. We couldn't believe that anyone would stoop so low and be so proud of their behaviors. Very, very, sad. Many kind people with good hearts reached out to us and offered condolences.

Shortly thereafter, I was given a vision of some mountains and surrounding scenery that I had seen about fifteen years earlier. I was told in my mind, "If you go to this spot, we will guide you from there." The grief and loss were short-lived. I was excited to receive the vision. I had never been knowingly led to a research area before by the Bigfoot Forest People. What the TROLLS intended for evil was ultimately used to for good.

Part 4

THE INTERACTION
RESEARCH METHOD

CHAPTER TWENTY-TWO

THE SOUTHERN OREGON INTERACTION AREA (SOIA)

In early January of 2016, I drove out to the area of the vision that was given to me. I was eager to find it and proceed to the next level of relationship development with the Bigfoot Forest People. Since Cynthia had to return home to Washington in order to go back to work, I asked a mutual friend of ours to tag along with me on this new adventure. Therefore, Jill Ligda joined me in my F-150 pickup truck as we navigated the logging roads for several hours. I always prefer to have one or more witnesses accompany me in order to verify and validate my experiences.

The first area we stopped at down a dead end logging road just didn't feel like it was the right spot to me. Nevertheless, Jill wanted to get out of the truck and check out the area. I parked the truck and we started looking around. Within a minute or less, we had found a snapped over tree, branches woven together, and some very large Bigfoot tracks walking through the area and up a hill. Although Jill was excited, I told her that I wanted to keep looking because this just didn't feel like the spot to me.

We climbed back into the truck and continued driving up and down logging roads for a few hours. Then I turned down a logging road, followed it for several miles, and ended up in a rather large area that would be perfect for a base camp. We drove down a skidder road leading away from this large area until I was forced to turn my truck around and head back to the base camp.

Jill got out of the truck and stood by the edge of the road guiding me so I wouldn't go over the steep embankment. I went forward and backwards, forward and backwards, and forward and backwards until I successfully turned my truck around. Then I parked my truck and killed the engine.

Jill stood outside the truck by the driver's door as I remained in my seat. I thanked her for helping me to turn my truck around. Suddenly, we both heard what sounded like four very loud foot stomps on the hillside about sixty feet below us. Then we saw a very tall skinny tree get pulled to the left and then pushed back over to our right and onto the ground. The tree had been snapped right in front of our eyes. If that wasn't a major confirmation from our Bigfoot Forest People friends that we had found the new area where they wanted us to come to, I don't know what is.

I climbed out of my truck and stood on the road, looking down the hillside with Jill. We couldn't see anything or anyone who could have snapped the tree over. It was pretty obvious to both of us that we had a cloaked Bigfoot Forest Person in our midst. We said "hello" and thanked him for the confirmation. Then we sat down on the nearby log.

Jill looked over at me and said, "This is pretty overwhelming for you, isn't it? I can tell by the look on your face."

I responded, "Yes, it is. When I was given the vision to find the new location, I didn't think that it was going to happen so fast. I most certainly didn't think that four loud stomps and a tree being pushed over right in front of our faces would accompany it. Although I have to admit that it was pretty cool."

Jill said, "Yes, that was very cool."

As we climbed back into the pickup truck, as Jill previously stated, I was very overwhelmed by the very overt interaction displayed to confirm the fact that we had successfully arrived at the new location. We drove back down the skidder road to the very large base camp area. I parked the truck again and Jill and I got out to explore the area. We hiked up a trail and found several large Bigfoot Forest People tracks in the ground. We also found some very large trees that had been lifted, stacked, and woven in ways that no human being could have performed.

After some lengthy hiking, we sat down on a log to rest. As we were sitting there and talking, we could both tell that we were being watched. It was a very cool sensation. I saw an Orb flash to my right. Our conversation continued until we heard a very loud 'thud' on the log just to my right. I looked down on the ground and there sat a very large pinecone that had been chucked at the log in order to get our attention. It most definitely did not fall from the tree above because there were no trees with pinecones on them in the surrounding area. Another confirmation that we had arrived at the right spot.

Jill said, "Well, they're going out of their way to let you know that you're in the right spot." I nodded my head in agreement. She looked at my face and asked, "Still overwhelmed?"

I responded, "Yup. Still overwhelmed but in a very happy way. I'm actually blown away by just how quickly this all has happened. I was thinking that the 'guiding process' was going to take six to twelve months. I didn't think we would find the area during our first trip out here."

As we walked back toward the base camp area, I heard some tree knocks emanating from the base camp area. I was hoping that we might have some visible guests waiting for us upon our arrival but no such luck. All I could think of in my mind was how grateful I was that SOHA had been breached and that I was being moved on in such an overwhelming and incredibly awesome manner. I don't think that too many people can claim that they were given a vision and led to their spot in the woods to be with the Bigfoot Forest People. This was truly special.

Jill and I drove on the logging roads and eventually left the area and reentered civilization with homes, livestock, cars, and roads. I felt compelled to stop my truck and get out to snap a couple of pictures of the mountains and surrounding area so I could send a picture to Cynthia so she could know what the vision looked like that the Bigfoot

Forest People had given to me earlier. As I stood on the road and faced the mountains, I snapped three quick pictures with my cell phone. I'm always in the habit of taking several pictures in the hope that at least one of them will actually turn out nice.

I dropped Jill off and I returned home. I began to look through my cell phone pictures because I wanted to send the right picture to Cynthia that would give her the best representation of the vision that was given to me in my mind. As I reviewed the three pictures in order to choose one of them, I eventually noticed something that I missed at first. Clearly, in the first picture, there was a distant Orb up in the clouds far away from me. In the second picture, the Orb had descended and came closer to me. In the third picture, the Orb was up close and personal to me.

I took those three pictures over a five-second period of time. In other words, that Orb covered a whole lot of ground in a very short period of time. It was like it was descending to say 'goodbye' to us and confirming, once again, that we were in the right place. As planned, I sent the pictures to Cynthia and didn't say a word to her. She spotted the descending Orb immediately and was equally blown away. She agreed with me that we had obviously found the right spot.

Not that long afterwards, I drove out to SOIA to spend one night all by myself. While I was out there, I saw two different orbs, heard several tree knocks, saw a Bigfoot Forest Person standing at the 2:00 o'clock position on the perimeter watching me for over fifteen minutes, and heard what sounded like young ones talking to each other just barely within earshot. As I slept out in the open on my cot that night, I heard footsteps walk up to the head of my cot. Then he squatted down beside my cot and audibly stated his name to me, "Onx." I asked in my mind, "Is that your name? Onx?" He replied utilizing mind speak, "Yes, my name is Onx. I am Ceska's cousin and I am now your guardian since you have been moved to our home." I replied, "Thank you for having me in your home." Onx stood up and walked away.

Shortly thereafter, I brought Alyssa Runswithwolves out to SOIA with me. Talk about a ball of energy. I want whatever she has because I believe that we could provide power for the whole city of Grants Pass, Oregon. I'm not talking about hyperactive energy. I'm referring more to a zest for life and a connection to the Earth. When I took her out to SOIA for a day trip, she immediately spotted a big blue Orb along the way. Amazing!

When we parked in the very large base camp area and got out of the pickup truck, she immediately commented on the energy that she could feel in the area. We hiked on a trail and found Bigfoot tracks and large trees that had been moved in ways that aren't possible for humans to do. We hung a right and started hiking up the side of a mountain on an old abandoned skidder road. The road had to have been abandoned about forty or fifty years ago.

While Alyssa and I were hiking up the skidder road, it became apparent to the both of us that something or someone had been placing freshly snapped trees and torn branches in piles. The very large piles appeared to be created as barriers and obstacles to prevent the ascension to the top of the ridgeline. Nevertheless, we made it to the top in spite of the strategically placed vegetative debris. Also, I must say, that I felt like a majorly out of shape old fart while hiking up the hill. Why? Well, because Alyssa could have run up to the top of the hill, back down to the bottom, and back to the top again before I reached the ridgeline. She was very patient with me along the way.

It was a beautiful sunny day and we enjoyed our stroll along the top of the ridgeline. There was nothing significant up there on the top. However, Alyssa noticed a line of energy up on top of the ridgeline. Perhaps there were one or more portals up there? Who knows. The scenic views were certainly worth the hike to the top.

On our way back down the mountainside, we stopped over by some very large stumps. Alyssa thought she had seen something large near one of the stumps. By the time we got there, whatever she had seen had either run away or had cloaked itself. While continuing our hike back down to the bottom of the hill, I couldn't help but notice that it appeared that a couple more snapped trees and branches may have been added to the various piles while we were at the top of the ridgeline enjoying the views.

A couple of weeks later, Mike Kincaid and Patrick Epistemon visited SOIA. Both were free to explore the area on their own and took advantage of their freedom to do so. They both found Bigfoot tracks and obvious signs of manipulating large trees and branches. A very large structure was found that was built with very large, long logs. They were elevated a good ten feet off the ground or more. It looked like a Bigfoot Forest Person was playing with large-sized Lincoln Logs.

SOIA was conveniently located much closer to home and, therefore, I could visit it more frequently. I would drive out to SOIA for day trips and spend a couple of hours at a time. While sitting out in the base camp, I would read from my Bible to the Bigfoot Forest People. Sometimes, I would hike away from the base camp to go see if I could find any new evidence. I also needed the exercise. One time, as I was hiking back to the base camp, I swear there must have been about one-hundred tree knocks sounding off in and around the base camp area. By the time I returned to the base camp, it was silent. I know I wasn't hearing things because Zeus, my six-pound Toy Fox Terrier, heard the tree. It was like an Iron Butterfly 'Inagodadavida' drum solo.

In the midst of all of the excitement regarding the new research area, my silent supporter, Cynthia, has had to live vicariously through all of my online reports, YouTube videos, and our daily telephone conversations. Maintaining a four-hundred-mile long distance relationship has most definitely been challenging but not impossible. It's been especially hard on Cynthia not to be present and share in the ongoing developments in my relationship building with the Bigfoot Forest People. Unfortunately, there's this thing called reality which requires us to have jobs and pay bills. I've been blessed to have her support while transitioning back to Grants Pass during the past year in order to be closer to Grady. Hopefully, she will join me soon in southern Oregon.

In April of 2016, Cynthia informed me that she was going to be able to take some time off to join me in SOIA. Needless to say, I was excited for her to have the opportunity to come south, spend time with me, and spend some time with our Bigfoot Forest People family. If anyone deserved to be there and enjoy the experiences, it was her. I was looking forward to spending this time with Cynthia in SOIA before we drove back north and hosted our annual Bigfoot University conference in Bremerton, Washington. Little did I know, Onx had some exciting plans in store for us as well.

CHAPTER TWENTY-THREE

THE BIGFOOT AGENDA REVEALED

Cynthia walked through the revolving door at the Rogue Valley International Airport in Medford, Oregon. I gave her a big long hug and a kiss on top of her head, as is customary for our initial reunions. She travels lightly so we bypassed the luggage area and headed straight out into the parking lot and climbed into my truck. Zeus, the 'official mascot of Team Squatchin USA', was eagerly awaiting his mother's arrival and greeted her inside the truck with enthusiastic licks and kisses all over her face. From there, we headed to the Black Bear Diner for breakfast and then on to the Southern Oregon Interaction Area (SOIA).

I was excited to finally be able to show Cynthia all around SOIA. It was now her turn to experience and interact with the Bigfoot Forest People in our new area. We planned to spend three nights in SOIA and then drive back to Puyallup, Washington so we could prepare for our annual Bigfoot University conference. Most people don't realize this because I'm the upfront guy but Cynthia is the background girl. She's the backbone of the conference and is the major reason for its annual success.

Upon our arrival to SOIA, we set up our sleeping cots, chairs, and table. Once we were settled in, I took Cynthia for a long walk and showed her the area. We walked down the skidder road and I showed her where the tree got pushed over in front of Jill Ligda and me. As we walked the full length of the dead end road and then back to the base camp, we didn't notice or see anything unusual, including tracks on the ground. We rested for a bit in the base camp and talked about the other past events that had been witnessed in SOIA by myself, Jill, Alyssa, Mike, and Patrick.

After a much needed rest, I took Cynthia in the other direction. We hiked up a trail for quite a ways and she was able to spot fresh Bigfoot tracks on the ground. Then she spotted the large trees that had been placed alongside the trail and leaning against other live trees. She was as amazed as I was because there's no way a human being could have lifted them and put them there. I showed her where Jill and I were sitting and resting on the log when it got thumped by the large pinecone. Cynthia was in agreement that there were no trees in the immediate area where the pinecone could have fallen from above.

Finally, I showed Cynthia where the abandoned skidder road was that went up the mountainside where Alyssa and I hiked to the top and then walked the ridgeline. The daylight hours were still short so we agreed to put that hike off until the following day so we wouldn't be rushed. Besides, we had already done a lot of hiking for one day. We walked back to the base camp and prepared for the evening.

At this point in time, I was instructed that I didn't need to put out the gifting bowls any longer. I was informed that we were beyond the habituation interactions. However, I was told that if I wanted to, I could leave some food for them on the table inside of the base camp perimeter. That was surprising to hear but made life a whole lot easier for me. I didn't have to walk outside of the base camp anymore while singing, 'Row, Row, Row Your Boat.' I also didn't have to clean the gifting bowls while wearing surgical gloves because we were no longer collecting fingerprints. In short, we were making a new transition from the habituation research method to the interaction research method.

As darkness fell upon SOIA, we sat in our chairs and enjoyed the clear skies and stars at night. We scanned the perimeter and hillside as we talked during the evening. We continued with our 'no lights' policy so we could see more clearly in the dark. Around 10 pm at night, we both noticed a very tall silhouette and eye glow at the 2 o'clock position on the perimeter. We were being watched and felt looked out for and protected.

About an hour later, we both saw a very tall cloaked image walk into the SOIA base camp and over by the table where we placed the food. The cloaked image looked like the shimmering image in the Arnold Schwarzenegger movie, "Predator." We both sat there with our jaws dropped in amazement. Eventually, the figure walked back out of camp from the same direction that it walked into camp.

As usual, I played my music via my MP3 player and portable Bose speaker. Cynthia played her flute. We both sang songs individually and together. Just because we were changing from the habituation method to the interaction method didn't mean that we were going to stop the utilization of music. The Bigfoot Forest People love, love, love music. When you think about it, at most social events involving humans, music is at least quietly playing in the background if not loudly at the forefront of the activity. Music is a social lubricant for positive interactions.

Eventually, both Cynthia and I hit the wall. It was time to crawl into our sleeping bags and go to bed. We lay on our backs while staring up at the stars and enjoyed our time alone in the middle of the wilderness. I fell quickly asleep while Cynthia lay awake for a while. She heard vocals around the perimeter of the base camp as well as bipedal steps inside the perimeter of the base camp. She was happy to be in SOIA with me and enjoying our time alone with our friends.

In the middle of the night, just after I adjusted my position inside my sleeping bag, I heard some bipedal footsteps over by the table which was about thirty feet away from us. It was too dark to see anything. I clearly heard two Bigfoot Forest People whispering to one another as they stood beside the table. Suddenly, I heard something go thump on the ground. It sounded like something was slid off of the table. Once again, it was too dark to see. Nevertheless, the unusual sound got my curiosity juices flowing.

Later that morning, after the sun rose, Cynthia and I eventually woke up. We laid there in our sleeping bags talking because it was still cold outside. We shared what we heard go bump in the night. We both had heard bipedal steps walking around the base camp, including near the head of our sleeping cots. We also heard what sounded like the young ones playing and talking to one another. Finally, I shared with her about the thump on the ground that I heard near the table in the middle of the night. I told her that it was too dark for me to see anything.

Once we crawled out of our sleeping bags, we put our shoes on and walked over to the table where I had placed two gifting bowls with Hawaiian Butter Sweet Rolls inside. The Bigfoot Forest People love, love, love bread products. The table sits about four feet off the ground and the only thing missing from the gifting bowls was one roll taken from the middle. I walked around the table and noticed the carton of one dozen eggs upright on the ground. Not one egg was missing or broken. It looked as if Onx had slid the eggs off the table and on to the ground. How they ended upright and unscathed is beyond my reasoning.

About thirty seconds later, I received a very strong and stern mind speak from Onx, "Please stop using the eggs as a control variable." Apparently, Onx did not appreciate the placement of the one dozen eggs on the table next to the gifting bowls. I didn't do anything to intentionally frustrate him. Matter of fact, it was just a leftover habit from SOHA. Every time I put the gifting bowls out at SOHA, I always placed a carton of one dozen eggs next to the bowls as a means of determining if the bowls were hit by little critters. There was no way that opportunistic little critters would ever leave the eggs untouched.

Anyway, placing the one dozen eggs out on the table with the gifting bowls was simply a habit that I developed during the habituation process. Once again, Onx was making it clear that we were beyond the habituation research process. We were now interacting with one another. He made it clear to me that they don't require me to leave out any food for them. Nevertheless, if I feel like leaving them food as merely a friendly gesture and not to document or prove anything, then they just might help themselves occasionally. But stop leaving the eggs out because we're way beyond that stage. I complied with Onx's wishes. No more eggs, no more control variables.

At this point, I should make it clear to the reader that by switching from the habituation research method over to the interaction research method, I essentially committed myself to backing away from the collection of most of the circumstantial evidence that I used to collect in the past, including casting tracks, looking for prints on the bowls, collecting hair and saliva samples, obtaining audio recordings of spoken language, etc. In short, during the new transition, the focus has shifted over from collecting circumstantial evidence to simply interacting with the Bigfoot Forest People and collecting witness testimonies.

The point being is that I have collected enough circumstantial evidence and witness testimonies over the years to establish my credibility as a Bigfoot researcher. In other words, there's absolutely no doubt that I don't lie and I don't hoax. If I said it happened, guess what? It happened. My word has been thoroughly vetted and verified by multiple eyewitnesses. My reputation is solid gold. Therefore, I don't need to collect any more circumstantial evidence unless it's been intentionally gifted to me. I'm not turning away a gift from our Bigfoot Forest People friends. The focus now is simply on relationship building, learning, and teaching.

Cynthia and I ate our breakfast, cleaned up camp, and went for our hike up the abandoned skidder trail in order to ascend to the top and hike the ridgeline trail. We got an early enough start that we had plenty of daylight to burn and no reason to feel rushed. As we made our way up the mountainside, I kept quiet and waited for Cynthia to point out the obvious signs. She was clearly noticing the same piled up debris and vegetative obstacles that Alyssa and I had noticed on a previous day hike. Cynthia was able to reach the same conclusions that much of it was freshly snapped or torn and recently placed in the piles. However, what she couldn't have noticed was the fact that there were more new trees and branches placed on top of the various piles that weren't there when Alyssa and I had hiked up the mountainside. I pointed out the new vegetation to Cynthia and she checked it out and verified that it had recently been snapped or torn based on the fresh light brown coloration of the wood.

Once we made it to the top of the mountain and reached the ridgeline trail, we rested for a bit. It was another beautiful day of hiking and enjoying the views from on top. Unlike the previous trip with Alyssa, we actually did find some fresh Bigfoot tracks up on the ridgeline. It was exciting to be learning about the local area, the trails they used, and the structures they were building. Most important of all to me, it was nice to finally be sharing that time in SOIA with Cynthia. Although I enjoy taking my other friends out there with me, they're not my soulmates. It was a beautiful day. By the time we made it back down the mountainside to the base camp, I was exhausted.

Once again, I placed some Hawaiian Butter Sweet Rolls in only one gifting bowl this time on top of the table. Two gifting bowls full of Hawaiian Butter Sweet Rolls seemed like overkill to me since Onx only took one roll last time. I did not place the eggs back on the table top. Instead, they were placed back inside the cab of my pickup truck. I did not want to offend him again.

Cynthia and I enjoyed another evening of sitting in the dark, singing, talking, laughing, whistling, playing music, talking, singing, laughing, playing the flute, and basically entertaining our friends of the forest for several hours. Once again, we noticed that we were being watched from the 2:00 o'clock position on the hillside above us. The eye glow was incredible. However, on this second night, we noticed more silhouettes and eye glow surrounding us. We also heard some occasional bipedal walking, tree knocks, and vocals. It was another beautiful starry, starry night. How awesome of a time was this? Incredible! However, I guess we could have gone golfing instead. Ho hum!

We reached that time of night when we were both hitting the wall and needed to go to sleep. We were both exhausted from the hike up to the top of the mountain and our bodies were demanding to engage in nocturnal dreaming. So we did just that. We crawled into our bags, stared at the stars and talked for a couple of minutes, and then said good night. I was out like a light and Cynthia wasn't that far behind me. It was another peaceful uneventful night in SOIA, or was it?

In the middle of the quiet night in SOIA, Onx woke me up from a deep sleep. He allowed me to lay on my back, enjoy the stars, and slowly orient myself to a state of being fully awake. Once he sensed that I was fully alert, he proceeded to engage in a two-hour mind speak with me. He shared information with me that was totally unexpected, overwhelming, emotionally moving, and exciting. There's absolutely no way to prepare for a moment like this. However, I will try my best to share only the highlights with you. Otherwise, this will become a thousand-page book.

As I lay there on my cot staring up at the stars, Onx said to me, "I need to talk with you about something very important to my people. We have never spoken to any humans about this. We trust you with this information. We are placing the future of our loved ones in your hands." I just laid on my sleeping cot feeling majorly complimented while at the same time feeling very overwhelmed. I thought, "We are placing the future of our loved ones in your hands? What in the world is he going to tell me?" I laid there waiting for Onx to proceed. After some silence, he continued to speak to me.

Onx asked me, "Do you remember the portal in the other location? The one that you and your friends stumbled across? The one that you were able to reopen several times? You were the first human on Earth to do that. No one else has repeatedly reopened a portal. The elders want me to talk with you and explain our plans and hopes with you. Are you willing to hear them? May I proceed?" I responded, "Yes, I remember all of it. Yes, please do proceed."

Onx shared, "The portal that you found is only one of many portals all over the Earth and across the universe. They were placed here and everywhere else, a long time ago before the human race came into existence, by an ancient alien race. A long time ago, some of our people learned how to manipulate the portals and travel through them. Not all of our people were born with the ability to do so. The portal that you saw with the red sky and the dark scraggly vegetation is our home world. Our planet has been dying for a very long time. Our sun has slowly been burning out. It takes a very long time for a sun to burn out. When our elders on our home world first realized that our sun was beginning to die, members of our race were sent out to find one or more worlds that we could colonize. Please remember, not all of our people can manipulate and travel through the portals. Also, we can only travel through the portal by ourselves. We cannot take anyone through the portal with us. Are you understanding me?" I responded, "Yes, I believe I'm understanding what you're saying to me."

Onx continued, "Eventually, one of our people found Earth and reported back to our elders. They approved a plan for all individuals who could travel through the portal to go to Earth and start a new home world. One quarter of our home world traveled through the portals and reached Earth. Three quarters of our people were left behind because they could not travel through the portals on their own. Do you have any questions?" I responded, "No, I believe that I'm understanding everything so far. Please continue."

Next, Onx shared with me, "Our people are all connected with one another. What one knows, we all know. What one feels, we all feel. We are all connected. Although one quarter of our people migrated to Earth, those of us who can do so have been traveling back and forth to our home world to visit with our family and friends ever since the great migration. When we arrive to our home world, what we know and feel while on the Earth, they get to know and feel on our home world. Also, what they know and feel on our home world, everyone on Earth also get to know and feel when we come back to Earth. We feel their despair. We feel their hopelessness. We feel their pending doom."

At this moment in time, Onx shared, only for a brief tolerable moment, all of those feelings with me. I cried. I'm crying now as I type this. It was very emotionally overwhelming. It was just like the time in SOHA when Ceska asked me what my intentions were, I told him to earn their trust and friendship, and he said, "Thank you!" I felt the emotions behind his expression of "Thank you!" Only this time I was feeling the despair and hopelessness of all the inhabitants from their dying home world. I was feeling their feelings of being trapped and the impending doom. It was very sad and overwhelming.

Onx shared, "We've been waiting a long time for the human race to develop technologically because we are not a technological people. We are a natural people and blend in with our environment. We are not engineers. After your second world war, we realized that the human race was almost at the point where they could help us so we created a plan. An agenda. In order to get the attention of the human race, we decided to start leaving many foot tracks in the mountains in northern California. Eventually, we were able to get your Patterson and Gimlin to film one of our people. We had her uncloak and slowly walk away from them. She could have cloaked right away or walked over to the brush and trees. Instead, we had her slowly walk away in the clearing because we wanted her to be filmed for a long time." I asked, "Why did you want her to be filmed?"

Onx responded, "We needed her to be filmed so we could get the attention of the humans. We wanted humans to start coming out to the forest to look for us. We hoped that kind people with good hearts and open minds would look for us and not be scared away. Those who were not scared away, we hoped that they would want to develop a friendship with us. Those who would develop a friendship with us, we hoped that they would stumble across a portal and not be scared away. Those who were willing to come back to the portal and study it, we were hoping that they would figure out how to reopen it. You're the first one on Earth who figured out how to reopen it. When you demonstrated that you could repeatedly reopen the portal, the elders decided to move you to a new area and have me tell you about our plans."

At this point in time, I feel it necessary to point out to the reader an analogy that makes sense to me from my own life experiences regarding the plan or agenda of the Bigfoot Forest People. In grade school, a lot of kids play basketball. In middle school, many of those kids get cut from the teams. Once high school is reached, even more of those kids get cut from the teams again. Then few of those high school kids actually make a collegiate basketball team. Afterwards, less than one percent of the graduating college seniors make it into the NBA. Once they reach the NBA, only a few players make the two NBA All-Star Teams. Finally, only a few of the NBA All-Star team members make the Olympic Dream Team. Last but not least, only one NBA player receives the Most Valuable Player (MVP) award. I call it the 'funnel effect'.

Onx then said to me, "We have spread our eggs out into many baskets. We have reached out to many people hoping that they would reach back to us, discover the portal, return to the portal, and eventually figure out how to reopen the portal. We are reaching out to many people because some humans may become frustrated and quit. Others may become ill. Some may die. Although I'm telling you this because you're the first human to figure out how to reopen the portal, we are still reaching out to others because you may quit, become ill, or die. Do you have any questions?" I responded, "No, I'm still following you. I believe I understand what you're trying to say to me."

Onx then said, "We need your help. We need you to put a team of humans together. We need you to create a shunt." I asked, "A shunt?" Onx said, "Yes, a shunt. We need a shunt. Do you understand?" I said, "No, sorry, I don't understand." Onx said, "We need a shunt. We need you to help us keep the portal open. A shunt. We need a shunt." I felt embarrassed because I'm not mechanically inclined. I asked, "Do you mean a stent?" I knew that stents are used to help keep blood vessels open. Onx said, "Yes, like a stent. But we need a shunt. A shunt. Can you help us? Will you help us?"

I said, "Onx, I will do everything I can to help your people. I will put together a team of humans to put our heads together in order to create the shunt that your people are in need of. What are we going to do with this shunt?" He responded to me, "You are going to help us keep the portal open so we can bring the rest of our people from our home planet to Earth. Will you do that for us?"

I laid there for a moment and thought, "Who am I to be making a decision like this?" Then I remembered what a bunch of knuckleheads we have in Congress, the White House, and around the world. I thought to myself, "I trust me and my judgment more than I trust those idiots." I asked Onx, "Wait a second. How do I know that you're not deceiving me and that you're asking me to help you bring over an invasion force to annihilate the human race?"

Onx paused for a moment and then said, "Please tell me about any time in human history where we tried to harm the human race? If we wanted to, we could have annihilated the human race a long time ago. You know from your experience with us that we have no other intentions but positive ones for the human race. We all come from the same God. Haven't we treated you with kindness, love, patience, and respect?" I said, "You're right. I apologize. Thank you for answering me."

Once again, Onx asked me, "Are you willing to put a team together to create a shunt for us? The end is near and there isn't much time left to help our people on our home world." I responded, "Onx, you need to understand that I'm not mechanically inclined. However, I know a lot of people and I believe that I have the resources and connections to help put together a successful team in order to help your people." Onx responded, "Thank you. We will wait for your success. In the meantime, please continue to come out and visit with us."

Before Onx left the area, I asked him one last question, "Are you willing to tell me how you are able to cloak and uncloak?" Onx responded, "Yes. Our natural state of existence is at a higher vibrational frequency than humans. Therefore, we are outside of your visual field of range. However, some animals can still see us such as canines and felines. Your cameras can catch images of us too even when you can't see us with your own eyes. Your pictures are often blurry because of our high vibrational frequency. If and when we are interested in having one of more humans to see us with their own eyes, we will intentionally slow down our vibrational frequency. When we do this, we become solid beings just like humans are solid beings." I laid on my cot in amazement because there was so much more to learn. I said, "Thank you for visiting with me and for trusting me. I will try my very hardest not to let your people down." He said, "We know you will. We trust your heart and intentions."

Our conversation came to an end and Onx walked away. I laid there under the stars enjoying the beauty of the universe. As I laid there staring at the stars, I was wondering where their home world was. Could I see their sun or was their planet located way beyond my field of vision? I also laid there totally honored that I was asked to help their people, while at the same time, I was overwhelmed that I was asked to assist them. I guess that's the price I get to pay for figuring out how to repeatedly reopen a portal.

I eventually fell back to sleep. When Cynthia and I woke up in the morning, I apologized to her because I knew that we had planned on being in SOIA for three nights, but I told her that Onx had spoken to me that night for about two hours and we needed to head back to Puyallup, Washington immediately. She asked me what Onx had said but I told her that we would talk once we hit the interstate five headed north. She patiently waited to hear all about it once we started driving north on I-5. I was feeling overwhelmed by the burden placed on me and I wanted to roll up my sleeves and get to work immediately.

As we drove north from Grants Pass, Oregon to Puyallup, Washington, I told Cynthia about what Onx had said to me. At first, she became worried that I was experiencing a heart problem because I had mentioned the words shunt and stent. Finally, I was able to reassure her that there was nothing wrong with my heart. I told her that the Bigfoot Forest People needed us to put together a team to create a shunt for the portal to help keep it open so all of their people remaining on their home world could come to Earth because their sun was dying. Cynthia was one hundred percent onboard with me. She understood my desire to cut our trip short by one day.

As we drove north, I was contacted via my cell phone from a gentleman out east who was retired but had a history of working with the Massachusetts Institute of Technology (MIT) as a physicist. He had heard me on Coast to Coast AM with Bob Gimlin. My description of the portal in SOHA had caught his attention because it fit exactly what he was learning about with his studying of the Bermuda Triangle. He concluded that the Bermuda Triangle was actually a very large portal that was taking our ships and planes and transporting them to another dimension. He wanted to learn more about the SOHA portal and my ability to reopen it repeatedly.

I immediately thought about the team that Onx and the elders wanted me to put together to help keep the portal open so their people could travel to Earth. I thought that this retired physicist would be a perfect candidate for the team. Therefore, I informed him about what Onx had just told me. He agreed to participate on the team. He was willing to brainstorm with me about how to create a shunt for the portal. Talk about serendipity.

At our conference near the end of April in 2016, I told everyone that Onx had engaged in a two-hour mind speak with me and shared information with me that I wasn't able to share with them yet. However, I reassured the attendees at the conference that I would let them know as soon as I was allowed to do so. I also shared with them that a retired physicist from MIT had contacted me and that we would be taking a scientific approach to our work at SOIA. The conference attendees were excited.

Throughout the past sixteen years, I have often been falsely accused of taking a non-scientific approach to my research, when in fact, I've produced more circumstantial evidence and multiple witness testimonies than most other researchers. The only thing I haven't provided is a body. No one will ever provide a body. Knowing what I know, it's not possible. By the way, I would say that it's scientific to discover how to repeatedly reopen a portal. Apparently, the Bigfoot Forest People think so which is why they asked me for my help.

A couple weeks later, I contacted the retired physicist from MIT in order to update him on what was happening in SOIA. He immediately asked me, "Can you please send me the device so I can tweak it so we can use it to kill one of those Bigfoot, bring the body in, and settle this issue once and for all?" I sat there in silence. Then I thought, "What the heck? Either he's playing both sides of the fence or he's thinking I'm someone else or he's experiencing some form of Dementia or Alzheimer's." I politely ended the phone call and never called him again.

I sat there totally stunned and depressed because I realized that I was right back at square one. I had absolutely no one on my team who was technologically savvy enough to help create a shunt for the portal. For the record, the definition of shunt is to provide an electrical current with a conductor joining two points of a circuit, through which more or less of the current may be diverted from one point to another point. Shunt can also be defined as to travel back and forth or shunted between two towns or two worlds. I would like to make it clear to everyone reading this book, once again, I'm not mechanically inclined. I had no idea what a shunt was. In other words, I had no way of creating a delusional conversation in my own mind that night because the word, shunt, was not a part of my vocabulary. Onx is the one who introduced the word, 'shunt' into our conversation and then tried to explain it to me.

To be honest, I had no idea what it was going to take to create a device that could help the Bigfoot Forest People with the shunt they needed to keep the portal open on both ends to help their family and friends travel to Earth. I had no idea how long this project would take at all. I seriously feared that it was going to take another sixteen years of my life. I also feared that I might not be able to help them at all. My mind was spinning and spinning regarding the massive responsibility that had just been placed on my lap. Nevertheless, I was going to do my best to proceed in helping them. I knew that I had Cynthia's love and support to help me through the possible tough times ahead.

CHAPTER TWENTY-FOUR

ARGUING WITH ONX

I was back in Grants Pass, Oregon. I had just finished showering and I was standing in front of the mirror shaving when Onx decided to engage in mind speak with me. He said, "Please come out here today. We need you to come out here please." I responded, "I'm sorry, Onx, but I can't come out to SOIA today. I have several private practice clients to see. Also, I have to go to my son's game later today. I just can't make it." Onx did not respond. Silence. I went on with my day as planned.

The next morning, I had just woken up and I was contemplating whether or not to climb out of bed and take a shower when Onx approached me again via mind speak. He said to me, "You don't have any clients to see today and your son doesn't have a game. Please come out here today. We need you to come out here please." Well, I had no idea how he knew my schedule but he was correct. He had me there. I had absolutely nothing on my schedule for the day. I responded, "Okay. I'll come out to SOIA today." He responded, "Thank you."

As Onx requested, I drove out to SOIA. When I arrived there, it was very quiet. I walked around the area, picked up some trash, and threw it in the back of my pickup truck. I sat quietly in the middle of base

247

camp for an hour, listening and watching for anything. Nothing. It was totally quiet. I thought to myself, "Well, this is confusing. Why was Onx so insistent, both yesterday and today for me to come out to SOIA, if nothing was going to happen once I got here? This doesn't make any sense at all."

I pulled out my Bible and read out loud from the gospel of John. Still nothing. An hour later, I packed up my camping chair and put it back in my truck. I started up my vehicle and slowly drove away while shaking my head. To be completely honest, I was very frustrated. I went out of my way to come out to SOIA as requested and then absolutely nothing happened.

About a half mile away from the SOIA base camp, I slowly rounded a corner in my pickup truck and then Onx delivered a very powerful and loud mind speak message to me, "Stop your truck and pick up the garbage on the side of the road." I responded, "You're kidding me, right? You were on my case both yesterday and today to come out here so I could pick up some garbage on the side of the road? Really? I've already picked up enough garbage today. Someone else can pick up that garbage. I'm going home."

I continued to slowly drive on the road when Onx said, "Please stop your truck and pick up that garbage on the side of the road now." I stopped my truck, shook my head, let out a frustrated sigh, killed my engine, and got out of the truck to pick up the garbage. As I picked up the garbage and threw it in the back of my truck, I was upset by the people who think that the forest is a big garbage can. I get so sick and tired of people who are too dang lazy to go to the dump or landfill to properly dispose of their garbage. I would love to slap these idiots upside the head for their laziness and stupidity. May they be infested with a thousand fleas of a camel.

I was about to climb back into my pickup truck when I noticed a wadded up piece of paper on the ground that was next to the pile of garbage that I had just picked up. I reached down, grabbed the paper, unfolded the crumbled up mess, and began to read it out of curiosity. The note read as follows: "I have pictures of your truck, your face, and your license plate. If you don't stop coming out here, I'm going to turn you into the Oregon State Police if I don't shoot you first." Well, needless to say, that got my attention.

Onx told me, "We need to move you to a new area. It's not safe here for you." Well, I sure as heck wasn't going to argue with Onx about going to a new area. The last thing I wanted to deal with was some psycho with a gun. I fear stupid humans more than anything else that I might run into out in the woods. Stupid humans are the most dangerous predators in the forest. More dangerous than cougars, wolves, and bears.

I asked Onx, "Where are you moving me to?" He responded, "Here", and then gave me a vision to a place that I had visited about thirteen years earlier. I reluctantly said, "Okay", because it was over two hours away from Grants Pass, Oregon. Although it was still located in southern Oregon, I was not looking forward to the long drive.

With the note in hand, I immediately drove to the satellite office of the Oregon State Police which is located in Grants Pass, Oregon. I showed them the note and asked if anyone had reported me or my truck. They told me that I had not been reported to their office. Then a State Trooper said to me, "Looks like you need to find a new place to go camping. I wouldn't go back to that area again if I were you. Also, this is outside or our jurisdiction, you'll need to go to the BLM office and report this to them." I thanked the officers for their time and left the building.

I drove over to the Bureau of Land Management (BLM) office in Grants Pass, Oregon and showed them the note. A gentleman sitting behind a computer asked me to come over and show him on a map exactly where my camping area was located. Don't worry, I didn't tell the State Troopers or this gentleman the real reason why I was camping out in the location. When I was finally able to pinpoint the spot on the Google Earth map, he hit a button on the keyboard and the software imposed a map over the top of the original picture. The overlaying map showed where the BLM areas were located.

The gentleman said to me, "Uh oh! It looks like you're camping on private property." I said, "That's impossible. I'm out in the middle of a forest and there's no private property anywhere near the area." He responded, "It looks like your camping spot is surrounded by BLM land but if this is your camping area, you're most definitely on private property." I asked, "Who does it belong to?" He said, "There's no way to tell. It could be owned by a timber company or a private party or by Josephine County. It really doesn't matter though. Given the fact that your life has been threatened, I would go find a new area to camp. There's plenty of forest out there to explore. I'm sure you'll find a new spot." I thanked him for his time and left the building.

A couple days later, I had the entire day off, so I started my drive to reach the new location that Onx and the elders wanted me to move to. I couldn't help but be in awe that this was the second time, in less than five months, that Onx and the elders had given me a vision of where they wanted me to go in order to establish a base camp so I could interact with them. Think about it. How many times has that happened to anyone that you know? I was both honored and blown away as I began my trek to the new SOIA.

Along the way, I opted to reach the new SOIA through the back door via the logging roads. I didn't want to drive on the highway when I could enjoy the beauty of the mountains and logging roads. As I was driving on the logging roads, I would occasionally take a turn and explore an area. When I did, Onx asked, "What are you doing?" I responded, "I'm just exploring this area to see if it would make a good base camp." He said, "I showed you where to go. Please go there."

I continued to meander along the mountain roads, slowly but surely heading towards the new SOIA. Once I stopped the truck to let Zeus out to go potty and Onx asked, "What are you doing?" I responded, "I'm just letting Zeus stretch his legs and go to the bathroom. Besides, I need to go potty too. Relax! I'll eventually get to the new area."

About an hour later, as I continued my snail's pace approach to reaching the new SOIA, I took a turn down a side road just to do some exploring. I love checking out new logging roads to see where they go. Every area is beautiful in its own majestic way. Every road is a treasure chest of unexplored natural wonder. Once again, Onx asked, "What are you doing?" I said, "I'm just exploring the area. You never know where a good place for a base camp might pop up." By this time, I was intentionally messing with Onx like on the Jack Link's Jerky commercials. He said, "I showed you where to go, please go there."

Well, after meandering on the logging roads for about five hours and enjoying the beautiful day, I finally arrived at the new location for SOIA. Zeus and I got out of the truck, walked over to the bushes on the perimeter of the base camp, and marked our turf. Onx said to me, "Welcome. We hope you enjoy your new camping area." I responded, "Thank you. It's certainly beautiful here. I can't wait to spend more time up here with my friends while we're visiting with you and your clan."

As I began to walk around and explore the area, I heard a couple different tree knocks all around me. It was a nice confirmation that I had reached the correct spot. I was surprised to see just how much circumstantial evidence was in the surrounding area. There were so many Bigfoot tracks on the ground that it looked like they hosted a convention in the area. Zeus and I hiked to different vistas and enjoyed the view. Finally, it was time to get in the truck and drive away.

While I was driving down the logging road, I saw a side road and decided to turn on it. Immediately I heard Onx ask, "What are you doing?" I said, "I'm just wanting to explore this last area to see if there might be a good spot for a base camp." He said, "You already know where we want you to set up your camp." I responded, "I know you did but it doesn't hurt to just check out one more area." Then Onx responded rather strongly, "If you go down there, something bad is going to happen." I disagreed with him and said, "Nothing bad is going to happen. I have my gun and I have you. It's not going to hurt for me to take a look at what's down there. I'll be okay."

I drove down the side road about a mile, stopped my truck, killed the engine, and Zeus and I got out and explored the area. It was a meadow surrounded by trees. A perfect fishbowl. An ideal place to set up a base camp. Zeus and I explored the surrounding area for a few minutes and then climbed back into the truck. I started the engine and the dashboard of my truck started screaming at me with an annoying sound. I looked down and saw the words, "Flat Tire."

I got out of the truck and checked out my tires. Sure enough, I had a flat tire. I dug through my truck to find the equipment to change my tire and it was nowhere to be found. I looked through the owner's manual to find out where it was supposed to be stored in my truck and it wasn't there. I thought to myself, "Crap! I'm stuck up on the mountain without any means to change my flat tire. I'm screwed!" I noticed that the sun was starting to go down. That's when I made the decision to drive off of the mountain with my flat tire because I wasn't going to spend the night up there alone in the dark.

As I slowly but surely began my descent off of the mountain, I finally reached a place where I had minimal cell phone reception. I called Shelley Mower for help and she drove all that way out to the mountains with the proper equipment to rescue me. I was finally able to change my flat tire. On my way back to Grants Pass, Oregon, I bought Shelley an ice cream cone as a 'thank you' for rescuing me. Finally, as I drove along the highway, in the dark to return home, I couldn't help but hear, "I told you that something bad would happen." That's when I decided never to argue with Onx again. Especially since that mistake cost me over five-hundred dollars because I had to put two new tires on my truck – not just one tire. From now on, Onx is always right. No more messing with Sasquatch.

CHAPTER TWENTY-FIVE

THE EXODUS

I was anxious to start bringing my team members up to the new and improved Southern Oregon Interaction Area (SOIA). First, since she lived locally, I brought Jill Lidga with me. We explored the area thoroughly and found several tracks in the ground. As we walked a logging road, we came across a very fresh, steaming hot to the touch, three-foot Bigfoot turd. How do I know that the three-foot turd belonged to a Bigfoot Forest Person? Well, it was surrounded by two twenty-six inch tracks on both sides of the stool. That was a dead giveaway. I was pretty sure that a Squirrel didn't leave it behind.

Guess what? I now have a three-foot shellacked Bigfoot turd in my possession that I proudly show off in a display case next to a pile of shellacked black bear scat for a means of comparison. There's a night and day difference between the two samples. I know it sounds pretty crappy but it's the best I can do.

Next, I was excited to bring Cynthia up to SOIA. She had some time off and didn't want to wait very long to see the new area that I had been guided to. We spent two nights out in SOIA. During the first night, we played the music, sang songs, talked, laughed, and Cynthia played her flute. We had the usual activity of bipedal walking, silhouettes, eye glow, vocals, and tree knocks. Eventually we went to bed.

In the middle of the night, while I was sleeping, I was dreaming about being visited by Onx at SOIA. During the dream, Onx introduced me to his uncle, who was the clan leader. In my dream, Onx was passing me on to him, since I was in his area. Also, his uncle had his very large hand on my head. His palm was at the base of my skull and his fingers were reaching over the top of my head and touching my forehead. He was gently squeezing my head, off and on, in a kind and caring manner. It was a very affectionate gesture.

When I woke up from my dream, I still felt the very large hand on my head, gently squeezing off and on, in an affectionate manner. As usual, I had a hoodie over my head and my eyes were covered with a t-shirt. Suddenly, the uncle leaned over me and gently whispered in my ear in a deep, bass, Squatchy tone of voice, "Zorth." I asked in my mind, "Is Zorth your name?" He responded, "Yes." I said, "It's nice to meet you. Thank you for inviting us to be here." Zorth said, "You're welcome. Thank you for being willing to help us." I couldn't wait to tell Cynthia all about it when she woke up later on.

During our second night at SOIA, while Cynthia was standing up in the middle of the base camp playing her flute, we both saw Zorth walk into camp. He stood at the 11 o'clock position on the perimeter and listened to Cynthia playing her flute. His cloaked shimmering image, much like the image in the Arnold Schwarzenegger 'Predator' movie, stood about ten feet tall. He was very broad shouldered and buff. Cynthia and I both said, "Hello", to Zorth. After he left the base camp, we both described seeing the exact same thing.

Afterwards, we took our 'juju' that we obtained from the Oregon House of Mystery earlier that day and started to explore the perimeter of the SOIA base camp. We came across a spot that behaved in the same manner as the portal did in SOHA. We saw sparkling lights and a fog of light appeared. It was incredible and very beautiful. I shared an amazing time in SOIA with Cynthia. It was so amazing that I wanted everyone on the planet to experience it. However, that obviously isn't going to be possible because I simply can't bring everyone who wants to come with me to SOIA. I really do want to but I simply just can't do it.

Every day, I receive emails and Facebook personal messages from individuals. Some of them simply thank me for being so open and honest regarding the reporting of my research data online. They enjoy the 'Team Squatchin USA' YouTube videos and SoundCloud audio files. Others want me to consult with them about how to improve their research so they can increase their visuals and interactions. Finally, several people always ask me if I'll take them to my research area because they would like to see and interact with a Bigfoot Forest Person.

If I had it my way, I would take everyone to my research area because I'm all about sharing and educating the public. In my heart of hearts, I'm truly a 'come one, come all' type of person. Matter of fact, Cynthia continually tells me to say, "No", to people. Yet, nothing thrills me more than to see the people that I do bring along with me enjoy their very first experience. It's like watching the kids on Christmas morning every time. It never gets old. However, if there's one thing that I've learned over the past seventeen years, it's that people can be untrustworthy.

People will smile to your face while they knife you in the back. They will swear on their mother's grave that they will respect my wishes for them not to return to my research area on their own without me. They will promise to never tell anyone where my research area is located. Then they will turn around and bring a carload of people to explore my area. Therefore, over the years, I've learned to say the following magical word, "No." See, Cynthia is having a very positive influence on me. Simply put, I'm no longer willing to risk my seventeen years of work so one bad apple can mess it all up for me again and again. I lost my first three research areas because I was being too nice of a guy.

That's exactly why I share my research data online so people can learn from what I've been doing and then replicate my research methods in their own areas back home. Those that actually take the time to learn and implement what I've been teaching online, experience increased visuals and interactions as promised. In short, there's no need for people to come to the Southern Oregon Interaction Area (SOIA). They can develop their own interaction area back home. Just read the testimonial letters at the end of the book and you'll see I'm telling the truth.

The problem is that some people don't want to put forth the blood, sweat, and tears to reach their goals. They want to take the shortcut to the top. Only a few privileged individuals get that opportunity to come to SOIA. They have to be a special person to accompany me. I have to vet them with a million questions and feel that confirmation in my heart that they're okay to bring along with me before I ever say, "Yes", to them. I've turned away many, many people, including the Finding Bigfoot TV crew.

One day, another email inquiry arrived in my inbox. I opened it up because I try to read and answer all of my emails. It's the courteous thing to do. As I read through this particular email from a guy named Steve Bachmann, he was very complimentary, and he told me that he was from Buckley, Washington. That got my attention because Buckley is a stone's throw away from Puyallup, Washington.

Next, Steve told me about his vocation as a contractor and how he had been working with his hands his entire life. Finally, he shared with me that he likes to tinker around with projects on the side like refurbishing antique tractors and building unique devices. He shared with me that he used Tesla's design to build an electromagnetic pulsating device and attached a picture to the email message. Well, both his kind-hearted personality and the picture of the electromagnetic device got my attention immediately. Perhaps this was what I've been waiting for in order to help the Bigfoot Forest People create a shunt for the portal.

I called Steve immediately and I think I caught him off guard. I don't think he expected to ever hear from me. Yet, there we were, talking with one another and getting to know each other. I don't think he realized it but I was vetting him during our phone conversation. I don't believe in coincidences and I told him so. Therefore, I chose to tell him about the Bigfoot Forest People's request for me to assemble a team to help create a shunt. Near the end of our conversation, I asked Steve if he wanted to join Mike Kincaid and me for three nights in SOIA near the end of June. He sounded shocked and very pleasantly surprised and agreed to come along. I asked him to leave his electromagnetic pulsating device at home. I just wanted him to meet the Bigfoot Forest People family in SOIA first and allow them to get to know him.

The day before Steve was to come to SOIA, I called just to check up on him and to make sure that he was properly prepared. There's nothing worse than driving four-hundred miles to your destination only to realize that you left something very important behind. I've done that before a few times. It sounded like Steve had everything in order and was ready and willing to go. Before we hung up, he asked me if he could bring his electromagnetic pulsating device along just to show it to Mike and me. He didn't want to turn it on. He just wanted us to see it and explain it to us. I thought that was a great idea and asked him to bring it along.

The next day, keeping with tradition, Steve, Mike, and I met at the Black Bear Diner on 6th Street in Grants Pass, Oregon. We enjoyed a meal together and got to know one another face to face. I was prepared to send Steve back home immediately if he turned out to be anyone other than who he was painting himself out to be. Well, my 'sixth-sense' was correct. He was a sweetheart of a guy and very sincere in his desire to learn about the Bigfoot Forest People. He also wanted to help them in any way possible. He is truly one of those 'salt of the Earth' type guys.

After filling our bellies, we left for the Albertson's grocery store on the south side of the Rogue River. We purchased our supplies for the evening along with fresh food for breakfast on the following morning. Finally, we drove through the Dutch Brothers coffee stand so I could caffeinate my body for a late night in SOIA. With goodies in hand, we proceeded to drive to our destination.

Once we arrived in SOIA, we set up camp. After the chairs, table, bins, porta-potty, and sleeping cots were in their proper places, we took a tour of SOIA. Then I enjoyed a rest in the camping chair while Mike and Steve did their own thing. They checked out the area and enjoyed getting to know one another.

After it got dark, I sent Mike and Steve out on a mission. I informed them that Cynthia and I had been up to SOIA a few weeks earlier. I told them that we had gone to the Oregon House of Mystery and brought the 'juju' back with us to SOIA. Finally, I shared with them that we explored the perimeter and found an area where a portal might be. I asked Mike and Steve to walk the perimeter and see if they could find the spot that Cynthia and I had previously found.

After two sweeps of the perimeter, they turned up empty handed. Quite frankly, that was to be expected since they didn't have the 'juju' with them. I told Mike and Steve that we would be going to the Oregon House of Mystery on the following day and then they could try it again with the 'juju'. They thought that was a good idea.

I began to play my music on my MP3 player and portable Bose speaker for the Bigfoot Forest People family. I also sang several songs to them. I could tell that Steve was getting tired. After all, he had left his home around three in the morning in order to meet Mike and me on time at the Black Bear Diner. Steve went to bed while Mike and I stayed up awhile longer. I'm sure Steve thought I was crazy and was probably unsure about what he had just got himself into. As usual, there was activity on the perimeter of the SOIA base camp. Bipedal steps, vocals, tree knocks, silhouettes, and eye glow. Eventually, Mike and I went to bed too.

Early the next morning, while it was still fairly dark, I was woken up by some very loud stomps on the ground on the other side of the bushes and trees. I'm talking twenty-six-inch sized stomping feet belonging to Zorth. The stomping was followed by a black bear grunting back at Zorth. He stomped his feet again and ran toward the black bear to intimidate it to leave. The bear snorted again, turned around, and ran off into the forest. Zorth walked back to the perimeter as I could see his massive shoulders, head, and glowing red eyes through a gap in the vegetation. I asked Zorth in my mind, "Was that you? You're keeping us safe at night, right?" He responded, "That was me. You're safe." I fell back to sleep.

After the sun rose later that morning, Mike, Steve, and I woke up and discussed the stomping as we laid there in our sleeping bags. I explained to them that it was Zorth and he had told me what he had done on our behalf to keep us safe. Afterwards, Steve proceeded to tell Mike and me all about the healing that he underwent for most of the evening. Apparently, when Steve went to bed, within a short time, he had healing hands and energy all over his body. They worked on him from head to toe for most of the night. Steve told me that he had to put into practice what I had told him. He said that I would have been proud of him because he was a navy seal and as strong as steel. He did not freak out during the experience. I was very proud of him.

Later on that morning, we left for a tour of the Oregon House of Mystery, otherwise known as the Oregon Vortex. We enjoyed the one-hour tour and left with our 'juju' intact. Then I drove Mike and Steve up to the Crater Lake National Monument Park. It was a beautiful day. I never grow tired of visiting the park with my guests. The expressions on their faces, when they first see Crater Lake for the very first time, are priceless. Afterwards, we enjoyed our Mexican meal at Miguel's Guadalajara Restaurant in Shady Cove, Oregon. The deck overlooks the Rogue River and the view is mesmerizing.

We drove back to Grants Pass, Oregon and stopped, once again, at the Albertson's grocery store for our evening supplies and fresh food for breakfast the following morning. I drove through the Dutch Brothers coffee stand to acquire my caffeine fix and then we were back on the road to SOIA. When we arrived, the guys wanted to do a walk about while I enjoyed a rest in my camping chair in the middle of the base camp. I get tired after driving my guests around all day long.

After the sun went down, I challenged both Mike and Steve to take another stroll around the perimeter and try and find the portal area that Cynthia and I found a few weeks earlier. I remained seated in the dark in the middle of the base camp because I didn't want to influence them one way or the other. Suddenly, Mike and Steve called me over to the same exact spot that Cynthia and I had found a few weeks earlier. Mike asked proudly, "Is this it?" I responded, "Yup! It most certainly is. Great job guys."

As we were standing there and enjoying the same sparkling lights and the fog of light, we suddenly heard a nine-hundred-pound owl sound off from the top of the hill adjacent to the base camp area. The elevation rises about one-hundred-fifty feet higher than the base camp area. We stood there and listened to the owl impersonation repeat itself over and over again. Eventually, the very poor owl impersonations were ending in a barking sound. We just stood there in the dark with our jaws dropped.

To be quite honest, as I can recall, it sounded very much like what Miss Andrea Billups and I heard up in SOHA during October of 2015. As suddenly as the sounds began, they stopped.

We walked back in the dark to the center of the base camp and sat down in our chairs. We were all excited and Mike started saying, "Let's go up there. Let's go up to the top of the hill." Steve let out an enthusiastic, "Yes! Let's do it!" I was about to agree with them when Zorth engaged in mind speak with me. He said, "No. Do not come up here tonight. However, you're all invited to come up here and sit before the 'Council of Twelve' tomorrow night." I repeated to Mike and Steve what Zorth had just said to me and we were all three excited about tomorrow evening. Wow! Sit before the 'Council of Twelve'! What an awesome invitation!

As usual, I played a lot of music and sang some songs. Steve was now a one-hundred percent bona fide believer that I've been telling the truth about my experiences in SOHA and SOIA. He was telling me that he already believed me after watching my YouTube videos but being there in SOIA and experiencing everything firsthand with his own eyes and ears was the icing on the cake. He expressed a genuine desire that everyone could experience what he was experiencing in SOIA. He understood why that wasn't possible but, nevertheless, he genuinely wanted to spread the love. That's the kind of guy Steve is. Eventually, we all grew tired and went to bed.

The next morning, after the three of us woke up, we shared what we had experienced during the night. We all heard walking around our cots during the middle of the night. I had a Bigfoot Forest Person squatting down at the head of my sleeping cot for a little while. I could hear him breathing and shifting his weight around. Steven reported that once again, he experienced healing hands of energy working all over his body from head to toe during most of the night. This time, he was totally relaxed and didn't need to be a 'navy seal as strong as steel' because he knew they weren't going to hurt him.

We ate our breakfast in camp, packed up, and drove off the mountain for another day of sightseeing. This time, I was taking my guests to see the Redwood Forest near the California coast. The Stout Grove is a very impressive place to visit. We took lots of pictures and then enjoyed eating lunch afterwards.

Needless to say, the three of us were very excited to return to the SOIA base camp because on our third night there, we were going to hike up to the top of the hill and sit before the 'Council of Twelve' after the sun disappeared. We returned to the base camp around 7:30 pm. I was exhausted from driving and told the guys that I needed to take a power nap for an hour before we hiked up to the top of the hill. I asked Mike to make sure that I was awake by no later than 8:45 pm. That would still allow us enough daylight to hike up the hill. Mike agreed to wake me up.

As soon as I lay down on my sleeping cot, I was catapulted into a vision. I was soaring about two hundred feet above a beautiful lush green forest. I kept flying and flying and saw nothing but green trees. Then I made my way over to a coastline. As I was flying up the coast, I noticed the beautiful blue ocean, blue sky, and the lush green forest. Suddenly, I noticed that the blue sky was starting to turn red. At first, I thought that the sun was merely setting. But then I noticed that the beautiful lush green forest was slowly transforming into dark scraggly vegetation. Then I heard Zorth say in my mind, "This is our home world and we need your help." After the vision was over, I slept until it was time to wake up.

At 8:45 pm, I was up and ready to go. I told Mike and Steve about my vision. We grabbed our camping chairs and took a couple of flashlights with us. It was light enough on the way up to the top of the hill that we didn't need to use the flashlights. However, we most certainly were going to need the flashlights when we walked back down the hill in order to avoid tripping on rocks, branches, and stumps.

When we reached the top of the hill, Zorth told me where to set up the chairs. I pointed to a spot and told Mike and Steve that we need to set up the chairs over there by the trees. Mike asked, "Are you sure this is where we are supposed to set them up?" I responded, "Yes, that's where Zorth just told me to set up our chairs." After we set them up, we walked around the top of the hill and enjoyed the three-hundred-sixty-degree panoramic views. It was a beautiful evening.

As the sun was slowly setting, we noticed the mountainsides across the valley. There were tiny pinpricks of light popping and flashing all over the place. It almost looked like a Christmas light display. Then I was asked to take some pictures so I did. Finally, as we were sitting there in the dark, waiting for the 'Council of Twelve' to arrive, Zorth began to interact with me.

As I sat there in the dark with Mike and Steve, Zorth pulled up a memory of my being in the northern Cascade mountains with Lori Simmons. We had gone to her research area that she took over after her father had passed away. Her goal was to further his research in the area in memory of her father. She had a very unique situation in her research area where she thought a Bigfoot was dwelling in the ground underneath a very large tree. I know, it sounds crazy, right? But then again, after all of my experiences in SOHA and SOIA, I'm living in a world that's beyond crazy. I'm living a science fiction novel, except it's all really happening.

We parked my Suburban and then walked over to her tree. I convinced her to walk up the hill and go on the other side of the very large tree. Fortunately, I was carrying my Bionic Ear parabolic microphone dish and Sony digital recorder with me and recorded everything I'm about to tell you. As we approached the tree, I recorded two of the Bigfoot Forest People talking to one another. Once we got on the other side of the tree, I was standing on the ground next to it while Lori was standing on a log about ten feet away.

I encouraged Lori to step off the log and come closer to the tree. She refused to do so because she was very scared. I walked over to her, gently put my arm around her waist, and pulled her off of the log and onto the ground. When I did that, her anxiety shot through the roof. When her anxiety shot through the roof, the tree growled at me. Literally growled at me. It was amazing!

Lori started sweet-talking to the 'big guy' and letting him know that she was okay. Apparently, when he heard that she was okay, we started hearing very fast tapping from inside the tree. I told Lori that I wanted to conduct a little experiment and received her permission to do so. I told her that I wasn't making a move on her but I just wanted to see how the tree would react.

Once again, I gently put my arm around her waist and slowly pulled her even closer to the tree. Once again, her anxiety shot through the roof. As a result, the tree growled at me again. I recorded everything and it's there on SoundCloud.com for you to listen to for yourself. This one thing was clear to me; the noise was not coming from the ground underneath the tree. Rather, the tapping and growling noises were coming from directly inside the tree itself.

Then Zorth brought back another memory for me while I was sitting in the dark with Mike and Steve. He reminded me of sitting in my office and answering the phone. At the other end of the line was Jon-Eric Beckjord. Although he was a member of Mensa, he was the most socially inept Bigfoot researcher that I ever had the privilege of crossing paths with. He would call my office twenty-five to fifty times per day trying to trick my secretary in allowing him to speak with me. If he got lucky and was patched through to me, as soon as I answered the phone, he would be screaming at the top of his lungs, "They're in the trees, Matt! They're in the trees!" I would tell him to please get back on his medications and then hang up on him.

After raising the memories of Lori and Jon-Eric, Zorth asked me to count the trees in front of me from my left to my right. I counted inside my head, "One, two, three, four, five, six, seven, eight, nine, ten, eleven, twelve." Zorth asked me to count the trees again so I did. I arrived at the same number as before. There were twelve trees in front of me. Then Zorth mind spoke to me, "We're in the trees." I thought to myself, "Oh my goodness, Jon-Erik Beckjord was right. They're in the trees."

Zorth then proceeded to tell me, "We are beings of light. We are the orbs. We live in the trees during the daylight. That is how we rejuvenate ourselves. We take in the energy from the sun as well as the nutrients from the ground through the roots. We produce 'Kvienchaka' in return to assist the trees. We have a symbiotic relationship with the trees. We are guardians of the forest and protect all who dwell within."

Zorth continued, "We can transform into anything we want to be. We can be a deer, bear, cougar, wolf, raven, or squirrel. We can be anything we want to be. We came over from our dying planet during the time of your dinosaurs. We've been here on the Earth longer than the human race. Eventually, we chose to shape-shift into an upright, bipedal, hairy human-looking hominid in order to get the attention of the human race. If we were a deer, we would just be another deer to you."

I sat there in amazement, listening, as Zorth continued, "We all come from the same God. Our souls are the same. We are all beings of light. We just have different bodies. However, the human race rebelled against God and sinned in the Garden of Eden. They fell from God's grace. We never fell. We never rebelled against God. That is why we keep our distance from most humans because they are self-centered and mean spirited. They are not kind to one another. They steal, rape, and kill one another. They go to war with one another. They do not take care of God's creation. We are only interested in interacting with kind humans with good hearts and open minds. We all go back to God after we die."

Zorth then told me, "The 'Council of Twelve' consists of two elders from each habitable continent on the Earth. I am the leader of the 'Council of Twelve.' We are humbled to be here in your presence. We are grateful for your diligence throughout the years and your willingness to help our people. Thank you."

I sat there thinking to myself, "Dang! The 'Council of Twelve' consists of two elders from each habitable continent and Zorth is the leader of the council? That means that he's like the 'President' of Earth. Wow! Who needs the president of the USA when I have the ear of Zorth?"

Finally, Zorth asked me, "Will you please ask your friends to count the trees in front of them from their left to their right. Ask them to count silently to themselves." I delivered the message to both Mike and Steve. They both arrived at the same conclusion. There were twelve trees in front of us. All of a sudden, they simultaneously stated, "They're in the trees!" I responded, "That's correct" and then proceeded to tell them everything that Zorth had just shown me and told me. This was an amazing experience. You can't make this stuff up. I know that some of you think I did make this stuff up but this is the truth, a truth that I freely share with you.

Zorth told me, "You may now return to your camping area with your friends. Thank you for visiting with us." I informed both Mike and Steve that it was time to return to the SOIA base camp. We folded up our camping chairs and carried them back down the hill as we used our flashlights in order to prevent one or more injuries along the way. Needless to say, when we reached the center of the base camp, we were totally stoked. We were so excited that we couldn't stop processing what had just occurred.

Then Mike got the idea to start asking Zorth some questions. I asked Zorth and he said it would be okay to ask him questions. Mike asked, and Zorth answered. Mike asked more questions and Zorth provided more answers. After a while, I said, "Wait a minute! I feel stuck in the middle here between the two of you." Mike joked with me about using me as a 'Squatchy Talkie' with Zorth. I asked if we could be done and Mike agreed.

You have to remember that Mike is the extremely intelligent computer geek who is constantly sifting through the data to make sure that everything is legitimate. He calls it 'debugging' the data. More often than not, he's usually so into his head that it's a challenge for him to be sensitive to what his heart is trying to tell him. Mike helps to keep things real. Actually, Mike and Cynthia are a lot alike. They both like to 'debug' and help me keep things real. It's just my opinion that Cynthia is prettier than Mike.

Since it was our third and final night in SOIA, Steve asked me if he could power up his electromagnetic pulsating device. I asked Zorth and he said, "Yes." Steve set up the device on the tailgate of his pickup truck. Essentially, it consisted of two 12-volt deep cycle marine batteries joined together to produce 24 volts of energy. These two batteries were hooked up to a very large inverter with a LED display to show the charge of the joint batteries. The inverter was hooked up to the electromagnetic pulsating device that Steve had made from a Nicola Tesla design. The device has a large wheel with sixteen very powerful magnets. As the device spins around at a very high velocity, it creates free energy. It also sends energy back to the inverter and on to the batteries so they never lose their charge. In theory, the device can run forever without ever draining the two batteries while creating free energy at the same time (i.e., Perpetual motion).

Steve fired up the device and we returned to our camp chairs in the middle of the base camp. Immediately, we heard heavy footed running from the forest to the back of Steve's truck. Then the heavy footed running went from the back of Steve's truck back out into the woods. Suddenly, Zorth mind spoke with me and said, "It's working! We are able to keep the portal open. Souls are coming through the portal." I told Steve and Mike and we were all excited.

Eventually, Steve got tired and went to bed. He had to drive all the way back to Buckley, Washington on the next day so he could complete a work project on time. Mike and I stayed up a little while longer. As time passed, Zorth was keeping me up to speed regarding the souls that were coming through the portal from their home world to Earth.

Suddenly, the inverter started buzzing an irritating high pitched noise. Mike and I walked over to it and saw that the batteries were losing their charge. We shut off the inverter. Zorth said to me, "We were able to get approximately two-thousand-three-hundred-fifty souls through the portal tonight. That's about ten percent of everyone who needs to come over." I responded, "Ten percent? Really? That means that there's only about twenty-three-thousand-five-hundred souls to bring over. That's not even the population of Grants Pass, Oregon." Zorth replied, "You are correct. However, you need to remember that our planet has been dying for a long time and that we would be doing this even if only one soul was left. Thank you for your efforts." Eventually, Mike and I went to bed. We were exhausted too.

The next morning, Steve asked who turned off the device. Mike said that he did because the inverter was screaming at us due to the fact that the batteries were draining. Steve said, "That's impossible. I've tested that machine over and over again in my workshop and the batteries never drain. It can run forever." We walked over to the tailgate of his truck and he turned the device on. Sure enough, the meter reader was showing that the batteries were drained. We left the device running as we sat down in our chairs and talked. Suddenly, we heard loud and heavy footed bipedal steps running from the woods to the back of the truck and then again back out to the woods. This was in the broad daylight of the morning hours. We couldn't see them running but we most certainly could hear them running.

After about fifteen minutes of running, the inverter began to scream at us again. We walked over to the back of Steve's truck and he turned off the device. We began to speculate why the batteries were draining. We reached the conclusion that the Bigfoot Forest People probably didn't realize that they needed to only take the energy from the electromagnetic pulsating device while leaving the deep cycle marine batteries alone. Therefore, they were draining the batteries in the process of trying to create a shunt for the portal.

Steve reminded both Mike and I that he had to return to his home in Washington so he could complete his job on time. He took great pride in always delivering his services in a timely manner and he didn't want to jeopardize his reputation that he had established in his community. Mike and I totally understood. However, we were standing there with the realization that we just helped approximately two-thousand-three-hundred-fifty souls make it through the portal and that was only ten percent of everyone who needed to come through the portal.

I asked Steve if he would please leave his device with Mike and I so we could complete the task of helping the Bigfoot Forest People make it over from their world to our world. I told Steve that I would be coming up to Puyallup, Washington in a couple of days to celebrate the Fourth of July weekend with Cynthia. Steve graciously allowed Mike and I to hang on to his device while he returned to Washington.

After Steve left the SOIA base camp, Mike and I devised a game plan to assure that we would complete the EXODUS mission on our fourth night. We decided to drive back to Grants Pass, Oregon and go to the AutoZone. We had Steve's two drained deep cycle marine batteries. I also owned a deep cycle marine battery. Mike decided to purchase three more deep cycle marine batteries so we would have a total of six batteries. Then, if he wasn't already spending enough money, he purchased six battery chargers. 'Mr. Debugger' spent around six-hundred dollars in order to help complete the EXODUS mission. Who's a totally sold out believer now? Mike's commitment to the task was amazing. I love that guy.

We drove to Grady's mother's home and set up the batteries in the garage and spent the entire day charging them. Mike and I went swimming with Grady and enjoyed the warm summer day. Then we ate an early dinner with Grady and his mother, Amanda. Although we are divorced, Amanda and I remain good friends. I felt compelled to ask Grady to join us in SOIA on the fourth and final evening. I reminded him that he was there for the portal with Adam Davies and John Carlson. I told him that the EXODUS in SOIA was going to be even more meaningful and I thought it was important for him to be there for that historic event too. Grady agreed to come along.

When we reached the SOIA base camp, I backed up my F-150 pickup truck into the cove area at the 12:00 o'clock position so the Bigfoot Forest People wouldn't have to run as far to reach the electromagnetic pulsating machine. Right around the time that the sun was setting, we turned on the device. Immediately, we could hear the Bigfoot Forest People running toward the device and then back into the woods.

As the evening progressed, Zorth engaged in mind speak with me. He told me, "We have managed to get four-thousand souls through during the first hour." I said, "How did you do that? That's almost twice as many per hour than you did last night." He replied, "We were standing by the three of you when you were talking about the batteries. We realized that we needed to only draw the energy from the machine and leave the batteries alone. Also, we were caught off guard by the success of the machine. We had no idea that it would work so well. So while you were gone during the day, we did a better job of organizing ourselves on this side of the portal. We also sent some of our people through to the other side to get everyone organized better so that they were waiting to come through the portal."

While the evening of the EXODUS was occurring, Grady said, "Dad, there's so many of them around us. I can see them everywhere. There are silhouettes, eye glow, and walking all over the place." Well, he was right. As the evening progressed, we had thousands of more souls showing up in SOIA. The place was being overrun with Bigfoot Forest People. Many of them stayed within their orb-like form.

Eventually, Grady grew tired and wanted to go to bed. As always, he wanted me to tuck him into this sleeping bag. He climbed into his sleeping bag and, suddenly, we both saw an orb by his legs. The orb slowly moved up his leg toward his waist and then zipped up into the air. It stayed about ten feet above us before it finally zipped off into the trees. Grady said, "Dad, that was really cool." I agreed with Grady, gave him a kiss on the forehead, told him that I loved him, and said, "I hope you never forget this historic evening for as long as you live." Grady said, "I won't dad. I will always remember tonight."

Mike and I continued to monitor the electromagnetic pulsating device. Occasionally, I would approach the back of the truck and say, "Okay, we're coming to check on the batteries. I need you to back away from the truck so we can take a look at the batteries." On one occasion, I literally saw five cloaked shimmering images of the Bigfoot Forest People back away from the truck. They ranged from seven to ten feet tall in height. The batteries checked out and I told Zorth, "The batteries are still okay." Then I asked him, "How is the EXODUS coming along?" He replied, "We're still getting them through. It's going really well. Thank you." They were averaging about four-thousand souls per hour through the portal.

Within five and a half hours, we were able to help Zorth get all of his family and friends over from their dying home world to Earth. He told me, "Please don't shut down the machine yet. We still need to find just one more soul. He's very sick." I assured him that we would keep the device running until they found their friend. Finally, Zorth said, "We found him and brought him over to Earth." Unfortunately, he died about a half-hour later. However, they were happy because their friend was able to see Earth and they were able to be with him when he died.

All in all, when the EXODUS was done, Zorth informed me that we were able to bring over twenty-three-thousand-five-hundred-forty-two souls. Out of the entire bunch, they lost three souls in the process. These three souls were older beings who were depriving themselves of the energy from their dying sun on their home world so the younger souls could survive.

I forgot to mention that while the EXODUS was occurring, there were obviously more and more souls congregating in and around the SOIA base camp. I was able to see red shimmering images, about three-feet by three-feet, that would float up to me. In the middle of these red shimmering images, I could see a feminine or masculine face. I would hear them mind speak with me as they would all say, "Thank you." Then they would float away into the dark. Mike and I were honored to help so many souls come over to Earth. It wouldn't have been possible without Steve's electromagnetic pulsating device.

Oh, and "thank you" Nikola Tesla for making the design that Steve used to create his device.

The next morning, when Grady and I woke up, Mike came walking back into the SOIA base camp. He told me about how he was woken up early in the morning while Grady and I were still asleep. Apparently, the Bigfoot Forest People wanted to address his skeptical debugging frame of mind. You see, even after everything that occurred, Mike was still having doubts as to whether or not everything really happened or if he was blindly following a manipulator of the truth.

Mike shared with me that as Grady and I were still sleeping, the Bigfoot Forest People woke him up. As he lay on his sleeping cot in the dark of the morning hours, he heard a tree knock in the woods surrounding us. Then he heard another tree knock. Then another. By the time the tree knocks were done, he counted a total of twelve tree knocks. He shared with Grady and I that he realized at that moment that they were speaking only to him to reassure him that the events of the previous two nights really did happen.

Mike got up out of bed while Grady and I were still sleeping. He went for a walk on the logging road. He told me that he was laughing, skipping, and crying all at the same time. He realized that everything that we had experienced during the previous two nights really did happen. We really did sit in front of the 'Council of Twelve' and the EXODUS really did happen. Mike was filled with enthusiasm and joy. He was finally in touch with his heart rather than being bogged down by his mind. I've known Mike for a few years and it thrilled me to see him reach this monumental moment in his life.

During those morning hours after the EXODUS, Zorth mind spoke with me and said, "Thank you for helping us to bring our family and friends over to Earth. All of you will receive a guardian for the rest of your lives as our appreciation for what you have done for our people." I thanked Zorth and then I asked him, "Am I done? Am I free from my sixteen years of compulsion? Can I go about my business without having to come out into the woods any longer?" Zorth responded, "Yes. You are free to do as you wish. However, we would still like you to consider being a teacher for our youth. Also, we would appreciate it if you would be our ambassador to the human race. You have much to teach others about us."

What Zorth said next shocked me. He said, "By the way, on that day sixteen years ago, that was me on the mountainside with your family. Welcome home. You are now free to write your book." Wow! Talk about a mind-blowing revelation. At that moment in time, I realized that Zorth and the 'Council of Twelve' had a game plan for me to follow for the past sixteen years. Although I tearfully, finally felt free to go on with my life, I knew that there was no way that I could deny their wishes to remain as a teacher to their youth as well as an ambassador to teach humanity about the Bigfoot Forest People.

Before we left SOIA that morning, Zorth told me, "Our life span is approximately two-hundred-twenty-years. Some of us live less and others live to be three-hundred-years old. We live about three times longer than the human race does. Also, we travel the power-line trails not because of the easy access or because the mammals follow the power-line trail. We follow the power-line trails so we can partake of the energy from the powerlines. Also, we do not eat mammals. We eat fish, eggs, birds, and vegetation. We do not eat mammals. It's the Treykon who eat the mammals."

I asked, "Who are the Treykon?" Zorth replied, "The Treykon were brought to Earth a long time ago to mine it for its minerals. When the aliens were done mining the Earth, they left the Treykon behind. They're a vile species. They stand about six to eight feet tall. They're menacing creatures and not very bright. They're the ones who eat the mammals and occasionally take humans in the forest. It's not us. We don't eat mammals and we don't harm humans."

Finally, I was joking as I asked Zorth, "What are you going to do now that the EXODUS has occurred? Are you all going to fade into the wood-work?" Zorth chuckled and said, "Yes we will continue to recharge in the trees. Also, we will not be as active in showing ourselves to the human race now that the EXODUS has been completed. However, if kind hearted people with good hearts and open minds reach out to us, then we will reach back to them. It is our hope to help improve humanity as well as their stewardship of the Earth, one person at a time. Please share this message with others of your kind."

As we drove away from SOIA after that fourth night up on the mountain, I felt like my life's work had come to an end. Sixteen years of field research had just been concluded with the completion of the EXODUS. Yet, on the other hand, I also felt like the next chapter with the Bigfoot Forest People was just beginning. The more that I learned, the more I realized what I didn't know. How could I give up on this adventure, even though at times I've wanted to move to Hawaii to get away from it all. With my luck, they're in Hawaii too.

While driving down the mountain, Zorth said to me, "Remember, we are in the trees and the trees are everywhere." Therefore, I ask those closest to me, "Where are the Squatches? They're in the trees. Where are the trees? They're everywhere!" In short, you don't have to go deep into the forest to find the Bigfoot Forest People because they can be in your backyard or city park.

CHAPTER TWENTY-SIX

A FIFTY-YEAR JOURNEY COME FULL CIRCLE

After the EXODUS had occurred, I drove to Puyallup, Washington to spend the Fourth of July weekend with Cynthia. As promised, I brought Steve's electromagnetic pulsating device with me. I invited a few special friends to meet at Cynthia's home in order to tell them about the EXODUS. Those present included, Cynthia Kreitzberg, Steve Bachmann, Anita Hlebichuk, Scott and Susan Taylor, and Lt. Col. Kevin Jones.

At first, we sat around the kitchen table visiting with one another while munching on delicious pizza and sipping on cold beer, soda, and water. As we were sitting there talking with one another, swapping stories, and laughing together, I couldn't help but think that we all wouldn't be sharing this moment together if it wasn't for our mutual interest in the Bigfoot Forest People phenomena. Everyone present had their own story to tell. All of us had been reeled in, one way or another, by our insatiable desire to learn the truth about our big hairy friends. Now my colleagues were about to hear the truth and I couldn't wait to share it with them.

After we had finished consuming our Italian cuisine, we moved from the dining room to the living room. Everyone found a comfy location to sit and then I began to share the story of the EXODUS with them. As I was sharing the story, I was watching my friend's eyes and body-language. I was waiting for someone to roll their eyes and say, "Matt, I'm sorry but you're full of crap." Never happened. Matter of fact, it was great to have Steve present because he was like an excited kid in a candy store and he had a whole lot of information to enthusiastically share with everyone present.

By the time Steve and I were done talking about the EXODUS, everyone just sat there for a moment in silence. Then they all began to take turns sharing their thoughts with the group. The consistent response was that the story makes sense and ties together a whole lot of loose ends. The information that Zorth shared with me explained many unanswered questions for Scott Taylor, BFRO investigator. Such as following a set of tracks that suddenly disappear and go nowhere or a Bigfoot going behind a tree but not coming out the other side. It also explains why most Bigfoot activity takes place at night because they're recharging, so to speak, inside the trees during the daylight hours. Finally, it also explains why there are so many myths, legends, and stories around the world in all kinds of cultures regarding the existence of Tree Spirits.

The discussion continued for a long while as we pondered the implications of the revelations about the Bigfoot Forest People. How would the community of Bigfoot researchers respond? Well, we were all in agreement regarding the "Three Thirds Principle." The first one-third will immediately accept the revelation and the EXODUS event without any doubts. They will become much more aware of their surroundings and start looking at trees a whole lot differently.

The next one-third of the Bigfoot researcher community will understandably have to ponder the information, chew on it for a while, kick the can around, ask me and others questions, and eventually will come on board the 'Woo-Woo Train' as it continues to roll down the tracks.

Combined together, approximately two-thirds of the Bigfoot researchers' community will start seeking to better understand Quantum Physics and Mechanics. Finally, they will start looking at the trees in their own backyard very differently. They will be talking to a whole lot more trees during the daylight hours and hugging them.

The final one-third of the Bigfoot researchers' community will continue to chase unicorns through the forest. They will disrespectfully blow me and my associates off as insane crackpots while they continue to try to find something that doesn't exist. In other words, the Bigfoot Forest People are not descendants of Gigantopithecus. They're not relic hominids. Perhaps after another fifty years of searching and not finding anything, these 'old school' paparazzi money-shot researchers will reconsider their theoretical position regarding who and what the Bigfoot Forest People truly are. For now, at least they're having fun in the woods with their friends and getting some exercise while they're hiking up and down mountainsides. It doesn't harm anyone else to have a group of people enjoying their Bigfoot social club together. It's all good.

After we were done talking and processing the EXODUS in the living room, we went back into the kitchen so Steve could talk about his electromagnetic pulsating device and turn it on for everyone to see, hear, and feel. Yes, I said feel. While the machine is running, you can literally feel the created free energy pulsating from the device. It's spectacular to experience it. Everyone was amazed by Steve's creation.

As everyone was leaving, I grabbed a hold of Lt. Col. Kevin Jones, former BFRO investigator, and asked him if he could arrange a breakfast meeting between Bob Gimlin and me. I told him that I would pay for everyone's breakfast. We both agreed that Bob needed to hear about the revelation of information from Zorth as well as the story of the EXODUS. It was time for a journey to come full circle and wrap things up for Bob so he could understand his role in helping the EXODUS to occur.

On Thursday morning, July 7, 2016, I met Lt. Col. Kevin Jones and Bob Gimlin at the Shari's restaurant in Yakima, Washington. I was grateful that Kevin helped arrange the meeting with Bob. I was also honored that Bob was willing to give me his time and ear. He is a very gracious and kind individual to everyone he meets.

At first, Kevin and I met at the restaurant and waited for Bob. While waiting, we playfully argued about who was going to pay for breakfast. Although I had intended to pay for breakfast, Lt. Col. Kevin Jones pulled rank on me and insisted that he was going to pay for the meal since he was hosting the meal. We also playfully argued about Bob's height.

Kevin estimated that he was somewhere up there with Kareem Abdul-Jabbar and I was estimating somewhere in the Munchkin zone from the Wizard of Oz. Apparently, we were both wrong.

While we were waiting for Bob to arrive, Kevin and I discussed our healing experiences with the Bigfoot Forest People. Kevin discussed how he believed that they healed people. I shared with Kevin about how the Bigfoot Forest People healed my leg, prostate, and abdomen. We agreed that they're able to manipulate energy and speed up our body's ability to heal itself.

While we continued to wait for Bob's arrival, Kevin brought up an interesting idea regarding the portal in SOIA. He wondered if it would be possible to obtain Zorth's permission to go through the portal and document their home planet. We discussed the ancient alien race that placed the portals all over the universe. We speculated about how many worlds and alien races existed across the universe. I played one of my favorite YouTube videos for Kevin. It's called 'Other Life in the Universe' by Howard Storm. It's only four-minutes and twenty-three seconds long but it's plum full of enlightening information.

Kevin talked about how things happen for a reason. He talked about a ranch in Washington where they have Bigfoot and orb activity. He also said that they've had some UFO activity occur at the ranch. He spent some time at the ranch and enjoyed his experiences. He learned about multiple beings as well as beings of light.

Eventually, Bob arrived and enthusiastically greeted both of us. He was very apologetic for being late. We encouraged him to order breakfast. He discussed his ailing back and neck and how it's been slowing him down. Kevin shut Bob down and told him to quit apologizing. He was on time and there were no worries.

Bob ordered some scrambled eggs, bacon, wheat toast, and coffee. Then he playfully dissed Kevin about not really telling him why we were meeting. Kevin joked with Bob that we were conducting an intervention on him about his crazy infatuation with Bigfoot. He laughed and said that the psychologist never helped him while he was in the military.

Since I finished eating right about the time that Bob arrived, I began to tell him about the story of the EXODUS. Before I began to talk,

I reminded him that he has heard me present three times. Although he clearly remembered my presentation at Johnny Manson's Sasquatch Summit in 2013, he didn't remember everything that I shared at my conference because so many people who wanted to visit with him were interrupting him.

Therefore, we agreed that it was important to quickly summarize my research experience that all led up to the EXODUS. When I got to the point where I had changed my theoretical orientation and started viewing them as a Forest People, Bob was pleased to hear about it. I talked about zapping, mind speak, healing, orbs, cloaking, etc. Bob said that he remembered listening to me talk about the Bigfoot Forest People healing my leg.

As I was continuing to talk, Bob told me that he didn't think I was crazy and that it wasn't new information to him. He said that he wanted to see more people do the kind of research that I was doing. He told me that he talked with the local elders of the Yakima Indian Tribe and they view them as a people. He shared that he doesn't like the aggressive approach that so many Bigfoot researchers utilize today.

I told Bob about the portal in SOHA in June of 2014. Then I shared about all our other amazing experiences in SOHA and how the TROLLS crashed it. I shared how the Bigfoot Forest People moved me on to SOIA and the subsequent experiences, including the two-hour mind speak with Onx. Finally, I was able to tell Bob all about our four nights in SOIA during June, including the story of the EXODUS on June 27, 2016.

I shared with Bob that the Bigfoot Forest People intentionally had 'Patty' slow down her vibrational frequency so both he and Roger Patterson could film her at Bluff Creek, California in October of 1967. They wanted to get the attention of the human race and have people come look for them. I further explained the 'funnel effect' and how it was all intended to get people to befriend them, discover the portals, figure out how to reopen the portals, and ultimately help them with the EXODUS. Bob said, "I believe you." He said, "What you're saying to me is what I've believed for a long, long time. I've talked with others who believe the same thing as you do about their paranormal abilities. Also, when I told you that I really enjoyed your presentation at Johnny's conference, I meant every word of it."

After I had finished telling Bob everything that I had to say to him, I shared that Zorth wanted me to thank him for helping to make the EXODUS possible. I also shared with Bob that Bigfooting as we know it was going to change. I told him that I know what I shared sounds really crazy. Bob responded by saying, "What you've shared with me are things that I've been thinking about for a real long time. I've never explained these things to other humans. I used to fly above the Earth out of my body. Also, I've been to places that I've never been to before, but I knew where I was because I had already seen it in my mind. The older I've been getting, I've been losing that ability." I found it amazing to hear this from Bob Gimlin.

Bob went on to say, "The Bigfoot people are here to protect us and heal us. When you talked about healing, that hit home with me big time. I strongly believe that they have helped me with all of my injuries over the years. What you shared with me is great and incredible. I never realized the tree thing until you told me about it. However, I believe that they have the ability to be what we can't see. It's all changing. I've heard others share with me similar things. We all thought Beckjord was weird but apparently, he was right. They're in the trees."

Bob continued, "I believe that they're beings of light and energy. Many others believe it too. I've talked with a number of them. It's so good that you shared this information with me. I never felt like I was helping out. However, many people told me that they had no interest until they saw the film. People your age had their parents take them to the movie. The thing that really bothers me is the people who want to try and bring a body in. I've been asked numerous times why I didn't shoot 'Patty'? It was never an option. I was too busy watching and trying to understand what I was witnessing. It happened so dramatically fast. She covered a lot of ground in that short period of time. I wanted to get on the horse and follow her but Roger asked me not to leave him alone."

Bob said, "Now that you're telling me this, I now believe everything happened the way it was supposed to happen. I didn't know that they had planned it but it's amazing. We weren't able to follow her up the canyon because it wasn't meant to be. You don't know how special it is for me to be here and listen to what you have shared with me."

Kevin piped up and said, "It's hard to believe but with Matt, it's much easier to swallow. Everything that Matt has described, I have experienced myself. I've experienced batteries draining and cloaking. It's easy to believe Matt because it's happened to me."

Bob asked me about the Bigfoot Forest People and how they created the shunt with the energy from the electromagnetic pulsating device. I took the time to explain the process to him and he was very fascinated. He was really happy to hear that so many souls were brought through the portal from their dying planet to Earth.

Kevin told Bob, "That machine, when you get close to it, you can feel the pulsating energy coming off of it." Bob said, "I will never tell anyone about what you told me and I will be at your conference next April."

Bob then shifted the discussion from Bigfoot to UFOs for a few minutes. He's very fascinated by how all the huge structures, like the pyramids, were built in the past. I told him that I had no opinion about UFOs and how the pyramids were built because I haven't been told about them. I said, "I can only comment on what I've experienced and what I've been told."

In closing, I said to Bob, "What I wanted you to get out of this is the fact that Zorth wanted me to thank you for your help. It was important for this journey to come around full circle. He told me that if kind people with good hearts and open minds reach out to them, then they will reach back."

Bob said, "I talked with this older Indian woman who was over a hundred years old. Her name was Mary. She asked me why we were going about looking for Bigfoot in the wrong ways. She said that we didn't need to yell at them, hit trees, and set up cameras. She said that all we had to do was go out into the forest with clear minds and be open to them. Then she said that they like music. Just go into the woods and accept them, talk to them, and tell them that you're there to be their friends. If people laugh at you, let them laugh at you. They've been among us long before we were on Earth. They've talked to my parents and my grandparents. They gave the medicine man great healing powers. He wouldn't have it if they didn't give it to them. That was about twenty-five years ago when I talked to Mary."

Well, my visit with Bob and Kevin came to an end. They had to go about their day and I had to drive all the way back south down to Grants Pass, Oregon. It was going to be a long day of driving for me. I can't begin to tell you how awesome it was to sit there at the breakfast table and visit with Bob, tell him all about the EXODUS, and be able to extend a 'thank you' to him on behalf of Zorth and all of the Bigfoot Forest People. Most important of all, Bob thanked me for helping to bring the bigger picture around full circle for him. He was thrilled that both he and Roger Patterson played a key role in helping the EXODUS to eventually happen fifty years later. Bob truly is a kind person with a good heart and an open mind. That is why the Bigfoot Forest People like and respect him so much.

CHAPTER TWENTY-SEVEN

THE REST OF THE STORY

I loved listening to Paul Harvey as a kid. I even made it into one of his write-ups when I was in the ninth grade at Leslie Junior High School. I had called into our local Statesman Journal newspaper in Salem, Oregon because the sports department had a hotline for sports questions. If they thought your question was worthy enough, they would answer it in the paper the next morning.

So I called the hotline and left the following message, "My name is Matt Johnson and I'm in the ninth grade. I stand six feet and seven inches tall. I know it's okay to dunk the ball in high school but are we allowed to dunk the ball while playing middle school basketball?" At that time in the 1970s, our middle school went from the seventh grade to the ninth grade. High school went from the tenth grade to the twelfth grade. The local sports writer answered my question the next morning in the newspaper and told me that it was legal to dunk the basketball in middle school.

Well, a couple of days later, Paul Harvey briefly touched upon my phone call in his article. He wrote, "Did you hear about the middle schooler in Salem, Oregon who called up the local newspaper and asked the sports writer if it was legal to dunk the basketball? Can you imagine how tall he must be?" I immediately became famous among some of my peers for the rest of the school year.

By the way, I averaged thirty points per game that season. I set a city record by scoring a game-high of forty-seven points while playing in only three quarters of the game. In the end, the Judson Junior High School basketball team beat me by a score of forty-nine to forty-seven. Fortunately, my teammates at Leslie Junior High School also scored twenty-eight points so we ultimately won by a score of seventy-five to forty-nine. But I digress.

Anyway, Paul Harvey always began his stories by sharing a teaser that would grab your attention. Once he had you hooked, he would utter his catchphrase line, "And now, the rest of the story." He would explain in detail everything that led up to the attention catching event and beyond. Then he would end his time on the radio by saying, "And now you know the rest of the story. Good day!" Oh, and his voice was so kind, gentle, and mesmerizing. I loved Paul Harvey and miss him very much. The world needs more people like Paul Harvey. With of the above said, I wish to share with you the rest of the story.

After the EXODUS occurred, Zorth brought back a memory for me that I had totally forgotten. I was five-years old and lived on 35th Street in Astoria, Oregon. One day, I walked a couple of blocks up the hill to my friend's house. They had enormous piles of lumber in their front yard because his father was a contractor. We used to crawl around and play in the lumber piles for hours. It was better than a tree fort because we didn't have to risk climbing up and down a tree. The only thing we had to do was watch out for the rusty nails that were still in some of the pieces of wood.

One day, after a few hours of playing in the lumber piles, we got bored. My friend's house butted on the edge of a vast forest just south of the residential area. He suggested that we go play in the woods. Well, Tom and I decided that Guy's idea sounded like fun so we followed him into the woods. We followed Guy up the trail for quite a long way until he came to a sudden stop. He looked up into the trees, pointed, and yelled out, "Bear!"

The bear was about thirty feet off the ground up in the tree. Both Guy and Tom turned around and ran down the path back towards the house.

I, however, remained totally petrified by fear. I stood there, looking up into the tree at the bear. Slowly but surely, the bear climbed down the tree. I literally could not move. I remember that my heart was pumping so fast. When the bear reached the ground, he turned around and walked over to me on two feet. He was a little taller than me. That's when I realized that I wasn't staring at a bear. Rather, I was staring at a real hairy kid who was standing about ten feet away from me.

After about a minute of just standing there and looking at one another, I heard inside my head, "Hello." That's when I turned around and ran all the way down the path and back to my friend's house. Once I reached their property, I kept running all the way home and I never went back to Guy's home ever again.

Zorth resurrected this memory for me to make a simple point, "We are all connected. What one knows, we all know. What one feels, we all feel. We have known you for a long time. We have been with you for most of your life. We will be with you for the rest of your life. We are friends. We are family."

Finally, Zorth asked me, "Please teach the other humans that we are their friends. That we love unconditionally as our Creator intended for all of us to do. The human race is broken and disconnected from the Creator, from one another, and from the Earth. We want to help the humans to reconnect with the Creator, with one another, and with the Earth. God has given the Earth to all of us to enjoy and we must take care of it. Please tell them that if kind people with good hearts and open minds reach out to us, we will reach back to them. Please remind the humans that we are in the trees and that the trees are everywhere."

And now you know the rest of the story. Good day!

Part 5

MULTIPLE WITNESS TESTIMONIES

RANDY RAY
(GRAHAM, WASHINGTON)

It was 1972 when I saw my first " Bigfoot Forest Person." Whatever it was called, as an eight-year-old kid, it was a "Monster." I was on the back of the old Johnson snowmobile with my mother driving. Normally, rides with my mom were boring. She rarely exceeded 5 mph, but on this day, as we headed across the frozen lake on the property in Maine, she started going faster, and faster until the sled was at full throttle. The beaver mounds and muskrat hills flew by as I screamed and laughed. I loved winters in Maine as a child and screaming across a frozen lake on a snowmobile were one of the reasons.

Mom let off the throttle completely and the sled came to an eventual idle. She yelled something to me but the motor was still too loud for me to hear what she was saying. I yelled back, "What?" She was looking intently to her left and as she yelled again, "Do you see it?" I was already turning to see what she was staring at. Her words resounded in my head because there, a few yards away, was this massive, tall hairy creature standing up beside a tree. Its right arm hung down past its knee's while its left arm was stretched way up along the side of the tree. It was pitch black. Maine has a ton of Black Bears and I had seen one myself while playing with my cousins. This was no Black Bear. It was too big and too tall. Plus, it was standing on two legs.

We stared at the Bigfoot Forest Person and he stared at us for what seemed an eternity. Mom apparently had enough and, thank goodness, she gave it full gas and off we sped to home. I jumped off even before the machine had stopped and started running to the house. My Mom stopped me and asked where I was going. I said I was going to tell the family what we had just seen. I had seven brothers and sisters. She grabbed me by the arm and swung me around. There was terror and yet something else in her eyes. "You are never to speak of this again, not to me, not to anyone, do you understand?" she said. My folks were old school and firm disciplinarians. I did understand and I did not speak of that day again until years later when I was an adult. Mom went to her grave and she never spoke of it again.

Thus began my fascination, and quite possibly, infatuation with the Bigfoot Forest People. I worked on summer breaks digging worms, cutting wood and haying to first pay the $96.00 for my entire school clothes for the coming year but also so I could buy any and all books, magazines, articles, or anything I could obtain about Bigfoot.

It may be hard to imagine, but my infatuation got even worse when the commercial came on the TV. A documentary about Bigfoot with video evidence. The wait was unbearable but the time came and I was glued to the set watching a man named Roger Patterson and his friend, Bob Gimlin, in some remote area in California. Although this Bigfoot Forest Person was a female, she was the same in every other way as to what mom and I had seen. I was hooked, line and sinker. More books. More documentaries. Even my 8th grade oral book report was about Bigfoot. Pretty much I stood up there, speaking of what I saw, and realizing quickly my mistake as the laughs and bullying began. It was a long while before I wanted to talk "Bigfoot" with anyone.

There were no more sightings on the property, although Mom and Dad went back up one night because my Dad said he heard voices, not human, and something banging on trees with a stick. They came back and told us all to go to bed and that it was nothing. We obeyed and so it was.

Life does what life does and I grew and enlisted in the Army. My permanent duty station was Ft. Lewis, Washington. "Ft. Lewis, Washington? Where's that?", I remember asking. Then I remembered from my books that Washington had a ton of sightings of Bigfoot. It took a while to get settled in and one was very busy being a soldier so "Bigfooting" had to wait but I did return. However, now I am in woods just like I had seen on that show so long ago. Rugged landscape, massive trees, and a total Bigfoot habitat. To me however, Bigfoot was a Monster to be feared. How could something so powerful not want to rip you to pieces? I read story after story of encounters. I agreed when the "victims" shot at Bigfoot and I longed for the day when a body would be brought in.

I have had multiple encounters over the years. I should say, soft encounters. No sightings. Once, while Elk hunting with a friend, we came across a large bi-pedal track in a mud puddle, clear as day. On another occasion, we heard tree's breaking and what sounded like wrenching of the branches, snapping and popping from being twisted. All for forty-five minutes and all at 12 a.m. Our rifles never left our white knuckled grips.

I've heard tree knocks. I have found tree breaks. My nephews came to visit from Maine and we went way up in the hills and came across five 15 inch tracks, in a straight line. It was this experience that got me thinking I may not have all the answers for the tracks just stopped. Where did whatever was walking barefoot go?

The scariest encounter was at the 9,400-foot level of an obscure mountain. I was deer hunting alone. Not by design but because my friend backed out at the last second and I had been looking forward to this for so long. I went alone, against my wife's wishes. One road in, one road out. I was alone just the way I love it. No other hunters. My tracks were the first. I pulled trees across road so as to be alone. Hunters scare me.

My 88 Ford rambled up the mountain and I found a perfect little flat clear-cut of which to set up camp. It was getting dark so I elected to cook some hot dogs and a hamburger on my little Hibachi. Best tasting hamburger ever, and now full, I closed the BBQ's lid and locked it, climbed up into my camper which sits in the bed of my truck and drifted off to sleep.

It was 2:38 a.m. according to my indigo when the sound woke me from R.E.M sleep. I strained to hear it. That deafening noise in your ears when there is utter silence. There it was again. A rattle. Something's messing with my BBQ left at the rear of the truck. Another rattle, only louder and with more force. Probably a coyote or a raccoon I thought to myself. This went on for a spell. I laid there irritated by this varmint. I gotta get up early for the hunt. When the rattling turned into full on shaking of the BBQ over the top of my camper, I reached for my 300 Winchester Magnum. 180 grain nozzler chambered and ready, safety off. I had never been so terrified in my life. I am on a mountain, alone, 2:30 a.m. in the morning and something is shaking my Hibachi violently over the roof of my camper. I know because it is fact and I am logical, that only two things can grab, as in, pick up a hibachi. Man or Bigfoot.

As I wrestled with this notion, and my own ability to hold urine, the shaking stopped. For a good three seconds, there was complete silence then the BBQ came crashing down twenty or so feet in front of my truck. I am now kneeling in my camper, rifle aimed at the door. I came to a quick conclusion. If whatever, man or Bigfoot tried opening that door, I was going to fire. If it was man, I would pack up and leave him there. Teach him a lesson for trying to get into a hunter's camper, during hunting season, at two in the morning!

Whatever it was did not try the door as a matter of fact I never heard it leave. No crunching on the hard pan I was on, nothing. I literally heard nothing and I stayed in that firing position until daylight. All I found was my Hibachi that had been thrown. Now a second encounter which had me thinking again. I may not have all the answers.

When I would go in to the forest I always would have an eye out, just in case. I would hide and get all camouflaged out hoping to get a glimpse. A couple times I thought I may have seen something. To increase my chances, I would bang a tree with a club. I would yell into the night with strangers with 9 mm's attached to our waists. There were FLIRS (forward looking infrared) night goggles, which are pretty cool by the way. Night vision camera's. Parabolic microphones and a whole bunch of beating it around in the forest, at night, scared to death. The definition of insanity comes to mind but yet, here I was doing the same thing over and over with nearly no results.

I still believed Bigfoot to be flesh and blood and some folks were saying it was an offshoot of Gigantopithecus Blacki which was a ten-foot-tall, lumbering bi-pedal ape that went extinct 400,000 years or so ago. Ok, why not? Seemed possible although I didn't see a lumbering ape that day, back when.

I was on social media and there was this Sasquatch research group called "Team Squatchin USA." I subscribed. Some guy named Dr. Mathew Johnson was the founder. Been a couple years now and I literally have lost count the times my mind has been blown. I could feel that what I was doing was wrong when I would invade their habitat and force them to hear me. To see me. To fool them. Dr. Johnson's research methods are polar opposites. He approaches their world with respect and kindness. I was at a symposium recently with Dr. Johnson as the distinguished guest and he made the analogy of entering someone's living room and banging on their furniture and yelling vocalizations as loud as possible. Maybe take a bunch of pictures and videos and for kicks and giggles, let's light a fire in the center of the room. Also, let's go to their master bedroom, pull back the covers on the bed, and look for hair samples. You most likely, wait, you definitely would not be invited back. No bells and whistles, just peacefulness. No FLIRS and cameras. No night vision. No fires or lights. Just doing as nature intended, under the stars with freezing nights.

Dr. Johnson's commitment inspired me. After sixteen years, he has been in the trenches, so to speak. His Habituation Research Methods have been a huge influence on how I think of these magnificent beings. They're not dumb giant mountain apes. They're not a leaf chewing relic hominid, but instead, a sentient being with families and loved ones. Beings who are as interested in us as we are them.

How could I have been so blind? The evidence was there. Dr. Johnson has opened my eyes and enriched my life by helping me to understand that we are on to something glorious. I no longer have fear toward them. I certainly would never think of harming them ever again. Dr. Johnson is the real deal. I am honored to have been allowed into his "Team Squatchin USA" Facebook group. I can barely stand it waiting for his sharing of miraculous things going on in the Southern Oregon Interaction Area (SOIA).

Now, when I go out into their domain, I am peaceful. Kind and respectful. I follow Dr. Johnsons methods and, to date, I have found a big branch broken off a tree in my yard, 4 inches in diameter, placed up against another tree. I have heard one speak to me although I did not understand what was said. I asked if they could show themselves to me, and awhile later, I was in my garage and something went bounding down the side slapping the walls as it went by.

I am here for the duration and Dr. Johnson is the pilot. Thanks to him for letting us ride shotgun. Bigfoot Forest people, Interdimensional travel, Portals, Orbs, Mind Speak, Telepathy, and Healing. You bet, we are living in exciting times. I feel Dr. Johnson has bridged the gap between species. I feel he was chosen by the Bigfoot Forest People for a multitude of reasons. His loving, perfect research methods are paying off big time and it has always been my life goal to interact with the big ones. I feel I am closer to that than I have ever been in my life. Fist thump to chest, Dr. Johnson. Fist thump to chest.

THOMAS FINLEY
(LONDON, ENGLAND)

Dear Matthew,

I must share with you my psychic connection with the Sasquatch people here in the U.K. I have told many about my experiences but after seeing your photo today, I feel like I can tell you in good faith.

My Bigfoot contact started after my vacation to California in 2009. On that trip I met several Bigfoot researchers Tom Yamarone and David Paulides to name a few. When my wife and I returned home I had my first lucid dream about Bigfoot roughly a month after I was back home in England. I was given a powerful connection and told by a shape-shifting female she was my protector and guardian in this place.

We have had loud heavy footsteps coming from the upstairs bedrooms when only my wife and I were in the house. We've had orbs on camera and the pets are sensitive to invisible presences also. Just the other morning when I woke up I found one of the pillows from my side of the bed leaning up against the recycling bin outside in the garden.

The heavy footsteps really are what impressed me and I have spoken to Arla Collett Williams and a few others in confidence and they have said it is possible for Sasquatch to interact with me as they live between worlds.

I've only shared with a hand full of people, yourself included. I had a very powerful thing happen on my first visit to the Ohio Bigfoot Conference. I was in bed at 3 am and was awoken to tapping at the window on my patio. My body was totally frozen but I could see out of my eyes. The finger tapping went on for over 30 minutes, yet my body was still paralyzed. I told my roommate what happened and he just smirked at me. I told another guest about what happened and she replied the same thing happened to her that Friday night!

Sincerely,
Thomas Finley

BARB SHUPE
(GREENWATER, WASHINGTON)

Dear Dr. Johnson,

I would like to thank you for all of the encouragement, insights and knowledgeable advice I have received from you over here the last several years. Not long after I discovered the Forest Folk were living in the forest around my home, I began to attend your monthly meetings where I met some amazing friends, I had my eyes opened to the true nature of the Sasquatch and learned how to create interaction through gifting.

Under your influence, I have developed my own interactions, gifts given and received as well as a deeper understanding of some of the Forest Folks "stranger" abilities. I have created a successful YouTube channel where I share what I have learned and now many of my viewers report similar successes as they continue sharing what you have originally passed on to me.

Thanks again, Doc, I couldn't have done it without you.

Barb Shupe

JUDY M. MORTON
(YREKA, CALIFORNIA)

In recent years I began sifting thru the internet about Sasquatch. There were stories of killing Bigfoot, being chased by Bigfoot, habituation with Bigfoot, and the entire spectrum. People who had spent their whole lives looking for them came up with nothing but a few foot prints and blurry pictures. In my mind, I simply thought it was a level of pure fantasy to try and get a good look or any connection to Sasquatch. I still found it completely fascinating. All of the things I read actually got me out of my chair and into the forest.

I began following Dr. Matthew Johnson's "Team Squatchin USA" Facebook group page. I decided to apply some of his methods, cut short to 20 minutes a week. I was, after all, driving thru a northern California forest, well known for Sasquatch sightings on a weekly basis. I selected a spot for none other than easy parking and an easy short hike to an area of seclusion but in no way a far reach from the road. I have as of yet to spend a night out there. I only spend 15-30 minutes each time.

The project is simple. I take the same pathway each time. I bring a simple gift, cookies, fruit, muffins, pretty stones, small drawings. etc. Sometimes I bring another person. After exploring and studying the pathway, gifting area, I meditate, trying to achieve a point of relaxation. During this time, I might pray for other people and always focus on nature and give Thanks to God. I always thank the Bigfoot Forest People for their protection of the forest and all who dwell with- in.

The first thing that happened right off the bat was that someone inter-rupted my sleep in the early morning hours at home. A voice asked me,

"Are you a Shaman?" I was taken aback and pretty sure the voice was referring to my prayers for healing in the forest, as I had just been visiting patients, as a nurse out in that rural community. I don't know if my answer met muster but it was pretty much what I just said in the last sentence. I projected the answer with the strong thought of the above as I was slightly shaken up at the time.

In the initial phase, no gifts were taken. Oddly, apples and oranges seemed to be ignored by all of the animals also. Some apples and oranges sat there for a long time. I began to only give them a week, taking up the old gift each week. Muffins disappeared, but I have no way of knowing what forest creature ate them. Dr. Johnson has said on numerous occasions that the Bigfoot Forest People love bread products.

Things went along quite boringly for quite a while. Then the dang road collapsed right near there. An entire lane caved in fell down about seventy-five feet off a cliff and into the Klamath River. This took a month of Sundays for the road crew to fix, forcing people to drive on the one remaining lane. With construction there most of the time, construction workers were often parked in my spot so I would not go there on those days.

One afternoon, as I passed on by because some vehicles were parked in my area, I continued my seventy-five-mile winding road up towards Yreka, Calif. I was overcome with drowsiness about a half hour later and pulled off to a wayside beside the river, parked and flat out fell asleep. It seems like just for a moment. I opened my eyes to be startled by a vision of a very hairy male face, pretty much covering the entire windshield of the car on the driver's side. The face disappeared as I leapt into wide awake and alert. The way in which it shot away, like up a tube, from huge, to pinpoint, to gone with a whoosh sound was the weirdest sensation. It was rapid and took a slit second.

I have continued to go to my project area until now, the end of the year, I will no longer be traveling this road on a weekly basis. But since this past year of such studies, I have had trees fall in my gifting area, unseen sounds of something falling from the trees above, noticed on a regular basis stick structures and changes of stick structures from huge to little glyphs on the ground.

There are times when the most wonderful scents, like flowers or perfume, just drift to me in the forest when there is nothing blooming. I know that Dr. Johnson has reported experiencing this phenomenon in his research area as well.

I now take note of every sound, every change in the forest, and very small bird. I went up to Washington state, visited my sister, walked in the forest near her home and pointed out classic stick structures associated with the Bigfoot Forest People. She, a week later, had a sighting of a Sasquatch at the very moment that a friend and I were meditating at my interaction area.

At the area of my studies, sadly, a forest fire raged nearby. At one point, a logging helicopter thundered on the mountain above. At another point, there was ongoing highway construction. There were many times I had to pass by and not stop, but somehow I hope that the failings of this human race is overlooked and I can continue with my interactions.

My new interaction area is now in the planning stages. I know exactly where it is without having been there yet. I suppose you would like to know how I know where it is? I will let you wonder. Cheers! Go out there and find an interaction area with whatever means you have. They are there. Thank you, Dr. Matthew Johnson, for removing the fear of Sasquatch interaction. I can now seek knowledge about the wonders of the universe and further my personal spiritual development. It is a wonderful thing to do.

TIMOTHY COLLINS (MADISON HEIGHTS, MICHIGAN)

What Dr. Johnson has experienced is more of a confirmation of many things I have experienced. However, his Clan is more open with him than my Clan is with me. We have experienced many similar things and the Forest People have followed a remarkable similar protocol in their nurturing, loving, caring ways.

We have both had healings from our respective Clans, the healings in Dr. Johnson's area are more well documented than in my area. I asked my Clan why they would do that for me (healing & watching over me). They said, "You are an Elder. That is what we do and your nature demands it!"

Reach out to them (the Forest People) and they will touch your heart. I never looked for them. Instead, they found me. I asked my Clan why they chose me. They said, "We didn't choose you. You chose us."

My methods are the same as Dr. Johnson's methods. But we never knew each other and he used several more protocols that I haven't used, such as sleeping out in the open in the great outdoors without campfires or lights.

Dr. Johnson and I have both experienced portals and other unusual phenomenon such as orbs. Again, similar to one another yet different. I never tried to trick or capture the Forest People on camera, however I have a few photos of them quite by accident. Dr. Johnson's Clan asked him not to use electronic equipment or bring cameras to capture their image. The Forest People told me that they feel the emotions of the people viewing their image and that is one of the reasons they don't like photos.

My Clan asked me not to talk about some things they have shown me. Dr. Johnson's Clan asked him not to talk about some things without their permission. I knew instantly when Dr. Johnson said things about his encounters, it was "TRUTH" because I experienced similar things in nearly the same way.

Finally, I was drawn to Dr. Johnson in friendship instantly as his words are from the heart. I could feel his intensions, just as the Forest People feel our intensions when we enter the Forest of their ancestors.

SAMANTHA RITCHIE
(TACOMA, WASHINGTON)

My name is Samantha 'Sam' Ritchie and I have been having interactions with the local Sasquatch clan here in the Cascade Mountains since 2013. Another local researcher and friend, Barb Shupe who had her own experiences for several years, directed me to the Team Squatchin USA meetings in Puyallup, WA led by Dr. Matthew Johnson early in 2014. From the very start, I was very impressed with Dr. Johnson's presentations of what he and others were experiencing at a location in the mountains of Southern Oregon referred to as SOHA, the Southern Oregon Habituation Area. Dr. Johnson used a method called habituation to continually go out to SOHA on a regular basis, usually once or twice monthly for three to four days at a time, in order for the local Sasquatch to get in the "habit" of his presence.

One area of documented evidence used by Dr. Johnson involved the use of food gifting bowls. By wiping the stainless steel bowls clean of any prints and arranging different types of foods he was able to obtain hand/finger prints as well as what foods were of interest to the Sasquatch and which were not. His "before and after" photos of these gifting bowls show clear evidence that something very intelligent was sampling the food in the bowls.

Being encouraged by the way Dr. Johnson went about the method of habituation I decided to make weekly visits to a certain area of the forest known to have Sasquatch activity. While there I would spend time sitting and meditating, often playing a flute (by the way, I have come to know that the Sasquatch love music and it's my experience that personal interactions with them will increase due to it).

At times I also shared a gifting spot with Barb to see how the local clan would respond. On one occasion, I left a half-gallon tub of peanut butter with the plastic lid snapped closed on the tree stump overnight. The next day I found the tub thirty feet away with the lid removed and most of the peanut butter eaten. However, when examining the inside of the tub it looked like it was poked numerous times with a stick to get the peanut butter out! This pretty much eliminates animals or humans from doing something like this.

The second important evidence he presented was audio recordings of the Sasquatch actually speaking intelligent words. Sometimes even calling out to Dr. Johnson using his first name, "Matt!" As in Dr. Johnson's case with the audio recordings, I was also able to record some pretty remarkable sounds by the Sasquatch. It was always important not to try and trick them by hiding audio recorders around a gifting spot. They will always know it's there and will cause it to either get shut off or cause the audio to be distorted. As with my camera, the small audio recorder was something I carried on me all the time. Developing trust with the Sasquatch over time made it easier to capture something on audio or video without them becoming alarmed. Likewise, Dr. Johnson always left his parabolic dish out in the open and was continuously recording so the clan simply got used to it.

I believe it was around August of 2014, at our monthly meeting in Puyallup, Washington, when Dr. Johnson first revealed to the group that he, Adam Davies and John Carlson had an encounter with a portal opening up in SOHA in June of that year. Their description of red skies and dark scraggly vegetation within the portal was fascinating. If that wasn't enough, Dr. Johnson spoke about the two short hairy guardians keeping watch in front of the portal that both Adam Davies and John Carlson also reported seeing. Even Dr. Johnson's son, Grady, saw the portal and guardians too. Perhaps to some hearing this for the first time it would have seemed like the ravings of a lunatic. However, I felt there was no reason why someone would make up such a story, especially if one's credibility and career as a clinical psychologist were on the line. Also, both Adam Davies and John Carlson are very credible witnesses so what incentive would they have in lying?

Personally, I had no reason to disbelieve any of this since I was already familiar with many personal accounts related in the UFO/Paranormal field. Also, I am a student of science and understand what is truly possible with quantum physics. So the saying, "truth is stranger than fiction", holds special meaning to me.

It did not take long for myself and others to experience the "stranger than fiction" part. On September 11, 2014, I was with a group led by Barb Shupe as we came across what can best be described as something right out of the 'Predator' movie, Barb saw something big and black jump down from a branch and run off. Thankfully, she was recording the whole event on her IPod. What the video later revealed was beyond belief. The being was literally translucent as the background greenery could be seen behind it as it jumped down, spun around and took off. The video can still be seen on YouTube by searching "Cloaking Bigfoot, Barb and Gabby."

The next day, I walked back to the same area alone without any recording equipment. To me, it was more important to experience meeting up with the Sasquatch than risk not seeing anything at all. What I did see was beyond my expectations. Here is my account of the incident from my book, "The Sasquatch: Journey Through The Veil" (pages 39-41):

"As I walked up the trail, I noted that the wind was picking up and upon passing to the other side of the little valley we now call the "field of dreams", a strange but euphoric feeling came over me. I began to talk to everything around me, the trees, the animals, the birds and especially the Sasquatches. I was up there alone and within a hundred yards from where the cloaked Bigfoot mentioned in the previous chapter appeared. I turned to go back and encountered an even more amazing sigh. Suspended in the air, a couple of feet above the ground, was four rods of glowing reddish/orange lights forming the shape of a rectangular box. This wasn't there a few minutes earlier and must have appeared after I walked past it.

At first, I thought that it was strong sunlight reflecting off the ground until, as I got a little closer, noticed that the light rods were above the ground and not reflecting off of anything. As I moved around it, the rods were stationary, as if they were part of a 3D object on a CAD software program. Also, if anyone has watched the *Tron* movies, this was like seeing a virtual light object in real life.

A strange calmness came over me as I was not in fear of this but was awestruck and said to myself, "Well, you don't see that every day." Did I come upon a portal of some kind and was this associated with the Sasquatch in some way? I didn't dare get closer to it though as I really didn't like the prospect of being thrust into some other dimension or world. I kept my distance, being no closer than fifteen feet from it, and felt it was best to just observe especially if I had no understanding of what I was really dealing with. As I passed it and looked back, a large beach ball sized orb appeared out of nowhere. It was translucent like a giant soap bubble and glowed with orange electrical sparks of energy. It slowly made its way between and into the four light rods and within seconds, the whole thing disappeared.

On September 28th, 2014, I came back to look for any evidence that the portal may have left behind. As I walked to the same spot, I looked down and discovered the ground area where the portal had been suspended, was completely sheered away and formed a nearly perfect triangle. It was if someone took a large sharp blade and scraped the leaves and undergrowth clean away. As I examined it closer, I even noticed that all the trees roots that were close to the surface were also shaved clean to the same level as the ground. It's one thing for someone to simply clear off an area down to the soil, but it's not possible for someone to precisely shave across a perfectly flat area cutting through not only dirt but also rocks and roots.

What could possibly cause this? All I can do is speculate, but since the light portal was over that spot, it's possible that whatever was within its energy field (including part of the ground) also disappeared with it as it pulsed out of sigh. This experience still affects me each and every day. It was like watching the special effects in a Sci-Fi movie but this was for real. The unseen reality that most people never experience was coming at me like a freight train. This was only the beginning as I would soon find out within that hour."

I mention this personal experience as a testament to the fact that portals do exist. As to the portal that appeared in SOHA, it has been witnessed by various folks and on different occasions giving further credibility to their existence. Although the portal I witnessed was different from the one in SOHA, I feel blessed to have had this experience. I also believe there is no such thing as coincidences. I was meant to see this.

Going down the rabbit hole a little further, I notice the last quoted sentence from the prior paragraph, "...this was only the beginning as I would soon find out within that hour." After I took a photo of the strange triangle on the ground, I hung around this area for a few minutes. The sky was clear blue and the sunlight was shining brightly. The shadows under the trees were just as dark as the sun was light. However, as I looked up at a nearby wooded ridge, I noticed an area between two trees that was extremely dark compared to the surrounding shadows.

Something was not natural about it as I stared intently into the blackness. The blackness was actually moving like a wave much like what you see when observing a mirage on a long stretch of highway during a hot day. Although my eyes could not focus on the form inside the dark mass I somehow knew the Sasquatch was there observing me. I waved at it as if I could see it as plain as day and took a picture with my cell phone. I then stepped a little closer and took another picture.

Once I had the chance to download these photos into my computer, I was able to use some enhancements to brighten and add contrast to the image. I was floored when I was able to see the full body of the Sasquatch standing there smiling and waving back at me. After I enhanced the second photo, I could see him point at me while his head was turned to the side. It is my opinion that he was speaking with another Sasquatch. I believe that he was commenting on the fact that I was able to see them despite the darkness they were cloaked in.

Perhaps the darkness I was observing may have been another portal that they were peering out from or it may simply be a case of their ability to affect their surrounding environment to produce that effect to remain hidden. Whatever the case, maybe it was becoming obvious that the Sasquatch had abilities beyond our human understanding.

As to the portal I witnessed, I kept that to myself for almost a year before producing a video about it on my Planet Sasquatch YouTube channel. I returned to the same area in August of 2015 and did a walk through with my camera as I told of that event. Once I posted the video, I received a comment from one of my viewers who asked me about the big black creature watching me from the side of the tree. I watched the video carefully and was shocked to see what the viewer was talking about. As I'm looking at this one spot next to the tree, I literally can see a face materialize out of nowhere. At first, it looks like a Grey Alien with the large oval eyes before shape shifting into the head of a Bigfoot. The video is clear enough to see it's changing facial expression along with teeth and the movement of its head as it slowly turns to go out of sight behind the tree.

A couple of weeks later, I took some more pictures of the ridge and examined them carefully on my computer. Positioned right in front of a tree was a complete face. It was smiling and staring down at me. The problem was that the face seemed to be sticking out from the tree while the rest of the body was behind it. I later took a comparison photo of that tree and the face was no longer there or any resemblance of it on the bark.

This really revealed to me something about the nature of what we call the Sasquatch. It's apparent they can remain invisible or cloaked from our visual standpoint. When they do appear, they seem to have the ability to change their appearance at will. Also, they appear to have no problem going through solid objects like trees. I do believe, at this point, that when you do see them, it is because they intend for you to see them. For me, they seem to have made a point for me to witness all these things to provide testimony of what they are and the true nature of their existence. Based on what Dr. Johnson has documented about his personal experiences with them, I would say that we are on the same page.

All the events I have mentioned have been documented on my Planet Sasquatch YouTube channel and the PlanetSasquatch.com website.

ERNIE HART
(UPTON, MASSACHUSETTS)

Dr. Matt Johnson's Bigfoot encounter, and subsequent research, experiences, and teaching about Bigfoot has helped me here in New England. I have found "Dr. J's" explanations and approach to finding, interacting and finally habituating with the Bigfoot Forest People to be the most believable and probable explanation of the subject. Once I began to listen and implement "Dr. J's" approach, things started happening quickly for me.

I went from being afraid of entering the woods, to finding the forest to be the most enjoyable, peaceful place to spend my time. I am not a longtime enthusiast in the Bigfoot community. However, I can only tell you what I have experienced over the past six months.

My interest began June 2014 in Alton Bay, New Hampshire. At 2:15 am, I was sleeping under canvas, it was pouring rain, and I have ear plugs in. I was startled awake with the most powerful, long howl I had ever heard. I was frozen in fear, unable to move. Even though I had never even watched a Bigfoot TV show, I knew what it was. It took me two more years to enter the woods and begin my own research here in New England. "Dr. J." taught me not fear the woods or the Forest People. By simply trusting him and what he taught, I began my research this way. Most Bigfoot proof is circumstantial. Even with photos of the Forest People to show to others, the vast majority of the world will still not believe. My evidence is the same.

Beginning in June 2016, a man invited me to his home in Berlin, New Hampshire. He took me out to one of his locations. As we left the parking lot and were walking towards the trail head, there, about

300 yards out on a rock cropping, I could see this huge black figure standing there looking at both of us. I was stunned! I was staring at it trying to get my friends attention. This large black figure with arms down to its knees turned left, and with two or three steps, disappeared into the tree line. It seemed to know we were coming. I was super excited and not afraid. We went into the woods and I was taught what to look for as far as signs of their present activity such as tree leanings, arches, teepee structures, tracks etc.

Since that day in June 2016, I've followed "Dr. J's" attitude and approach to interacting with the Forest People. As a result, I have experienced the following:

1. The Forest People have visited me at my summer camp, I've heard footsteps near me as I'm hiking without seeing them, and I know I am being shadowed and followed by them.
2. Hearing a click/pop language between two individuals very near me as I just stood and listened to them as they were approaching me.
3. I have had all my electronics malfunction while trying to use the high tech equipment when they are near, such as my Camera, GO-PRO, cell phone, and GPS.
4. I have heard and felt them "stomping their feet" twice near me even though I couldn't see them.
5. The Forest People have responded to me when I ask questions by tossing small stones and acorns.
6. I have heard the woman "screaming in the woods" while just talking to myself asking them to give me something new and different as evidence that they're there.
7. I have heard loud branches snap and break nearby me to announce their presence.
8. I have had a thirty-foot log spin clockwise, right in from of me, as I was kneeling down to take a photo at the root base.
9. The most telling of them all is when, somehow, the forest people selected a You-Tube video on my phone of "Dr. J." and it began to play loud as I was hiking. It was in my pocket so I took it out and tried to turn it off but could not turn it off. "Dr. J." was teaching of

a time when he was asking the Forest People to provide him with a teacher. Instead, they told him, "We want you to be a teacher for our youth." So I lifted my phone into the air and asked: "Did you turn this on? Do you know Dr. J?"

I'm saying all this as I am hiking and I can hear them nearby. I sat on a large log with the cell phone in the air, "Dr. J." was still coming through and I simply asked, "Do you want me to do with you what "Dr. J." is doing in Oregon?" Immediately, three or four small stones were tossed at me from different directions. This happened in early August of 2016. I've never seen anything like this before.

Dr. Johnson has taught me that the Forest People are as interested in us as we are in them. My next hurdle is to stay out at night, all night, and wait for them to come to me. Maybe by the time you read this I will have done that. Everything that I shared in my testimony happened over a six-month period of time. Once I got away from my computer, walked into the woods during daylight hours, it made all the difference in the world. Nighttime, here I come.

CAROL DAVISON AND NOLA LIGHTHART (TWIN FALLS, IDAHO)

When your grandmother tells you that there are other people that live in the forest, you listen. She told us that if we should cross paths with these people, we were not to bother them or chase them. She said they wouldn't bother us if we treated them with respect. That was my first awareness of the existence of the Bigfoot Forest People. I'm guessing that the year was 1954 or 1955. The location was Happy Camp, California, where my grandmother was born and raised.

I had forgotten all about Bigfoot until I was nearly half a century old. I can't say what called me back to the mountains and forests in an effort to get to know the Forest People. I started reading about encounters, sightings, and vocalizations. I found myself with a strong desire to have a personal relationship with the ancients.

When I saw the video account of Dr. Matthew Johnson's daytime sighting at the Oregon Caves National Monument Park, I knew he was telling the truth. I mapped it, and his encounter took place within 25 miles, as the crow flies, from the Karuk Reservation at Happy Camp, California. I searched for Dr. Matthew Johnson, found him on the internet, and asked if I could join his Facebook group, "Team Squatchin' USA." I became an official member by the Fall of 2014.

After months of active participation in the group, Dr. Johnson invited me and my partner, Nola Lighthart, to spend some research time with him at SOHA. We were both ecstatic over the opportunity, yet cautious, not wanting to be influenced into agreeing with soft evidence, just to fit in. I was determined to seek and find the truth, no matter what everyone else said. Nola and I arrived at SOHA to begin our study, exactly one year to the day after John Carlson and Adam Davies had been there and experienced a portal two nights in a row.

We tried to work out our own system of scrutiny, each of us having the other's back, and being hyper vigilant to our surroundings. Nola would watch the forest behind me and vice versa. We were determined that nothing could sneak up on us without one of us noticing, and certainly, no one was going to hoax us.

After setting camp, I braved using the porta-potty first. After standing to adjust my clothes, I witnessed a peculiar glowing light about 12 feet from where I was standing. It was circular, light green in color, and was emitting its own light. I estimate it was dinner plate in size and had the luminescence similar to a firefly. I mentioned it to Nola, but by the time she had finished using the porta-potty and turned around, it was gone. I have no idea what it was.

The first night sleeping out in the open under the stars wasn't as difficult as one might think. Dr. Johnson doesn't allow his guest to sleep in tents or campers. After placing the gifting bowls as per Dr. Johnson's protocol, we settled in for a restful night.

The next morning, in the pre-dawn light, the five of us gathered and went down the path from the SOHA base camp to inspect the bowls. Nola and I had chosen fresh brown eggs and several soft molasses cookies to add to the feast. Matt told us that the bowls were usually untouched the first night, so we were happy to discover that "something" had helped themselves during the night. Most of the eggs had been cracked open, the insides consumed, then the shells were placed one into the other and placed back into the carton.

We knew by the evidence, that no raccoons, squirrels, or birds had taken the food. There was NO mess at all. The sandwich halves looked untouched at first, but Nola lifted one piece of bread and saw a small finger swipe through the peanut butter. The cookies were gone.

The second and third nights were much the same, some items taken, but no mess at all.

We were treated to a set of four finger prints on the inside of the shiny bowl. When Nola lifted it to inspect the underside, we all saw the large thumb print on the bottom surface.

Before being taken to SOHA, we signed a NDC (non-disclosure contract). I'd like to make it clear that by signing the contract, we were agreeing to not disclose the location of SOHA, and to not return to the area without Matt's approval. There was no fee or charge to go to SOHA. We selected our own items to put in the gifting bowls. We were in no way restricted from exploring the entire area, taking photos or videos, or told not to speak to anyone about our experiences.

Matt encouraged us to have a good look at the tree structures and surrounding landscape. After seeing how the trees were arranged, entwined, and stacked, we knew that it was not natural. The structure area was too dense with trees, saplings, and underbrush to have been built by any kind of machinery. Many of the logs were just too heavy for even a strong person to lift.

On the third morning, Nola and I were treated to a large clear hand print on our truck. Not to be fooled by one of the three men that were with us, we asked each of them to put a print on the other side of our truck for comparison. We got them to cooperate before telling them our reasons. The print did not match any of us.

The third night was my favorite. The three men and I walked down the path toward the location of the "portal" which was witnessed in June of 2014 by Dr. Johnson, his son, Grady, and his guests, Adam Davies and John Carlson. It was moonless, so pretty dark, and there was a stiff breeze from the west. As we approached the trees that formed a canopy over the path, I could see a distinct mist or fog lingering up above my head about eight to ten feet from the ground level. This caused me some confusion, because it didn't seem to be effected by the breeze. It just seemed to hang up in and around the foliage.

Approximately one hour later, as we sat in a circle back at the SOHA base camp, I heard close, clear bipedal footfalls right behind me. I could see every person within the camp, all accounted for, yet when I whipped around to see what was making the step sounds, I could see nothing at all.

During our visit to SOHA, neither of us were under any peer pressure to agree with anyone else's observations. I wouldn't hesitate to go out researching with Matt again, in hopes of learning more about these fascinating beings. His methods may seem strict and on the verge of obsessive, to the inexperienced, but in the end, his protocols paid off for us. You have to remember that he has spent years trying various methods to see what really works. I would tell anyone who is interested in the Bigfoot Forest People, to try Matt's approach. Go out to the forest, be patient, and let them come to you.

ANDREA BILLUPS
(HASLETT, MICHIGAN)

It is 4:30 a.m. when I am awakened in pitch blackness, in my cot, high in the mountains. Far from the safety of Florida, where I have been staying — or even my home in Michigan, which is located in the forest and near a lake.

If something is going wrong up here, in the middle of nowhere, one thing I realized, "Ain't no one coming to save me. Not even Dr. J., who is next to me, asleep, and unaware of the creep-tastic symphony that is beginning."

I have asked for this experience. At this moment, I am not yet a knower — but close. I've been a distaff student of sasquatch for several years, finally reaching out to Dr. Matthew Johnson, a man whose honesty and credibility speak to me. I have spent years of following him online and reading damned near everything I can about the subject - from hominid anthropology to genetics to tales of Native American lore. Now, I have been invited to see for myself and I am petrified.

When I am not in a cot, cocooned on a distant mountain in a forest coming alive, I am a rational explorer. After much study, the evidence has added up for me. I don't take the truth lightly. It's my livelihood. I've come to a conclusion that something, some people, do share the planet with me and they are way more than legend. They also have managed not to be seen much. For centuries. Who are they?

But back to tonight in October of 2015. Let me be clear, I am not a camper. The last time I did so was in 1973 when I was an unhappy Girl Scout, traumatized by a weekend of cabin sleeping. I am an admitted froufrou. I wear make-up every day and au natural is a look for someone else - not me. But curiosity has triumphed. I've flown to Oregon to put something to rest.

This journey, I have taken alone, and it is personal — and also in some sense professional. I am a veteran journalist of more than 25 years. I'm old school. If you really want to know if something is true — you get out there and report it yourself. You go. You see. You decide — based on what you uncover. Not what someone else said — in a chatroom, on Facebook, in some grainy video claiming "proof."

So, I am hunkered down in the mountain chill, my first night in camp, wearing two pairs of leggings, a sweatshirt, a ski jacket, a toboggan and under not one but two sleeping bags and a tarp. I am still cold but I feel safe. Until the noise begins and I cannot ignore it.

It is disorienting. Odd sounds. Whoops and barks. It's also frightening. We have no lights. No fire, and nothing but the starry open sky above, which offers comfort amid the pin pricks of light. But I can see no further than the tree canopy that surrounds our clearing.

I pull the bedding down so I can get a peek. I am afraid to look but I must know. Who or what is whooping and barking? A vocalization I've never heard in a zoo or even online. We are at 5,000 feet on a remote mountainside in Oregon at 4 a.m. I know we do not have dogs or owls, whose back and forth "Hoo-hoo-hoo-hoo" grows louder and closer with every minute. But are they owls? Their calls do not trill at the end like the sounds I've heard at home. It's like someone is mimicking owls. And whoever that is, is huge.

"Dr. J., are you awake?" I tap on his shoulder. I am trembling. Do you hear that? "Yes", he whispers.

I do not want him to know that I am now in a state of panic. His truck is beside us, parallel with my cot. Fight or flight. Do I get up and get inside the truck and lock the door in terror or do I listen with wonder for something I knew could happen and now is happening?

They, it, them, were surrounding us. Hooting, barking, and moving around the camp. I could not see them. I would later listen to the recordings of that night — and feel my blood pressure quicken and that sense of terror revisit.

Could this be real? But it was and it was happening. As if someone, somethings, wanted me to know: "Yes, we are here. Yes, we know you've come. Yes, it's ok to believe in us. We are real and we are not going to hurt you."

That last point took me about six months to understand because, in my fear of the second night of a camping expedition to Dr. J's beloved SOHA, I was not able to fully process all that had gone on - it took some time.

For the record, our second night episode went on for about two hours. There were distant muffled voices, whistles, and perhaps even more creepy to me — the faraway tree knocks — or were they? Not the kind of tree knocks I've heard on "Finding Bigfoot," the "whack" of a bat sound, but gentle, resonant, taps on wood that permeated the hillsides and unusual intervals. Something out there was communicating with its kin or with me.

It was that morning, as I lay still in my sleeping bag on my cot and prayed for daylight, I wished for a valium, a shot of tequila — something…. that I realized that more than likely — Bigfoot was real. I for sure didn't think my friends back home would believe me. But after this night, I knew that I'd had an experience of a lifetime. I was now a knower.

If you are not a native to the Pacific Northwest, then its beauty and expanse are staggering. I was exhausted when Matt met me at the airport after a 4-leg cross-country flight. But the next day, as I traded my girlie attire for something far less attractive, the majesty and reality of where we were headed started to sink in.

We drove, thru rutted hillside, into tiny crevices of road, up and away and winding until we met a clearing where Dr. J. had been visiting for almost a decade. So this is it, I told myself. This is SOHA. High atop a mountain with sweeping vistas. A good place NOT to be found.

Also a place where he was cultivating a relationship with a clan of people who were interacting with him regularly. Here I now stood, where the stories of encounters — visual and cloaked — had fascinated me late into the night when I poured over blog posts in search of something definitive.

We set up camp. Dr. J. was a pro. Afterwards, he explained the perimeter, the protocol and the surroundings. So far so good.

We went on a hike. And once we crossed the threshold of the clearing on a path into the deep forest, the complicated markings posted in photos by other bigfoot researchers - things I'd only seen in photos became clear. There were weavings, logs placed inexplicably, a jungle gym for someone. But then who drives deep into the mountains to twist trees, bend branches, to oddly build and play?

I was, on edge. And for whatever reason, real or imagined, I felt like we might be being watched. I said so. Dr. J. nonchalantly advised: "They know we are here. They are watching our every move." We did not see the "they."

Dr. J. talked with me about his ten-year history in SOHA and all that had occurred. I calmed down, but my nerves went haywire as dusk slowly melted into dark. On the side of the mountain. Was it out there? This thing I'd traveled so far to find?

We sat in chairs facing each other, our backs in different directions to the forest, so we could better see all around us. Whether it was my imagination or not, at some point around 10 p.m. that first night, I felt something sweep across my forehead. It felt light, like a feather or the touch of soft hands. At first, I thought it was a leaf. Except I was not under a tree and no leaves were falling.

I shared this with Matt who nodded. He slowly explained that others had been touched, quite literally, by something that was cloaked. I'd read about cloaking and wondered if it could be true. I'd wanted to keep an open mind. There I sat, and reconciled that something had gently touched my forehead. "I am not making this up," I told myself, "It HAPPENED." But what had happened?

We talked deep into the night, playing music, singing, and walking the perimeter of the clearing. I saw what I thought was eye glow. At first, I dismissed it. Then Dr. J. asked, "Did you see that?" Indeed, I had.

Something had flickered in the trees. I thought I saw movement too, but the darkness made it hard to discern.

"Did something...." I started to ask Matt, and he finished my sentence, "Move at 11 o'clock position on the perimeter? Yes, we are not alone."

I felt frozen but not unhinged. Excited but afraid. When nothing dramatic occurred that night, I got in my sleeping bag on the cot, and to my surprise, drifted off to sleep, awaking only briefly. I was so tired from my travels that the gravity of all that was going on in SOHA had not hit me.

Around 3 a.m., it started to rain or at least I thought. I had my phone inside my sleeping bag so I saw the time. A tarp had been pulled over our cots. Matt had put it at our feet on our cots, if indeed it showered, and so I figured he had pulled it over us during the night.

"Tap. Tap. Tap," I heard above my head. That HAD to be rain, I thought as I was too afraid to pull down the covers to see. There were just three taps and then total silence. I fell back asleep. While it was still dark outside, Matt rolled over to ask, "Did you pull the tarp over us in the middle of night?"

"I did not," I told him. Then he recounted being awakened by three sharp tugs that moved that cover to his waist, then his shoulders and over his head as he'd slept. I had not touched that tarp.

When daylight came, I got up to use the facilities and came back to my cot to find that I had not been alone after all during the night. A five-inch footprint, clear as could be, was at the head of my cot. I wear size 6 women's shoes. I have small feet. The juvenile footprint was about a half inch shorter than my own sneaker. There was just one.

Somewhere, I have a photo. To be candid, I cannot come up with any rationale that would put a small barefooted child at the top of a mountain, far from people, and in a place I knew I did not have the stamina to hike to. Something or someone small with a five-toed foot had stepped into the moist dirt behind me during the night and that, I had to allow, was real. I saw it with my own eyes. It wasn't someone else's YouTube video. It had just happened to me.

As a journalist, I've been trained to keep an open mind and to think rationally about things I did not understand. Read, study, digest, be discerning, find credible sources, ask them, and read some more.

I was always deeply curious about Bigfoot. I believe I'd been reading about Bigfoot for two years solid before I ever talked to anyone about my fascination. The internet, I'd discovered, was filled with lots of hoaxes, lots of posers, but also a quiet community of people who knew what they'd seen and who joined a club with relatively few members.

The best conclusion I'd drawn, and later shared with many laughing, skeptical friends, was that there was plenty of evidence. Not just the footprint casts from all over the world. Where were they all coming from? What about the thousands of anecdotes saved online — with similar descriptions, fact patterns, accounts?

The best of it, I'd surmised. was the record left in Native American writings, from Florida to Vancouver BC. Native peoples had recounted the Bigfoot Forest People they had encountered, even giving those people names. Could they have emailed one another to get their stories straight? No. That was not possible. Somehow from state to state and tribe to tribe, they were identifying something that was similar. That was a real thing, that lived among them and was a constant.

And so I concluded, unscientifically, un-journalistically, but based upon my own premise, that the Indians were not making these stories up. They lived in the forests, communed with nature, and across our continent, were describing the same thing. To me, that record was the truest of all.

By the third night in camp, my emotions had balanced. Now, I knew the eye glow I started to see at dusk was indeed real. That the movement I charted in the trees, back lit by the ambient light of the sky, was real. The feeling that things were nearby, well, there were things nearby. Stealthily moving up the mountainside and assembling for the evening's entertainment. I could hear them quietly take their places. I felt them there under the cover of the trees.

Dr. J. and I talked, even started a heated political argument to draw attention to ourselves. It must have worked. We soon had an audience all around us and there was no denying it. Eye glow all over. I told myself they were curious. If they wanted to attack me, well that would have happened days ago. I had a tiny bit of peace.

Around 10 p.m. or so, as I walked around the circular area of camp, now on my own, I was overwhelmed by the smell of beautiful, heavy-scented flowers. Like expensive perfume and it was staggering.

"Matt, did you put on aftershave to freshen up," I asked him. He was standing twenty-five feet away. "No, he laughed. What is happening?" He walked over and caught wind of the beautiful scent. "It was like Hawaii with floral leis," he said. To me, it smelled like the perfume counter of Neiman Marcus, where rich scents were bountiful. But what would smell so fragrant and so lush on the side of an Oregon mountain in October? Especially when the air temp was near forty degrees and nothing floral was blooming?

I have no explanation for it, save to say it was amazing, beautiful, and female. I wondered had I been sprayed with some sort of being's pheromone? Dr. J. said, "It could be a female presence expressing pleasure that you're here with me." He noted that his fiancé, Cynthia, had smelled it before earlier in February when it was cold and absolutely nothing was blooming. In any event, it was shocking and amazing. If someone in the forest did that to show their feminine side, I was impressed, wowed, and stunned.

This was not the only shocking moment that evening. Later, I walked the perimeter of the base camp with Matt, who was holding a lighted smartphone playing music. I noticed at the 11 o'clock position on the outside of the camping area, a very tall shadow. I looked down, as it was dark, readjusted my eyes, and then I looked again. It was still there, I froze, and then it swayed.

"Did you see him?" asked Dr. J. I don't remember if I spoke or nodded, but not long after, I hit that place where fear consumed me. Whatever the big shadow was, standing several feet back into the forest canopy, it was now swaying as the music played. Not quickly, just ever so gently.

At that point, I could no longer look up or into the trees. I was so shaken, I stared at my feet. I clung to Matt's side. If he took a step, I was stuck on him like glue. "He won't hurt you," Matt implored. I tried to sing. I tried to take heart. My legs shook. I know I saw what I saw.

What I'd flown across the country to confront, was out there, and he was at least two feet taller than Dr. J. who is 6'9". Awed, amazed, paralyzed, I was all of those things that evening. I believe I only slept because I was, at this point, filled with so much stress hormones that my system just crashed. But there is more.

The next morning, I awoke at dawn and looked over into the clearing of our area. I asked, "Matt, did you leave a drum mallet out on the ground last night In camp?"

"No," he said, getting up to examine it. "We brought this up here a few months ago," he said. "It had gone missing," he said. ""They" must have returned it," he said with a smile. That, in itself, was bizarre because I knew for sure it wasn't there the previous evening.

I went to the bathroom, which I'd insisted on keeping close to camp for fear of fear itself. Then I came back, wiped my eyes, and looked down on the chrome running board of the truck, right next to my cot. There were fingerprints, like someone had gripped underneath the bottom of the truck and grabbed ahold of the chrome. Five fingers on one hand. Five on the other, about six inches apart. Dr. J. laughed. "Belly crawlers," he said. "They wanted to check you out, so they crawled under the truck." Six inches away from where I'd been sleeping. Oh, God.

If you had told me five years ago that I would have had ongoing experiences with the Sasquatch, I would have laughed you under the table or asked you if you were high. But the truth is that after I left the beautiful SOHA, and went home to my own house, which stands in the woods, things started happening to me that I simply could not explain. I'll write them here straightforward, to put them on record, because I have no other more thoughtful or explanatory way of sharing.

I live in central Michigan in a very modern two-story house. Its whole back side is primarily glass, and it sits at the edge of a massive forest trail system. The back of our property is wetlands. Our home looks into a dense forest where you can hike for miles. On one end, power lines abut this greenway. No too far away, there is also a lake. It is beautiful and I have a game trail and three-foot-deep gully that snakes about 50 feet from my downstairs back porch. I see and hear all kinds of critters nearly every day.

For years, my forest had been my haven of peace. I would walk nearly every day when the weather was good or trail run for exercise. But there was always one area, a pine thicket about a mile and a half in, where I just stopped. Where it felt odd. Where the hair would stand up on my arms and where I'd get that feeling, "Turn back now." So I did. I called it my "Enchanted forest" and I joked with my partner, Steve, that it was spooky.

One day, I got the nerve to enter. Once inside, I found a beautiful area and lots of signs. Arched trees and tee-pee structures. I found a clearing that had a massive tree that had been hit by lightning. After the top tumbled over, it left a three-pronged statue, about thirty feet high. I called it my angel tree. It looks like a giant angel with arms outstretched. I went there as my comfort grew, to sit, to pray, to read my small Bible, and to meditate.

Maybe six months later, I discovered nearby, another massive structure. A tree had toppled and then literally, hundreds of five and six feet long broken branches had been stacked or woven through it. There was an inside corridor where I could nearly stand up. I am 5'3" tall. There were branches hanging off of it in certain places. It was simply wild that day. There it was. Intricately arranged, and seemingly out of nowhere.

The more that I examined it, the more I knew that someone had built it. Yes, the tree had toppled and it was a massive hardwood. But someone had come along later and created what looked like a shelter. It was intricate and many of the logs were so embedded they would not move. They were jammed into the ground. This piqued my curiosity and also scared me.

I began gifting like Dr. J. used to do. Just for fun. Apples high in trees, some plastic toys, and jars of peanut butter that disappeared. Later, the cleaned out jars, minus lids, were left in their place. I imagined there were just raccoons and deer. I continued to visit.

One day, in October of 2016, in mid-afternoon, I went out for a long walk. I sat in front of my angel tree, where I'd also left a letter A with a pinecone beside it — my glyph for me. I spoke inside my head: "If you are out there, if this is real, please show yourself to me. Give me a sign that what I am feeling and thinking isn't just crazy."

I sat a while longer and then got up and began to walk from my tree to the trail, about twenty-five feet. For some reason I looked to the left where the trail moves ahead. Then it happened in a slip second. Red fur went flying, like a jet about thirty yards away. I could not get my breath, and my heart was beating so hard. My brain immediately went to rationalizing, "That was a fox. No, probably a squirrel. Wait… what was that?"

I started to walk toward it inexplicably, realizing fully now that it was longish red hair moving in the wind, about four or five inches long. The color stood out against the greenery of the pines. If it were a squirrel, or a fox, how was it at least eye level? Whatever I saw moving was at least five feet off the ground.

I stopped and turned around, petrified. The forest was eerily quiet. It was Mid-afternoon. I was at least a mile and a half walk from where the forest clearing meets my home. I looked around. Was I being watched? It was silent. Still utterly quiet. I followed the trail back quickly, looking over my shoulder, but too afraid to run. I crossed the wide marsh and got into a new forest of mature hardwood, maybe a half mile from the angel tree area. I was beating a familiar trail back, wondering if I were alone. Then I looked up and saw, about seventy-five feet away, the strangest sight. A log was tossed out of the top of a massive tree.

When I say tossed, I use that word deliberately, because it was cascading horizontally, not end over end, as it fell to ground with a giant thud. Maybe a limb had broken, but it looked about four feet long and at least eight inches wide. It seemed like it got launched. Like someone took two-hands and sent it out of the top of a tree.

At that point, I had to sit down. Was that for me or just bad timing? It wasn't close to me, but coming from a place directly ahead. Was it to get my attention or just a scary fluke?

I had my phone and nervously began to text a message to Dr. J. "Call me," he responded immediately. He picked up on the second ring. With a calm voice, he asked me to slow down and to go back over each detail. I struggled for words to describe what had happened. No, he didn't think I was nuts. Yes, what I saw, he assured, was likely meant for me to see.

He was excited. I was petrified. After about fifteen minutes of counseling in the forest, so to speak, I was able to hike back out and get to home. We later convened another call where Dr. J. helped me to debrief. His wisdom helped me to think more thoughtfully about all that had gone on that day.

That was the most intense outing I have ever had in my forest, but only the beginning of many other happenings of which I do not fully understand. Among them:

I travel a lot and am often gone from my primary home for months on end. Last May, after being gone for nearly 5 months, I went walking in my forest area on my way to the angel tree and where I gift. I got owl called in mid-afternoon. It went on for about two minutes and then stopped.

When I hike in my forest and am about to enter the pine stand area where I gift, sometimes I will feel light-headed. One particular time, I "lost time", meaning I was walking and then I came to about a quarter mile up the trail. I have no recollection of traveling that far. It's like I was coming around one corner and then, poof, I am walking a long way away. That was scary. Two other people have felt the same light-headed and energy shifting of this area. It's very unusual. There are also structures and such nearby.

Oftentimes, my 11-year-old Lab will wander in our backyard. She does not go too far because there are wetlands and such nearby and because she is a quirky shelter rescue. Sometimes, she will ask to go outside and then I will have five to ten minutes or so where I cannot find her at all.

I was talking on instant message with a woman who channels the Bigfoot Forest People. I do not judge her talents, although some might think I'm simply crackers. She is honest and lives in an area of Michigan where she has had contacts since she was a little girl. I'd reached out to her at the behest of another friend who has a clan on his property. What she shared with me was staggering. "They are trying to heal your dog. They say she walks funny," this woman told me.

What made this message to me so staggering was that my dog, a black lab, takes medications for her seizures that weaken her back legs and sometimes she wobbles. She does walk "funny." Few people, if any, know that about my dog. How was it possible that this woman could share such information with me? Who told her this? We had no real friends in common. We had never met. She lives hundreds of miles away.

The woman went on, "You have a small clan who know you and who watch you." She offered names for some of them. There is a young girl, the daughter of one of the clan males. "She likes your blonde hair," the woman told me. "She watches you all the time. She loves you." Then the clincher. The woman said, "She likes the rocking chair in your office. She thinks it's pretty."

That bit of information, maybe three people know that I keep an antique red velveteen rocker and footstool in my private office at home. The office, like our bedroom suite, is downstairs in our home, which has glass windows that open direct onto an open forest. You would have to walk up to our covered back deck and peer in the window to see the rocker. I rarely take anyone into my office. So how anyone might know about my rocker is beyond me. You'd have to look into my window to see it. This news has stayed with me and forever changed me. Both the information about my dog and my office furniture is simply unexplainable. And I will leave it at that.

It is frustrating trying to understand what you feel might be going on around you but it isn't concrete. One day, in my mind, I simply said to them: "Please let me know you are there. I feel your presence, but could you give me a sign." Two days later, a giant vine weaving turned up about 75 feet into the forest directly behind my house. It was intricate, beautiful, and it hadn't been there before. If nature did this, nature was quick.

I have learned to trust my dog's behavior as a cue that I am not alone. Sometimes at night, we will step on our back porch when I let her out. She is older, now eleven, and she will wake me up to go in the middle of the night. Occasionally, she will simply stop on the porch and become rigid staring at the same area where I suspect they climb into a four-foot gully/creek bed/game trail area behind our house, and watch. The dog frequently stares there at night and sometimes will simply refuse to go out at all, wanting to go back inside the house.

One evening, in the dark, I opened my door for her only to hear a giant thud and running. It was two-footed, this sound, and it came from one of a several giant hardwood trees about 15 feet from the back porch. I could not see it because it was 3 a.m. It sounded louder than a raccoon dashing out of the tree. Whatever it was grunted, in the same way we might grunt if we dropped several feet from a height to our feet. It was enough to send me back inside quickly. The dog growled, but did not give chase. My hunch tells me it was a juvenile Bigfoot who was hanging out nearby to watch us inside at night.

There have been many smaller incidents here. Close to my house and deeper into the forest where I continue to hike, sometimes sitting out at night with a Bigfooting friend. They are similar to what others have experienced and written about. The whistles, the tree knocks, the small glittering sparks of energy, even a pane of iridescent energy floating one evening that seems to appear from nowhere. I can't explain any of it except to say that I saw it and I was not alone.

In conclusion, I have thought long and hard about writing my own account. You see, I am a journalist and so exposing this information publicly is harder for me. After some soul-searching, and because of my respect for Dr. Johnson's work, I have decided that I should share my truth. What I have recounted here is true. It has happened over the past several years here in Michigan. My experiences have intensified after my trip to SOHA. It seems that after you become "a knower," they know you know and are with you. They are quietly watching. I have come to give them my respect. I believe we are dealing with a Bigfoot Forest People who have always been with us. They are very unique with special energies and qualities that we have only begun to understand. I do know that I am not alone in the woods. I feel honored to know that, too.

SHELLEY MOWER
(HUGO, OREGON)

I have always believed in the possibility of Bigfoot being real. I have wished that I could interact with them, even if just once in my life. In 2013, I had the pleasure of meeting Dr. Matthew Johnson and Cynthia Kreitzberg. I enjoyed discussing my thoughts about the Bigfoot Forest People with them. Also, I tried to learn as much as I could by reading testimonials and whatever I could get my hands on. I was invited to visit the Southern Oregon Habituation Area (SOHA) with Dr. Johnson and Cynthia a few times. I had a few experiences that I couldn't explain to myself and left with the belief of that there really is something or someone out there that we can't explain.

The first time I was able to visit SOHA, it was a rainy night. We had a tarp over us hanging down the back of our chairs. The front was open to listen and watch for movement on the perimeter in front of us. There were different sounds around camp that night, but the one that stands out to me is that there was a sound of a crying baby at the 9:00 o'clock position on the perimeter. It was an eerie sound, hearing a human sounding baby crying out in the black darkness of trees in the rain. But it didn't last long. You could hear other muffled sound in the same direction, as if they were consoling the baby.

We had ways of saying where we were hearing or seeing things without pointing at them. We didn't want to draw attention to ourselves by pointing and talking about it. Dr. J. would make it known to new visitors where the positions were located on the perimeter. It helped eliminate pointing and kept us focused for the next thing that could happen.

During another visit to SOHA, I got to experience eye glow. I hadn't said anything about what I thought I saw, because I didn't want to seem crazy, like I am sure some people think of Bigfoot believers. Nevertheless, I kept quiet and listened to Dr. J. and Cynthia telling each other and me what they were seeing. Oh my, Cynthia said that she was seeing exactly what I was seeing. At about knee level in the bushes, there were two white spots that seemed to be blinking at times and moving slightly in either direction. The blinking was not a fast blink like normally done. It was a slow open and close movement. I couldn't believe she had described exactly what I was seeing and I hadn't said a word about. I told her I was seeing the same thing. How exciting!!! I couldn't believe that I had what I believed to be was my first sighting of something in the Bigfoot world.

In July of 2015, when I was up at SOHA, Dr. Johnson, Mike, and Jamie accompanied me. It was a busy night around the perimeter of the base camp. Something or someone other than us was making different noises around our camp. The sounds were in all different directions around the base camp, as if we were being watched from all sides.

We had been trying to investigate a portal in the SOHA location that had been witnessed the previous year by Adam Davies, John Carlson, Dr. Johnson, and his son, Grady. The guys had walked down to the location while I stayed up in camp in the pitch dark of night. We were trying to see if the portal would open with them down by it after they had visited the Oregon Vortex/Oregon House of Mystery in southern Oregon.

While they were down by the portal area, they were discussing what they could see and called me down to see if I could see it as well. It was a really dark night, but I walked the dirt road down to where they were standing. On my way to them, I was focusing on the road to see where I was going. It was so dark and the guys were quite a ways down the road, so I was trying to hurry. About half way down to where they were, I had a feeling come over me that I believed I was not alone by the road and I am not talking about the guys. I felt that others accompanied me in the tree line along the side of the road. At that moment, I heard a dog bark right by my left knee but I couldn't see it. It was like it was invisible.

It sent chills up my spine and still does to this day. It was such a close sound and didn't make sense to me, since there were bushes on both sides of the road.

I got down to the others as fast as I could and sucked up to the side of them trying to get their attention. Literally standing as close to them as I could, because it was something I couldn't see and didn't understand. I was able to tell them what I had heard and later found that Dr. Johnson had recorded it on the portable parabolic microphone dish that he had set up.

While at that location of the SOHA portal, we were noticing that there was a strange white fog of light in the surrounding area. I know it wasn't actually misty fog. I tend to cough when in fog like that, because I have asthma. Also, the wind was blowing but the fog of light was not moving. We don't know what made it appear like that, but it was interesting.

That same night, I was sitting with Mike by the 12:00 o'clock position on the perimeter of the base camp. We were playing music loudly to entertain the Bigfoot Forest People. It was a nightly routine that Dr. J. would play music while walking around and singing to them. We would take turns doing different things for entertainment. Jamie had a beautiful drum to play music. Mike and I played music from his phone. As we played music, we could see something right in front of us moving to the music. It was mesmerizing, to say the least. We couldn't stop watching it. The next morning, we went and looked at what it was. There was a leaf hanging from a spider web thread. It still is amazing to me to think of the movement that was happening the night before.

While visiting SOHA, every evening there were two gifting bowls placed out on the trail for the Bigfoot Forest People to take what they wanted. There were items moved and taken from the gifting bowls, but never was it apparent that small animals or birds had bothered the bowls. They were always neat and clean. Small animals and birds come by my house and they make a mess of things while eating. At my home, birds peck at the bread items that were left out and make a mess. Small animals break all of the eggs into little pieces. But I had never seen that happen up at SOHA. Also, little animals and birds don't leave human-like finger-prints on the gifting bowls.

I am thankful for being able to experience SOHA, thanks to Dr. Matthew Johnson. I am so excited to experience more with the Bigfoot Forest People. I believe they are out there and choose who they will interact with. I hope I am blessed with being one of those individuals that they will choose to interact with in SOIA in the future. Squatch on my friends!

STEVE BACHMANN
(BUCKLEY, WASHINGTON)

Like the largest percentage of Bigfoot enthusiasts, we sit at our computers and type away and watch Bigfoot YouTube videos. That's who I was, nothing more than a one-in-a-million whom would die to get the chance to experience the Big Hairy Guy. Yep, I believed in him, 100%, from a young kid. Why? No idea, I just did.

So one evening in the summer of 2015, I spotted two individuals online that I truly believed were telling the God's truth. There were many others I also watched as well but I wasn't sure if they were telling it straight up. One of the two people I believed was a man named, Dr. Matthew Johnson. The best thing was that he was located close by with most of his experiences occurring between Washington and Oregon. The other gentleman was located in Florida. I knew that would never happen because I wasn't going to be going to Florida anytime soon.

A year had passed by, it was now the summer of 2016. I believe late May, the guy in Florida had taken down his YouTube channel and went by subscribe or pay-per-view. "See you later! I'm not paying to watch your videos!" There were a couple others that took the same approach, but not Dr. Johnson. He was still broadcasting his YouTube videos for the world to hear and see for free.

Like I said, it was now May of 2016. I began to get an itch to get up in the mountains. I just knew that the Bigfoot Forest People were there, but no way was I going by myself. So I took the next totally out of character and brazen move I would ever do, I wrote Dr. Johnson a letter. I shared with him how I would like to go camping with him in the southern Oregon mountains to meet Bigfoot. Really now, the letter I wrote him was a quick and short biography of my life in sentence by sentence form. In one of those sentences, I mentioned that I had built an Electromagnetic Power Generator System. Like the government says, "Over-Unity" is impossible and Bigfoot is just a myth. Little did I know but I would find out later that both the Electromagnetic Generator and Bigfoot would be the two most real phenomena of my life.

At the beginning of June 2016, my phone began ringing in the evening. I looked at my phone and saw an Oregon pre-fix. I just thought, "Who could this be?" I answered the phone and to my surprise, it was Dr. Matthew Johnson. He immediately explained to me why I was chosen by him. My "Over- Unity" Electro-Magnetic Device might be of need to help the remaining Bigfoot Forest People leave their dying home world and come to Earth.

Well, this was way over my head but I thought, "Well, if this is my ticket to get to the Southern Oregon Interaction Area (SOIA), then I'm going to give it a try." While in SOIA, I learned that there were approximately 23,500 Bigfoot Forest People trapped on a dying planet. They did not have the adequate electromagnetic flow in their bodies to pass through the portal. Therefore, they were stuck on a dying planet.

Matt, also during the next couple of weeks, during several phone conversations, coached me on how to conduct myself in SOIA. Basically, I was to behave as a Navy Seal and not freak out when the Bigfoot Forest People touch me and I see nothing because they're cloaked. I responded, "Okay, I'm all in. Let's go!" On June 23, 2016, Matt called me and said "Steve just leave the Electromagnet Device at home because this is your first time to SOIA. I just want the family to get to know you." I replied, "Sure, okay."

The night before I'm ready to depart, June 24, 2016, for Southern Oregon, I gave Matt a call and asked him, "Would it be okay with you if I bring the device so that I could show you and Mike? We don't have to turn it on. I just want to show it to the both of you." He thought it was a good idea and agreed.

So at 3:00 am, I left my home in Washington and drove to Grants Pass, Oregon. Once I arrived, we ate breakfast together at the Black Bear

Diner on 6th St. I finally got to meet Mike Kincaid, who's a friend of Matt. After we finished eating our breakfast, we drove to the Albertson's grocery store for supplies, through the Dutch Brothers coffee stand, and then up to the mountain location to spend time in SOIA.

By the time we reached SOIA, it was the late afternoon which left us plenty of time to set up our sleeping cots, chairs, and tables. Remember, I'm totally new to all this Bigfoot research stuff. When evening arrives, Matt starts talking and singing to the Bigfoot Forest People. I'm thinking, "Wow, what have I got myself into?" To be honest, it seemed a little crazy to be talking and singing to the forest. However, I kept an open mind and open heart. I was hoping to experience something during my three-night camping experience.

A couple of hours had passed and nothing much happened. There was a bright moon and a sky full of stars. It was beautiful. At 11:00 pm, I couldn't take it any longer and I needed to go to bed. I had been up since 3:00 am, drove four-hundred miles, and I was tired. It was time for me to go to bed. So while Matt and Mike stayed up, I fell fast asleep under the stars.

Now, this is where the world is to be forever changed as I know it. There are no words that can truly describe what's about to happen to me. Around 1:00 am, I was fully awake, and there are hands all over my body. No, not Matt's and Mike's hands. Mostly, the hands were in my stomach, liver and kidney area. That 'Navy Seal' thing kicked in and everything Matt told me that could happen bombards my brain. My heart was beating out of my chest, and the first thing I thought of was to ask the Bigfoot Forest People to slow my heart rate down. About sixty seconds later, my heart rate drops back down to normal. I finally could pay close attention to what was happening to me. This was like some kind of Godly divine miracle.

I was never once touched inappropriately nor can I say that my body was violated in any way. I could feel the care, love and warmth that was just flowing from their hands. Later on, I figured out that they were doing a full body physical on me and healing any part of me that may have needed healing. After they had finished, I looked at my phone again to see what time it was and it was only 1:20 am. Shortly after that, Zorth laid his hand over my head. His hand went over my head from ear to ear. He leaned down and breathed in my ear three large breaths of air. He was very large and you could feel his power through his hand and breathing.

After Zorth was done, there was someone else who stayed with me the entire rest of the morning rubbing my feet from 1:30 am until 6:00 am. I got up that morning and told Matt and Mike what had happened to me. I could hardly believe the words coming out of my own mouth while explaining everything to the guys.

The next night came quickly, there we were, once again, waiting to find what surprises the Bigfoot Forest People would have in store for us. During the second evening, Mike and I were looking for one of three Portals that were supposed to be in the area. We found the area and called Matt over to confirm our find. We nailed it. Suddenly, while standing in the dark, we heard several owl and barking sounds coming from the top of the hill adjacent to our camp. Once again, just like the first night, I was touched constantly but somehow, probably from pure exhaustion, I was able to fall asleep.

On the third and final night for me (Mike, Matt, and Grady spent a fourth night after I had to leave), it also proved to be an exciting night. We climbed a short mountain next to the SOIA base camp where we were to be greeted by the "Council of Twelve." While sitting on top of the mountain, I was touched several times. It was an amazing experience.

Afterwards, we hiked back down to the SOIA base camp. I asked Matt if I could bring out the Electromagnetic Generator Device that I had built and start it up. We wanted to see if the machine would help to open a nearby portal in order to help approximately 23,500 Bigfoot Forest People trapped on the other side of a portal on their dying planet. I dropped my tailgate on my pick-up truck and proceeded to make all the electric connections to run the generator. I attached the final wire and, BAM, it was up and running.

As the Electromagnetic Generator Device was running, I explained to Mike and Matt exactly what was happening as the Generator ran. I told them that it will run off the set of batteries (24volts) for hours and never drain them because of its repulse affect. I told them that I had tested this process many times at home, up to 8 hours at a time, and that the batteries never drained.

We decided that we would let it run and allow the forest people to examine the effects of its running. While the machine was running, I decided to lay down for a while to catch up on some much needed rest. About an hour and a half later, I woke up to a beeping sound and asked Matt where's that sound coming from. Mike and Matt explained to me that the batteries lost power after about an hour of me lying down. I said that's impossible. I got up and viewed the charge indicator on the Inverter it had lost 4.5 volts of power. The inverter was beginning to shut down so I turned it off.

The next morning, Matt and Mike stood there next to me while I explained what just occurred is impossible for this machine to do, and that I have tested it several times at home with no failure. But after thinking a moment about what just took place, we postulated that the Bigfoot Forest People were drawing energy from the Electromagnetic Device as well as the two Deep Cycle Marine Batteries. Zorth told Matt that the machine was working and that they were able to get some souls through. WOW! They figured out how to charge themselves, go to the portal location nearby, use the additional charge in their bodies to hold the portal open, and help their stranded Bigfoot Forest People families to pass through to their new home, Planet Earth. That first night I believe Zorth told Matt that about ten percent of the souls made it through the portal.

I had to return home to Washington because I had to get back to the kitchen remodel I was currently working on. I wanted to complete my job on time. I pride myself in completing my work on time or early. Matt asked me if he and Mike could keep the machine and run it one more night in SOIA. He would return the machine to me over the Fourth of July weekend when he returned to Washington to visit with his fiancé, Cynthia. I agreed. Then Mike and Matt devised a plan to drive to Grants Pass, Oregon and purchase some additional batteries so they could have more than enough to complete assisting the Bigfoot Forest People with their EXODUS to Earth.

Before I left SOIA to return to Washington, Matt was standing next to me and in a silent moment, he spoke to me and said, "Steve, Zorth says you have a guardian for life." I looked at Matt and thought, "Okay, whatever." I had no idea what exactly that meant.

On the fourth night, I was informed by both Mike and Matt that they were able to help Zorth and the other Bigfoot Forest People at SOIA to get the remainder of the 21,000 souls through the portal. Well, I would like to report that the batteries did not fail. In fact, the one set of batteries that were re-charged ran a full six hours without draining. Mission was accomplished. The EXODUS was complete.

The EXODUS occurred six months ago, and my life has profoundly changed. I now live with the Bigfoot Forest People every day, in ways that would blow your mind. Much of it's very personal as I have great respect for their race and would never want to offend them. They have been the kindest most generous people. I would like to give a great big 'High-Five' to God for creating such a hi-quality race of Bigfoot Forest People. I would also like to thank Dr. Matthew Johnson for reading the letter I sent to him and for giving me the life changing phone call. As a result, I am forever blessed and grateful.

MIKE KINCAID
(SAN FRANCISCO, CALIFORNIA)

One of my earliest memories was one of my scariest. My family was living in Bellingham Washington close to the lake in a new home that was built on the edge of the woods. I must have been 3 or 4 years old at the time. I shared the room with my brother and my bed was closest to the window. The window was high up on the wall. I remember waking up in the middle of the night and seeing a face in the window staring down at me. I covered my head hoping it was not real. But when I peeked, the face was still there. I then remember bolting under the window, screaming, "It's a bear," while awaiting the sound of smashing glass with an arm trying to reach down and grab me. I knew it wasn't a bear but didn't have a word for what I was seeing. Fortunately, the glass remained intact and I made it to my parent's room. Years later, after seeing the Patterson and Gimlin Bigfoot film (1967), I had a new theory of what I saw.

In April of 2016 I went back to this house. It had the same windows. The current owner was nice enough to let me take a picture with the window. From the outside, the bottom of the window was just over my head. I am 6' 2". You can do the math from there.

That experience inspired my present day interest in the Bigfoot phenomena. At least interest enough to participate a bit online and study the evidence that field researchers posted or eyewitnesses reported. Ultimately I joined the TS-USA Facebook group. Little did I know that I had started a new journey.

In the Bigfoot researcher field, credibility is extremely important. Although I watched Dr. Matthew Johnson get routinely beat up online, he appeared to me to be the most credible researcher who was actually reporting real results. In my eyes, his credibility came from his reporting all evidence regardless of controversy or reputation and his willingness to invite guests as eyewitnesses to verify the research.

Over the past three years, I've been with Matt to the Southern Oregon Habituation Area (SOHA) five or six times, the Washington Habituation Area (WAHA) twice, and the Southern Oregon Interaction Area (SOIA) twice. I've helped at his annual conferences and met a many of his guests. When you spend this much time with someone, especially camping, you really get to know someone. I find Matt to be funny, generous, patient, smart, driven, and a teacher. He is really a great person with a huge heart who cares passionately about Bigfoot and educating others about the subject matter. I am proud to call him my friend! I found that he is that credible researcher who doesn't shy away from telling the truth like I had originally believed.

When Matt offered to bring me to SOHA, I was thrilled to get to go and experience field research first hand. But I also had to rein myself in a bit and study my motives for going. Ultimately, I determined that I wanted to go for personal expansion and to help Matt -- pure and simple.

At first Matt was extremely strict about protocol: no snoring, no breaching the perimeter at night, always say "Just going potty" while peeing at designated spots on the perimeter. He told wild stories about mind-speak, orbs, belly crawlers, and Beings of Light. Wild and weird stuff! So on my first visit I was hoping to be terrified. I was hoping for huge foot stomps, shadowy figures, orbs - something to make my jaw drop.

Instead, on my first night I had a wild "dream" experience. After staring at the stars and listening to the forest for an hour, my first dream starts immediately. I feel my cot picked up and I am thrown off the mountain. As I fall I think, "But I came here to see you." I wake up. That dream felt real.

I lie awake again, staring at the stars confused by the falling dream then slowly drift off. The next dream starts immediately again. I feel like I am asked "If I want to continue." I answer "That is why I came." Boom I feel my left leg being grabbed at the calf through the sleeping bag. I struggled, then open my eyes only to see a terrifying, huge wolf head by my leg. Then, BAM, energy shoots up my leg into my torso and I am "connected back into the universe" and I feel eternal love, and life makes sense.

I fall back asleep laughing; feeling like I had been "there" before. Was this a dream or real? I had never had a vivid dream like that! This experience was wildly scary then weirdly welcoming. From that point forward I felt very comfortable and welcomed at SOHA.

For the first several SOHA visits, going to check the gifting bowls felt like Christmas morning. The anticipation while walking to the gifting location was exciting. And often the results were baffling. Fingerprints, bites, slobbered M&Ms, finger scoops - really compelling stuff when you see it firsthand.

On one of my visits I played "chef" for two nights in a row. On the first night a single pinch was taken from one sandwich on the right bowl. Interesting! But on the second night the same behavior occurred! The same sandwich in the same bowl with the same behavior. No critter does that. That was a demonstration of subtle communication.

During my SOHA visits, I experienced other evidence like voices, a gifted stick, bug sound disguised voices, a weird dancing leaf, items being moved in camp, things buzzing past my head, a shadow figure next to my cot that disappeared after I stared at it for two seconds, a small orb entering into the back of a guest's head, and more traditional stuff like tree structures and prints. Most things I experienced were puzzling, subtle, gentle, and fun.

One of the strangest events happened when I was purposefully pretending to sleep. I lay with my eyes peeking out under my sweatshirt hood while I listened to the forest sounds. Suddenly, an electric sounding buzzing object came flying into camp straight to my face. It paused and slowly scanned from right to left across my eyes, then quickly buzzed off. What does that in the middle of the night?

On another occasion I was slowly panning my phone across the campsite wondering if I could see more through the screen than I could with my eyes. When I pointed the phone at the 11 o'clock position on the perimeter of the SOHA base camp, something exploded through the bushes from left to right for about 30 feet crossing a gap at the 12 o'clock position to about the 2 o'clock position on the perimeter. Unfortunately, I wasn't recording.

Another morning while waking up at SOHA I looked down at my bedding and was surprised to find that the extra sleeping bag and tarp that I was using as a comforter was lying on the ground at the foot of my cot. I was puzzled because it could not have slipped off naturally to the far end. I reset the bedding to see how that could have happened and determined that it could have slipped to the left or right, but not neatly and all the way off the end. After a few minutes of walking around I suddenly realized that my Achilles tendon, which had been sore for around a month now felt strong. The injury had disappeared. They healed my leg.

At WAHA, something zapped my phone in the middle of a video. The video was recording in full daylight, then POW (like an electric snap), the phone's screen went black. Later, when I watched the video it looked like the video was completely black except towards the end. You can see the sky as I panned upwards in shock. An added twist is a weird voice that appears at the moment that my phone, to my eyes, went black. I call this "the black video."

I had all of these great experiences and an awesome guide and friend in Matt. I had grown as a person. But, still never a visual of a Bigfoot in the traditional hairy bodied sense. They had only tickled my conscious perceptions with hints that they exist without giving me that in-your-face WOW moment of "there's a Bigfoot."

But, apparently, I had gathered enough faith in my prior experiences and in my belief in Matt to end up camping deep in the mountains with the goal of attempting to help them with a problem (i.e., The Exodus). Faith to trust in the journey, faith to trust your friends, faith to accept things that you experience even if they appear unbelievable.

And note that I struggle with faith evidence-wise. I'm a mathematician by schooling and database programmer by trade. I have spent the last 30 years debugging code daily. So I end up discounting quite a bit and try and make a purposeful effort to be objective. I guess that is my counterbalance to keep me grounded while weird stuff was happening.

The journey of experiences is how I ended up spending four days in the woods as Matt narrated an impossible story for four days. Even though I had no direct evidence that the details of what Matt was saying was happening, I'm "all in" because of personal evidence, journey, faith, and credibility.

And, finally during my last trip to SOIA in June of 2016, for me, some really cool stuff happened:

1. I heard huge, thunderous, flat footed, foot stomps with heavy breathing - Cool!! Again! More huge, thunderous, flat footed stomps with heavy breathing a minute later - This thing is HUGE!! Apparently, it was Zorth.

2. While walking towards the 7 o'clock position on the SOIA perimeter, something explodes out of the grass and shoots down the hill knocking away branches and leaves. I immediately yell, "I'm sorry! I didn't mean to scare you." I go back to apologize again a few minutes later, and the Bigfoot explodes again and shoots down the hill and walks away, this time with a shriek!! Again, I apologize by saying, "I'm really sorry!!"

3. I get poked in my side while standing in the dark inside the SOIA base camp - Weird!!

4. I get poked in the back of the leg a few minutes later. Wow! It's now happened twice!!

5. I can barely see a shadowy figure and as it slowly drifts to the left inside the base camp.

6. Sparks of light in the tree tops in the valley across the way. Weirdly, I had seen this in a dream ahead of time before it actually happened.

7. And, a repetition of super loud owl like sounds, combined with barking noises, came from up on top of the hill just outside of the SOIA base camp. I wanted to go up to the top of the hill immediately but Matt said that Zorth told him that we couldn't go up there that night. However, we were invited to sit before the "Council of

Twelve" up on top of the hill the next night. This is crazy stuff, but then again, what an honor!

8. While driving around the next day, while off the mountain, we pondered what will happen when we sit before the "Council of Twelve." Meanwhile, apparently Zorth is listening to our conversations somehow and Matt is responding for him throughout the day. That gave me the idea later to use Matt as a "Squatchie-Talkie" to learn more.

9. When the evening arrived, Matt, Steve, and I hiked up the hill to sit before the "Council of Twelve." I was hoping to see twelve hairy beings come walking in before us. Nope, apparently the twelve trees in front of us were housing the "Council of Twelve." This was kind of a disappointment, but we get our instructions after a series of questions, go down the hill, and turn on Steve's electromagnetic pulsating machine. Steve was tired and went to bed early. The batteries die after about an hour.

10. The next morning, Steve was perplexed that the batteries died so quickly. But according to Matt, Zorth told him that they were able to get approximately 2,350 souls through the portal from their home world. We then regroup and discuss plans for the day. Steve has to go back home to Washington to complete a work project. He agreed to leave his machine. Matt and I bought batteries and chargers to continue with our task on our fourth night at SOIA. We charged everything at Grady's mother's home, and then we went back up into the mountains with Grady. Eventually, we turned on the machine before dark and let it run. Wow! On this night, the forest was alive with activity. Things were moving all around us. At one point, we hear a thunderous crash and Matt responds "Zorth says some of the newbies are getting used to gravity." We end up staying up until 2am while Zorth, through mind speaking with Matt, counted down to zero.

11. Finally, we shut the machine off after Zorth told Matt that everyone has made it through. Matt and I do a brief toast to the accomplishment of helping the Bigfoot Forest People with their Exodus from their home world to Earth. Matt was visibly drained. He began

reconciling that he had reached a major milestone in his bigfoot journey after sixteen years of dedication. Possibly the end of his journey. He felt released from his obligation and compulsion.

12. However, I still have no direct evidence that his narration was a reality. At one point I say, "Don't we at least get some applause?" We finally go to bed in the pitch dark of night. Then, just before dawn, it was still dark but there was changing light. Something woke me up and I was staring at the stars. Matt and Grady were still sleeping. Then I hear the first sound. KNOCK! LOUD, CLEAR, STRONG, and directly next to basecamp, with a slight electric twinge. Then after four seconds, KNOCK! Two of them! Awesome! KNOCK! Wow, each is identical and evenly spaced! KNOCK! Dang, I'm kind of lucky. KNOCK! Five! KNOCK! Six! KNOCK! Awesome! KNOCK! Uh oh, where is this going? KNOCK! I keep counting. KNOCK! Ten now! KNOCK! Eleven! KNOCK! Twelve!!!! Silence. I just heard twelve, evenly spaced, identical, super loud, knocks. Matt and Grady are still sleeping. I'm simply stunned as I lay there on my cot. I feel like I got my own personal applause. Then after a few minutes, my doubt creeps in. Remember, I told you that I'm a debugger by profession. "Did that really just happen?" KNOCK! Yes. KNOCK! You... KNOCK! #$@W* (translation - nice guy in the woods). Pause... KNOCK! Get... Crunch! Over... KNOCK! It. Pause... KNOCK! We... KNOCK! Do... KNOCK! Exist.

Okay, I don't really know the meaning behind these last three sets of knocks. They could also be a tribute to each participant or a tribute to three Bigfoot Forest People who died shortly after making it to Earth. But I do feel strongly that the first twelve knocks was a message directed towards me. I teared up at the confirmation and I was stunned. After a bit, I finally fell asleep again.

When I woke up again later, it was a bright morning and I was staring at a tree. I felt like I was supposed to stare at this tree. Suddenly, I see a white cue ball sized object jump from the top of this tree and fall towards the ground. But it never hits the ground. Instead, it jumped out sideways and falls in a parabolic arc. It wasn't a leaf, a bug, a bird, but a solid white ball of light. Maybe someone was enjoying their new home?

My ultimate take-away from my trip to SOIA in June of 2016 was that I either helped a friend come to closure with his bigfoot journey of sixteen years or I helped my friend, Matt, plus helped him accomplish something really cool (i.e., The Exodus). Either result is a win in my book. Six months later, I still wrestle with this experience at SOIA. It seems so long ago. It was weird and cool and it really happened. Thank you, Matt. I lived a movie!

ANITA HLEBICHUK (PUYALLUP, WA)

My name is Anita Hlebichuck. I was born and raised in Puyallup Washington. I moved away to Idaho for a few years. In the Fall of 2015, I moved back to Puyallup. My life has become more amazing than I ever expected because of meeting Matt and Cynthia, and my experiences with the Forest People. Through them, I have met other very special people involved in the Bigfooting community.

I have personally had so many things happen in my Forest Person journey, but for now I would like to talk about when Matt came to Puyallup, Washington to tell us about the EXODUS.

Cynthia and I had known about what help was needed by the Forest People. I had been told by them that Cynthia and I had the ability to help them as well, which we had been working on doing. When Cynthia told me what had happened in Oregon, I was in awe and amazement at the realization of the magnitude of what had occurred.

I was invited to Cynthia's and Matt's home for pizza along with the Taylor's, Steve Bachman, and Lt. Col. Kevin Jones to hear first-hand the details of what had happened, and to see Steve's machine up close. I arrived before everyone else. Steve's machine was sitting on the island in the kitchen. It was turned on and I came around the other side of the island to look at it up close.

I am an empath. I also can feel and sometimes see energy. The amount of energy I felt coming off of the machine was literally staggering. I felt the energy moving through my body very strongly. My legs began to feel very weak and I had to go sit down at the table.

After eating pizza, we all moved to the living room and Matt relayed to us all that had transpired. He told us how originally Steve had brought the machine to Oregon with him just to have Matt take a look at it.

A little bit of a back-story here. The Forest People had contacted me using mind speak. It was very off at first, because what they were telling me did not make sense to me. At that time, I did not know Matt and Cynthia very well, so I was concerned they would think I was nuts if I shared what the Forest People were telling me. When I did share what I had been told, Matt confirmed it matched what he was told, and I was able to understand the situation the Forest People were facing. I knew what they needed, and sitting in the living room I learned how it was accomplished.

Matt told us how when they turned on Steve's machine the Forest People came running over to it. They could hear the footsteps. Using the energy from the device they would hold the portals open, so the others who could not hold the portals open themselves, could pass through. Finally, they could have their families, their species, reunited on Earth.

Just as none of us expected this to happen so quickly, neither did they. The first night the Forest People drained the batteries as well as absorbing the energy from the device. Once that was figured out they left the batteries alone.

They were able to bring their families and loved ones all through the portals in SOIA. Sadly, there were a three who passed away, but were not left behind on the dying planet. I had also been told that somehow, Cynthia and I could open and hold open a portal, because of something in our make-up. Matt passed the information on from Zorth that we did help three souls come through up here in Puyallup. Matt also relayed that we were all assigned guardians for the rest of our lives for what we each did to help the Forest People. I have since learned my guardian's name, and felt her presence numerous times. I am very touched, honored, and grateful that they would do that.

I believe that Matt's willingness to stick with it all the years he has, leading up to the actual EXODUS, and wanting to know what was really happening, combined with his willingness to check out the "Woo" side helped to gather in all of us who played a part in helping another fellow species be saved.

Thank you, Matt, for all you have done!

Moving forward from here, my hope is that my relationships with the people I have met through a mutual interest in Bigfoot, and my friendships with the Forest people will continue.

HOWIE GORDON
(CHICAGO, ILLINOIS)

I have been fascinated with Bigfoot ever since I saw the Bigfoot Episode on The Six Million Dollar Man in 1975. I was 4 years old at the time. Later in life, I was on the Reality TV Show, Big Brother 6 and Big Brother 7 All-Stars during the Summer of 2005 and the Summer of 2006.

I became friends with past and future Big Brother Alumni. Kail, from Big Brother 8, owns a Resort in Rainbow, Oregon and started having Big Brother Alumni on fun get-togethers.

After our first trip in 2008, we all planned another trip for May 2009. I started Googling on the Internet. The Oregon Bigfoot and Dr. Matthew Johnson's name came up. I read up on Dr. J.'s Bigfoot Encounter at the Oregon Caves National Monument Park on July 1, 2000.

I decided to write to Dr. J. I mailed my letter to Dr. J. on April 27, 2009. A few days later, (Thursday April 30, 2009) I arrived in Portland, Oregon. I was with my "Big Brother" friends (James BB6/7, Chelsea BB9 & April BB10). We had a rental car and a 3-hour (roughly) drive to Rainbow, Oregon. We were all having some fun and talking a little Bigfoot as well. But then I received a text message from Dr. J. Dr. J. wrote, "Howie, I received your letter and I was rooting for you on Big Brother. If you want to talk about my Bigfoot encounter, then I would be glad to. Also, if you want to go to the site where I saw Bigfoot or if you want to camp out in one of my research areas then that would be fine as well."

I started yelling and getting excited as we were driving eating and drinking. I told the Big Brother Gang that this Bigfoot Researcher that

I wrote to has just invited me to go Bigfooting with him. So I replied to Dr. J. that I would love to go out in the Bigfoot wilderness with him. Next, I changed my flight and extended my trip. Since May 2009, I have been going to visit Dr. J. on average at least once per year (1) May 2009, (2) May 2010, (3) September 2011, (4) February 2012, (5) September 2014, (6) April 2015, and (7) August 2016. I went to dinner in Chicago/Schaumburg, Illinois with Dr. J. in February of 2012 as well.

I would like to share my notes from my most recent trip to the Southern Oregon Interaction Area (SOIA) with Dr. Johnson, Scott Taylor, Susan Taylor, and Tammy Kennedy:

SOIA Bigfooting
(Night One: August 25, 2016)

Dr. J. talked about how things are attracted to Howie (10:30 pm-is). Scott and Susan Taylor went to bed at 11 pm-ish on Thursday Night August 25, 2016) in the Southern Oregon Interaction Area (SOIA).

On the first night in the new area, it only took about an hour for this to ring true. We got into our cots at just around Midnight (so now this is Friday August 26, 2016). Within about an hour (1am or so), everyone was asleep, except for me. Next, I heard a wood knock at about the 8 o'clock position on the perimeter of the SOIA base camp. Some crunching at the 4:30 o'clock position. And some crunching at the 2 or 2:30 o'clock position.

A few minutes later, I heard what sounded like twenty people were running straight towards me in the dead, black, and quiet night. It sounded as if somethings was about to go down. I started breathing heavy as I was going through my mind, "Is it a bear or some crazy guy in our camp?"

I was thinking, "Do I wake everyone up?" It was happening so fast. But at the end of the locomotive sound running at me, a seven-foot-tall Bigfoot was standing at the foot of my cot. He had a happy looking smile on his face. He looked me in the eye for a two-second count and then ran off or cloaked. It was just awesome and I was super scared for a little bit. But I was saying in my mind, which he can read, "I am scared, but please come back because I want to see you again."

354

Dr. J. later told me in the morning, that I saw Tuqua (Too-Kwah), the son of Zorth. It turns out that Zorth is who Dr. J saw on July 1, 2000 at the Oregon Caves National Monument Park. Tuqua is about 7-feet tall and was assigned as Dr. J.'s Guardian. About thirty-minutes later, Tammy Kennedy and Grady woke up. I told them what I saw. We kept hearing walking around and branches moving. About twenty-minutes later, I heard loud footfalls coming right at me again. Tuqua was off to the left corner of Tammy's cot. I saw his entire body but his face was not too clear. As quickly as he came in, he vanished. But Tammy and Grady heard him.

He continued to follow the same pattern every twenty-minutes or so until I fell asleep around 4:30 am or 5 am in the morning. Before I passed out, he would come to within 10-feet or less of our cots several more times. We could hear him breathing, snarling and walking around. I spoke out to him and asked if he would show himself to Grady and Tammy. He would come close but he would never reveal himself again.

He shook Tammy's cot two or three times and mine the same. Also, I felt like he had healing hands on me as well. I fell asleep around 5 am and woke up at 9 am. I heard two or three times zippers opening and closing. I was talking with Tammy and asking her if she was going in my suitcase or her suitcase. In the morning, Dr. J. said his bag was closed when he went to sleep and it was open in the morning. Tuqua was opening and closing the zipper on Dr. J.'s bag.

That morning, driving down the mountain, we saw two Black Bear cubs and their mother. Three bears total. We were driving down the mountain and the bears were walking up the mountain. They saw us and the momma bear froze. She then darted off to the (left/east) side and down the hill and her two cubs followed her.

(Night Two, August 26, 2016)

I got in bed early from lack of sleep from travel and being up all night the night before. So I was probably in bed around 9:30 pm-ish while Dr. J., Susan and Scott Taylor sat in the chairs and walked around and played music.

I heard tree knocks before I fell asleep. I heard a Bigfoot walking behind me near where Scott Taylor moved his portable bathroom too. Dr. J played music and saw an incredible light show (Orbs) throughout the presentation, and especially at the end.

(Night Three, August 27, 2016)

Micah, Dr. J.'s 20-year old son came out with us. Right as the sun was going down I was up the path in the 9 o'clock position on the perimeter of the SOIA base camp. We were hearing this sound. A silent stalker type of sound. I told Tammy that doesn't sound like a Bigfoot. It sounded more like a mountain lion creeping around. A cougar. So we walked back into the SOIA base camp.

About ten or fifteen minutes later, a cougar gave chase to a deer ending up down the hill a few yards in the 12 o'clock position. A Bigfoot jumped in and threw a log at the predator. I think to just scare the Cougar away and not harming it. The crashing sound of the log was super loud as it scared Zeus (the Team Squatchin USA Mascot) and he ran back into camp. The deer continued on an angle and ran through camp as well. But this was an amazing sight and impressive to listen to as well. While sitting in the chairs after dark, some Bigfoot Forest People were throwing pebbles that were landing near the cooler and table.

(Night Four, August 28, 2016)

We played music and sensed a lot of Bigfoots cloaked and in the base camp area. I felt a tug on my sweatpants. I believe that was their way of saying hello to me. Then I began to receive some healing hands full of energy near the food and cooler where they stopped me at. I could feel light energy going into my back where my broken vertebrae is located. I felt some pulls on my hoodie. And this happened on two to three to four different occasions. This energy feel was greatly reduced compared to what took place in the Southern Oregon Habituation Area (SOHA) during October of 2014, about two years earlier, when I could feel the touch no different than human hands.

Tammy, Dr. J., and I all went to sleep around 1:00 am or so. I saw a three-foot by three-foot misty, red, smoky orb of energy, that Dr. J had mentioned before, about 50-feet or so above the middle of base camp. It descended down and towards me and my cot. It ended up about 10-feet in front of me and less than 10-feet off of the ground.

I said, "Doc, is that the red orb you have been seeing?" He saw it as it hovered and moved past him and towards the 6 o'clock position on the perimeter and up into the trees. Dr. J. said he was glad I saw that as he thought he was seeing things until I saw the red glow and we both saw it move in the same direction.

About fifteen minutes later, Tammy and Dr. J. fell asleep. I heard a tree knock and a Bigfoot walk into camp from the 12 o'clock position on the perimeter of the SOIA base camp. Heavy foot-fall. He got to inside of our camp and then I could no longer detect him. He stayed cloaked or turned back into an orb and left the area.

SOIA is most definitely the Squatchiest place on Earth. There were an un-limited number of Orbs, tree knocks, and heavy bipedal foot-fall. More than anything, I have never seen so many Bigfoot tracks in one place ever. The SOIA base camp's ground is too hard so not many there. But just outside the base camp, and all around the perimeter in the tree growth areas, there is just foot-print after foot print of Bigfoot Forest People tracks.

TAMMY KENNEDY
(CHICAGO, ILLINOIS)

At the end of August, 2016, I took time off from life, as I knew it, to visit the Pacific Northwest. This would be my first time in Oregon, first time camping, and most importantly, my first time at the Southern Oregon Interaction Area (SOIA).

I did a lot of research over the years on the existence of Bigfoot by searching the internet, reading books, watching shows, and through discussions with others. I am aware of the hoaxing, money schemes, and television shows that have grown in popularity over the years as did the Bigfoot phenomenon. I am aware of the different species many think Bigfoot is and the different places they think this species has come from. I knew that "if" Bigfoot existed, which I believed in by "faith" only to this point, it was not and could not be an animal species or Gigantopithecus. After this trip, I hoped to have a few more answers.

The ride up the mountain, that first day, was beautifully breathtaking and exciting. I could not believe I was one of the privileged to actually be visiting SOIA. This was not a mountain, campsite or "place" of any kind. This was a supposed home and visiting site of the Sasquatch. However, I had planned to take it all in and would not be convinced of anything I did not experience myself. I have heard stories, testimonials, seen videos, and met those that have seen/encountered Bigfoot. Others' experiences were not my personal proof, however, and my first night proves to change that.

After sitting and talking under the moonlight at camp, we did not use camp fires, I witnessed the first ritual Dr. J. does for the Squatches.

He does not set cameras up, put food out, put up special lighting, set traps or record information. He introduces us to them and invites them to visit us. He speaks to them like we speak to each other and is very polite and respectful. He then takes his speaker out and plays music. He knows, and I do too now, that the Squatches absolutely love hearing music. This lasts for one to two hours. Although the selection of music is varied, it is always soothing or uplifting music. During this time, I saw orbs begin to come out everywhere in the trees. Some remain longer than others and some float by quickly. I was having my first experience with their presence.

Once Dr. J. believes the music has played long enough, usually for an hour or two, he again thanks the Squatches and invites them to visit us while we're sleeping on our cots. Now, we are all ready to get comfortable and stare up at the beautiful star-lit sky from inside our sleeping bags. For me, the night was magical enough but this was only the beginning. That night, it did not take long to begin hearing things. Once I did, I was frozen. Not frozen cold but unable to move with my senses heightened more than ever before, as I did not know what to expect. I was not afraid of a Sasquatch but of what they may present or do and how well I would handle it. I did all I could to be remain calm and relaxed.

There was a lot of obvious curiosity around the camp that first night. A couple of us that were awake could hear the same constant rustling of branches and leaves and bipedal footsteps all around us. Some footsteps were further away, while I could also hear and feel some that were only feet or inches away. This lasted for an hour and then I fell asleep only to be woken a short time later by more bipedal footsteps very nearby.

As I lay listening for more, feeling ready to fall back asleep, I felt a strong tug two times on my blanket. Without moving, I looked everywhere I could but did not see anything or anyone. I asked if the person next to me had tugged my blanket but he said no. His hands were tucked inside his sleeping bag.

The continued movements could be heard around camp very near us and I was glad that two others were also up at this time. Incredibly, I heard a walking and stomping sound followed by heavy breathing and snorting just feet in front of us. I whispered, "Did anyone else just hear that?" The response was, "That snorting? Yes." All three of us heard the same breathing and snorting type sounds.

A short time later, as the movement continued in that same area, I heard something else and slightly lifted my head to look toward our truck but could see nothing. I looked to my right to see if anyone had left their cot and most were asleep. Did I just hear zippers? Those were on our luggage. One other person was awake on his cot and asked if I had just heard zippers? I was trying to make sense of hearing that because it meant something that had the ability to open and close a zipper was feet in front of me. I answered, "Yes" and we joked about whose luggage could be of interest to a Bigfoot. Nothing more was heard that night.

However, in the morning, one piece of luggage had the zipper undone and it was confirmed that no one ever left their cot during the night. My first night, needless to say, proved to be surreal and what could have been a once in a lifetime event. Having one or two others hear and experience what I did, confirmed it was real and that the Squatches were just as curious about who we were as much as we were about them.

The next day, large footprints all around camp could be seen. After a full day of activities and little sleep the night before, I fell asleep early and quickly that night and did not awake. It was the third night that something new and incredible happened.

The usual nightly ritual of introductions followed by music once again took place. The last song Dr. J. played was a Whitney Houston song called, "I Will Always Love You." As soon as the song ended and Dr. J. began to thank the Squatches, loud, nearby tree knocks began. It was like applause. There had to be at least a dozen quick tree knocks or more and I was unsure if they were disappointed that the music had ended or if they were just pleased with that song. It was a communication with us nevertheless, and aside from the orbs that appear once the music begin, I was sure this was another sign of the appreciation the Bigfoot had for the music Dr. J. played.

My last night provided yet another new experience. By now, I had slept three nights at SOIA, saw nightly orbs, heard tree knocks, heard bipedal footsteps, heard breathing and the zippers, and felt them tug on my blanket. I felt more of a comfort level with their presence.

During the last night, sitting around before the music played, I saw shadows out of the corner of my eye go past me twice. I also felt my hair, not blown in the wind because there was none, but rather swooshed or flipped with a hand. I thought they were preparing to show themselves to me this evening. I was calm and ready for anything they may have done and had no idea what was about to happen to me.

Later that night, I felt a strange feeling come over my body. It was almost like I was cold and shivering, but I was warm. Just then, as I closed my eyes to relax, I could see strange pictures clearly appearing in my mind. I opened my eyes to ensure I was not dreaming. As soon as I closed my eyes again, the images began to appear once again in my mind. They were a single picture at a time. A wooden bird, a doll with no eyes, a picture of beach and other things that had no relationship to one another. They were just some of the approximately fifteen images I had shown to me.

I have never experienced anything like this. After a minute or so, it ended and so did that feeling. As a matter of fact, I felt very relaxed and tried to envision things but could not. Ironically, a short time later, another person at camp shared that they had the same similar experience with other different, strange images. I could not make sense of why this happened but nothing more followed. To me, either I was being tested or my mind was being looked at.

There is not a doubt in my mind that the existence of the Bigfoot Forest People is real. These are not animals to be hunted and captured or feared. SOIA is called an interaction area for a reason.

This is a meeting and learning place. A place both of us have a high level of comfort with each other. Nothing happens by accident here.

Dr. J. has built a level of trust with the Bigfoot Forest People over the years. The relationship that he has established with them provides much more amazing things than I have ever experienced in my life. There is no proof other than mutually shared experiences. The Bigfoot Forest People have abilities beyond our comprehension. They are peaceful and friendly.

I am thankful I had the opportunity to be enlightened at SOIA, thanks to Dr. Matthew Johnson. I wish everyone respected Bigfoot as Dr. J. does. We may not know or understand exactly what part they play in our world, but they do exist and knowing how to interact with them is important. You cannot undo something like what I saw or experienced. It just happened and my world today is a different place because of it. A better place.

SCOTT TAYLOR
(SPANAWAY, WASHINGTON)

I have been researching the Sasquatch phenomena ever since I had my first encounter in October of 2005 while deer hunting in western Washington state. I went on a Bigfoot Field Research Organization (BFRO) expedition the following summer, and shortly their-after, became a BFRO Investigator.

Over the years, I have met a lot of people, who have a lot of different ideas about Sasquatches. Some seemed truly strange and "off the wall" with what they were reporting. I wasn't ready for what those people were telling me. However, I learned to be polite, withhold judgment, and file away what I was hearing in case later evidence clarified the issue.

I found that in time, some the "way-out" things that I was hearing were actually happening. I also discovered from following up on reports that the people who were most knowledgeable about our forest people friends were those who just happened to have a home in a rural area where they shared the land with these secretive, elusive, yet curious beings. They were using the "Habituation Research Method" by just the fact that they shared their space with the Sasquatch people.

I had heard of Dr. J., as his friends call him, from several TV shows about Bigfoot. I heard him speak on a couple of occasions. Then, at the second Oregon Sasquatch Symposium in 2011, Dr. J. was a featured speaker, and he talked about witnesses having all the symptoms of Post-Traumatic Stress Disorder (PTSD). That resonated with me, as I had experienced PTSD myself, and recognized that very many, if not most eyewitnesses were dealing with the same thing.

We talked about that at dinner that evening, and I got to know Dr. J. better. We became friends and kept in contact. I followed his work at the Southern Oregon Habituation Area (SOHA). Then, Dr. J. moved up to Puyallup, Washington, which is near-by to where I live.

One evening, he invited a few people to meet he and Cynthia for dinner. Then we were invited to his home for more Sasquatch related discussions. He asked me, "Scott, as a new person around here, where would be a good place to establish a research site?" I just walked over to his back door, and pointed to the green-belt behind his house, and said, "Right down there." Dr. J. was surprised, but took me seriously. He started doing night sits, and putting out his audio recording equipment, and sure enough, they were there. He established the Washington Habituation Area (WAHA). I went there with him the night after he was playfully shoved by a Sasquatch in front of two other witnesses. It was an enjoyable night. They could be heard moving around us.

Dr. J. started a monthly meeting at The Hanger Inn Restaurant, at the Pierce County Airport to talk about anything Sasquatch related. I was a regular attendee and sometimes speaker. I was able to follow the latest news from SOHA, his Habituation Research site in Southern Oregon. I never got the opportunity to go there, and I wish we could have made the schedules work. It would have been educational to see for myself what so many other people, some friends of mine, experienced while visiting the forest people there.

Dr. J. liked to take people there who he thought he could trust. Having other people come visit the site provides corroboration of what Dr. J. was reporting. However, keeping the site location secret was very difficult with so many people going there with him. Someone talked, and the site location was discovered. However, the Bigfoot Forest People had already started the process of guiding Dr. J. to a new location.

My wife, Susan, and I had the opportunity to accompany Dr. J., his friend Howie Gordon, and Howie's friend, Tammy, to the new location at the end of August 2016. The Southern Oregon Interaction Area (SOIA). We only were able to stay for two nights due to a previously scheduled event, but those two nights were eventful.

Susan and I found a pair of scissors about one-hundred yards up the road beyond the SOIA base camp on the first evening just before dark. We picked them up and upon returning to camp, I asked Dr. J. if he was missing any scissors. He said, "Hey, those were in the bottom of this tote last time I was here." Crafty and playful beings these Sasquatches are.

We had activity as soon as it got dark. We could see their eye-glow as they were peeking around the trees. The next morning, we found track impressions at that spot. One walked right up to Howie, gave him a stare, and then walked away.

The second night was even better. The Bigfoot Forest People came within about twenty feet as soon as it got dark. Susan and I sat in our chairs holding hands as they approached. They were stick tapping almost on request. SOIA was very interactive. One was messing with the porta-potty. It lifted and dropped the lid.

Dr. J., who had been taking a nap so that he could stay up late, got up and opened his truck door. He didn't know that they were right there. Well, as soon as the light came on, the one by the porta-potty sounded like he was tripping over his own feet in a mad scramble to get out of sight. It was comical to hear. I got up and walked over that way, which caused that Sasquatch to flee down a trail. The next morning, we found its footprints on the trail.

Later, as he often did, Dr. J. was playing music for them. After about an hour, he told them that he was done, and that this was the last song. As that song ended, two of the Bigfoot Forest People walked away into the woods. I could hear them grumbling and complaining. We went to sleep on cots in the open, as is the custom with Dr. J. It makes us observable and approachable. In the morning, Susan reported being "scanned" from her feet to her head about five times during the night. We sure hated to leave.

So, having said all that. One cannot spend a lot of time with a person and not get a sense of the integrity and character of that person. I have found Dr. J. to be 100% genuine and honest. He some time ago abandoned the "spot and gawk" method of research, turning to the Habituation Research Method, which has resulted some very significant discoveries.

Many of these discoveries make him the target of people who are getting nowhere or don't even actually get out in the field. Some of these discoveries are hard to accept if you are not ready. There was a time when I was not at that point either, but having the context of my own personal experiences, the testimony of other experienced Sasquatch field researchers, as well as the rural accidental habituation witnesses, who have had similar experiences, I know that what is being reported by Dr. J. and others is actually happening.

Many term it derisively, the "Woo-Woo" or the "paranormal." It is not something that one can easily convince others of, but then the very idea of Bigfoot is still considered a paranormal myth to most people who have never had an experience. Which is exactly the point, in order to begin to understand it in a personal sense, one has to experience it. So, if you are not there yet, that's okay. Keep Squatchin' and you will eventually get there. Dr. Johnson's Habituation Research Methods work.

SUSAN TAYLOR
(SPANAWAY, WASHINGTON)

I met Dr. Matthew Johnson ("Dr. J.") when I started going to monthly meetings at the Hangar Inn Restaurant. I had read about Dr. J.'s Sasquatch encounter near Grants Pass, Oregon in July of 2000. I used to live in Grants Pass, Oregon and had read numerous stories and heard of people having encounters in the area for many years. I got to hear about the encounter from Dr. Johnson in 2014.

I have been interested in stories and encounters with Sasquatch since I was young. I would watch TV shows and read books every chance I got to learn more about this subject. I decided in 2013 to start doing some field research and attending expeditions to learn more about the elusive Sasquatch. I had planned to become a BFRO researcher to learn more about Sasquatch behavior from witness observation and interaction. I learned a lot from accompanying a BFRO investigator on many witness interviews and visiting sighting spots.

I had the opportunity to have a lot of interactions with Dr. Johnson over the past couple of years with attending meetings, conferences, and dinners. I find Dr. Johnson to be very honest and reputable about his sightings, experiences, and interactions with the Sasquatches.

In August of 2016, my husband and I had the opportunity to visit the Southern Oregon Interaction Area (SOIA) with Dr. Johnson, Howie Gordon, and Tammy Kennedy. I was not expecting much interaction with the Squatches due to the fact that with all of my field experience, it seems to take a few days for the Squatches to even attempt to interact to someone new in their surroundings. I was just hoping that maybe I would hear a wood knock or a howl.

The first afternoon that we arrived at SOIA, we set up our cots and left the area. We came back while it was still light out and my husband Scott and I went for a walk up the main road. We walked about a ½ mile and saw a pair of scissors lying on the side of the road. They looked new, like they had not been there long and I thought it was very odd that we found a pair of scissors on the road, because this is a road that is not traveled often at all. We picked them up and brought them back to the main camp with us and jokingly asked if Dr. J. had ever seen these particular scissors? I was shocked when he said "Yes" and went on to say that the last time he saw them they were in a tote of his.

That night, when it got dark, we heard some movement around base camp, bipedal footsteps, and saw an animal of some sort walk by us right around the perimeter. We observed eye glow around the perimeter of camp also.

The second day we were there, we left the SOIA base camp and came back about dusk. Everyone laid down for a nap. Scott and I stayed up to see what we could observe or hear. We heard movement around the perimeter of camp but could not see them, then the wood knocking started. It was very close and very loud, they repeatedly knocked, it was very clear what we were hearing were wood knocks. We heard bipedal footsteps on the perimeter directly in front of us, we could not see them but they were there. Dr. J. started playing some music on a speaker for them and they liked the music, when he stopped they wood knocked approximately ten times.

Throughout the night I sensed and heard them coming into camp and on the edge of the perimeter. I had been having some serious stomach problems for the previous few months and had several gallstones that had caused me a lot of pain on a weekly basis. Dr. Johnson had talked to the Squatches earlier and asked that they maybe help heal my stomach.

When I went to sleep the second night in the SOIA base camp, I didn't sleep too soundly. I kept hearing bipedal footsteps and it was very clear and cold. I was awakened sometime in the middle of the night by a sense of energy and some sort of electrical impulse starting at my feet and climbing upwards in my body. It went to my mouth and I could feel the tingling sensation in my lips. This happened five times consecutively. I was not dreaming. I know that I was wide awake. It was a little unnerving to say the least, however, I was not scared at all.

Four months later, I have not experienced any more stomach pain since leaving SOIA, whatever happened there to me was very real. I still have no explanation except that the Bigfoot Forest People are healers.

Dr. Matthew Johnson is a man of integrity and truth. He tells it like it is. What I have witnessed and experienced at SOIA is very real and humbling, and I believe that others have experienced things that are just as amazing. There are many things out there that are very real and science cannot yet explain. Keep Squatchin' and you will eventually believe.

JACQUI DAVIS, MS, LPC, NCC (ROGUE RIVER CITY, OREGON)

I attended the Southern Oregon Interaction Area (SOIA) for the first time at the beginning of October, 2016, along with some of the other SOIA team members. I originally met Dr. J. when I responded to a post on his website, introducing myself as another therapist interested in Sasquatch, who lived locally.

Matt offered to meet me for dinner one evening after work, and at the end of the meal, invited me to go with him and his team to SOIA. He carefully questioned me during dinner, and little did I realize I was being "vetted" to go to the area. I was honored and also a bit intimidated, but being an adventurous sort, I agreed to go a week later. Little did I know, my rational mind and world was about to be changed forever.

I first met the Team when we met for breakfast at the Black Bear Diner, before leaving for SOIA. The site is remote and very difficult to get to. I drove with Dr. J. On the way, he explained the rules of the game: Have an open heart, open mind and be open to new experiences. That's it! I believe he did not want us to go there with any preconceived ideas of what to expect or how to behave, just to remain in innocence and let it happen.

We reached SOIA in the early afternoon, set up the camp, and let the evening gently settled in. Our group had many varied and unique experiences with the Bigfoot Forest People. All of the experiences were unique with many varied levels of exposure to our big friends. As I had no experience, I just sat and soaked up the richness of the conversation. Little did I know that the "Locals" were already observing us!

As evening settled in, I noted some red and white twinkling lights on the perimeter of the SOIA base camp. The more experienced members picked up "eye glow" and some Orb like activity. They played music and sang, as the Bigfoot Forest People seemed to really like music. As soon as that started the activity increased, and we began to hear whoops, some tree knocks and hear twigs breaking in the forest. We all heard some bipedal footsteps in the forest, as they appeared to come closer to listen.

When I retired around 11 pm, one of the members, from the June, 2016 trip to SOIA, prepared me by stating not to be surprised if I felt my feet poked through the sleeping bag occasionally throughout the night. About an hour later, I heard heavy bipedal footsteps around our cots but I pulled the covers over my head, feeling a bit intimated. Later, my feet were indeed gently prodded with a soft leg massage for over an hour. It seemed gentle and respectful, I got the impression that they were introducing themselves in a way that would not be so intimidating.

Whenever the Bigfoot Forest People were around, I noted my heart rate picked up noticeably, and I felt a vibration in my chest area, this continued for the entire stay at SOIA. Some of the other members also noted this same experience. I observed the activity around our cots seemed most active between 11 pm to 4 am that first evening. That next morning, we found many footprints of adults and juveniles at the 12:00 o'clock position, on the perimeter of the SOIA base camp in the damp earth.

The next day, after going off the mountain for breakfast and on an outing to Crater Lake, we returned to another evening of interaction. During the day, the activity appeared very quiet. That second evening, one of our members, Steve, who had been to SOIA in June 2016, brought an Electro-Magnetic Pulsating Device that he had built out of the back of his truck and fired it up. This was the machine that was part of the amazing Exodus in June of 2016 at SOIA. He stated he did this for the Bigfoot Forest People alone, as they loved the electro-magnetic field generated by the machine. They would come around camp to soak in the energy.

As soon as the machine started, the woods became lively with more twinkling lights, orbs and eye glow. We heard loud heavy bipedal footsteps, sticks cracking in the forest around the area, and a large light being appeared, witnessed by Dr. J. and myself, and asked to come near the generator. It appeared that more than just the Bigfoot Forest People alone were interested in the energy field.

Dr. J. stated that there was a portal in the general area and that the Being of Light may have come through that. Matt stated he had never seen so many beings around the area since the June activity. Shortly thereafter, Dr. J. also witnessed some tall beings coming down the road from another active area, approximately one mile from camp and asked them if we had permission to touch them on their fingertips. Permission was given and although I could not see the being clearly, it appeared translucent and about 10 feet tall. I gently reached out my hand and with Dr. J. guiding me, touched the fingertips and immediately my arm felt tingly and somewhat numb.

After that we played music for them into the wee hours of the morning, and I went to sleep watching the twinkling lights around our cots and listening to a conversation of what seemed to be adults and young children off to the side in the woods. This was also heard by some of the other team members. When I woke up the next morning, I found the gift of a rock placed under my foam mattress and sleeping bag. I made the bed the evening before, and no such rock was there.

On the third morning, some of our members were feeling drained and ill, perhaps due to the intense electro-magnetic field we had been exposed to the evening before, and left to seek medical aid in nearby Grants Pass, Oregon. After we packed up their gear, getting ready to go to see them in the hospital, Matt sat for a minute with Zeus in the extra-large-sized camping chair. I noted a shimmering oval light, with a slight gold color, over his head, approximately fifteen feet up in the air. I first noticed it as the trees behind it appeared distorted. He did not see it but told me to take a picture. This was later published in the "Team Squatchin USA" Facebook Group. Other independent observers noted several Bigfoot Forest People looking through the trees near the oval. I did not see those myself when taking the picture.

I found that the activity did not end once I left SOIA. I have been experiencing some gentle prods, pokes and massaging at night for the months following to the present. I believe from my experiences with them that they are gentle loving beings. They are also great Healers. They're excited at interacting with us as we are with them if we come to them in proper spirit and attunement.

I got the message at SOIA, from a female Forest Person, that this site is much more than an interactive area. It is a school, where they are learning from us as well as we are learning from them. She called it their University. I am grateful and honored for the experience and opportunity I was given there. It indeed changed my outlook forever and I feel much more connected to our Universal Friends.

KEVIN IAN BEEGLE (MUKILTEO, WASHINGTON)

This is my endorsement of Dr. Matthew A. Johnson's narrative. I will verify our mutual experiences which we had at SOIA and the conclusions that I have made after spending time with him. I will share my observations that support my endorsements.

For those of you who do not know me, which in all honesty will be the vast majority of readers, my name is Kevin Beegle. I consider myself to be a very logical person, a person who endeavors to explain things in a logical way. When there is no logical answer, however, I will detail phenomenon for the readers' contemplation. The following statement to many may seem of a chapter from J.R.R Tolkien and I know that will immediately put some people off and they will stop reading, however, I will tell the course of events to the best of my understanding.

I firstly want to address my interactions with Dr. Matthew A Johnson and make some relevant refutations that this is all some kind of elaborate hoax that he has cooked up. Let me play devil's advocate for a moment and say if he is a hoaxer and a fraud, he is really bad at it. Just like in a crime investigation, one would have to look for the motivating factor that would allow a sane person to perpetrate such a fraud. Primarily, this would be money, in which case Matt Johnson has missed the boat. He charges no one money to go to SOIA, not me, not anyone.

He may charge nominal speaking fees for conferences and speaking engagements, but he is never to my knowledge asked for huge research grants or publicly funded research as many others have. He freely shares his information and protocol and in many interesting twists of fate, you can watch many people using his habituation method while at the same time criticizing him about his results. In other words, interestingly enough people, who are intellectually honest, would have to say that there is a hint of either jealousy and/or frustration afoot.

He continuously exposes himself to freezing temperatures and inclement weather for his experiences. These are not the actions of a person who would be doing this for any other reason than to experience a relationship with a being that he has come to understand. Discomfort and hardship being only worth it to a person who is trying to have an experience, not to perpetrate fraud.

If, for example, it was a foregone conclusion that something was about to happen (i.e., a hoax was being perpetrated), surely he wouldn't be spending Christmas night on a mountain top with his wife sleeping without a tent. To what end does that prove? If you don't believe him, the fact that he is doing this will make no difference at all and wouldn't further the hoax in anyway. I ask the reader to contemplate this while reading. He, in all fairness, is prepared to do things that I would not do. Yes I have had Sasquatch experiences, but I am not willing to act like a homeless person on the top of a hillside to make this happen. Maybe you would but my knowing that the being exists is more than enough for me to wait until at least springtime to do my work.

This is especially true in a field where people increasingly tell you how long they have been researching Bigfoot as a method of expressing expertise. This, in my opinion, is mostly a logical fallacy which really only backs up time and not results and begs the question of the two types of people who are in this field. To my mind, although there are different camps on flesh and blood vs. paranormal beings, these two camps could easily coexist on a research expedition, because although they may have different ideas of what the quarry could be, the methods of tracking the being would be the same, looking for sign etc.

The huge gulf in this community is more people who want to prove a being exists vs. people who want to understand the being without having to prove anything to anyone. I fall into the latter category and so given the nature of the conflict will not be heard or understood by many. To put it in terms of today, as a previously insured person who survived cancer because of the Affordable Care Act, they will never be convinced that it wasn't a good idea, conversely, a previously insured person that saw their health insurance rates and deductibles skyrocket that it was. It's all a matter of personal perspective.

History

Our Paths first crossed at a TS-USA Bigfoot Conference in Bremerton, Washington. To be honest, I didn't really want to go. I really thought that it was a waste of time because if Sasquatch wanted to tell me something, they would tell me directly and it seemed like the Bigfoot community as a whole ate their own young. People who should be working together for a common goal bickering over who was an expert, who wasn't, who had scientific proof, who didn't, etc., etc. Frankly, I believed that most people were more in tune with the need to feed their egos than they were with interaction with the Forest People. Sam, my wife, and I really had everything we needed in a spot that had interaction and was filled with love and understanding, did we really want to enter into the quagmire of "they" don't get it but "we" do.

But as the universe does, it brings things together and we did go after all. This is when I met Dr. Johnson, who was running himself ragged, putting on a Conference with Cynthia and seemed genuinely stressed out over being called a fraud over the portal that had been witnessed recently before. I observed him quite honestly like I would a student that I felt was having a hard time in their life and I approached him and entered into a conversation to get a sense of what was going on.

Now, call it a gift or call it a curse, I have a natural born gift to look 99% of the people I meet in the eye and "know" whether they are lying or hiding something. It has to do with my minds ability to see micro expressions, which is a fascinating subject on its own, and how people can't help but make small instantaneous facial movements to give themselves away. Dr. Johnson gave no indication of telling a falsehood or exaggeration and it was at that point in time, I decided to really give him my attention to listen to him. We spoke again briefly in small talk during the remainder of the Conference and left it at that. It wasn't until I was visiting my family in Northern Ireland in the Summer of 2016 that I knew things had changed.

While in Northern Ireland, which had only recently legalized Celtic Hand Fasting as legitimate, due to the efforts of a druidic order which I am a member of, we spent a lot of time going to ancient sites of spirituality. Druids being animists, believe that all things have power, the Oak tree being a major representation of wisdom and connection to the earth. While in an oak grove, I touched a tree and became electrified with energy, like a small current was traveling from the tree to me. I knew then that trees where the integral part of knowledge. In terms of today, I would imagine it being a WIFI access point to the internet or Cloud based computing.

The idea bore out to one worth testing. Being on Lay lines most stone circles such as Stonehenge and Averbury, are believed to be connected Along the lines of an energy web that encircled the world. Given that there is evidence that many of these structures were predated by "Wood" Henges similar to an Oak Grove, it begged the question that these where points of commutation that many of our ancestors had used for telepathic communication.

I hypothesized that the Forest People would do the same. It had always puzzled me that a group of beings, more intelligent than ourselves, would leave cryptic glyphs in the woods for the benefit of communication between themselves. If anything, they were doing it for the benefit of humans, who have interpreted them in so many different ways that it is not usable for anything other than a sign of intelligent construction. Placing a palm on a tree and using the world's "internet" on the other hand was a beautiful solution to store and retrieve archives.

It was at this time that I came to the conclusion that the Forest People could use these access points. It was not unheard of for shamanistic people to speak about merging into trees to enter into the spirit world and so it made sense to at least test this knowledge out to theorize that the Forest People would be a component of this. I was directed by the information that I was seeing in my mind after reputably going to different Celtic sites that I should proceed. The idea that testing all information that comes to you is an integral part of most cultures, to ward off the "trickster" element that plagues us all at times, when the head overrules the heart, and impels us to take short cuts, mostly to follow red herrings.

It was at this time that I felt compelled to speak with Dr. Matt Johnson about what I had experienced. In fact, although there are multiple people in the Sasquatch world that I had come to respect, including Dr. Jeff Meldrum, I was hardly going to drive to Idaho, to try to speak with a person who had never experienced the type of phenomenon that I had experienced. I wanted to speak to a person who was a highly educated individual, who was open minded, and I could think of no better person than Dr. Johnson, because if this was an item of super-fluousness, that he would keep it confidential, as he has done with information that he has about many people who actually attack him publicly. In other words, he stood by an ethical standard that many people do not.

It was a lengthy process in order to get Dr. Johnson to finally meet with me, and he appreciated that I wanted to tell him my conclusions personally in a face to face setting. I live approximately a day's drive away from Dr. Johnson but it was worth the trip down and back to tell him my story and gauge his reaction. When we finally did speak on the telephone, he without hesitation asked Sam and me to experience SOIA. He barely knew me and although knowing only that I was predisposed to the idea of the paranormal, that was it. I asked him if I could take a firearm to SOIA because I never sleep in the wilderness without one and he agreed. This is not the action of a person who would perpetuate a hoax given the fact that I had a deadly weapon on my person and, if push came to shove, would use it to protect my wife and myself.

So it was under this understanding that Samara and I spoke in depth with Dr. Johnson at the Black Bear Diner restaurant in Grants Pass, Oregon. We finally fleshed out the details of what I had been told to do through this mental communication. That I was directed to assist Dr. Johnson in his research and to verify my information. Dr. Johnson seemed genuinely surprised by what I told him and he actually questioned me a little about how I could know what I said. He said that what he was about to tell the group was something that he had only shared with a select few people and I think that the accuracy of what I had said on first reaction made him question whether someone had told me his secrets which he has explained in this book.

He introduced me to two other people who were going to camp with us at the location, Steve Bachmann and Jacqui Davis. The former who was introduced as a interested party in Bigfoot Research and the latter a fellow Mental Health Professional. We caravanned to the location in separate vehicles and set up our location and discussed how the arrangements for the next few days.

Sam, Steve and Jacqui went up to see a promontory spot but I went the opposite way. Although Samara and I are married and go to the woods together, we do experience things in separate ways. I do like to be alone while looking for tracks, etc., while having another person there to verify experiences. So I hiked to the highest spot that I could reach in the opposite direction. Partially because if I were another entity, that's what I would do, get a high vantage point and sit there and observe for a while to check out who was below me. If the proverbial hit the fan, I could be over the ridge and out of there at a moment's notice.

I walked and felt quite happy that there was nothing of a man made nature up there that would emanate lights or could project any kind of sound. After that I came back down toward the camp and thought I would "talk" to the biggest tree and see what, if anything, that I would be told. It was at this point the numbers 12 or 13 came into mind. 13 being the most relevant number for some reason and to follow a trail arcing around the camp at, what Dr. Johnson would call, the 12 o'clock position.

Dr. Johnson amused or bemused by what I was doing, just sat quietly in camp giving me the occasional look. As I walked back through the brush, not actually knowing where I was going, I was continuously drawn in the arc up to where Samara, Steve, and Jacqui were. Knowing that Samara would sense anything strange up there, I just headed back through the opening at the 12 o'clock and sat next to Dr. Johnson at which time I stated to him. "The only thing that I can't tell is whether it is 12 or 13, which is it?" A couple of things came to mind as he reacted to this statement: (1) he was again in befuddlement to what I was saying, and (2) his reaction to the way that I was traveling around the camp.

It was at that time that he discussed the fact that he and two others had been told that 12 beings from the 6 habitable continents had come to him and stated that he had been asked to facilitate an EXODUS from a dying planet and that the only way that this could be done was by the use of an energy device that could be used to power the portal gate on this end. He made some comment about waiting for the others to come back to finally explain the whole scenario, but added that he thought it was strange that I took the exact same route as the Forest People when traveling out the upper grove to the 12 o'clock position, to which I just stated "that's what I was told to do." Strangely enough, if I were Dr. Johnson at this point, I personally would have wondered if I was not perpetrating some kind of elaborate hoax on him as I was speaking things that no one could know.

When the other's returned to the camp, Dr. Johnson sat us all down and detailed the strange synchronicities that had occurred bringing us all together. I was not the first person that had contacted Dr. Johnson saying that Sasquatch could dwell in trees and that many others had also shared this belief. I know that I can't take credit for an idea that is millennia old when vast amounts of people throughout the world had believed this. It was just a strange connection that through the melding of shamanistic tradition and new ideas of quantum physics that I could, among others, put these ideas to the test.

Dr. Johnson then started to tell his story about how Onx had proceeded to tell him of how the portal needed to be powered from this end to work. That he had been the only person contacted to try to figure it out because he was the first person on Earth to figure out how to reopen a portal. He also shared that many people had been exposed to portals, however, had not been able to understand the information or could come up with the device needed to power the portal from this end.

He then said that he had been contacted by an individual who had built a zero-point energy device (or close to it) that could be run for hours on end for that purpose similar to a Tesla device. I immediately said, "So that's why Steve is here" to which the group again said a collective "Wow." I was being told things that again no one in the party knew except the two of the five people. I know that Jacqui and Samara were pretty much in wonderment as to how I was getting this information.

I won't go into the details of the night of the EXODUS. I wasn't there and I didn't witness it. Hopefully, it is fully explained to the reader's satisfaction in Dr. Johnson's book. However, I will say that at no time did I feel that he wasn't telling the truth and that I didn't believe him. I will say however, that it was at this point that I figured out the meaning of the number 13. That Dr. Johnson was placed in such high regard by his efforts and success in assisting the Forest People that he was accepted into their clan. Whether or not Dr. Johnson wants to claim this as accurate, that's up to him, however, that was my interpretation.

On the second night at SOIA, the device was put into use. I don't understand or pretend to understand how it was made. However, there was an overwhelming sense of power emanating from the device. Apparently this use of free energy being absorbed by the forest people is like manna from heaven for them. I could, being a sensitive person, feel the energy flow. It became too much for me and it physically made me ill. In my initial SOIA report, I could not say what the problem was, but it was due to the running of the device for hours that night. I have come to the conclusion that I don't want anything further to do with it, because of health concerns.

That being said, I did have some anomalous X Rays that still can't be explained after being at SOIA. Being a person with a Chronic Illness, people ask me why did you not ask the Forest People to heal that. It was discussed at the Camp and Dr. Johnson did ask if I wanted them to attempt some kind of healing on me. I declined. This can be attested to by all other members in the Camp.

My logic is this, I don't know how these strange abilities have come to me, one way or another, I want to keep them. If this is some kind of zero sum game, where it comes down to having one or the other, I would rather things stay the same. Dr. Johnson at no time promised me healing. He only wanted to know if I was open to the idea, to which I said no. I know that he had benefited from a healing personally. However, it was not put to me like he was some kind of faith healer, where the Forest People would touch my forehead and I would rise up healed.

Please understand that this story is not to portray myself as an expert in Forest People or as some kind of person who you should follow like some kind of guru. I am neither. I am just a person who is a small part of a puzzle. A puzzle that takes all of us to put into place. There may be a small group (very small) of people who can tell you the name of your Sasquatch guide or know what a glyphs mean, if anything, I am, however, not one of them or claim to be.

This is the truth as I see it and would attest to it.

Below is my initial report posted on Teem Squatchin' USA and with the additional information that I can now share I feel is complete.

Environmental factors:

The average temperature high was 72° during the time that I was at SOIA with the low being an average of 50°. The average humidity during the time that I was there was 72%. There was no appreciable rain or thunderstorm during the time that I visited. It was not out of the ordinary range that an average person would feel uncomfortable or be affected by climatic conditions. The average wind was less than 2 mph.

The geology of the location shows that there is a high concentration of Quartz and also gold, Quartz being an indicator of gold, hence the number of gold claims in the area. Some people believe that quartz acts as a capacitor to store energy, including myself.

Location protocol:

There are no tents or structures allowed that would obscure the vision of anyone in camp. It should be noted, as it is indicative of Dr. Johnson's approach to this Sasquatch people, which is very open and in many cases puts us on show rather than them. In essence, we are there for them to learn from us and interact with us rather than any kind of domination over the forest people. There is a lot of respect shown to the forest people and we packed everything out of the location including human waste so that we did not offend their house in anyway. We did not sleep in tents we slept in the open. We did not use any artificial light sources or use any fire or heat method at all at camp. With the half moon and clear skies after a period of adjustment our night vision was more than enough to see and maneuver in the dark. White light being a huge problem for experiences, as the eye cannot adapt to bright lights from a flashlight for up to 20 minutes after. We did not share common meals or drinks; there was no alcohol or use of recreation drugs.

Health statistics:

I am a 45-year-old male, with a height of 5'10" and I weigh 220 pounds. I have an average heartbeat of 59 bpm as recorded by my Apple Watch and that is historically been my average for over three months. I do have type one diabetes and I am medicated by an insulin pump. During the time that I was at SOIA my average heart rate jumped to almost 150 bpm on an average due to some factors, which remains unknown.

Experience:

My initial feeling when coming to SOIA was that there was an inordinate amount of energy, feeling much like the positive ions felt after a thunderstorm. This gave me a lot of energy and I felt powerful when I showed up, we arrived at the location during the afternoon where it is reported that there is very little Sasquatch activity. I am a person who has followed Native American and European (Celtic) philosophy on Nature and the power of the flora and fauna, I immediately felt at home and welcome to the location. There never was any feeling of malevolence during my time at SOIA. Dr. Johnson allowed me free reign over the location to explore and have personal experiences. We did and do have an agreement that some of the reasons that I was there and some of the experiences that I had had at this location and others remain confidential until the spring conference. We had never spoken about the messages that I was receiving and what he was told by Zorth, however, it became clear that there was an uncanny overlap; to the point that we both could finish each other's sentences at times.

On the first night, after Dr. Johnson spoke to the forest and explained who we are and why we were there, I also addressed the forest and the forest people in Upper Salish. I told them that we were there to learn and to interact with them, that they were not afraid, nor were we afraid of them and that anything that we had was theirs to take and examine.

I believe Dr. Matthew Johnson implicitly, a statement that I have never made about another person in this field. It should be noted that I am not a follower by nature; in fact, I am the type of person who tries to poke holes in people's arguments all the time. I expect you to do the same to me, as it is only through the process of discussion that learning occurs. I encourage debate, however I am not a conspiracy theorist. I believe that there are things that are unknown and remain unknown because I believe for whatever reason; we as researchers aren't intellectually honest at times, forming data and experiences around a previously formed conclusion that fits our paradigm, and ignoring the salient facts at times. Enough about that for now.

During the time I was at SOIA, I experienced multiple things that were unexplainable. The preeminent thing was the constant shimmering red and white light that surrounded the camp. This was very similar to the fiber optic lamps that you could buy back in the 90's. The points of light were separate and flowed the same way in unison when moving. The other connection that I made was the hollow hair of a polar bear that reflects the color of the snow. Polar bears actually having black skin.

I did see and hear what appeared to be a large figure, 8-foot-tall, in my estimation on the road on the way into camp. Dr. Johnson, who believed it was me at one point as I was drawn to that area and was talking to the forest at that specific location multiple times, also spotted this figure. On the way back up from that location on the first night, I heard a large being crashing through the forest about 10 feet from me. This was heard and noted by all in camp who were at that time 30 feet from the noise.

Interestingly enough, my wedding ring was taken from my finger twice. This was totally bizarre as I was experiencing swelling in my hand and feet and it was a much tighter fit than normal. I do not remove my rings at night. The significance to me was that this ring depicts the spirals found on the Newgrange stone in Ireland, which is commonly under-stood to be a neo lithic depiction of the spirit vail, or in modern terms, a portal. This ring was also blessed on St. Patrick's grave in Downpatrick, Co. Down, Northern Ireland. The ring was examined and returned both times undamaged, however, not placed back on my hand.

On the second night, Samara Terpening and myself walked into the woods while playing music and we experienced at least 3 forest people standing and swaying to the sounds. Two were in front of us and one to my right; they were so close that I could feel the energy emanating from them.

By the third day, I was becoming overwhelmed by the locational energy, my heart rate was racing constantly. I was nauseated to the point that I could no longer stand and had to lay down. I had no experiences on the 3rd night other than when I was retching, there were large creatures moving through the bushes surrounding me. Others witnessed this and I believe that the forest people were very concerned for my health.

During the night, I lost bladder and bowel control and it was early the next morning I was taken to the hospital and admitted into the CCU. This was not, however, before we witnessed a pterodactyl flying over the camp. The sound and the down force of the creature amazed me. It was honestly like a helicopter washing over the camp like it was coming in for a landing.

There are certain things as I stated before that I cannot comment on in addition to this, but I must keep my word of non-disclosure and I hope that this at least gives you some hints on how the camp is set up, the protocol, and how interaction may be accomplished.

SAMARA TERPENING
(EVERETT, WASHINGTON)

I didn't really know Dr. Matthew Johnson when he invited my husband Kevin and I to the Southern Oregon Interaction Area (SOIA). We had attended his Team Squatchn' USA conference in April of 2016. It had been a little over a year from my first experience with the Sasquatch or Forest People. At the conference I was in a group of people who were talking with Dr. J but I mostly just listened and we were never introduced.

His conference was the first Bigfoot Conference I had ever attended. It was so wonderful to share experiences with others who have had unusual happenings with the forest people. I was in quite a bit of pain during the conference and had to take pain medication even with that I missed several of the speeches because of the pain. By the time Dr. J was giving his speech I had a terrible migraine in addition to my regular pain. Admittedly I was a bit cranky and when he started to speak it was very loud as he was extremely passionate about the topic. He was saying that he does not lie and he does not hoax. He referred to a portal and portal guardians but did not go into detail about it. He seemed to think everyone there knew about his history.

I was a new member of his Facebook group and I had only seen him on a TV show that talked about his first experience and feeding the Forest People behind his house. During his presentation at the conference he talked about how some people had found the site that had the portal where he had been researching the Forest People. He was very upset about them publicizing the location. I could completely

389

understand why that was so disturbing to him. I was new to the Bigfooting community but that seemed to be a breach of code and a very ignominious thing to do.

I had been researching Bigfoot for a year and at the conference was the first time I had heard the term "Woo". I had to ask someone what it meant. Bigfooters have their own vocabulary. Instead of telepathy they call it "mind-speak". I don't understand why; as telepathy perfectly describes how the Forest People are said to most commonly communicate with Homo sapiens.

I didn't know the back story behind Dr. J's speech so I was confused most of the time and concluded that I would have to research more about his experiences when I got home from the conference. Over all, my impression of him was that he believed what he was saying. He did not seem to have an ulterior motive to just getting the reality of what he had learned and experienced out there. To me he came across as stressed out, arrogant and overbearing. I could also see that he was guarded and hurt which led to the ultra tough persona he was portraying. He was very driven to speak the truth and not withhold any information. I believe that he is smart enough to know that, if his goal was to influence people into believing the seemingly bizarre things he was saying, he would have not come across as a tyrannical dictator. He did not seem like the kind of person that I would be friends with or want to hang out with.

I have some natural talents that have helped me throughout my life to tell if a person is being honest and what their motives are. I have always unconsciously used tools like reading and interpreting micro-expressions and body language and how they transmit thoughts, desires, fears, emotions, and intentions. There are behaviors, gestures, or expressions of the face that do occur without conscious prompting which leak or reveal our true feelings or sentiments. Some of these behaviors or expressions flash before us very quickly (1/15, 1/25 of a second). Unlike regular facial expressions, it is impossible to hide micro-expression reactions they cannot be controlled as they happen in a fraction of a second. I had only learned that I was reading micro-momentary expressions several years ago when my husband, then boyfriend, noticed what I was doing and encouraged me to get tested. I had never heard of micro-expressions. Involuntary facial expressions can be hard to pick up and understand clearly, and it is more of an inherent ability of the unconscious mind.

Daniel Goleman created a conclusion on the capacity of an individual to recognize their own, as well as others' emotions, and to discriminate emotions based on introspection of those feelings. This is part of Goleman's emotional intelligence. In E.I., attunement is an unconscious synchrony that guides empathy, and report. It is very rare that people do this instinctively. In the Wizards Project, previously called the "Diogenes Project", Paul Ekman and Maureen O'Sullivan studied the ability of people to detect deception. Of the thousands of people tested, only a select few were able to accurately detect when someone was lying. The Wizards Project researchers named these people "Truth Wizards". To date, the Wizards Project has identified just over 50 people with this ability after testing nearly 20,000 people.

I have been labeled an "Empath" or a "Sensitive", "Psychic" in the esoteric, metaphysical community and general public. I do believe that there are scientific or physiological explanations for many of the so called paranormal, extrasensory perception or ESP abilities that I have. I may unconsciously be more aware of pheromones and have an overdeveloped vomeronasal organ that senses pheromones and the body responds to those cues. The best-known case study of this involves the synchronization of menstrual cycles among women based on these unconscious odor cues.

In the past when I have walked by radios they will go to static until I move away. I am one of those people whose watches stop working after a little while. I have read that the HeartMath Institute (HMI) researches heart-brain communication and its relationship to managing stress, increasing coherence and deepening our connection to self and others. HMI's scientists also explore the electrophysiology of intuition and how all things are interconnected. They measure the heart's magnetic field around the outside of the body and how it changes with emotion and affects others in the fields range.

"It is proven that some women have four cone types that could serve tetrachromatic color vision," said Dr. Jay Neitz, a color vision researcher and ophthalmology professor at the University of Washington in Seattle. The genes for the cone cells that process red and green are found on the X chromosome, of which females have two. Tetrachromatic women are believed to carry the genes for three normal cone cell types and one mutant type. Neitz estimated only about 2 percent of women have the genetic mutation that results in the extra retina cone. Women with tetrachromacy have retinas that contains four types of higher-intensity light receptors with different absorption spectra. This means that they may see wavelengths beyond those of a typical human being's eyesight, and may be able to distinguish between colors that, to a normal human, appear to be identical.

My intention in listing these different scientific explanations of measurable abnormal and unconscious abilities is to get away from the immediate dismissal of personal experiences and perceptions based on thinking it is magical or "woo". Science seemed to be magic to the uninformed and uneducated population in the past. We fear what we do not know. People were killed for studying corpses to learn anatomy and more about what killed a person. People were considered heretics and killed for using the modern medicine of the time. I believe that some day we will understand how to do some of the extraordinary things reported by Bigfoot experiencers, that are considered "Woo" or crazy or unbelievable. I was raised in a very religious home. I have been sober my entire life including never trying marijuana even though it is legal in Washington. I had paranormal experiences as a child but suppressed them and tried to deny them until I was confronted with the Forest People.

Kevin and I went target shooting in the mountains with a friend. My daughter told us the area we were going to was on "the Bigfoot Highway" nicknamed after all the Sasquatch sightings. She had seen a scary movie about Bigfoot and warned us not to go. I never thought I would come across a Sasquatch but believed that they were real. When we got to the spot Kevin had to pee and said "this will keep the Sasquatch away". Immediately we smelled an awful smell and I knew we were being watched. I was overcome with fear and felt angry (I have only been angry a handful of times in my life and I didn't have any reason to be angry or afraid at that time. At the same time, I seemed to hear a voice in my head that said "I could just easily kill you." I instantly felt sad and wondered what we had done to make this person so upset with us. It was as if I could feel the Sasquatches emotions and thoughts. He thought it was Ridiculous that we thought urine would frighten them away.

He was shocked and embarrassed that I knew what he was thinking. I did not feel threatened at any time. I "knew" he would not hurt us. I, right away, knew that he was upset because he thought we should be down at the popular shooting area and that he did not want a big mess up in this pristine area of the forest. Then I heard Kevin say, very randomly and loudly, "we need to be sure and pick up all of our shells and clean up like we always do". Why did he say this and state the obvious? I had a picture of the Bigfoot in my head and where he was, but could not see anything. When I looked at Kevin he was looking in the direction that I thought the Bigfoot was. Yes, I "knew" it was a Bigfoot and that there was more than one. After Kevin spoke I felt a calming feeling and words in my head like "Okay, you can stay, but you better keep your word."

The smell went away. I walked the 25 to 30 yards back to Kevin. He asked if I had smelled that awful smell. I said, "Yes, it smelled like dead animal and rotten salmon." But we could not figure out where the smell was coming from as there was no wind and the smell was gone. We were not close to the river where salmon would be. We sniffed around and could find nothing. It was too early for bears to be out of hibernation. There were some patches of snow around and I looked for tracks. There was no logical explanation. We had just had a three-way telepathic conversation with a Sasquatch, but that is crazy right?

We both seemed to know that he would not harm us but just in case Kevin set aside a loaded 40 caliber gun in case we needed it quickly. Our friend from New York noticed the smell but kept on loading the guns oblivious to anything else. While we were shooting, I kept getting the feeling we were being watched from different areas. Several times, when I looked back at Kevin, he was looking in the same directions that I felt we were being watched from. At one point, I was shooting at a steel target which is fun because you can hear if you hit it and you don't have to stop to see if you did. The boys had been having a difficult time hitting it because it was small. I was farther away from the target than they were and hit it quickly several times in a row. I looked at the boys and our friend was shaking his head and Kevin was just staring with his jaw dropped. I felt pretty full of myself and Kevin said jokingly under his breath, "Bitch." We all laughed and I seemed to see that same Sasquatch in my head smiling and heard a deep laugh, in my head. That's crazy, right? I would have probably dismissed the "minds peak" or telepathy if Kevin had not experienced it also. It kept happening so much with physical backing that I could no longer deny it.

The Sasquatch followed us home. I could see them in my head. I think maybe I can unconsciously see them on a higher color or smell them or see their aura and that is how I "know" where they are. They left foot prints and fingerprints at my house and hit the side of the house. I saw one in my mind coming up to my bedroom window and could hear the heavy footfalls. The window was three feet from my head and open with an air conditioner in it. I saw in my mind or third eye a black Sasquatch with a round head. I thought that could not be right because they don't have round heads. Later I found out that some do. I also found black hair stuck in the air conditioner and foot prints on the ground. I could feel his excitement to interact with me as he got closer to me. I also "knew" he was a young adult male and had a playful sweet personality.

I was excited and smiling. I was kind of in shock and a little nervous too. I couldn't believe this was really happening. I have never felt threatened around the Sasquatch and I knew he would not hurt me. I had filed a report with a Bigfoot research group online and was contacted earlier that day. The Bigfoot researcher of over twenty-five years said that they take women for mates. He confirmed that lots of people have telepathic communications with them and they do follow people home and peek in the windows and hit the house.

I could hear the Sasquatch breathing and then I heard two short sniffs in and one long breath out. It was so loud and reminded me of being by a large bull as a child. They have very large lung capacity. Why was he sniffing me? That was a primal thing to do and I started to think about my daughter worrying about them taking me and what if I was wrong and he did want to take me like the professional researcher said. I said in my mind, "Please don't come in the house." I immediately knew that he was crushed that I thought he would take me against my will. He was devastated and disgusted. I knew he knew why I asked him not to come in the house. I felt so bad. He left and I was so sad thinking I had blown my chance at learning more about them and building a relationship also I had hurt his feelings.

I thought they would stop coming to the house, but the next day I heard a "Whoop" in the neighbor's yard. Again I was in disbelief. I didn't think that they would make such a loud noise in a neighborhood. No one was living in that neighbor's house at the time and I could see in my mind the same Sasquatch as the night before up in the neighbor's tree. I had not heard their voice before and was in awe of how loud and powerful it was. The only thing I could compare it too was a lion's roar. I was so happy that he came back and then I saw him smile and I heard very clearly in a cheeky sarcastic tone, "Is this far enough away for you?" That made me laugh out loud. He thought he was so clever and was pleased that I got his humor and thought he was funny.

Different ones came by the house for two weeks teaching me that they were real and wanted to be friends. They left gifts and clear signs that they were really there and this was really happening. I saw one walking outside my house in my mind. When he got to the tree, I heard the tree branch get brushed at the same time I saw him move it with his hand in my head. This is how they taught me to trust the telepathy. I still doubted it all and went to three different psychiatric professionals. They all said that they didn't have any concerns about me hallucinating or having a mental condition that would cause this. One was very excited and encouraged me to pursue more communications with them.

One night I saw in my head a female Sasquatch in the bushes behind my house. I felt her essence and knew her as the mother in my area. The dog started to growl. He usually barks at everything and chases after it but now he was cowering and scooting closer to me on the bed. I asked in my mind, "Is that you?" Then I heard rocks clicking together in the bushes. I had heard them do this in the woods before. She was answering my telepathic questions in a physical audible way to teach me to trust my telepathy.

I had been arguing on the internet with someone who said that the forest people were demons. I started to question my ability to trust my intuition and thought, "What if they are tricking me?" Then I thought there is no way that they are evil. Like I said before, I have unfortunately been exposed to evil beings and I have never felt anything close to that around the Forest People. She stayed all night with me to comfort me and show me that they thought of me as family. They were grateful for me sticking up for them on the internet. I fell asleep and woke up to my dog growling again. I asked in my mind, "Are you still here?" Again, I heard the rocks clicking together in the bushes and I saw her sweet smile in my head. This happened a couple of more times that night.

SOIA REPORT

Before we left home, I reached out telepathically to the Forest People in "Dr. J's" area. I felt a connection to two males and a young girl that I believe is the one he calls Chatty Kathy. I could feel the Forest People watching us as soon as we started up the mountain. I felt their excitement as we approached. I have an ability to "see" or "feel" the Forest People. I "feel" them and take a picture of the area where they are and they show up in the picture but I don't always see them with my eyes, at least not on a conscious level.

Our brain filters out things that it interprets as hallucinations and gives us a report on what we see over an average of 10 seconds. I think I may actually see them but my brain interprets it differently. I still "know" what I have seen on a subconscious level and with other senses and my body reacts accordingly. Like when you are watching Jurassic Park and your heart jumps. You know it is not real but your body does not and reacts to what it sees.

Kevin and I went to Northern Ireland for a month this summer to have a traditional hand-fasting wedding. We visited high energy areas on ley lines and many ancient structures and sites. We were visiting a large estate like Downtown Abbey. As we sat on a bench overlooking the sea, I said to Kevin, "I feel so powerful and happy right now." He laughed and said he knew that I would feel the ley energy. He told me that we were on a spot where the ley lines intersect.

Powerful was the word that best described what my interpretation of being full of energy felt like. I am drawn to and love to absorb earth energy. SOIA has this same high energy. I felt powerful as if I had been recharged by a huge battery. The area is beautiful and filled with great hiding spots for the Forest People to watch us. I felt them watching us the entire time we were there. We always had at least two watching us that I sensed or saw with my eyes and third eye or felt with a heart connection to them.

It is hard to describe but it is mostly a Clairsentient or clear knowing. The air was full of cedar with a sweet sage like smell too. As the Doc was giving us a tour, I remembered that I had dreamt this area the night before. I blurted out in my ADHD way, as I giggled, "I was here last night." Doc was like "Okay?" and continued with the tour. I had not really talked to him much before this, just at the restaurant that we met at and had breakfast with the two other members of our party earlier that day.

Kevin and "Dr. J." stayed in camp and three of us hiked up a small hill. At the top the energy was so intense I could feel my heart racing. I believe it was the axis of the power there or where the ley-lines crossed. I was glad to have another female with us. Jacqui Davis is a mental health professional who had worked with "Dr. J." This was her first time Squatchin'. We both felt like this area was sacred land. I later found out that this was the area that Dr. J met with the 'Council of Twelve.'

On the way down the hill, I noticed a rock in the path. It was on top of the ground where as the other rocks were pushed in the ground. I felt drawn to it and, from my experience with the Forest People, I knew this was there modus operandi for leaving gifts. I had many times walked down a path in the deep woods and on the way back a gift would be placed right in the middle of the path. Sometimes they put the gifts on leaves or in the middle of stacked rocks or with a "glyph".

I always pay close attention when going in. Usually it is very obvious though like a perfectly stacked pile of blue jay feathers with no bird body around, something we would have noticed on the way in. I felt two Forest People go with us up the hill. When I pointed to one of the areas that I "felt" them, we saw shimmering lights and movement. I saw with my real eyes a little black head pop out and back down behind cover very quickly.

I saw groupings of little lights all throughout the visit with very large amounts at night close together in the form of a Sasquatch. The best way

I can describe the lights is similar to when I have done a cartwheel or right before a migraine I "see stars" or twinkling lights in my peripherals. I liked Kevin's description of fiber optic lights too. I also saw light just like static electricity in your sheets.

At night there was a cricket like sound but it seemed to only be coming from one area. Not like crickets that I have ever heard before, it was more like the electrical arcing sound from the electric fence my neighbor used for his cows. It was not a chirping sound more of a little clicking sound.

On the first day I felt like I was being watched from the 9 o'clock hill behind the vehicles. I saw the familiar "very black absence of depth darkness" between two trees. Later the darkness was half as tall and I could see trees where the top had been solid. Even later, I could see trees and plants all the way from the bottom to the top of the once solid black area. This is typical in photos of the Forest People. They appear as solid black in an area. Then in a later photo, there are plants etcetera where it used to be solid black. Most of the black areas have depth to them but if a Sasquatch is there it is solid. They are great at blending in and hiding.

I noticed that there was not only no sound but even a vacuum of sound when we arrived for the first couple of days. What I mean is not only were there no bird noises or bugs or wind in the trees but it was as if we were in a bubble. Being inside a force field is what came to mind or time had stopped for everything but us. I did not see a single animal or bird that first couple of days. On the third day I saw a mom and baby deer walking right towards us. I told them it was ok and they kept walking up to us. Zeus chased the mother off but the fawn stayed for a little while and then walked away.

I saw lizards, squirrels, different birds and more. I had a Blue Cardinal that was squawking at me and following me around that day too. It was just oddly quiet that first two days. I cannot think of a single time that I have gone in the woods and not seen any wild life before this. I was talking to "Dr. J." and the Blue Cardinal was sitting behind him staring at me. I felt a huge presence over my head and in my mind I saw a huge pterodactyl flying behind me. The word thunderbird came into my mind. I was looking at "Dr. J.'s" face in front of me. His jaw was dropped and his eyes wide open, looking at what was over and behind me. I turned quickly but it had flown out of view.

I asked what that was. "Dr. J." just sat there struggling to find the words. He said a large bird and started to describe the feathers etc. I interrupted and said like a thunderbird? He shrugged and shook his head as if giving in and said yes a thunderbird. "Dr. J." described it and its movements as I saw them in my mind. I felt and heard the wings flap. It was very powerful. The air was forced down on me like a blast from an air gun times ten. The flapping of the wings was colossal and imposing. Kevin was on his cot looking up at the sky above me so he got a perfect view.

"Dr. J." had a hard time putting into words what he had just seen. I was laughing at him after we made our SOIA report video. It seemed like he didn't want to tell people that he had seen a thunderbird, knowing how much grief he got over the portal. He said he was just having a hard time describing it. He never tried to coach us on what to say and did not try to describe things for us he just let us experience. He never suggested that we edit our experience. He is very adamant about telling the truth and the whole truth.

On the first night, "Dr. J." played music over a portable speaker and I played my Native American flute. Kevin took over as DJ and I stayed up with him as the others lay down for the night. When we played music for the Forest People, they liked whatever moved us. It is like they are experiencing the music through you. If the music makes you feel happy they are happy. If the music feels sacred the mood turns reverent. Kevin and I walked into the dark forest at the 12 o'clock position, where we had seen the large silhouette of a Forest Person move in between the trees. As we stood there, I could feel them moving in closer all around us.

I have abnormally large pupils and can see exceptionally well at night. I saw shadows and mists moving around us. When I say shadows, I mean shadows standing right next to us without light casting them. They were alive! They seemed to be moving rhythmically, like dancing or swaying. I felt this was the Sasquatch/Forest People in a simple or pure form. The beings at SOIA had the same energy that I have felt around angels, except angels are more serious and Forest People are more playful and childlike but dignified.

I had seen a shadow type being in the day at our location in Washington, right before we came to SOIA. It was standing by a tree and as soon as I looked at it the shadow being went behind a tree. It was waiting for me to see it. The shadow being had the same energy, size and shape as the Sasquatch it just looked different, like solid smoke. With my religious upbringing, my first thought was "evil spirit" but I have been around evil and this was nothing like that. When you are in the presence of evil you know. I wasn't scared of the figure at all. I felt he was alien energy but was a Sasquatch. I asked what type of being the Sasquatch were and got a very clear answer of Extra Terrestrial and Terrestrial but they were the same beings.

When "Dr. J." was telling me about the Exodus, it all made sense to me. They are all the same but some have been born here and some are new to our realm. I feel like this first shadow being was new. Zorth's energy is very strong and stoic like the Elder in my area. The new beings at SOIA in the night were sweet and pure, more gentle and innocent. I wish that they did not have to learn about us and what we have done or how some of us have treated them or what some think of them on our planet. They are so worried about frightening us. They do not want to be thought of as monsters or scare us.

We started to feel a bit of trepidation as more and more came in closer and closer to us. I could see some solid Sasquatch silhouettes moving in towards us in the distance. We were in the dark woods and out of view of "Dr. J." and the others. Kevin does not have great night vision and I could tell that his PTSD was triggered by the feeling of being surrounded.

I want to make it clear that we have never felt threatened by the Forest People but it is a constant struggle to overcome your instinct to flee from giant hairy beings when you are defenseless in the dark woods. We usually are carrying a gun on us and have concealed carry permits but we did not have them on us at this time. We carry to protect from humans and there were none around so we left them locked in the car. Not that a gun could protect you from a Sasquatch if they wanted to harm you, but they never would.

With my connection to them I can contact any of them around the world. I asked them to look after Kevin in Northern Ireland. They knocked the side of the house like they do here to let us know that they got the message and were there with him on the other side of the world. When you can feel each other's emotions and intentions and essences, there is no lying. You wouldn't want to hurt someone else because you would just be hurting yourself. I hope that eventually we will all be connected by the heart connection like this and the world would be so different. I always feel such love around the Forrest People.

Having the Sasquatch so close to us was amazing. It felt like there were five to ten of them very close to us and even more a little further away. It was hard to go to bed after that. Kevin went to bed and I played some of my music. I played Maria by Ricky Martin (Spanish version) and every time he yelled out, "Whoopi", I would yell out, "Whoopa" too. I think I startled them the first time I did it and laughed. I did a little salsa/bachata type dance to the music too. They loved it. I was just letting go and having fun. They were rushing all around me. It was exhilarating. I don't speak Spanish and I don't know what the lyrics mean. I was just enjoying the music. Then I took it down a notch. I played Dirty Paws by Monsters and Men and sang along. The last song I played was Cindi Lauper's, "True Colors". I sang along, "I see your true colors shining through, I see your true colors and that's why I love you, So don't be afraid to let them show, Your true colors are beautiful, Like a rainbow."

I was singing from the heart. I love to sing but do not think I am very good at it. I went to bed and had a very hard time getting to sleep. During that night I awoke to a beautiful young girl's voice singing from the woods. It was so enchanting. Her voice was gentle and sweet, yet very loud and echoed through the forest. I felt like it was Chatty Kathy giving back to us after we were sharing our music and opening up to them. I felt such a strong heart connection to her during the singing. It is indescribable the soul fusing that took place during that singing. It was a beautiful melody and I could not understand the words. I felt drawn to the woods like I was being pulled in by the heart strings. It was as if our souls were one. I was lost in the music. I have tears in my eyes as I type this.

The next day I took an amazing photo where the FP did show their true colors. It was in the sacred area at the hilltop. Jacqui and I went back up the hill and I was drawn to a specific tree. Jacqui has had training from spiritual teachers about the esoteric. I have just recently been open to it all and do things intuitively. However, she knows what it is called and some of the history behind much of it.

I felt drawn to sit with this tree. This is not something I had done before. I used to laugh at my sister who talked to trees and never thought I would become a tree hugger. But I have learned that there are physiological reasons why I am drawn to certain geological areas. I can use the EMF app on my phone to verify some of my findings. Jacqui told me, "Grok with the tree." I had never heard of that before. The word is coined from a 1961 science-fiction novel, "Stranger in a Strange Land." It is "to understand intuitively or by empathy, to establish a rapport with" an "to empathize or communicate sympathetically (with); also to experience enjoyment."

Jacqui said that she learned from a Polynesian Shaman that trees take one breath a day. Also, they move much slower than us, so we have to be with them for a while before they notice us. She suggested that I lay with my spine along the tree. I thought it was different but tried it. I felt like I was being hugged by the tree and that it was a wise old tree. I felt prompted to touch a new tree that was by my hand and at the same time a fallen tree. As soon as I made contact with the tree, I felt a rush of energy flow through me. I have never "connected" with a tree before.

I honestly thought it was a hippy kind of thing. I am finding that I am becoming more of a hippy every day. I try hard to keep an open mind after I have experienced the Forest People. I am experiencing things that I did not believe in two years ago. So when "Dr. J." said he saw a portal with guardians, I just thought that is different and accepted that anything is possible. I try not to judge people as crazy for having strange experiences anymore because I honestly would have called myself a nut two years ago.

I got up from "Groking" and thanked the tree. I took a picture of it. In the photo, there were rainbow colored streaks of light and a face seemed to appear in/on the tree. I was shown the tree's "True Colors" like I had sung about the night before. It also seemed to back up what "Dr. J." and my husband had said about the Forest People being in trees. I felt the photo was just for me to see for now and for "Dr. J." to share at the conference. I have given it to him to share when he feels it is right and am sure he will put it in the book. The Forest People have given me many photos to share. Some are for others to share like this one. I have photos in two other Bigfooters' books published this year.

Every night around dusk, we would hear this strange indescribable sound. I have never before or after heard anything close to it. It was like a suction sound with a popping at the end. It was combined with a growl and it sounded as if it was moving like a bullet through the woods. "Dr. J." said that was them coming out of the trees. It was astounding.

At SOIA, I saw little lights every night. I have seen the little lights before but "Dr. J." told me about the lights outlining the shadow shape and that made it easier for me to train my eyes to see them. Sometimes the lights are all together more densely in shapes like a square and sometimes you can see a face in the middle.

The bushes by Kevin's bed seemed to be full of little red lights every night. I checked around for wires, but they would have to be projected to appear as they did. You can't project through to the inside of bushes like that. Even being projected, you would not be able to reach the same effect of the lights I witnessed.

I also saw the large Sasquatch shaped shadows at night. Some had an outline of tiny little lights. I have seen this again recently around a person. I have learned that to see auras, you have to train both hemispheres of your brain to communicate better with each other. I am ambidextrous and am good at logical thinking and math as well as being artistic. I already use both sides regularly but I have done exercises to improve the balance. Just telling your brain that you want to see the "cloaked" Sasquatch and taking time to look around for unusually shapes or distortions in the woods will help develop this part of your brain. I did not believe in auras a few years ago but now I know they are real. The lights around the beings are in their aura, I believe that is what we were seeing. We might not have been able to see the Sasquatch but we could see their auras.

On the third night Kevin went to bed early and Steve went home. Jacqui, "Dr. J." and I stayed up and we saw many shadow beings. I had been arguing or strongly debating with "Dr. J." and Steve earlier. We agreed to disagree and they said that they appreciated my commitment and passion. After I told my personal experiences that led me to my strong opinion on the matter, "Dr. J." was very empathetic, and understanding where I was coming from. We made peace but stood our respective ground.

I believe that the forest people come into people's lives or follow them home to heal them. Whether emotionally or physically, the forest people seem to show up when people are in a low point in their lives. Two men, who had never met, had very similar stories at another conference I went to. They were both suicidal when they had their Sasquatch sightings. They both said that it changed their lives and saved them.

Earlier that day when we went into town we heard a story on the news that was very similar to something that I had experienced and it led to my PTSD being triggered. A year ago, I would not leave the house alone. I started shooting competitively and even learned to load my own ammunition. This helped me to feel a little safer but I still did not go out alone unless someone I trusted was meeting me at my destination. After not being afraid of a large hairy man following me around in the woods in the dark, while I walked to the campground restrooms alone, my PTSD oddly got better. The Forest People said that I did not need to carry a gun for protection because they would always protect me. After the events of the day though I could not stop thinking about the events that led to my agoraphobia.

I found myself again debating loudly and enthusiastically with "Dr. J.' During the conversation, I asked Zorth if he would just answer the question so we didn't have to debate our different philosophies. I can be very stubborn and surprisingly so can "Dr. J." I knew that Zorth was listening and I could see exactly where he was in my mind. I was waiting for him to answer me directly but instead, "Dr. J." interrupted himself and said that Zorth kept telling him to tell me something. It was very wise of Zorth to answer through "Dr. J." It confirmed to me that Zorth was real and could hear me and that "Dr. J." could communicate with Zorth and interpret correctly what he was given telepathically. If "Dr. J." wanted to manipulate people and was a fraud, he could easily just say Zorth said this or that and many people would not argue with him.

I always question everything, including what the Forest People tell me. In fact, I passed several tests that the Forest People gave me by using my own knowing and reasoning to figure out that the Forest People were testing me. I did not just accept the obvious easy answer. This is the "trickster" that the Native American's speak of. It is not to be mischievous, it is to see if you are ready for the next lesson or step. Many times people talk about how the Forest People stopped coming around and they feel abandoned. But in reality, they are teaching you to "find" them with your heart not your eyes. Also, I think they do it when people become so obsessed with them that they start thinking of them as a God type figure and thinking that everything that happens is the work of the Sasquatch.

Because I was not in a good space in my mind the third night, it was harder for me to see the Forest People in their basic light bodies. "Dr. J." and Jacqui could see them easily but I had to try very hard to pay attention to the forms. I do believe that they vibrate at a higher frequency then we do. Just like each color has a different frequency. Red is slower and blue is faster or higher. I think that while I was upset I was on a lower slower frequency and it made it difficult for me to see them as clearly.

After meditation, it is easier to see auras and focus on telepathic communications because you have raised your body's frequency. Just like the heart energy study I talked about earlier. Your magnetic field changes with emotion and can be measured. I thought I saw a shadow being in the road and then "Dr. J." said there are many around us. I could see them in my mind as very large hairy Sasquatch but I could not see them with my eyes. "Dr. J." and Jacqui were looking in the same directions all night. It was obvious that they were seeing the same thing but I only got glimpses with my real eyes.

"Dr. J." asked one if he would touch his hand. He reached it out I could feel them around me but was frustrated that I could not see them. I saw a fingertip touch "Dr. J's" hand and he said thank you. It was very magical and beautiful. I felt honored that they felt safe enough to come right up to us. I reached my hand out and asked if they would touch me. I was trying desperately to see them with my eyes and should have just trusted and focused on my third eye seeing. "Dr. J." grabbed my wrist and directed my hand up higher and over a bit as I was just blindly holding it out in front of me not thinking about how tall they are. I am embarrassed thinking about where my hand might have been.

Thank goodness for "Dr. J." A few seconds after "Dr. J." held my hand up, I saw a very faint outline of tiny lights and felt a shock on my hand. It was like a static electric shock but did not hurt at all. It makes sense that it felt like that as my energy was not flowing freely and rapidly so I was static and the light being's energy was much higher and moving freely and quickly. It was such a wonderful. I felt the emotions of the beings around us and it was that of pure love. It was amazing and almost overwhelming love. "Dr. J." said that the being in front of him was his new guardian, I forget his name. I saw "Dr. J." reach out his hand and I could see a solid smoke hand touch his. It was truly marvelous.

I went to check on Kevin, as he had not been feeling well. On the first couple nights, they had the machine running so the Forest People could get energy from it. I heard and saw it arcing at regular intervals. Steve said that it does not do that at home. I know that arcing can happen when there is an overload. In this case, I guessed that the FP were taking a lot of energy as it would build up. They turned off the machine.

Later, "Dr. J." said that a new Forest Person said that he just got there and asked if he would turn the machine on again. "Dr. J." did and a little bit later it quit working. Steve said that it had done that on the first night they used it. He figured out that the Forest People were taking energy from the battery and not the machine. He got a new battery and told them to take it just from the machine. This new guy did not know about that apparently.

The machine was very interesting. I had Steve explain it to me and it is a beautiful design. I could feel the strong energy from it similar to getting an MRI. Kevin seemed to be having a hard time dealing with the high energy in the area. His blood sugars were off and he had to adjust his insulin. Stress and illness can cause a change in the amount of insulin he needs.

During the previous night, I woke up to the sounds of Kevin vomiting. I quickly unzipped my sleeping bag and jumped up to check on him. I heard what sounded like a bipedal elephant crashing through the woods. It sounded like trees were being thrown from its path and huge fallen trees were being crushed underfoot. I saw a very large Zorth in my head rushing over to check on Kevin. He seemed to be stable during the day, but during the last night, he was weak and retching through the early morning hours. He had to use the toilet urgently and regularly. He kept saying he would be fine and didn't want to go to the hospital. He gets like this when his sugars are very high. I told "Dr. J." that I might need him to get Kevin in the car. He was so helpful and attentive during the whole visit. He was not all stressed out like he seemed at the conference and I was surprised that he was actually very sensitive. He was very respectful and considerate. He has a strong moral code and I found him to be elevated in integrity and very honorable. Much like me he will defend his beliefs and principles with extreme conviction. This is what I was seeing at the conference.

"Dr. J." helped me get Kevin in the car. He and Jacqui said not to worry, they would pack up our stuff. I felt bad leaving them like that but they were wonderful. Jacqui called the hospital because she had worked closely with them and made sure they were ready for us when we got there. "Dr. J." arranged for a place for me to sleep and shower while Kevin was in the Hospital. They came to the hospital to check on Kevin. "Dr. J." kept checking on us and was very gracious.

When I went to pick up my camping gear at his garage, the rock I got from the trail was on the top of the pile. I had forgotten about it. He said that Jacqui said it was mine. I put it on the floor of the car in the back. The day after we got home the rock was in the house but we did not bring it in. Then I set it on a little table. I later found it on the bed. I thought maybe the dog had moved it, even though he has never messed with rocks before. I finally took notice of the rock when I found it inside my shoe. Jacqui said it was in the cup holder of my camping chair. I showed it to Kevin and he said that's gold. After investigating I found out it was gold and quartz. Both are high energy. If you take a stone and quarts out of a freezer and measure the temperature of both to make sure they are the same, you can put an ice cube on each of them and it will always melt faster on the quartz because of the higher energy. It is my reminder of the energy at SOIA and a healing stone.

I have many medical illnesses. Before we went to SOIA, I had an appointment with my kidney specialist to schedule a kidney biopsy. My kidney function has been in the stage three kidney disease ranges for three years. I asked for the Forest People to heal me. I went to stay at a cabin with a girl who said that the Forest People were there all the time. I got there before her. I did a sweet grass offering and rang my Tibetan singing bowl. I didn't know how to do an offering. I tried to light the sweet grass but it did not burn as easily as sage. I couldn't get it to light. I gathered some dry pine needles and put them with the sweet grass clippings. The needles burnt but the sweet grass fell under as I tried to move them so they would light. I felt the Forest People watching and they were laughing and very amused at my failed attempts and awkwardness. I said in my mind I am doing this for you and laughed out loud at myself. I finally just hung the remaining sweet grass braid in a tree.

I looked up and there were two black Sasquatch standing about 20-30 feet away. I could see their whole body except for the face. One had a small tree trunk in front of his and the other had a spindly bush in front of him. I said 'hello' and they did not move at all. I waited for some communication but they were quiet. I felt as if they were scanning me. After a while, I looked down to navigate the trail and when I looked up they were gone. Many of my symptoms where much better after that encounter.

Then I went to SOIA. I heard breathing in my ear at night and felt and heard them around me several times during the night. I found a knuckle print on the ground by my head. When I got home and went to the Nephrologists, they postponed my surgery indefinitely because my kidney function was within normal range for the first time in three years.

Dr. Matthew Johnson is, in my humble opinion, a man of great integrity and great character. I consider him a friend and am very grateful for the experiences I had at SOIA.

GRADY JOHNSON
(GRANTS PASS, OREGON)

You all know Dr. Matthew Johnson as the Bigfoot researcher. Some of you even call him Dr. J. Well, I just call him dad. My name is Grady and I'm nine years old. I've been out in the woods Bigfooting with my dad since I was two-years-old.

One of my favorite times in the woods was when I saw the little guardians and the portal in SOHA. It was funny when Adam shushed a Bigfoot while everything was happening. I was kind of creeped out but I didn't do anything like scream. I knew we would be safe because Bigfoot is nice and doesn't harm anybody.

One time, right after I woke up in the morning at my home, I saw a Bigfoot walking down our backyard toward the Rogue River. He looked big, tall, and he was kind of black and brown. My dad said that the Bigfoot was in his room the night before and made his room stink really bad. He said that it is his Guardian.

I like that the Bigfoot are nice to my dog, Zeus. They play with him really nicely. He likes them too and has lots of fun with them when we are in SOIA.

But my most favorite time in the woods with my dad was when we had Steve's machine out in SOIA. That night, there was a lot of movement all around our camp. I said, "Dad, they're everywhere." I could see the portal light off in the distance. I heard lots of them walking all around our camp. I also heard some tree knocks.

I got tired and asked my dad to tuck me in bed. When I was getting inside my sleeping bag, my dad and I both noticed a white orb down by my leg. It sat there for a moment and then it flew up into the air and into the trees.

The next morning after I woke up, I saw some Bigfoot tracks out in the woods. They were really big. Much bigger than my dad's feet and he has big feet.

I like going Bigfooting with my dad because we get to hear cool things and see Bigfoot too. I love interacting with them. I'm sure that other kids my age wish that they could have this kind of experience too.

I'm lucky because not that many people get to have this kind of experience with the Bigfoot Forest People. I can't wait to tell my children someday about Bigfoot and the interactions that I've had with them and that they can have with them too.

CYNTHIA KREITZBERG
(PUYALLUP, WASHINGTON)

I had a childhood fascination with the creatures of myth and legend. I read all of the books I could find on Sasquatch, the Loch Ness monster, theories to explain Easter Island and the large, complex figures worked into the Earth that could only be seen from high above. However, with time those stories faded from memory and imagination as I graduated from college, entered the workforce, and began raising my family. "Patty" was relegated, in my mind, to the status of a relic of a species that mankind had pushed to extinction.

I created a MySpace account in order to understand the environment, and provide protections for my 15 year old daughter. I was certainly not an early adopter, the few friends I found on MySpace informed me they had left for Facebook, their MySpace accounts rarely checked remnants of the rapidly evolving social media. I cringed, just barely feeling competent in MySpace, and opened a new account in Facebook. My daughter had already departed MySpace, so High School, Facebook was where it was at for college students, and graduation loomed. I reluctantly created a Facebook account, entering a world people seem to love to hate.

The Facebook network is amazing. Within weeks of setting up my new account more faces from my past began to pop up in my friend requests. I learned more about my cousins from the Eastern seaboard than I had learned in the previous ten years! Then one day an announcement popped up – the thirtieth class reunion for South Salem High School was being scheduled. Wouldn't that be interesting? However, I did not want to go alone. I started recruiting friends to go to the reunion with me.

411

Buttressed by two friends who agreed to attend the festivities with me, I registered to attend the reunion.

Of course by the weekend of the reunion, my friends had bailed on me. So, I walked in to the Friday night pre-function without the armor of people I KNEW would talk to me. Luckily everyone else was in the same boat, and some familiar faces emerged from the crowd, as eager as I for someone to talk to. Mine was a fairly large graduating class, so people naturally congregated into familiar groupings, exchanging news and relaxing into an unexpected level of comfort with people not seen for twenty or more years.

I people watched as I visited, trying to dredge up names and associations for the faces in the crowd. A few people were fairly easy to recognize and identify. Matt Johnson was no longer the skinny blonde giant of High School days, but his height still made identification instantaneous. We introduced ourselves in passing, both moving on to more familiar personalities than we were to each other. At one point I overheard a couple of women talking about Matt, pointing to foot casts spread out on a table, and commenting they were surprised he would be sharing such things given his professional standing. I'd missed the presentation of the foot casts, and so was clueless as to what was going on and why. I wandered off looking for more people I knew.

I had set a goal for myself regarding the reunion. I was really going to push myself to interact with as many people as I could over the weekend. Although my parents still live in Salem, I booked a room at the reunion hotel in order to force myself to stay engaged. The best laid of plans – there was no one I recognized in the restaurant when I showed up for breakfast Saturday morning. I was mulling over plans of what I could do on my own that day as I worked my way back to the bank of elevators to return to my room.

Just as I reached the elevators, the doors opened and Matt Johnson stepped out. Matt had always been a courteous and friendly person, though we had never known each other well. Everyone knew Matt, so here was my chance to perhaps get involved in any groups planning activities for the day. Grabbing my courage, and stuffing my shyness in the handy garbage can, I stepped in front of Matt and uttered what was to become a very life-changing phrase, "Would you like some company?" Matt's head snapped back on his neck, and he appeared totally surprised, but kindly invited me to join him for breakfast. So, I found myself sipping on a fresh cup of coffee, and talking to Matt as he consumed his breakfast. Our conversation took off, shyness and hesitancy rapidly fading behind me. One of my goals was achieved, I'd made a new friend at the reunion.

Matt and I exchanged phone numbers, and he took off to drive a friend and his wife around Salem. The Long's had taken the train in to Salem, and had no vehicle. I decided to make some phone calls, then set out on foot to explore downtown Salem. While I was on the phone, Matt called and left a message. He had his temporary phone set up, his friends had decided to go walking, and he would see me later. A quick return call confirmed his location in the lobby, and we set off walking Salem together.

Food being the frequent bridge in new social situations, we wound up once again sitting across a table from each other with food in front of us. As we ate, Matt told me the story of his encounter with a Bigfoot above the Oregon Caves, July 1st, 2000. The encounter that rocked him to his core, and catapulted him on his journey to understand, and prove, what he had until that day, dismissed as myth and legend.

It was fascinating listening to Matt recount his experiences. Hearing that story from anyone else, I might well have dismissed the tale out of hand, or at least decided the person should wear glasses when hiking. But Matt had always had a reputation as being honest and not taken with flights of wild imagination. There was also the evidence given by his body as he recounted his tale. I don't believe it is possible to fake the physiological responses Matt evidenced as his story unfolded. The quaver in his voice could have been affectation, but not the pounding pulse I could see in his temple as he shared how terrified he was for his family. His eyes looked inward, not at me, not gauging my reaction, as he described how he felt his mind "reboot" when he couldn't identify what he was seeing against any animal he has seen in the wild or a zoo. Matt is no outdoor neophyte, his 20 years in Alaska had exposed him to eyewitness encounters with animals most people only see in photos. I was convinced.

Matt and I wound up spending most of the day together talking, sharing, getting to know one another. Our mutual attraction grew steadily, but we agreed that we had registered to attend the reunion in order to renew acquaintance with old friends, and make some new friends, so we parted company when we reached the party that evening. I never expected to have as much fun at a reunion as I did that evening! I did reconnect with some old friends, and made some new friends as well. Matt had to leave Salem a little after midnight to catch a flight out of Medford Oregon. We caught up with each other and talked some more before he climbed into his Suburban and headed south. A totally unexpected and unlooked for relationship had ignited in a very short period of time.

We stayed in touch by phone and e-mail. Four-hundred miles separated us at that time, and our plan was to maintain that long-distance relationship for at least a couple of years. I've seen the cartoon a number of times: "If you want to make God laugh, tell him your plans." We made God laugh. Events unfolded rather quickly that made it clear that Matt needed to be in a larger metropolitan area, and guess where I was? So, by early spring we were moving Matt into an apartment complex about a mile from my home, and we were adjusting to being in a non-long-distance relationship. No complaints!

Over time, Matt shared the stories of his subsequent research and experiences after his encounter at the caves. I think my most perplexing question was a very common one, "What is Sasquatch?" Matt was meticulous about explaining the varying theories regarding a definition of Sasquatch – all while never really giving me a position statement of his own beliefs. At the time I thought he was letting me make up my own mind – but it was a very un-Matt-like behavior. It wasn't until June 2011 when all the pieces of the puzzle came together and I finally understood the reasons for Matt's reticence.

The Oregon Sasquatch Symposium (OSS) was hosted by Toby Johnson in a camp near the MacKenzie River outside of Eugene Oregon. Matt was scheduled to be one of the speakers, presenting on witness treatment and Post Traumatic Stress Disorder (PTSD) in witnesses. I was nervous, a total know-nothing, without so much as a brief encounter to my name, attending a conference with a group of people who had been involved in the field for years. Matt warned me before we went that there would be people at the conference, and people presenting at the conference, who believed that Sasquatch had "paranormal" abilities, and some even believed that Bigfoot might have extra-terrestrial origins. But, we would be polite, and chose to hang out with the serious researchers. Thus armed, I adopted the role of "technical assistant" to Matt, and helped out with the laptops and audio equipment for the speakers.

A lot of the conference is a blur to me. I remember Ron Morehead's presentation, turning to Matt in shock and consternation, telling him "I've heard sounds like that before in Montana!" I enjoyed listening to Matt, hearing him speak, sharing his own experience, and the experiences of a number of people who contacted him over the years to share their stories, their trauma, and how that trauma was compounded by not being believed, or not even being able to share what they had experienced.

Then Thom Powell took the stage, and began his presentation on "The Coconut Express". I tried to catch Matt's eye, to get a read on what that might mean, but Matt was listening intently, with a pronounced focus on Thom's words. I eased back in my seat and positioned myself to see Matt's profile as I listened to Thom's story.

Thom was sharing stories of his experiences from years in the field, in particular the frustrations and aggravations of the total failure of all electronic equipment to capture evidence of the elusive creature named Bigfoot. Matt had shared a lot of the same experiences, track-lines approaching a camera trap, and diverting around the cameras. Bait-piles stripped before the men could react to the seismic sensor and turn their lights on. However, Thom began touching on phenomena beyond even the frustrations expressed by Matt.

Thom talked about brand new packages of batteries inexplicably being totally drained. Trail cameras turning off, then back on, of their own volition. Thom spoke of being a good little researcher, miles and miles in the mountains, tree-knocking three times, always three times, because that is what good little researchers do. Then arriving home, miles and miles from where he had spent his day, and hearing "knock, knock, knock" emanating from the woods behind his home.

Through it all I watched Matt's posture and physical reactions as he watched Thom. There was nothing dismissive or impatient in his attitude. He was intent, and relating to everything Thom had to say in a way that surprised me given our conversation before attending the conference. Thom started talking about being called out to interview a witness who claimed to have Sasquatch living on her property, and furthermore, claimed the Sasquatch were talking to her in her head. Thom listened to her story, examined the evidence, and was convinced that at least the presence of the Sasquatch was true. Thom proceeded to follow his standard research methods, placing trail cams in likely places, advising the woman to leave food, and onward he marched. And the results continued to match his experience everywhere else he had mounted trail cams, set elaborate traps, and sought to obtain evidence of the presence of the elusive beings of the woods.

Thom received another report of Sasquatch activity, this time near Seaside Oregon, about 100 miles from the woman he was already working with. The gentleman in Seaside was also reporting that the Sasquatch were communicating with him in his head. Throughout all of this time Thom was speaking in a lively manner, but with an underlying sense of exhaustion. I felt he was a man who had reached the end of his rope in some manner I did not fully understand. It was at this point Thom said "I am a science teacher. I've always been methodical, systematic, and I decided to use a double-blind approach to this problem to solve this question once and for all."

I felt, as well as saw, Matt shift to totally concentrated attention at this point. Matt sat up straighter in his chair, he leaned forward, and his eyes narrowed as he focused every ounce of his attention on Thom. Thom saw and felt the response as well, I saw him hesitate for a brief second as he took in Matt's change in demeanor. Thom went on to explain that there was no relationship between the woman outside of Portland, and the man in Seaside. They had never met, had no knowledge of each other at all. So, Thom told the man in Seaside to tell his Sasquatches to tell the woman's Sasquatches that he wanted pictures of them. A couple of days later the woman called Thom to tell him that the cameras had gone crazy! They had turned off and back on, all by themselves, all night long. And in a couple of frames there were shadows of rapidly moving humanoid figures. It went on and on. Thom paged through the photos captured on the trail cameras as he talked.

I don't remember all of the details of the subsequent challenges Thom issued. I just know that by the time he yielded, the preponderance of coincidences was overwhelming. The scientist had proved to himself, beyond a shadow of a doubt, that there was a level of communication occurring between groups of Sasquatches separated by a significant distance that he could not explain. Thom concluded his talk by drawing a correlation to the abilities of certain aboriginal tribes to also communication across large distances without the use of technology.

I don't remember if there was another speaker after Thom, before the lunch break. All I remember was sitting next to Matt at lunch when Thom Powell sat down across the table from us. He looked at Matt, and asked "What really happened up there on the mountain that day?" Matt didn't say anything at first. He just looked at Thom. Thom sat silent, waiting. Matt finally told Thom that he needed to talk to me first, that he owed it to me to tell me what happened before he told Thom. Thom glanced at me, nodded at Matt, and told him he would be waiting.

Matt has written of "Paul Harvey's the rest of the story." After Matt talked to me, we returned to Thom, and Matt told Thom what had happened at the caves. When Matt finished, Thom smiled and said "Now I believe that you really saw a Sasquatch that day."

That was a game changer. I think Matt was more than a little anxious that I would write him off as crazy and leave. I didn't, I'd heard too much, listened to too many stories from people that weekend to discount all of them as kooks. Also, that weekend, I met my first BFRO researcher, and asked him what he thought Sasquatch was. And I heard him say – they are a people. I didn't get it then, it simply confused me. Did he mean humans who lived in the wild? How did you account for their size? Was the hair an evolutionary development to allow them to survive the elements? Overloaded with new information and the transition in thinking left me confused, and very excited.

It was about one month later that I first went out with Matt in his Southern Oregon Research Area (SORA). I had been in Northern

California with my two younger children for a family reunion, and we stopped in the Rogue Valley area on our way home for a new kind of adventure.

From this point on I am not even going to try to pretend I am relating events in chronological order. The first trip out is pretty clear in my mind, but the others begin to blur together. I walked in with the advantage of Matt's ten years in the field as a "old school researcher" intent on solving the mystery in order to put his world back on an even keel. The world had turned out to be too large, and too surprising, to allow Matt to re-impose order upon his experiences. He was moving to habituation before I met him, and he encouraged me to learn from the lumps on his head, and just enjoy the experiences.

Not that I've always succeeded in just absorbing what I experience. My mind has still attempted on numerous occasions to categorize, rationalize, and otherwise shove the inexplicable back into an explicable box. But, I'm getting ahead of myself with that.

So, our first trip. Matt had gotten to the campsite ahead of us, and had everything set up. He met us down in town, where we ate, then stocked up on coffee drinks at an espresso stand. We were ready for our very first night sit. We would be nocturnal, meeting the Sasquatch in their world. We set up our chairs in the light, and as Matt encouraged us to do, we laughed, sang, played games, and generally made our presence known as the light faded. I played my recorder, pulling a few songs out of memory, but mostly just making noise. The wind came up as the sun went down.

In the shifting trees, the sound of the wind, it was impossible to tell what might be the movement of observers. Our eyes were aching, and we were all shivering by 1am. We decided to call it quits, and headed back to our camp. It was a relief to be out of the wind, in the warmth of my sleeping bag. However, I am VERY susceptible to the effects of caffeine. Warm and sleepless I stared into the dark and listened to the wind until the dark turned to grey, and finally color began to return to my sight.

I tried napping the following day, but it was warm, and the tent was hot and airless. Instead we hiked around the area looking for tracks. My two children, the skeptical neophytes were of course the individuals who located the tracks. It took my son's sharp eyes to spot the smaller imprint inside of the mother's print. My daughter laughed when she saw it, saying she remembered following me and jumping in my footprints on the beach. Matt added food coloring to the plaster to make the juvenile track stand out from Mama's.

We had decided to only stay up until about midnight, then retreat to the tent to give the Sasquatch a sense of security by having us "contained." I was already starting to drift off when Matt grabbed my arm. I listened, and for the first time in my life heard the unmistakable sound of a very, very large creature walking through total darkness (at least by our standards) on two feet. I'd heard people talk about hearing "bi-pedal" walking, and wondering what they meant. Hearing it for the first time I knew, and understood that the bi-pedal motion is unmistakable.

I wasn't sure how many individuals I was hearing. At times I thought only one, at others I thought there were two or more. I couldn't tell exactly what they were doing, just subtle movement around our camp, and the rustle of items being moved. They were very quiet, and very careful. My sleepless night was catching up with me. Matt had to keep shaking me back awake. He finally gave up on me, and I faded into sleep listening to the quiet sounds outside the tent.

In the morning we examined the campsite. The ground was very hard packed, so we found no foot impressions beyond a hint of a shape in the dust. However, when we had gone to bed the previous night my son's gym bag was sitting on one of the chairs. In the morning the bag was sitting upright, not tumbled, on the ground in front of the chair.

The rest of these events are highlights that remain vivid in my memory. Other details have faded, but these experiences were significant to me:

Our base-camp is at the end of a logging road, on the top of a ridge. Where the road ends, the ridge forms a "choke-point", narrowing down for a period where it drops off sharply on both sides. There is a wooded area here at the choke point, traversed by a trail to a higher area where the ridge widens out. One day we had headed away from the choke point to explore a lower area of the ridge. After we returned we rested for a time before heading back up toward the high point of the ridge. I don't know how many steps I took before I realized that I was following a straight line of pine cones, carefully arranged in the center of the path. At the end of the line of cones was a pattern of sticks laid out on the ground. There was nothing "random" about the layout of the pinecones, or the shape we found in the path. Additionally, it was all put there during the time we were exploring in the other direction away from base camp, it had not been there in the morning.

On one journey up the mountain to the base camp I saw what I later came to believe was a juvenile Sasquatch. Matt was intent on driving, so missed seeing the figure that I just barely glimpsed. We drove around a corner, and I saw a flash of black, a figure running on all fours, disappearing down a trail that bisected the road and continued down the hill. It sounds very cartoonish in description, but there was literally a cloud of dust still hanging in the air behind the figure. I have spent a lot of time in my life in Montana, and over the years seen numerous black bears. This was NOT a black bear, though the shape was somewhat similar. There is no way a black bear could move that fast.

One morning the two young Sasquatch apparently got bored with our lazing around in the tent. We were "rudely" awakened by the loud thump, and crashing sound of a log being tossed down the hill behind our tent. Seconds later we heard the sound of running feet retreating from our area. I could just imagine them giggling as they ran. We decided to do some exploring in the area where they had tossed the log. Where we started out there was a well-defined trail, with small trees stripped of their branches laid horizontally to form a very rough staircase. We thought we had found a major trail down the side of the ridge.

The trail quickly became smaller and smaller, with poorly defined animal trails branching off from the main trail, until all of the trails were equally poorly defined. The hill became steeper and steeper, and we were soon creating our own switchbacks to work our way down the hill. We wound up at a flatter area scooped out of the side of the hill. The sun was shining down into the small bowl-shaped indentation, and we rested there for a time. Matt looked around, and wondered if it might be a sunning area for the Sasquatch. It would have been perfect for the purpose, sheltered from any wind, inaccessible, at least for humans, and warm with the sun. After we rested for a time we decided to head back up the ridge. The hillside was getting even steeper, and we did not want to risk a fall.

I was climbing out on hands and feet when I spotted what looked like a trail. I followed it as best as I could, still scrambling on hands and feet, when I realized that directly under my face was a large footprint. The details of the toes in the dirt were very clear. Approximately the front third of the foot had been pressed into the dirt of the hillside. For some reason the footprint on the side of the hill like that made me start to laugh. There I was scrambling for all I was worth to get back up the ridge, and directly under my face was the evidence we had been searching for.

Matt and Grady stayed in camp one time, while I followed the path through the wooded area towards the higher part of the ridge. Matt was fairly certain that the main bedding area was below a certain section of the path through the woods. I had my penny whistle with me, and was going to play for a while to see if the Sasquatch would respond. I found a stump in the area I wanted, and climbed on top for the best vantage spot. As I started to get settled silence settled in around me. The birds became totally silent. I had a very strong sense of being observed from a higher point on the hill, and more than just being observed, a sense of warning, you are being watched because we will not let you do anything bad. I turned and scanned the hill for any sign of movement. There was nothing.

My heart was beating faster, and my breathing was a little ragged as I pulled out the penny whistle. I don't remember what I said, something about just wanting to play a few tunes for them. The sense of being watched began to fade, and the birds began moving around again. I wiped my sweaty hands on my jeans and began to play. When I walked back to camp later I did not look behind me.

We had been putting out food on every trip to SOHA, and it was never touched. Which was interesting. Matt explained that it sometimes took time for the trust level to reach the point where the Sasquatch would take the food. But what about all the other animals? NOTHING was touching our food. There were no peck marks in the sandwiches, even though we saw crows around. None of the berries were flown off, or pecked open. The sandwiches weren't dragged into the dirt, nibbled at, and left. The food should have been attracting the squirrels and birds we would see in the woods, but it wasn't.

Then one morning the sandwiches were gone, lifted cleanly out of the bowl and consumed. There were no crumbs, no sandwich bits scattered around. The berries were intact, not smashed, not scattered, just left exactly where we put them. A few mornings later the sandwich bowl was not exactly where we had left it. That morning we did not have to clean the smeared peanut butter and jam out of the bowl, it had been licked totally clean. Another time we found a section of the crust that had fallen off smashed totally flat in the dirt next to the bowl. I held that paper thin piece of crust in my hand and marveled at the weight it would have taken to flatten the whole wheat bread crust so completely.

At the same time these events were occurring in Southern Oregon, we were also experiencing activity in Washington. Our night-time recordings echoed a world we would never have guessed existed in the daytime. We heard a lot from nine-hundred pound owls, patterns of calls and behaviors that repeated night after night. For those who suspect the owls were merely Barred Owls, and our projecting weight and volume on them is wishful thinking, I ask you, how much data you are going to write off as being "coincidental" before you concede the patterns in what we were hearing were significant? Owl call, owl call, tree knock. Owl call, owl call, tree knock. Or, on other nights, owl call, coyote howl, owl call, coyote howl, owl call, pack of coyote's yipping together.

Yes, there were nights that we heard from the fluffy, feathery Barred Owl that nests in the area. It would be difficult for a Sasquatch to mimic the effect of an owl flying through the woods quietly whoo-whooing. But those other times? The patterns became more and more clear as Matt reviewed hour after hour of recordings.

I also heard for the first time a Sasquatch howling in full-out voice. I don't know if they were hunting, or if it was simply a song to a beautiful night. I do know that I responded to the sound with a combined sense of awe, and goosebumps. I was happy the source of that howl appeared to be a couple of miles distant, and NOT getting closer. To rationally know they have never sought to hurt us, or in this area even attempt to intimidate us, is one thing. To hear that voice, the power and volume of it for the first time in person, is quite intimidating.

Then came the series of events that catapulted me into complete appreciation of what Matt experienced in his first encounter with Bigfoot. Up until this point I was buffered by Matt's stories, prepared by his explanations of what to expect, what me might experience. Then I left the marked trail.

We had been hearing so much activity in our recordings that we finally carved out time to arrange a night sit. We invited a woman we had met at a conference, a local Bigfooter, to join us. We became aware of their presence around us almost immediately after we got settled into our chairs. They were being fairly subtle, but we heard the rustle of the leaves as they moved around us. Occasionally we would see a glint of eye shine. We talked to each other, laughed, and talked to the indistinct figures whose presence we felt more than saw. We couldn't stay out all night, we all had obligations the following day, and we were starting to think about leaving when CRACK, not thirty feet from where we were sitting one of the Sasquatch hit a tree. I don't know how high the others jumped, but I left the seat of my chair. Even skeptical me couldn't argue the origin of that "hello!"

That experience in the greenbelt behind our house was ultimately eclipsed by my first experience with "cloaking", the term generally used to describe knowing full well a Sasquatch was present, but unable to see it, or having a Sasquatch disappear before your very eyes.

Howie Gordon had flown out to visit us in Puyallup, Washington. The first night we were out in the greenbelt I looked over at Howie to see a soft white glow illuminating his right arm and part of his chest. Matt noticed the light also, and instructed Howie to turn off his cell phone. Howie responded by telling us he had left his cell phone at the house. We all stared at the glow along Howie's arm, until it moved up to his hand, then back down to his elbow, and then up to his shoulder. Then it zipped off up into the trees. I don't know how long it took me to stop staring. I had never seen anything like that before in my life.

The experience with the orb left us eager for another night-sit the next day. After dark, we grabbed our chairs and headed out into the woods. We were sitting in a semi-circle and talking quietly together, aware of the soft footsteps and rustling brush that indicated the locals were moving in closer. Matt spoke up, and in the tone he calls his "calm psychologist voice" he told our audience that we would love to see them, would one or more of them please step out and say hello.

Within moments we heard distinct and deliberate movement heading our way. Howie kept saying "Doc, he's coming, Doc, he's coming right at us." Matt and Howie were sitting closer to the path, and apparently they briefly saw the silhouette of a large male Sasquatch before it disappeared from view – but the sounds of the footsteps continued towards us. I felt totally frozen.

I watched Matt stand up, but I was submerged in a variety of sensations. I heard the fall leaves under the Sasquatch's feet, but it also sounded like they were rolling in front of him like ocean waves. My mind felt fuzzy, the best word I've found to describe what I was experiencing is dissonance, an inability to focus either my mind or my eyes, every thing around me was fuzzy and indistinct. The hair on my left arm was standing on end, and I could feel energy coursing through the left side of my body, the side closest to the Sasquatch.

I saw Matt swing around to his left, and look behind him. The sound, the energy, the dissonance, all began to fade. It was only after we compared notes that I learned that Matt swung around because the Sasquatch had bumped his shoulder and pushed him around.

We did not sleep for hours after than adventure. We each told, retold, and retold our stories again and again. We were definitely heading down a rabbit hole none of us had expected to fall into.

I have more special memories of times spent in SOHA and southern Oregon than I could possibly share, but I would like to share some of the most impactful experiences of my times there. After the sun set, and darkness set in we would begin our socializing with the Forest People. I play the recorder, and also like to sing, mostly well-known tunes from musicals or the folk songs I learned as a child. When I sang I would walk towards the perimeter of the cul-de-sac, and slowly pace around the front of the bushes. I had just finished singing a song, when the branch of a small Pacific Madrone bush in front of me began to shake vigorously. The shaking continued for far too long for the effect to have been caused by a squirrel or a bird jumping out of the bush.

I choose to interpret the shaking of the bush as applause, and dearly hope that is the correct interpretation, rather than relief that I had finished singing.

During one trip in February, we were sitting in a semi-circle in the dark. The stars were amazing, brilliant in the cold night sky. It had been a very quiet evening, with almost no activity on the perimeter of the camp. While sitting there I suddenly smelled a very sweet, floral scent. I was the only woman there, and definitely not wearing perfume, so the scent was unexpected. I stayed silent for a time, finally asking if either of the two men smelled that gorgeous scent. Matt smelled it also. He said that it reminded him of the tropical scent of a Hawaiian Lei draped around his neck, underneath his nose. The other gentlemen present smelled nothing.

In early 2013, I returned to working full time. I was no longer able to travel to southern Oregon as frequently as Matt. My role shifted from participant to sounding board, a ready ear to process the stories of Matt and those who traveled south with him on a monthly basis. The transition to that role was not easy, listener instead of active participant, armchair enthusiast rather than boots down at camp. Rather than getting easier over time, not being able to go to SOHA became more and more difficult.

The longer Matt continued with his new patterns of habituation, leaving the cameras behind, turning out the lights, and spending time simply singing, playing music and talking, the more interaction he and his companions experienced. The Southern Oregon Research Area (SORA) had become the Southern Oregon Habituation Area (SOHA), and the results were encouraging.

In June of 2013, Matt drove to Oregon and picked up Grady for a father son trip to SOHA. We were still sleeping in the tents at that point, but the Sasquatch were spending more and more time in camp at night. I woke up at my normal 5:30am to get ready for work and found my phone blowing up with text messages from Matt. During the night his memories had been read by an adolescent Sasquatch, and after breaking free and asking for a chance to ask questions as well Matt had mental contact from an adult Sasquatch. They were guardians of the forest, and all who dwelled within, they read human memories so they could keep track of, and understand the humans on the planet. Even in the limited format and communication capabilities of texting I could hear and feel Matt's shock, awe, and total mind-blown amazement at this new development. Matt was finally a huge step closer to his dream of interacting with this elusive species, seeing them face-to-face, holding a young Sasquatch on his lap.

After the nighttime mind speak, Matt began walking along the edge of the brush perimeter of the camp after dark. Matt would play music on his cell phone, walking around the edge of the brush, holding the phone up for the Sasquatch to view the music videos on his screen. At times he would see young Sasquatch on their bellies in the brush, oblivious to the fact that he could see them in the glow of the light from the videos.

One night, Matt experienced a new, and profoundly moving experience. Behind the row of juvenile Sasquatch on their bellies, two translucent beings of light appeared, the light from their bodies floating around their feet like fake smoke on a Broadway stage. Matt experienced an intense sense of unconditional love from the beings of light before they faded away and disappeared. He cried in wonder and emotional catharsis when he returned to his chair and told Michael Beers and Gunnar Monson what he had just experienced. They had admittedly seen the light, but been at the wrong angle to see the beings of light.

Matt's protocol evolved, and consistent patterns began to emerge. At this point I think there was value in my being external to the main action. I was able to provide the external evaluator role to the stories that Matt and his companions shared. Reviewing and processing the variety of experiences everyone shared enabled us to identify some of the patterns that were developing over time.

I will never forget the weekend of the portal incident. Matt called me from camp, and almost immediately turned the phone over to Adam Davies to tell me their story. I could occasionally hear John Carlson in the background, confirming and expanding on Adam's narrative. Although Adam and John were laughing, there was a hysterical note to their voices, and they were emotionally extremely volatile and stressed. Adam repeated several times that he was feeling very negative energy from the beings in the portal, and that the whole experience was very inimical and frightening.

I had a terrible time trying to reconcile what Adam and John were telling me with the experiences I had in SOHA. I always felt so at peace when I was there. I slept better there, on a cot in the open than I ever slept at home. I was greatly relieved when Matt's subsequent mind speak with Ceska explained that the portal was a device, it opened to another world, bright light would turn it off, and there was nothing to fear from the guardians. Our experiences and years of habituation to the SOHA environment made it easy for us to embrace the information Matt received from the local clan.

For several years we had been watching as a wave of light would wash up the trees in front of us, and wondering what caused the periodic illumination. Now, in a flash of understanding, we understood that the light on the trees was the light from the portal. We had never looked behind ourselves to see the cause of the phenomena. The portal had been there all along, and we had never experienced danger. Lacking the experience and the relationships we had, John and Adam were unable to reconcile their experiences as being benign.

Even after he was reassured by the local clan, Matt came very close to abandoning his research after the discovery of the portal. Prior to that point Matt was feeling like he was breaking through the barriers, and getting very close to achieving the next level of interaction with the Forest People. Now, there was the question of the portal, and the relationship between the portal and the Forest People. New, unique sounds were captured on Matt's recordings, I heard a "sonar ping" that repeated randomly all night long, varying in direction and intensity. Matt deeply questioned if all of his conclusions to date had been erroneous, and if the solution would forever elude him.

It was almost exactly a year later that Matt figured out that exposure to the Oregon Vortex magnetic field was the "key" that made the portal manifest. Once again he was off and running.

On a subsequent trip to SOHA with Matt, I was busily singing and playing a variety of instruments for the Forest People. Matt asked if I was taking time to watch for signs of the portal, or portal activity behind us. I had been focused on the entertainment, and trying to discern any shapes or movement in the trees around us.

After Matt's reminder I began scanning behind us periodically for activity. All of a sudden a perfect rectangle of light appeared in the vicinity of the portal. The rectangle of light was oriented towards my right, angled away from the road into the trees. Then, as if a shade had been pulled down over a window, the rectangle of light disappeared. I did not see anyone or anything emerge from the light, but the experience was so totally unexpected that I flapped my hands in the air and stammered for a few seconds before I could describe what I had seen to Matt.

Matt and I spent the eve of Christmas day in SOHA in 2015. Not long after, the location of SOHA was identified by TROLLS and broadcasted to others. Matt was given a vision in a dream of where to start looking for our new habituation area. Matt met up with Jill Ligda, and they began their exploration of the area. After a long day driving snowy roads, and finding two possible locations, they headed out of the mountains. Matt stopped on the main road out to take a picture of the image the Forest People had given him to bring him to that spot. The sun was setting over the mountains, and Matt wanted to share the picture with me.

Matt, as is his norm, took several shots in sequence. When he reviewed the shots to pick out the best picture to send to me, all thought of sharing the shots with me disappeared in a greater excitement. In the sequence of pictures was a very clear orb descending from over the mountains, getting progressively closer to Matt. As quickly as Matt takes picture like that, the orb had to have been moving at an incredible rate of speed. Unfortunately, Mike Kincaid was able to identify the location where Matt had taken the pictures within minutes of Matt sending the images to him. Matt could not publish the orb pictures without giving away far too much information about the new location.

In April of 2015, I was able to join Matt in Oregon the weekend before our spring conference. We spent a couple of days at the new site, that Matt was calling the Southern Oregon Interaction Area (SOIA). The name of the new site was intended to reflect the higher level of interaction and acceptance from the Bigfoot Forest People. The weather was warm, the snow was gone, and it was a beautiful site. Our original intent was to stay for three nights, but after the second night Matt scared me to death. When I woke up, Matt was staring at the sky. He informed me that plans had changed; we were going to head to Washington that morning. When I asked for an explanation, he said he would tell me what was going on once we were on the road. He refused to say anything more, other than asking what a shunt was.

Hearing shunt and stint my mind immediately jumped to the possibility that the Forest People had told Matt that he had heart problems and needed to get to a medical doctor for a check-up. Matt was adamant, he would explain when we got on the road, so I swallowed my fear and helped knock down our camp and pack it up.

Matt explained his mind speak with Onx during the night. The need to find a way to create a shunt to hold open the portal so those Forest People, unable to manipulate the energies needed themselves, could escape from their dying world. We didn't have a clue how to proceed, but our commitment was immediate and unequivocal.

Matt has recounted the subsequent events that led to the EXODUS, so I will not repeat his story. However, the Bigfoot Forest People have spread a wide net, and a woman who had recently returned to the area where she grew up, the Puyallup Washington area, soon reached out to us.

Anita Hlebichuk had been strongly drawn to return to Puyallup after several years of living in Idaho. Not long after returning to Puyallup, Anita found the TSUSA group, and reached out to several local people in the group. Anita and I met up one day to explore her local area, and quickly felt very comfortable with each other.

A while later Anita started experiencing mind speak from the Forest People. The messages were hard for her to understand, but she was being encouraged to trust Matt and me. When she shared the message it began to appear that the Forest People believed that Anita and I might have some innate ability to open the portal for those who could not manipulate the portal themselves. Baffled, totally unsure of what we could accomplish, we started spending time in the greenbelt behind the house trying to figure out what we were supposed to do.

We located several areas in the greenbelt where there was energy that we could both perceive. At one point when we were trying to decide which direction to follow, Anita was told "down" repeatedly, and a moment later we found arrows drawn in the dirt pointing in the opposite direction I was intending for us to travel.

We eventually found a spring that resonated strongly with Anita. She can still sit there for hours watching the play of the light on the water, and the half-seen flows of energy in that spot. From there it took Anita dragging me through a large patch of nettles for us to find a small hillside, topped with a group of trees. In broad daylight we could both perceive a fine mist surrounding the hillside. When we climbed up there we were both knocked to our knees by the energy swirling between the trees.

Anita and I never did figure out what we were doing, or supposed to do. The events at SOIA over-ran all of our expectations, and almost before we understood our objective, to use Matt's words, mission accomplished, mystery solved. Matt sent me progress reports the second night, once they understood how to manage the EXODUS. As Zorth updated Matt, he would send me text messages reporting the mounting number of souls who had made it through the portals at SOIA. When Matt reported the death of the final Forest Person to cross over, I cried along with them, at the same time we rejoiced that they were all successfully reunited.

Matt later told Anita and I that we had brought over three Forest People during our efforts. Comparing what happened in SOIA, and what we experienced, I believe that somehow, some humans have the ability to collect and concentrate energy that the Forest People can then tap. Human batteries, powering the Forest People so they can hold open the portals for others.

The weekend after the EXODUS occurred in SOIA, Matt made the drive north to Puyallup. He was simultaneously exhilarated, exhausted, and physically amped up. He talked and talked about the events, the feelings, the impact of being surrounded by so many Forest People at one time. He told me about the red mist containing faces, obviously male and female, floating near to say thank you before fading away. He shared again Zorth telling him that they had to go retrieve the final surviving member from the old world, and we grieved together once again at his passing after making it through the portal. Words, impressions, emotions, poured out of Matt as shared the final events in SOIA.

We invited a group of trusted friends to join us for dinner at our house, and Matt shared with them the story of the EXODUS at SOIA. Steve Bachman joined us, to add his perspective to the story, and also to share the background of his device that had powered the Exodus. Matt was restless and excited, but also drained to a degree that at times I had to remind him of details in the earlier sequence of events to help the story make sense to his listeners. Watching the faces of our friends, I could see the impact of Matt's words, and also recognize in them when the experiences of Matt, Mike and Steve caused pieces of their own experiences to fall into place, a puzzle finally becoming clear after years of the pieces not quite fitting into place.

Mission accomplished, mystery solved. We all needed transition time, time to process and reflect on the cascade of events. Matt was reassured by Zorth that the Bigfoot Forest People still wanted to pursue relationships with kind humans with good hearts and open minds. They too needed time to transition, time to acclimate the newcomers to their new home. The compulsion driving Matt back to the forest over and over was lifted, and a new future awaited us all. Our new journey is just beginning.

Part 6

AN OPEN LETTER
TO MY PROGENY
JANUARY 25, 2017

DEAR BIOLOGICAL DESCENDANTS,

Please forgive me, I know that doesn't sound very warm and endearing. Nevertheless, my point is that I'm writing to all of you (i.e., My children, grandchildren, great grandchildren, great great grandchildren, etc.). I'm writing to all of you who are my direct biological descendants because I think there's information that you need to know. By the way, I love every one of you and I can't wait to see you someday in eternity.

I believe that everyone is a unique creation and that there's no one else on the Earth who is like anyone of us. Yet, my progeny, we share the same DNA and, therefore, we also share many similarities too. When I was a child, I saw some pictures of my grandfather and my father and I couldn't believe how much I looked like the both of them when they were younger. When I look at my sons, Micah and Grady, I can't believe how much they look like me. Although we are very different and unique, we are also similar in many ways. We are merely separated by generations.

With that said, here's what I think you need to know. I truly believe that within our DNA comes the ability to be more sensitive than others might be to the unseen paranormal world. I'm not saying that all of you have been born with this gift, I'm simply suggesting that some of you have possibly been born with this gift.

Why is it important for you to know this? Well, thank you for asking because I'm going to take the liberty to tell you. If you have this gift and you don't know it, then the gift may feel more like a curse. Case in point, in January of 1995, I had a new client come to my office for counseling in Anchorage, Alaska. He desperately wanted me to help him get rid of a curse. I'm always interested when new and unique cases come into my office so I informed him that I was all ears and please tell me what was going on with him.

He said, "Doc, I wasn't able to make it down to my parents' home for Christmas this year in Minnesota. I just couldn't afford the airline ticket. Anyways, I was sitting in my living room and I called them up to wish everyone a merry Christmas. All my siblings, nieces and nephews, go to my parents' home on Christmas day. All of a sudden, Doc, I could see all of them. I could see who was sitting where and who was standing where. I could see who was grabbing the next present out from underneath the Christmas tree. I was on the speaker phone and I started telling them everything that I was seeing. They thought I was outside my parents' home, looking through the window, and playing a trick on them. So I told them that I was on my landline telephone at my home in Anchorage, Alaska. I told them that I was going to hang up and to please call me on my landline. Well, Doc, thirty seconds later, my home phone rang and it was my parents. When I answered the phone, everyone started freaking out on me. You've got to help me, Doc. I need to get rid of this curse."

Well, I immediately thought he might be dealing with some kind of psychosis because it sounded pretty darn crazy to me. Then spontaneously, I asked him for his parents' home phone number. I asked, "Your parents are retired right? They should be home right now, right?" He said, "Well, Doc, yes. They are retired. Unless they're out running errands, they should be home."

As I was dialing his parents' home number, I asked, "I have your permission to talk with them, right? They're going to be able to confirm everything you just told me, right?" I was expecting to have him stop me right there and then because I was making a bold move to call him out on his delusional and psychotic thinking. Instead, he said, "Yes, they will confirm everything."

I thought to myself, "Well, calling him out didn't work so now I'll be able to have his parents' input. Perhaps they can help me to gently confront their adult son." When his parents answered the phone, I said, "Hello, my name is Dr. Matthew Johnson and I'm a psychologist in

Anchorage, Alaska. Your son is in my office. He told me what happened on Christmas day and he gave me permission to call you and confirm his story."

His parents were on the speaker phone and immediately responded, "Dr. Johnson, you've got to help our son. He was able to see everything that we were doing even though he was at his home in Anchorage, Alaska on Christmas day. We called him back and he was there. He saw who was sitting where and who was standing where. He told us about what was inside the present that one of our granddaughters opened up. Please, you've got to help him."

I thanked his parents for their time and assured them that I would do my best to help their son. After I hung up, my client just sat there with a big 'I told you so' smile on his face. I said to him, I'm sorry but I can't help you get rid of your curse because I don't think it's a curse. I think that you're looking at it all wrong. Instead, I think you have a gift. I am willing to work with you to help you better understand your gift and see how you might be able to use it to help others. If you're willing to proceed down that path, I think I can help you." He agreed to proceed. After a few months, he left my office with a new and positive perspective regarding his gift.

You see, my loveable progeny, I'm sharing with all of you about this curse/gift scenario because my mother, Joann Johnson, struggled with it. She only opened up to me about it. She told me that I was the only one of her four kids who appeared to have it. Although she would secretly expose me to articles and books covering extra-sensory-perception (ESP) and other paranormal phenomena, she dealt with her gift as a curse.

She grew up in a generation where such things were not talked about. Heck, who am I kidding? My generation isn't very keen about discussing such matters either. Nevertheless, although my mother encouraged me to learn more and embrace by gift, she drank alcohol like a fish in order to anesthetize herself and avoid her gift. She couldn't handle it. She turned to alcoholism to cope with something that she could not understand. She wanted me to do better than she did.

During the last few days of her life, my mother laid in a coma in a hospital room. I spent time with her every day reading to her, talking to her, singing to her, brushing her hair, and putting water in her dry mouth. On the day she passed away, she woke up from her coma for a few minutes. Although she wasn't able to talk, she looked at me and mouthed the words, "I love you." She died a few hours later.

We took my father, Art Johnson, home from the hospital and sat down in the living room with him. We were attempting to console his loss of my mother who he had been married to for over fifty years. As I was looking out of the large living room window on to the porch where my mother enjoyed sitting, smoking her cigarettes, and watching the birds on the river, the Christmas lights came on. My mother had Christmas lights hanging all over the porch all year long and never took them down. My dad said to me, "Go outside and turn off those damn Christmas lights."

I walked outside to unplug the Christmas lights from the wall socket, but to my surprise, the Christmas lights were not plugged in. Yet, they were glowing brightly. I immediately sensed my mother's presence near me and I said, "Hi, mom! I love you and miss you already. Thank you for being a great mom to me. I can't wait to see you again in the future. I'll go get dad for you."

I walked back inside the house and into the living room. My father said, "I thought I told you to turn off those damn Christmas lights." I stood there in silence in front of my dad. A few tears were rolling down my cheeks. I responded, "Dad, the Christmas lights aren't plugged in. Mom's outside and she needs to say 'goodbye' to you. I think you need to go outside and talk with her."

My dad just sat there staring at me like I was crazy. He went outside and saw that the lights were not plugged in. He spent about five minutes outside talking to my mom about who knows what. He never told us what he said. When he came back inside the house, the Christmas lights turned off. I don't need any more proof about 'life after death' nor do I need any more proof about the unique gift that some of our biological family members appear to be born with. It's in our DNA.

My son, Grady Johnson, has been involved with my Bigfoot Forest People research since the age of two. At present in January of 2017, he is ten years old. He has seen them. He has talked with them. He can tell when they're around. They have reached out to him on multiple occasions. Ultimately, what he chooses to do with his gift and his relationship with the Bigfoot Forest People is up to him. I have no expectations of him to carry on with my research. His life is his life to live as he wishes. I just hope that no matter what he chooses to do with his life, he will at least consider it a gift and not a curse.

Likewise, Grady's older brother, Micah, also appears to have the gift. Micah was five years old when our family encountered the Bigfoot up on the mountainside above the Oregon Caves National Monument Park on July 1, 2000. His mother strongly discouraged him from being involved in my Bigfoot research.

At the age of twenty-one, Micah decided to join me in the Southern Oregon Interaction Area (SOIA) on two separate excursions during the late summer of 2016. He was motivated to join me after he had his own personal encounter with a cloaking Bigfoot. Both he and his friend saw the Bigfoot while they were sitting in a car, overlooking the city lights of Grants Pass, Oregon.

While in SOIA with me, Micah was able to see and interact with the Bigfoot Forest People. Matter of fact, he was playing his music for them while using my portable Bose speaker. He was dancing up a storm and was surrounded by them. Off in the distance, I saw a Being of Light observing Micah while he was dancing. Eventually, the Being of Light began to mimic Micah.

At the end of our trip, Micah told me that I wasn't crazy after all and that the Bigfoot Forest People are real. Once again, I have no expectations for Micah to carry on with my research either. His life is his life to live. I just want Grady and Micah to be happy and embrace their gifts – not deny their gifts.

With all that said, my dear progeny, I wish the same for all of you. I was only one of four children who inherited the gift from my mother. Micah is one of only three children born with the gift. Finally, Grady was the only child from his mother and he has the gift. If you too are born with the gift, please embrace it. Don't hide from it. Don't deny it. Don't drink or drug it away. You have been gifted by God for a reason and I strongly encourage you to embrace it, explore it, understand it, and use it to help others. In my particular case, the gift was used to help save 23,542 souls (minus the three souls that died within an hour or less of crossing over) during the EXODUS by helping to bring them over to Earth. I know I sound crazy but it's all true.

Last but not least, just as the Bigfoot Forest People are real and live among us, so is God. Zorth openly spoke about the existence of God, Jesus, and our need to be connected to them. He said that we all come from the same God. He said that we all have the same souls but different bodies. Finally, he said that we all return to the same God after we die. Please strive to live in love and to be connected with God, Jesus, and your fellow man. Love, love, love like there's no tomorrow.

Thank you, my progeny, for taking the time to read my book and this crazy impersonal, yet very personal, open letter to all of you. I love all of you. I look forward to meeting you on the other side with God. Until then, cling on to faith, hope, and love. The greatest of these is love.

In the love of Jesus Christ,

Dr. Matthew A. Johnson
(Your father, grandfather, great grandfather, great great grandfather, etc.)

P.S. To the rest of you who have just read my open letter to my progeny, if you're experiencing something similar, please embrace your gift. Don't deny it or attempt to run away from it. Eventually, you'll have to talk with your progeny about it too. God Bless!

Part 7

HOW TO GET A HOLD OF DR. JOHNSON

CONTACT INFORMATION

Website: www.TeamSquatchinUSA.Com

YouTube.Com: Team Squatchin USA

Sound Cloud.Com: Team Squatchin USA

Facebook Group Page: Team Squatchin USA

Twitter: @BigfootDoctor

Email: BigfootDoctor@Yahoo.Com